VICTORIAN
Murderesses

A True History of Thirteen
Respectable French and English Women
Accused of Unspeakable Crimes

VICTORIAN
Murderesses

Mary S. Hartman

Dover Publications, Inc.
Mineola, New York

Bibliographical Note

Victorian Murderesses: A True History of Thirteen Respectable French and English Women Accused of Unspeakable Crimes, first published by Dover Publications, Inc., in 2014, is a republication of the work originally published by Schocken Books, Inc., New York, in 1977.

International Standard Book Number
ISBN-13: 978-0-486-78047-4
ISBN-10: 0-486-78047-3

Manufactured in the United States by Courier Corporation
78047301   2014
www.doverpublications.com

A version of some of the arguments and cases in this book
first appeared in an article, "Crime and the Respectable Woman:
toward a Pattern of Middle-Class Female Criminality in
Nineteenth-Century France and England," *Feminist Studies,* 2, no. 1 (1974):
38–56, Feminist Studies, Inc., 417 Riverside Drive, New York, N.Y. 10025.

Portions of Chapter 2 were first published in an article, "Murder for Respectability:
The Case of Madeleine Smith," *Victorian Studies,* 16, no. 4 (June 1973): 381–400.

Portions of Chapter 2 were first published in an article, "Child Abuse and Self-Abuse:
Two Victorian Cases," *History of Childhood Quarterly: The Journal of Psychohistory,*
2, no. 2 (Fall, 1974): 221–248.

FOR MY PARENTS,

Dorothy M. Robertson
AND
Kenneth W. Robertson

CONTENTS

PREFACE AND
ACKNOWLEDGMENTS

THESE LADIES are no friends of mine, but I shall miss them. Notorious women they surely were, or most of them at any rate, but it is their very familiarity which makes them disturbing. They are uncomfortably ordinary. There are thirteen of them, French and English, and twelve cases—one accusation involved a mother-daughter team. The cases span the period from the 1840s to the 1890s, a critical time when the middle classes to which the women belonged were taking on their modern appearance.

These accused daughters, wives, and mothers have little to teach any would-be twentieth-century practitioner about the art of murder; nearly all of them bungled badly in the act, and those who got away with it relied upon methods that required special circumstances and relations between the sexes which no longer obtain. What their stories do offer are some glimpses into the domestic confines of middle-class families and some hints of the problems and even the terrors that women faced there. Some of the accused murderesses would make superb individual subjects for psychological analysis; but this study, while not ignoring these more particular aspects, will stress the ways in which the women's lives were linked to those of their more typical female peers. The accused women will be the center of attention, but the accounts will focus on their collective contribution to our understanding of their less sensational sisters.

Many persons have generously helped me in preparing this study. I trust that I can thank them all while mentioning only a few. Thanks, then, to the editors of *Feminist Studies,* the *History of Childhood Quarterly,* and *Victorian Studies* for permission to reprint portions of earlier versions of the cases published in those journals. Thanks to the administrators of the National Endowment for the Humanities and to the Rutgers Research Council for funds which permitted research in England and France. Thanks to the librarians at Rutgers University, Princeton University, the New York Public Library, the Archives Nationales, the Bibliothèque Nationale, the British Museum, and the Public Record Office. I am indebted to M. Henri Polge and M. Jean d'Orléans, directors of the Departmental Archives of Gers and Indre-et-Loire, for their kindness in locating materials on the Lacoste and Lemoine cases. I am grateful to Dorothy Christie who directed me to the documents collected by her late husband, Trevor L. Christie, for his excellent study of the Maybrick affair, *Etched in Arsenic* (London, 1969), and to David Crosson, research historian in the Division of Rare Books and Special Collections at the University of Wyoming, who graciously made the Christie Collection available to me.

Special thanks, too, to Rudolph Binion, Marc Hollender, Elizabeth Jenkins, Maurice Lee, William O'Neill, Elaine Showalter, Peter Stearns, Hilah Thomas, and Judith Walkowitz, all of whom read versions of the draft, offered helpful criticism, listened patiently to the theories I concocted, and offered some better ones of their own. Thanks to Katherine Finnegan and Margaret Nierenberg, who collected many of the materials, to my fine editor, Christopher Kuppig, who was a hero of patience, to Judith Kahn, who improved my prose, and to Inez Elkins and Shirley Meinkoth, who deciphered my handwriting and are the best typists I can imagine. Thanks, finally, to my husband Edwin, who wishes to assure anxious friends that he is alive and well.

MARY S. HARTMAN

Douglass College
Rutgers University
June, 1976

VICTORIAN
Murderesses

INTRODUCTION

THE SUBJECTS of this study are thirteen nineteenth-century English and French women of "respectable" middle-class status, all of whom were accused of being murderesses or accomplices in murder. They include the independently wealthy wives and daughters of merchants, industrialists, and professional men, as well as near-resourceless shopkeepers' wives, and one spinster governess. The victims were the women's husbands, lovers, rivals, pupils, siblings, offspring, and grandchildren. Two of the victims were suffocated, one died of a skull fracture, two were shot, another succumbed to knife wounds and body blows, and the remaining six were poisoned. Most of the accused women were probably guilty as charged, although only six were convicted and none was made to suffer the death penalty. Furthermore, five of the six who went to prison were freed before their full sentences were served. Six of the seven others were acquitted, and the thirteenth was never brought to trial. It is possible to conclude that it was wise to be female and respectable if one intended to dispose of somebody in the nineteenth century. Middle-class women were literally getting away with murder.

The cases of several of these women have long fascinated the practitioners of true-crime literature.[1] Most of these writers, however, have trotted the women out for display in the spirit of tour guides in Madame Tussaud's Chamber of Horrors. Armed with obviously sensational material, they have been more concerned to shock, amuse, or titillate than to understand. Few of them have risen above easy categorizations of their subjects as freaks or lunatics, and none has attempted to look at the "respectable" murderesses collectively. Of course, the middle-class women accused of murder were a small group, and in an obvious sense their acts alone united them. The notion that they might be considered together as in any way representative of their

1

social class is, on the face of it, implausible. Their involvement in criminal investigations appears to make them automatically atypical creatures fit only to the interest of collectors of the bizarre and the macabre. But these women do not deserve to be dismissed so lightly. The circumstances which prompted their actions, the strategems they employed, and the public responses to their reported behavior display a pattern which suggests that, far from committing a set of isolated acts, the women may all have been responding to situations which to some degree were built into the lives of their more ordinary middle-class peers.

To argue that this handful of women may have been closer to the typical women of their class than might be expected is not to suggest that untold numbers of middle-class women in the nineteenth century were undiscovered murderesses. Nor is it to imply that some qualities characteristic of several of the accused women, such as a peculiar sort of ruthlessness or an apparently well-developed sexual appetite, were necessarily common among the non-criminal women of the class. It is, however, to suggest that the women in this study may have been among a group which was especially sensitive to certain problems and tensions which were common to a large number of middle-class households.

Such a view is clearly hard to reconcile with received notions about middle-class women in the nineteenth century. The "code of manners through which the Victorian damsel smiles" [2] is a familiar one, and was hardly restricted to English shores. That code defined the proper young woman as a frail but appealing, intellectually inferior but morally superior being, whose duty it was to be passive, decorative, and sexually pure. Such creatures, it now appears, existed mostly in fantasy, but their image has been slow to fade. For many, it still requires an effort of will to conceive of any respectable young woman of the period performing an arduous task, making an important decision, or wrestling with a real problem. And it remains awkward, for some at least, to accept the inescapable fact that when she married, this unearthly creature had sexual intercourse with her husband. The suspicion lingers that she submitted only to achieve the high calling of motherhood and that she must have endured the act itself in a semicoma.

Difficulties in imagining that women of the so-called respectable classes had either problems or sexual experiences are simply a reflection of the persistent conviction that these women were not "real," but we are slowly learning not only that these women existed, but that they were far less ethereal than the popular image would have it. The influence of a code of femininity was genuine enough in their lives, but more compelling still, it appears, was the reality of the changing, sometimes bewildering, world to which they had to adapt. As the outlines of these women's collective experience begin to emerge, it becomes possible to interpret more sensibly the information about a small number of individual women for whom the records are more complete—including these accused murderesses, whose lives were thrown open to public scrutiny when they became involved with the processes of the law.

The problems of more ordinary middle-class women in the nineteenth century are now being seen as less pat and trivial than before, no longer just boredom or frustration over domestic isolation. Historians agree that in this period women were for the most part confined to the home as their husbands moved out to mind the marketplace, but they are challenging earlier views that women necessarily lost status and options as a result, that their problems were reduced to irrelevant domestic minutiae. Admittedly, middle-class women no longer filled the economically productive roles which had been theirs earlier; the redirection of their energies toward housekeeping and motherhood, however, actively engaged women in the process which is fashionably called "modernization," a process which produced a collection of new and shifting problems for them. A variety of evidence from health literature, fertility records, and consumption data shows that women were taking advantage of higher incomes and new chances to improve the quality of life. Abandoning earlier fatalistic attitudes, they showed new concern over problems of infant mortality, maternal disorders, and general family health. They welcomed technological innovations for home use and even, in England at least, participated actively in family planning and the choice of newly available contraceptive devices.[3] Women were carving out greater domestic autonomy, albeit in a context still laden with traditional habits and views and in the face of growing public criticism which made them scapegoats of all those who were fearful of change. Their problems, in this view, emerged more from their willingness to welcome and encourage change rather than passively to accept or even to resist it, and so were related more to frustrations and anxieties over new and changing expectations than to alleged deprivations resulting from declining status.

Not all of women's problems in this period can be seen as products of conflict over their new domestic initiative, but the awareness of the fact of their assertiveness clearly expands the ways to interpret evidence about their troubles. Only on rare occasions do we see individual women actually in the process of coping—or failing to cope—with their difficulties, and the women we know most about are the ones who, for one reason or another, look far from typical: Florence Nightingale or Charlotte Brontë or the subjects of this study. No one, on learning of their poisonous adventures, would be tempted to call Madeleine Smith a run-of-the-mill *jeune fille en fleur* or Adelaide Bartlett a humdrum housewife. But unlike Nightingale and Brontë, Smith and Bartlett in important ways were ordinary women who found extreme solutions to ordinary problems. The lethal proclivities of these lady killers have hitherto blinded observers to the ordinariness—the typicality, indeed—of their circumstances and the difficulties they faced.

These thirteen women, then, were persons who in many ways were quite unexceptional. Before the acts which suddenly exposed their lives to public view, they had apparently conformed to expected standards of behavior for women of their class. None of them led a reform campaign or participated in a political or social movement. Until their trials, none had ever written anything for publication. Only one followed an independent career, and not because she chose to, but because she lacked the requisite dowry for marriage. All received an average or somewhat above average education by the standards of the time, either at home or at convent or boarding schools. All either managed their own homes or helped their mothers in managing theirs. Of the nine who were married all either had children or hoped to do so. All were reported at some time to have spoken fondly of children and motherhood. All would have called themselves Christians. In these ways and more besides, this group of women shared the experiences and aspirations of most of their peers.

When their involvement with the law opened the closed doors of these women's lives, one of the most "shocking" (though to our post-Freudian world, hardly surprising) revelations had to do with sexuality. This was a taboo subject in the class and one which, despite all the recent discoveries about secret Victorian lives, the historian rarely encounters being discussed in public by ordinary nineteenth-century persons. The topics include pre- and extramarital sex, abortion and miscarriage, birth control techniques, sexual frequency and satisfaction in marriage, masturbation in women, and venereal disease among proper women. Again, though the revelations indicate that some of the women were sexual as well as criminal deviants—adultery was then regarded as a form of deviation—the context of their sexual relationships, and the public responses to them, tell us a great deal about the intimate problems of more ordinary women who transgressed neither moral nor criminal codes.

However, sexuality and sexual relationships were only a part of the hidden history of domestic power relationships revealed in these cases. In view of recent evidence that the majority of middle-class women were acting in ways which shifted domestic power more in their favor, the strivings of all the accused women to enhance their own authority in relation to fathers, husbands, and other domestic authorities are hardly peculiar, nor are many—but obviously not all—of their methods. The cases provide support for the theory that women of the class were gaining greater autonomy in some areas, though concentrating as they do on individuals who chose or were driven to drastic and even murderous solutions to their problems, they are more properly a collective record of some of the casualties which accompanied that achievement.

The focus of this study is on the accused murderesses as women rather than as criminals. In order to ensure the availability of evidence necessary to reconstruct the circumstances which led to their being suspected of murder, only the "sensational" cases were selected. The group includes nearly all the cases of French and English women which became *causes célèbres* in the period of Victoria's reign,[4] and the materials permit the sampling of a large number of public responses. Clearly, it would be useful to know something more of the less celebrated middle-class murderesses, but there is no straightforward way to determine even the total number of such women brought to trial, let alone their motives, since available aggregate statistics provide little or no information as to the social class of offenders by crime category.[5] However, a consideration of general data for all those tried for murder helps provide a context for the women here in their identities as accused criminals rather than as middle-class women.

Unsurprisingly, fewer women than men were accused of murder in both England and France, although the percentage of women charged with murder was (and remains) higher than for many other sorts of crime. For example, in England from 1855 to 1874 the annual totals of women tried for murder, which ranged from twelve to forty-two, twice exceeded those for men and normally were at least half as high, whereas women were only a fifth to a quarter of those tried in assize courts for all felonies.[6] A similar pattern in murder applied in France, although there the number of women tried for all serious crimes was relatively less than in England, remaining at about a sixth of the total tried in assize courts throughout the century.[7] It has been argued that greater social freedom accounted for the larger representation of English women in crime statistics. All the same, the middle-class French woman may have murdered more than her English counterpart. This study in fact provides some evidence that she did.

Admittedly, women's representation in statistics of those tried for murder (and in crime statistics generally) is probably artificially low for several reasons.[8] The records of coroners' inquests reveal that only a fraction of the known cases of infanticide led to an indictment for what is largely a woman's crime, and infanticides which were never detected are also believed to have been numerous. Moreover, the demonstrated greater popularity of poison among women and the fact that several women were multiple poisoners apprehended only on the "last" occasion supports the view that many deaths by poison which went undetected were women's crimes.[9] Then, too, it is possible that social attitudes of greater leniency toward women kept some murderesses out of the hands of the law, and also that women's own socially conditioned skill in dissimulation gave some of them an edge. Taking all these factors into account, it may be that women's "real" figures for murder exceeded those of men.

Not many women were executed for murder—as has been pointed out, none of the middle-class women considered here went to the scaffold. Data from a recent study of English women executed for murder indicates that of the forty-nine put to death between 1843 and 1890, the majority were miserably poor.[10] These lower-class murderesses, like their middle-class sisters and, indeed, like most male murderers, chose their victims largely from among spouses, relatives, and acquaintances. An analysis of their motives reveals that they murdered far more frequently for money. Twenty-two of the forty-nine did so, often for very small amounts, such as the pitiful sums obtainable from burial societies. The next largest category of motives was sexual triangles; in five such cases a wife murdered her husband for a lover and in five others wives took revenge against husbands or lovers for infidelity. Of the seventeen remaining cases, half a dozen women had unclear motives, though all appear to have been influenced by the brutalizing effects of poverty. Several murdered children they were unable to care for. One woman drowned her eleven-year-old daughter because the man she was living with forced her to make a choice between him and the child. Another, the mother of seventeen children, poisoned her husband of twenty years because she could no longer bear his savage beatings. Poison was the most common means used; no fewer than twenty-nine of the forty-nine women used poison, and twenty-three used the old standby, arsenic.

This sampling, of course, is not representative of all murderesses, since it excludes the majority who were reprieved, acquitted, or never brought to trial, but it does permit some initial comparisons with the subjects of this study. These middle-class women's crimes conformed to the general rule of domestic murder, and poisoning was clearly the preferred means. Desperate want was not, by definition, a factor, and though financial gain cannot be overlooked, it is not a dominant feature in any of the sensational cases here. Similarly, though infanticide may have been employed by the lower middle classes when a child threatened to disrupt an achieved standard of living, it was largely a crime of the poor, save when, as in one case here, it was resorted to as a means to preserve respectability. The personal incompatibilities and sexual problems which do account for substantial numbers of female homicides in the lower classes emerge as dominant among respectable murderesses, but an examination of the latter cases suggests marked differences of method and motive which were peculiar to the changing circumstances of middle-class women. The women in this study were trapped in situations involving choices between traditional and modern authorities and lifestyles which women of the lower classes could hardly have experienced in quite the same ways.

It is certainly possible that examination of court records will reveal other middle-class murderesses, whose cases did not become *causes célèbres* like the ones here, and that more of the motives uncovered will be related to economic hardship. An attempt to gain some impressions about this possibility, however, suggests that in any case the number of middle-class women tried for murder was surprisingly small. A survey of the summaries of cases in the London Central Criminal Court for three selected years for each decade from the 1840s through the 1890s revealed just 6 out of 117 cases of women tried for murder in which the perpetrator appears to have of the middle class.[11] Of these six, three killed their children and were declared mentally unbalanced. Two others killed adult women, a mother and a servant, but the deaths appear ro have been the unintended result of blows administered in a sudden quarrel. The sixth, a widow, poisoned her landlady for money. The conclusion tentatively to be drawn from this survey is that the murderesses dealt with in this study should not be considered unrepresentative merely because their cases were sensational, but that, in fact, the sensationalism was a product of the very infrequency with which a respectable woman went on trial for her life.

Two main subjects will be considered in tracing the accounts of these sensational murders. First, the behavior and motives of the accused women will be explored in their social context. Second, the development of a discernible pattern in the alleged crimes and in responses to them will be discussed. It will be argued that circumstances which led respectable women to contemplate murder, as well as factors which influenced public reactions to the women's behavior, did shift throughout the period and also that distinctive features came to characterize English and French cases which were apparently related to different paces of modernization in the respective countries.

The twelve case studies, which are paired chronologically, treat their subjects not only as suspected or actual criminals, but as middle-class daughters, wives, and mothers, persons who are intriguing in themselves and who also offer clues to an understanding of the hidden and intimate lives of the majority of women of the class who remain anonymous. The attempt to discover some of the experiences and problems of a larger group of women through a small and "aberrant" group has obvious risks. Historians are only beginning to explore the uses of the exceptional individual in defining hidden features of the typical, an enterprise which more intrepid sociologists and psychologists have long engaged in.

It is evident that detailed biographical material on a limited number of individuals does not lend itself easily to quantitative treatment or extended generalization. For this reason many social historians have made it a principle to avoid such evidence, on the ground that it cannot provide verifiable answers to their questions concerning social relations within the group to which the individuals belong. This unduly restrictive attitude will not be adopted here: the questions will be asked, even though the answers are recognized as perhaps partial or tentative. The difficulty of constructing a satisfactory picture of domestic relations in a past age should not discourage the exploration of the available evidence on some aspects of those relations, including the intensely personal aspects which are least susceptible to the forms of analysis which many social historians currently favor.

The evidence not only provides the occasion, as it were, to capture whole households by surprise, but also to explore the range of public responses to the cases. All touched upon aspects of women's behavior and beliefs about women which preoccupied many people. The articulate who had the means to do so expressed their views publicly in the press and commented on those of others. Those who were not so well placed, including many women, adopted less official means of making their opinions known. Consciously or unconsciously, all passed judgments of varied sorts, not only on the accused women, but on women in general.

Durkheim's brilliant formula that the deviant person is created by and necessary to the community, both as a focus for group feelings and as an indicator of prevailing social boundaries of attitudes and behavior, is now a commonplace. Taking a human life, of course, has always been considered an extreme form of deviancy in most societies, but even with the accused murderer, as with all lesser deviants, community attitudes and modes of control vary immensely and depend upon many factors. It has already been suggested that in the cases here both their social status and their sex could prove useful to the accused women. The fact is not surprising. Women, in particular socially well-placed women, still enjoy special favor under criminal justice. But this favor, though real, has hardly been a static and fixed quantity. It has depended in part upon the capacity of a society at any given time to incorporate the deviant behavior of an individual accused woman into a generally acknowledged positive image of womanhood, and thereby both to explain that behavior and eliminate or lighten ordinarily prescribed punishment. Of course, a favorable view of womanhood did exist in the nineteenth century; indeed, perhaps never before or since have women—middle-class women, that is—been so popularly idealized for their alleged virtues. Still, as these cases reveal, the effectiveness of the prevailing cult of womanhood in protecting the accused murderesses was limited. What is striking in the "official" responses to the cases is less the evidence of special favor toward women than the evidence of the changing conditions under which such favor applied. Those conditions involved judgments on alleged facts about the women's lives which often had little or nothing to do with the charges, but everything to do with shifting attitudes toward women.

Most well-publicized trials, of course, elicit dubious theories of guilt or innocence as well as a variety of prejudiced opinions. In these cases, however, it is striking that the actual situations of the accused women, which can be reconstructed with some confidence, coincided so rarely with the ways in which the courts and press perceived them. To take just one example, in ten of the twelve cases, false beliefs about a sexual issue prompted either the verdict of the jury or that of the public or both. The disparity between the judgments and the reality was perhaps bound to be greatest in sexual matters, but it gives some concrete meaning to the often cited "distance" between the sexes in the middle classes. Men and women were coming to live in different worlds, and their understanding of one another was often limited. It was other women who, almost alone, gave evidence of comprehending the situations of the accused women.

These criminal trials reach into some of the private areas of women's and men's experience in the past which have rarely been explored. They contain some surprises, of course, but many of these even now are surprises of recognition. For us, as for many who attended the trials, the experience is less one of attending a freak show than of looking into a distorting mirror—the features are altered, but they are unmistakably our own.

1.

ARSENIC AND MATRIMONY:

The Cases of Marie Lafarge and Euphémie Lacoste

Marie Lafarge

ADJUSTMENT TO MARRIAGE may never have been a simple matter, but in nineteenth-century middle-class society the ordeal was intensified, especially for women. At no time before or since has popular self-consciousness about marriage and the "marriage market" reached such heights; and it is no wonder, since for larger numbers of people than ever before, marriage held out the great hope for bettering oneself in society. For the majority of women, whose destiny was the domestic sphere, changes in actual social roles as well as in the image of the ideal wife made initiation to marriage, even at best, an awkward and uneasy time. At worst, the new pressures of matrimony could lead to disaster, as they did in the cases of two young French women of the 1840s, Marie Lafarge and Euphémie Lacoste.[1]

The details of the tensions of their early married lives would have gone unrecorded, save for the fact that both their husbands died rather suddenly and under peculiar circumstances. Suspicion settled on the wives who, in the end, were tried on charges of poisoning their spouses with arsenic. The evidence against the women was circumstantial, as it is bound to be in the very private crime of poisoning, but many found that evidence to be compelling. Still, Mmes. Lafarge and Lacoste each publicly and repeatedly denied the charges, and one of them, at least, may have been telling the truth.

Marie Lafarge and Euphémie Lacoste were both members of the bourgeoisie, but each came from a distinctly different segment of the class. Mme. Lafarge, the wife of an iron manufacturer who owned a forge in the Limousin, was a Parisian with an excellent education and upper-middle-class and aristocratic connections. Mme. Lacoste, by contrast, was a provincial woman from the tiny village of Mazerolles in southwestern France. Married to a small tradesman who had retired to live off the proceeds of an inheritance,

10

she inhabited a far more traditional world than Marie Lafarge. Yet both young women were obliged to face a variety of new experiences, many of which were peculiar to a transitional class. Their responses to the bewildering pressures of change in their lives, as well as the responses of their societies to their behavior, reveal stresses which could hardly have been unique to the two women. At a time when the bourgeois "mistress of the home" was being set up as the new class ideal of womanhood, the cases of Marie Lafarge and Euphémie Lacoste suggest some of the obstacles women were encountering as they moved toward that elusive ideal.

Of the two affairs, that of Mme. Lafarge was clearly the more sensational. By the summer of 1840 the literate public all knew at least the outlines of Mme. Lafarge's life, and women, it was reported, talked of little else. One of the most celebrated trials of the century, the Lafarge case has continued to arouse an interest which is reflected in a steady stream of publications.[2] Its central figure was an elegant, dark-haired twenty-four-year-old woman. If the male commentators (who, as was usual in the case of an accused woman, addressed themselves first to her physical appearance) disagreed over whether she was beautiful, most concurred in praising her intelligence, talent, and charm. Some observers did remark that her profile was not really good, that her forehead was too prominent, and her nose and mouth too large. But nearly everyone agreed that her eyes were extraordinary, her smile enchanting, and her soft, deep voice both appealing and seductive. The interested public learned, too, that the accused was a woman of considerable cultural achievements; she sang and played the piano, read the fiction of George Sand and Victor Hugo, and even wrote poetry. Marie Lafarge, in other words, was a recognizable romantic heroine—or so it seemed.

Born Marie Fortunée Cappelle in Paris in 1816, the young woman was the daughter of an artillery officer who had served in the Imperial Guards. She was illegitimately related to the reigning royal family, since her maternal grandmother was one of the natural daughters of the king's father, Philippe Egalité, and Mme. de Genlis. Her father died in 1828, when Marie was twelve, and her mother, who remarried two years later, died in 1835.

Marie, at eighteen, was sent to live with her mother's sister, who was married to the secretary-general of the Bank of France. But despite the advantages of wealth, comfort, and opportunities to develop her interest in literature and music, Marie complained with some justice that her aunt disliked her and made her painfully aware of her status as the "poor cousin." The dowry of 90,000 francs left her by her parents was not impressive in her aunt's social circles, and Marie soon realized that her relative regarded her as a marriage liability.

The problem of finding a husband for this orphan was first taken in hand by an aristocratic married friend of Marie's, who arranged a meeting with the brother of her former governess. Though the man was a respectable subprefect, Marie understandably considered him beneath her and confessed her delight when a former friend of her father advised her that no marriage contract should be made with a man whose only income was his salary as a subprefect. In the meantime, however, one of Marie's uncles had engaged the services of a matrimonial agency, which proposed an apparently more suitable candidate in one Charles Lafarge, son of an honorable justice of the peace from the Limousin. His dossier included warm letters of recommendation from his priest and the local deputy from Uzerches, as well as flattering watercolors of Le Glandier, his estate, which had originally been a Carthusian monastery. Advertised as a wealthy ironmaster with property worth at least 200,000 francs and an annual income of 30,000 from the forge alone, Lafarge was praised as the mayor of his commune and a pillar of the community.

To prevent Marie's learning that Lafarge had been turned up by an agency, the uncle arranged a "chance" meeting with his "friend" at the opera. Marie found the twenty-eight-year-old ironmaster both boorish and ugly, but four days after their first meeting in August 1839, her aunt announced that she had published the banns. Fearful that Marie might balk, she even withheld the information that Lafarge was a widower. Within a few weeks the civil and religious ceremonies were performed and the couple set out for the Limousin.

In memoirs published after her trial Marie described the despair and illness she suffered on the trip, the terror inspired by the sexual advances of the stranger who was her husband, and the disillusionment upon arriving at her new home.[3] Her in-laws seemed no more than vulgar farmers and the estate was a shambles. The vaunted ironworks, she would later learn, was bankrupt. In desperation she locked herself in their bedroom on the first evening and composed a letter to Charles, announcing that she had deceived him and that she loved another man, who had secretly followed them from Paris. She added, somewhat implausibly, that she intended either to take arsenic or to depart alone for Smyrna.[4] With credulous horror Charles read the document and ordered the guns loaded and the dogs to be kept on the alert against the interloper. But after a terrible row involving family and visitors, Marie finally admitted her ruse and agreed to stay on. Charles, for his part, promised that he would not demand his "marital privileges" until he had fixed up the estate and arranged for a loan in Paris to finance operations at the forge.

In the ensuing weeks relations between Lafarge and his new wife reportedly improved. On the advice of his lawyer Charles saw to it that Marie, in deference to her Parisian background, was provided with subscriptions to newspapers, membership in the local lending library, numerous visits, and renovated surroundings. In November 1839, as remodeling proceeded at Le Glandier, Charles left for Paris with two projects: he intended to apply for a patent on a new smelting process he had developed, and he planned to negotiate a loan to perfect the process in his forge and publicize it for sale to other ironmasters. He did manage to receive the patent, but as the weeks passed, his efforts to get the loan proved fruitless. He returned home early in January 1840 complaining of an intestinal illness from which he said he had suffered ever since mid-December. Indeed, he traced the condition to the very day on which he had received a cake sent to him by his wife.

After his return home Charles's condition worsened; he suffered constant attacks of cramps, vomiting, and nausea which kept him in bed from the evening of his arrival. Marie attentively watched over her husband, brought him food and drink, and summoned doctors, but Lafarge's health continued to deteriorate. A friend visiting at Le Glandier a week after Charles's return claimed to have seen Marie stirring a white powder into a drink intended for her husband. Marie insisted that the powder was merely gum arabic, a substance commonly used for intestinal complaints, but her mother-in-law confided fears of poisoning to a friend, who suggested that a local chemist examine the dregs of a now suspect eggnog. Analysis revealed the presence of arsenic, and Marie was forbidden to minister further to her husband. Charles, however, died the day after the test was conducted. His family then launched an investigation which culminated in Marie's indictment for murder. After a trial rich in social and psychological revelations, but almost universally condemned as a travesty of justice, Marie Lafarge was found guilty with extenuating circumstances and sentenced to life imprisonment.

Four years later, in July 1844, news of another alleged arsenic poisoning of a husband by a young wife, this time in the southwestern department of Gers, prompted the press to speak of a new Lafarge affair. But the case of Euphémie Lacoste was a very different matter. True, the young Euphémie had married a man who never would have been her choice, one who had been married before and whom she found ill-mannered and difficult. She had also nursed him practically alone through a fatal gastric illness, and her suspected resentment of her husband did arouse gossip. Still, the only feature of the case which echoed the romanesque flavor of Marie Lafarge's story was Euphémie's disappearance after a warrant was issued to bring her in for questioning. Rumors spread that she had fled to Spain, where she had either joined a religious order or become a shepherdess, and when she finally returned voluntarily with her hair cropped short, there was much speculation that she had been masquerading as a boy. In its other particulars, however, the case was more prosaic in appearance, although no less puzzling.

The daughter of small landowners in the department of the Hautes-Pyrénées, Euphémie Vergès was twenty-two years old in May 1841 when she married her sixty-eight-year-old great-uncle, Henri Lacoste. Several years before her parents had received an offer from Lacoste, a retired shopkeeper, who had informed them that he stood to inherit a considerable amount of money and property from an elder brother who owned vineyards near the village of Riguepeu in the neighboring department of Gers. Seeing an opportunity to provide well for their daughter and to ensure their own future security, Euphémie's parents agreed to the match and offered a dowry worth 20,000 francs. Lacoste, in turn, agreed to pay for the education of his intended bride at a convent school in Tarbes. In this instance, as in many similar ones among the wealthier peasantry and lower provincial bourgeoisie, the parents made the marriage agreement without informing the daughter; Euphémie learned of her forthcoming marriage only a few months before the wedding took place.

Mlle. Vergès, à dutiful daughter, apparently put up no resistance. As neighbors and friends subsequently testified at the trial, the marriage initially seemed to be a happy one. Admittedly, there were rumors that the young bride, in marrying an uncle more than three times her age, had sacrificed her inclinations toward a young grocer from Tarbes, but most agreed that she was very solicitous to her new husband. Even for this part of France, where bourgeois women were frequently noted to be "merely the first among their husband's servants," [5] Euphémie stood out as especially attentive. Lacoste boasted to his friends that his new bride was perfection itself, that she shaved him, washed his feet, and even cleaned his fingernails. He promptly made out his will, leaving everything to Euphémie, and announced that he hoped soon for a son and heir.

Two years passed, however, and Euphémie failed to become pregnant. Lacoste reported his concern to his friends and began to complain that his wife had become difficult and moody. Euphémie, in turn, confided to their friend, the local schoolmaster, that her domestic life was increasingly trying. Henri, she said, was not only parsimonious, he was jealous; he refused to allow her to see friends or even to make visits alone to church. Moreover, there were rumors that Lacoste had attempted to proposition two of the maidservants, who subsequently had left service with the couple. Neighbors assumed that Euphémie had discharged them because she was worried that her husband intended to father a child and disinherit her.

Henri Lacoste was suddenly taken ill in mid-May 1843, after the couple had attended the local fair in Riguepeu. His attack, which was attributed by his wife to indigestion after a meal of beans, onions, and garlic, resulted in vomiting and weakness, but since he distrusted doctors, Lacoste allegedly refused medical help. When his condition worsened three days after his first attack, he finally had Euphémie write to a doctor and request a written diagnosis of his symptoms.[6] In the meantime he was visited by a public health officer summoned by Euphémie. But the numerous plasters and purges did not avail. Lacoste died a few days later.

His widow, according to local reports, was not unduly troubled over her loss. As the maid put it, "Madame shed a few tears and then promptly went off to look for the will." [7] Euphémie's subsequent behavior was also regarded as suspicious by the townspeople. She decided to move into nearby Tarbes, first staying in rooms which she and her husband had rented for their visits to that city and later renting a larger apartment. Local gossips talked about how she had made extravagant purchases, including a coach and ponies, and they also claimed that she was entertaining young male visitors as late as midnight. This was highly improper behavior, especially in the provinces, where new widows were expected to spend two years in full mourning.

The growing rumors that Lacoste had not died of natural causes finally reached the public prosecutor, and when the body was exhumed the following December, it was discovered to contain traces of arsenic. Acquaintances recalled that on the day he took ill Lacoste had complained of a foul glass of wine given him by the schoolmaster, Joseph Meilhan. This, in conjunction with the discovery that the widow had provided Meilhan with a small pension, was sufficient for the authorities to bring an indictment for murder against the pair. However, testimony at the trial failed to produce any evidence of a conspiracy between Euphémie and the seventy-year-old schoolmaster, and the two were ultimately acquitted. The decision was prompted in part by the fact that experts who testified on the presence of arsenic disagreed sharply about the source of the poison and about the quantity discovered in the body. But Mme. Lafarge, from her prison cell in Montpellier, had a different opinion on the acquittal of the accused. "My condemnation," she declared, "saved Mme. Lacoste." [8]

The evidence in neither case allows for a conclusive determination of the actual guilt or innocence of the young women, although in both cases it is possible to make a considered judgment. It should be noted that the number and variety of sources of evidence for the Lafarge case far exceeds that for the Lacoste affair. The testimony in Marie Lafarge's case permits a more detailed reconstruction, partly because more persons witnessed the events. At the time of the alleged crime the residents at Le Glandier included the young couple, Lafarge's widowed mother, a cook, two male servants, Lafarge's hired business associate and his wife, a niece of Lafarge who was visiting Marie, Marie's servant Clémentine Servat, and a spinster friend of the family who was staying there while she painted portraits of Marie and the niece. In addition, throughout Charles's illness there were numerous visits from friends, relatives, and doctors. In the Lacoste home, on the other hand, there was, in addition to the couple, only one servant, the housemaid Jacquette Larrieu. Visitors were limited to a few friends and the public health officer.

The smaller number of witnesses reflects the more limited world of the Lacostes, and especially of Euphémie. The village of Riguepeu itself comprised only seven private dwellings, four little farms, an inn, the mayor's establishment, and the home of the priest. The Lacoste residence, which was set apart from the village and referred to as the Chateau Philibert after its previous owner, Henri's brother, was actually just a more elegant version of the local style of white, one-story dwelling with a red tile roof. Journalists who visited the community reported that the residents, who spoke an incomprehensible patois with a strong admixture of Spanish, distrusted all outsiders and, save for the priest, refused to talk about the Lacostes. The priest said only that he had a high opinion of the couple and that as Euphémie's confessor and spiritual guide, he had complete faith in her moral character. [9]

The witnesses called upon during the investigation to describe their acquaintance with the couple did include a fair number of the town's residents: the mayor, the priest, the innkeeper and his employee, farmers and masons employed by Lacoste, former servants, and a few others. There was also testimony from some persons outside the town, chiefly acquaintances from nearby Tarbes. However, detailed evidence about daily affairs in the Lacoste household is limited, and the natural reticence of those closest to the town's most prominent couple makes reconstruction still more difficult.

Henri frequently went out visiting on his own and thus his friends could provide a fairly clear picture of him. About Euphémie, however, much must be inferred. Her married life was almost completely restricted to the home, and her reluctance to discuss personal affairs obviously relevant to the case further complicates an effort to retrieve her situation. The court, moreover, on the grounds of protecting her modesty—and occasionally on the unspoken grounds of protecting her husband's reputation—repeatedly avoided issues pertinent to the charges.

In addition to the more detailed testimony in the Lafarge case, other documents permit a clearer understanding of Marie herself. Much of her correspondence from both before and after the trial has been collected.[10] Marie also wrote two volumes of memoirs while waiting for her appeal, and after the appeal failed, she wrote a series of pieces which were published by a relative after her death and entitled *Prison Hours*.[11] Finally, before her murder trial Marie was a principal in another trial which concerned her alleged theft of a diamond necklace. The affair came before a correctional tribunal in July 1840 and resulted in extensive publicity being given to many aspects of her life before her marriage. We therefore know a great deal about Marie Lafarge. And yet a mystery remains.

Euphémie Lacoste appears far less complex than Marie and probably more representative of middle-class provincial women of the period than Marie was of upper-middle-class Parisian ones. But this impression may be inaccurate. Euphémie left no memoirs, no correspondence to enlighten, or perhaps mislead, her contemporaries and future generations about her private thoughts and feelings. She did testify in her trial and a few others spoke about her life after her arrival in Riguepeu, but there was no one to give detailed information about her before she married her great-uncle.

There may, indeed, have been little to tell. Her mother might have had something to say, but she had died by the time of the trial. Her father, perhaps overwhelmed with shame or grief over Euphémie or perhaps simply unable to make the journey, did not appear at the trial, although he did send a curious letter in his daughter's defense. Only her older sister was present in the courtroom to provide familial support for Euphémie, and public opinion, which was so strongly in sympathy with the accused in Marie Lafarge's case, was far less favorable to Euphémie Lacoste. In the tiny departmental capital of Auch where she was tried, many of the eight thousand residents thought there was good reason to condemn Mme. Lacoste, and they did not hesitate to say why. Others obviously absorbed in the case, including many women, volunteered no opinions.

Any attempt to explain the two women's responses to marriage and their alleged roles in murder must contend with available evidence on their different experiences and expectations before marriage. There is a large volume of relevant material on Marie Lafarge, but since most of it consists of her own writings, much of which were devoted to her long campaign to prove her innocence, it must be treated with extreme caution. For Euphémie Lacoste, trial accounts alone must be used to reconstruct early experience. But fragmentary and biased as the evidence is in both cases, it does allow some perception of the different emotional and intellectual states which the two women brought to marriage.

Not surprisingly, both courts and press showed special interest in suspected prior romantic attachments of the two women, not only because they bore on the question of motive, but because they touched upon the special preoccupations of a society which was shifting its views on the theory and practice of courtship. One historian has identified a sweeping "romantic revolution" underway in France in this period and suggests that courtship habits in all classes were being affected by what he describes as a "surge of sentiment." [12] Simply, his theory argues that in thinking about a marriage partner, more and more young people were beginning to give priority to the individualistic goals of "affection and compatibility" [13] as against the older criteria of family and community goals, which placed greater emphasis upon property and financial security. It can be argued that this trend was not broad enough to be considered a "sweeping revolution," but there is no question that in the 1840s sentiments in favor of romantic love were agitating the bourgeoisie at all levels.

But the romantic ideal was far from triumphant in France at the time Marie Lafarge and Euphémie Lacoste were tried. Indeed, it was especially among the growing bourgeoisie that issues of financial calculation and what the French called "interest" were apparently gaining in importance as new male recruits to the class increasingly sought to pave their way to success by making "good," that is, lucrative, marriages. At the same time though, it was the bourgeoisie, especially in Paris, whose young were most influenced by the one area in which the theory of romantic courtship clearly held sway, namely, the literary milieu. In what emerged as a more general youthful rebellion,[14] prophets of the new movement preached the priority of feeling and sentiment in courtship and, in doing so, won the attentions of a wide and sympathetic middle-class audience. It is perhaps not paradoxical that a generation whose options to marry for "inclination" continued to be restricted—in some ways more than ever—should have responded to a liberating romantic ideal for escape, however illusory.

It is not easy to grasp the roles and responses of marriageable bourgeois women, surrounded by the appealing new reading material, yet obliged to wear the price tags of their dowries. Were these young women actually denied access to romantic literature until a "prudent" marriage was arranged, as official pronouncements suggested,[15] or did they contrive to lay hands on it before then, as seems more likely? And if they were exposed to this new ideal, how did it affect them, given the fact that for most such women, there was an arranged marriage in store? Whatever the answers for women of the class as a whole, it is likely that more sensitive bourgeois daughters exposed both to social changes and to new romantic ideals came to perceive apparently contradictory impulses in their society.

Parisian daughters, at least, were aware that the marriage market was expanding, as ambitious young provincials such as Charles Lafarge flooded into the capital in search of wives and fortune.[16] Romantic ideals were unlikely to dominate among men newly enabled to achieve economic ideals, yet for the already well-dowried young women, the options were at least theoretically increased. Then, too, while it was true that their daily lives continued to be more restricted than those of their brothers and their more "advanced" female counterparts in England, young French daughters, and Parisian ones in particular, had access to varieties of vicarious experience through literature which were arguably greater than those available to English girls.

The new popular romantic novels in France had not yet been sanitized by stern middle-class canons of respectability, as they had been in England.[17] Many of these French works attacked the arranged marriage as "bourgeois," glorified love-matches which overcame social barriers, and featured active roles for female heroines. Of course, much of this literature, most notably the wildly popular works of George Sand, emerged out of a basically aristocratic tradition of freedom for women, with its older conceptions of "salon feminism" merely given some new twists. But this fact made it no less potent in a bourgeois milieu which remained powerfully attracted to aristocratic ideals. The natural result for the avid readers of such fiction, especially given their limited experience, must have been the creation of a huge "credibility gap" as the realities of actual courtship and marriage in their society dawned upon them. But documented evidence of such casualties among bourgeois daughters is difficult to uncover, except in literary portraits themselves, such as that of Emma Bovary. Both Euphémie Lacoste and Marie Lafarge, however, do supply historical substance to many aspects of Emma's demoralizing fictional experience. And each young woman adds some ingredients of her own.

Both the accused women were proved to have nurtured romantic fantasies before marriage, but, not surprisingly, Marie enjoyed wider experiences and a broader education in her more elevated social milieu. It is often difficult to distinguish fact from fancy in her memoirs, but since the overall outline of events she describes was still verifiable by others at publication, it can be assumed to be fairly accurate. In the cases of both women, youthful experience does appear to have conditioned initial responses to marriage and, more especially, the strategies of escape—criminal or otherwise—which they adopted.

Marie Lafarge's memoirs portray a creature who from the very beginning was unwanted, unloved, and unattractive, although she appears to have exaggerated all these qualities for dramatic effect.[18] According to Marie, her father, who had hoped for a boy, was disappointed with her, despite her own intense childhood attachment for him. And to make matters worse, the sister named Antonine, who arrived when Marie was five, was promptly pronounced prettier and more endearing than she. At age nine Marie was sent to the convent school of Saint-Denis, but she complains that her already marked individualism set her apart from her two hundred fellow pupils, who were absorbed in nothing but their miniature versions of the social battles between the old and Imperial aristocracies. Rescued from the school by her parents after an allegedly serious illness, Marie declares she finally won the love of her adored father by showing her pluck in tomboyish escapades, including romps with the young officers under her father's command and mock jousts on horseback. But after her father's death when she was twelve, Marie swears she was inconsolable and records her fury over her mother's decision to remarry.

The only relief Marie admits in all her misery is the happy summers she spent with her grandfather on his estate in Picardy. She hints at her own aristocratic lineage, proudly describes the noble visitors, and relates that on one occasion she was even permitted to live a medieval romance by supervising the lands and staff as a make-believe chatelaine. Still, she constantly returns to the disapproving mother who would not let her forget her ugliness and recounts that at age fifteen or so she decided that if she could not be pretty, at least she would be intelligent. The reading campaign she embarked upon included Voltaire's *History of Charles XII*, which she reportedly preferred to the memoirs of the Empire, which she declared too harsh on her *demi-dieu* Napoleon, especially during his "sad defeats." [19] She loved Racine, Corneille, and especially Molière, enjoyed the accounts of the conquests of Pizarro and Cortez, and devoured *Paul et Virginie*. Most of all, she says, she adored the novels of Sir Walter Scott, and she recounts that before going to sleep she used to imagine that she was galloping along with her friend Diana Vernon "when, on her white horse, she went hunting across the mists of Scotland." [20] Later, it was an easy transition to the heroines of George Sand.

Confessing that she continued to feel awkward and unloved in the world outside her books, Marie relates that during her last visit to Paris with her mother, she was obliged to attend a ball at the Tuileries where, at age seventeen, she was "royally bored." [21]

I knew no one, the friends of my aunt de Martens were serious men, politicians and diplomats of an anti-dancing persuasion; moreover, after having admired all my sumptuous surroundings, the beautiful dresses and the pretty faces, and after having endured the torture of feeling myself carried away by the quadrilles of Tolbecque while the paucity of dancing partners kept me riveted to my chair, I finally went [home] to bed at midnight, exhausted by boredom and grateful to rest at last from all the pleasures of others.[22]

A year later the mother she said never loved or understood her became seriously ill, and Marie maintained that she felt great guilt for the love she herself had withheld. Still, she supplies a final death-bed reconciliation in which her mother's last words were, "Poor child, I loved you." [23]

This rendering of her early years at least reveals much about what Marie wanted her contemporaries and posterity to believe about her and her society. Written with charm and style (so much so, indeed, that at least one contemporary reviewer insisted it had to have been ghost-written! [24]), the volume portrays a gifted, misunderstood, and sympathetic young woman. It appealed especially to a female audience (the English translation in 1841 was explicitly dedicated to the Women of England [25]) and women in both France and England were reported to have bought many copies.

Marie's superb descriptions of personalities and events make the memoirs well worth reading as an account of the age, but what is more important for this investigation is that they offer some possible clues to Marie's alleged part in murder. These clues, however, are difficult to extract and interpret. Most obvious are the direct admissions concerning her self-dramatizing intellectual and romantic nature, her pride coupled with an inferiority complex, her individualism and scorn for the petty conventions of bourgeois and industrial society, her intense need to be loved, and her feelings of rejection. Yet all these qualities were the standard literary baggage of the romantic school, and Marie's facility in using them may tell more about her skills as a writer than about her actual self-perceptions. At the least, it is possible to say that Marie Cappelle was immersed in romantic culture when she moved in with her aunt in Paris in 1835.

It is notable, however, that by age eighteen, Marie claimed to have made numerous observations about young women in her society which, by the time she recorded them at least, constituted a harsh critique of women's position. She constantly refers to the necessity of a young woman's keeping silent and to her own obligation to express her feelings in indirect ways. She once remarks bitterly, "I was mute because I knew that a young girl ought to be concerned about others without pretending to concern them with herself, and that she ought to use her good sense to listen gracefully and hold her tongue intelligently." [26] Elsewhere she records her disdain for the showy, contemporary education for women in institutions such as the school her sister had attended in Paris.

It is impossible to imagine the importance given in these *pensions* to the rather ordinary beings we call men, persons who are neither much worse or much better than ourselves. They are fashioned into serpents, demons and spirits of the unfathomable depths, ceaselessly occupied in deceiving and beguiling us. A young woman must never look them in the face; if she is self-respecting she must answer them: "Yes monsieur, No monsieur." One syllable more might compromise her, two more dishonor her. Finally I am certain that if such sermons had been made to our mother Eve in forbidding her the Tree of Knowledge, she would have eaten two apples and we would be doubly wretched for her fault.[27]

Evidence of a feminist consciousness appears frequently in Marie Lafarge's writings, but again it is difficult to know how much she affected these utterances as part of a conventional romantic image, much as other women, who may or may not have been sincere, adopted the more typical romantic model of the passive, delicate, and submissive woman who outwardly acknowledged masculine intellectual superiority. However, to say that these opinions may have been affectations is not to say that Marie's behavior was not influenced by them. Having constructed her romantic castle, she may well have decided to inhabit it.

The developing period in the life of Euphémie Vergès Lacoste is nearly hidden, but there is little likelihood that her experiences duplicated those of Marie Cappelle. Like Marie, Euphémie had one sister, although hers was older and, according to all reports, less attractive than she. This sister was married—it had been at her wedding that Henri Lacoste had noticed his lovely, unmarried niece and arranged the marriage settlement. But the fact that Euphémie's sister had married first was only natural since she was the elder. That Antonine Cappelle had married before Marie, who was five years her senior, was yet another blow to Marie's ego.

Euphémie's father, a hard-working landowner of peasant stock, had become a small bourgeois *rentier* and mayor of his town by the time he arranged his younger daughter's engagement. She is pictured then as a religious and faithful daughter, carefully educated about the serious responsibilities of married life. In accordance with the agreement with her great-uncle, she went to Tarbes to a convent school in her late teens, and there she seems to have enjoyed her first opportunity to mingle with many young women her own age. Her movements were probably quite closely watched, however, since her parents moved to Tarbes for the duration of her stay, and she lived with them and attended the convent school as an "outside student."[28] Still, there is some evidence that she may have used her tenuous new freedom to form at least one friendship of which her parents disapproved.

The young man in question, Hippolyte Bérens, owned a grocery store in Tarbes. Nothing is known of the circumstances of his meeting with Euphémie. At the trial one of the residents of Riguepeu, a carpenter who had worked for the Lacostes, admitted that he had acted as a go-between for some of the new widow's suitors and stated that when Euphémie had expressed a preference for the grocer, he had urged her to consider the offers of some professional men who were better placed in society than Bérens. The eagerness of these suitors, who reportedly numbered fifty or sixty, was comprehensible, since Euphémie's newly inherited fortune was known to be worth about 700,000 francs. What was unclear was the nature of the widow's early relationship with the grocer. This relationship was considered crucial to the case, since an attachment before marriage provided Euphémie with a plausible motive for murder.

At the trial Bérens denied he had known Euphémie before her marriage, though he admitted calling on her when she moved to Tarbes after Lacoste's death and proposing to her a few months later. (His offer had been finally refused since Euphémie, in the meantime, had been persuaded to accept the proposal of a local lawyer, an offer which was subsequently withdrawn after the charges against the widow became public.) Euphémie herself denied knowing Bérens before her marriage, but both a maid and the carpenter stated in preliminary interrogations that Mme. Lacoste had asserted that she would marry Bérens since he had been her "first love" from her days in convent school. Realizing too late the serious implications of this admission for his friend Euphémie, the carpenter tried to withdraw it in the trial, but by then the probability of a prior understanding between the pair was evident. Indeed, it may have been the discovery of her "understanding" with Bérens which prompted Euphémie's parents to inform their daughter at last that other plans had been made for her.

The rumored existence of Euphémie's mysterious lover added a special element of excitement to the trial proceedings, but journalists reported that his appearance in the flesh was a sharp disappointment to the crowd of women in the ladies' gallery, many of whom stood up to get a better view when his name was called. Bérens, at twenty-seven, was described as a short, squat, and awkward young man, who stood nervously twisting the brim of his hat in his hands. "They expected him to be a hero out of a novel," [29] said La Presse, but the witness, who responded to questions in a stiff, rehearsed fashion, hardly qualified. His heavy blond mustache and sidewhiskers, which might have pleased in another era, were an added disillusionment at a time when the ideal romantic hero was not only tall and thin, but also dark-haired. Bérens, it was agreed, was thoroughly unsuitable.

Marie Cappelle would not disappoint the expectations of the curious in this regard. They learned that before her marriage to Charles Lafarge, her name was linked to no less than three romantic-sounding personages. The fact that none of these actually appeared in court permitted her public to maintain intact the image of their intriguing relationships with Marie, although each, in different ways, was exposed as less than the hero Marie had first imagined. She later described her vision of this paragon in her memoirs.

I saw in the development of my talents a means of being loved, and I adorned my mind for that being I could not yet see in my imagination but whom I hoped to find in the future, and whom I awaited as the complement to my existence. When I had written thoughts that were lofty, I read them to *him,* when I had conquered a difficult piece of music, I sang *him* my victory. I was proud to offer *him* a good action, and I dared not think of *him* when I was not satisfied with myself. He was not a man, not an angel, simply someone who must *love* me.[30]

The first possible embodiment of this ideal was to appear in 1836, shortly after the newly orphaned young woman moved in with her mother's sister. Marie soon adopted the habit of visiting an elderly great-aunt, another of Mme. de Genlis' daughters, who bought her a piano and filled her head with tales of the Old Regime. It was through this relative that she met Marie de Nicolai, the friend with whom she would have her first adventure with a romantic hero. Her guardian, Aunt Garat, later stated that she thoroughly disapproved of the girls' friendship, not only because Mlle. de Nicolai's family was not from her own "circle," from which she wanted her niece to select all her friends, but also because the de Nicolais' aristocratic connections were bound to give Marie ideas of a future marriage which were beyond her limited means.[31]

The friendship nonetheless was permitted to continue, and Marie de Nicolai one day confided to Marie Cappelle that she had noticed a handsome, elegantly dressed stranger with a worshiping look who seemed to be following them on their chaperoned daily walks. Enchanted, the enterprising Mlle. Cappelle discovered through an acquaintance that the young man was a Spaniard and a poet named Félix Clavé. But the two girls soon learned that far from being the creature of noble birth they had both imagined, Clavé was the son of a mere teacher who ran a school in the Boulevard du Roule. Disillusioned, Mlle. de Nicolai was ready to abandon any intrigue, but Marie Cappelle said she criticized her friend for her snobbery: "If you wished to make a marriage of convenience, I would understand your hesitation, but if your heart belongs to him, can you take it back?" [32] She persuaded her friend that they should send Clavé a note which she had composed: "For our health, a walk in the Champs-Elysées at two o'clock; for our salvation, a prayer at St. Philippe du Roule." [33]

The delighted recipient kept the appointment, but Marie Cappelle soon realized that the young Clavé's affections were devoted solely to her prettier companion. Although Mlle. de Nicolai remained nervous about pursuing the relationship, her friend volunteered to act as a go-between and urged Clavé to send his letters to the home of her great-aunt, who fortunately did not examine her mail. He readily complied, with unctuous outpourings of fine sentiment—now in poetry, now in prose—which would later produce hilarity when they were soberly read aloud in court.[34]

Marie Cappelle, who did her best to transfer Clavé's love to herself, was forced, as she said, to be the "second Marie."

> I had loved him first for Marie, then later for the noble, strange and proud sentiments which he permitted to escape from his heart into these letters. I understood them all, I shared some of them, and if he sent all his love to Marie, all his thoughts, all his sorrows were for me.[35]

The young man admitted to a male friend that he had unintentionally aroused Mlle. Cappelle's love for him, and he felt obliged to remind her firmly that his affections were elsewhere.

> Say that I am an egotist, that I am ungrateful, a vile and contemptible man, say all that, dear Mariquitta, and God knows you will not have lied. I am worse still—I am in love. . . . How could it be that I have neglected to thank you for the charming present you made for me? Yes, I will wear it in memory of you and in order that God will forgive me for being so ungrateful and thoughtless. I hope, Mariquitta, that you, who are so good, so devoted, will not resent my unpardonable conduct and that in spite of everything, you will continue to give me the support I need so much. You can write *to her* that since that day she has caused me to commit so many idiocies that I no longer recognize myself, my head is so turned about.[36]

Marie de Nicolai, meanwhile, began to grow frightened over her participation in this innocent though possibly compromising adventure. Exhibiting more typical behavior than her love-struck girlfriend, she confessed all to her governess and was told she should write promptly to Mlle. Cappelle and request the return of the letters in which she had discussed Clavé. She did so, but received instead a thin volume of poetry by Clavé, which contained an ardent but respectful good-by letter apologizing for having caused even a moment's anxiety. Marie Cappelle told her friend that she was most upset with her for having confessed to the governess, but she finally returned most of the letters.

The incident produced hard feelings between the young women and they became temporarily estranged. Clavé, meanwhile, declared himself heartbroken and late in 1836 left France for Algeria. Marie continued to write to him for a while, but it was clear that his ardor for Mlle. de Nicolai cooled as his business interests in an agricultural concern there developed. Marie Cappelle, now twenty-one, was deprived of even the vicarious pleasures of being a go-between.

Marie's two other romantic adventures were more fleeting, but in one of these, at least, she would taste the joys of being herself the object of a young man's attentions. Again, the meeting took place on a walk, although this time her companions were her three-year-old niece Gabrielle, the English governess who served as chaperon, and a dog. Marie admitted that her pleasure on these outings was in pretending that she was Gabrielle's mother: "I called her my child, and it seemed to me that everyone envied me my beautiful angel, and that I was doubly a woman and doubly worthy of respect." [37] Marie well understood the special prestige of the married woman and mother in her country, although she was distracted from this impersonation one day when she noticed that an elegant young man, dressed in the height of fashion with yellow gloves and highly polished boots, smiled at her and seemed captivated by Gabrielle. Thereafter, Marie and her companions encountered this man every day on their walks. Far from urging Marie to discourage his interest, the governess seemed impressed by the gentleman, or so Marie said, and assured her that in England many "young misses" began the "stories of their marriages" in just such chance encounters.[38]

Marie confessed later that she might not have been so enchanted had she not recently been deeply impressed by a novel whose hero was a man who followed his female idol everywhere, wrote her delicate letters, saved her life, and sought her love without ever daring to approach her. After six hundred pages of this exemplary behavior, Anatole, as he was called, was revealed to be a deaf-mute, and his readers, by then madly in love with him, dissolved in tears. The tragic ending was averted, however, for Anatole's beloved was moved to return his love. A kind priest taught her sign language and, needless to say, the pair married and lived happily ever after.[39]

It was not to be so in the case of Marie and her hero, although he reportedly did do a good bit of following her about, waiting for her in churches, handing her notes and flowers, and standing around beneath her window. They regularly exchanged letters in the Tuileries gardens, but Marie, perhaps wishing to conform to her novel, said she never spoke a word to her admirer. Unfortunately for her, however, her aunt discovered the little intrigue and assured her that the young man was doubtless showing her letters about for sport. If he was a person of any standing in society, she insisted, he would never be so imprudent as to marry a girl who would dare to write to someone unknown to her family. If, as was more likely, he was a scoundrel, he had doubtless mistaken her for a rich heiress and now all her dowry would be insufficient to buy his silence.

As her niece trembled in fear for her good name, Mme. Garat set out to discover the young man's identity and recover Marie's letters. She returned with the galling news that the young admirer was none other than a druggist, a M. Guyot, whose income was a paltry 600 francs a year. He had given up the letters without protest, she said, and was even willing to marry Mlle. Cappelle. Mme. Garat snidely remarked that if Marie wished, she could reign over Guyot's turkey rhubarb and senna before the year was out. Then, in family council, the aunt obliged her humbled niece to listen as she read all her letters to Guyot aloud in a mocking tone.

Despite her sermons against snobbery to Mlle. de Nicolai, Marie Cappelle had no wish to marry a man who kept a shop. She nevertheless attempted to put the best light on her feelings.

> I would not have hesitated about marrying an educated peasant or an honest working man; but to marry a druggist . . . and without love! It was enough to drive me to despair.[40]

Of course, she would have more than hesitated over any *actual* peasant or working man, just as she was appalled by an actual druggist. Like most girls of her station, Marie understood the practical imperatives of class. But the episode had more tragic consequences. Several years later when the intrigue with the druggist was publicized during Marie's first trial, young Guyot, who was on holiday in a hotel, reportedly leapt to his feet in the guest parlor and exclaimed that Marie Cappelle had killed him. He was later found dead in his room, having cut his throat with a razor.[41]

The third and final figure in Marie's gallery was a genuine nobleman, but unlike the other two he is linked with the young woman in one source alone, her memoirs. There was an actual Comte Charles Charpentier, who owned properties not far from her grandfather's in Picardy. This man interested Marie because she had heard stories that he had a reputation for being both charming and immoral, indeed, even depraved. But her experiences with him appear to have been limited to a few neighborhood social gatherings and some chaperoned excursions on horseback. With these, however, she managed to construct an elaborate, but transparent tale. She alleged that this dissolute man, who was rumored to keep a demanding mistress in his chateau, had confessed to her that she was the first pure love of his life. He had even proposed to her in secret, she said, though he later told her in tearful, self-sacrificing tones that he could not destroy her young life by chaining her to someone who was aging and financially ruined. The two therefore parted in a dramatic scene for which Marie provides a complete script.[42]

The sole truth in the story is probably a psychological one. After the humiliating experiences with Clavé and Guyot, Marie seems to have decided that the only safe hero was an imaginary one—or a near-imaginary one—who, if he failed to marry her and carry her away, at least could not hurt, disgrace, or disappoint her. This was the fantasy figure whom she would briefly resurrect in her desperate letter to her new husband as the lover who had pursued her on her wedding trip to the Limousin.

It was no wonder that the same set of bourgeois women who would dismiss Euphémie Lacoste's pathetic grocer was enthralled by Marie's heroes. And no matter that these included a schoolteacher's son and a druggist, for that pair had learned their fictional roles well enough to pass for the studied and soulful young worshipers who peopled the women's romantic fiction. (Guyot, indeed, learned his role all too well.) Yet for most such young men, the practical concerns of scrambling for a "respectable" place in a Parisian world overcrowded with ambitious would-be professionals made romantic masquerading and literary posing no more than a brief episode in their lives.[43] To be sure, the young men's attempts to establish liaisons independent of family intervention and their use of elaborate costumes to disguise their class origins did underline a growing defiance of traditional norms of "interest" in favor of the new romantic ideal. But that defiance was itself hardly so disinterested as it appeared. Guyot and Clavé, like many other young hopefuls, were not beneath preaching romantic ideals when these held out the fortuitous consequence of a fat dowry.

Euphémie Lacoste's understanding with the grocer and her timid reference to him as the "first love" she had hoped to marry are part of the evidence that in the face of parental power the "romantic revolution" was cautiously making itself felt in the younger generation of the provincial bourgeoisie. But it took Marie's more bold behavior and her appeal to literary ideals to capture the Parisian audience. Her small intrigues were already more than most of her peers would have dared, yet her actions were less an aberration than they were an intensification of the urban girl's experience. The romantic literature and daydreams about men, the walks, the small adventures with peers, the authority struggles with more practical female relatives, were all the stuff of the urban middle-class girl's experience. Marie dramatized them, and her story, which sharply contrasted the extremes of new ideals and traditional imperatives, struck resonant chords in the young women who applauded her.

Both Marie's guardians and Euphémie's parents were criticized in the national press for the husbands they selected for their charges.[44] The fact that neither young woman had a real role in the decision was deplored more in Marie's case, for although Lacoste appeared to be a worse choice than Lafarge, greater regard was expected for the wishes of a young woman of Marie's status and "romantic" credentials. In any case, a young woman's right to participate in the choice, and even to seek a love-match, was an emerging urban ideal which provincial girls were not seen to share. For Euphémie, criticism centered less on the failure to consult the bride-to-be than on the choice of a husband who was three times her age.

It was true that in France the more traditional pattern of large age disparities between married couples persisted and that at this time approximately sixty percent of all married women were at least five years younger than their husbands.[45] Still, the age disparity between the Lacostes surpassed permissible limits even for traditional communities. Expressions of resentments among rural men against husbands in such cases—and especially against widowers who remarried, as Lacoste had done—persisted through this period in organized public demonstrations by groups of local young men to punish the husbands for removing eligible brides from the available supply. These protests might take the form of charivaris, that is, mock serenades at the offender's house with drums, cowbells, cooking pots, and anything else capable of interrupting his sleep.[46]

If Lacoste was spared this instrument of the enforcement of communal will—and there is no certain evidence he was—it may have been due to his elevated status in the village, and the fact that his bride was not from the immediate neighborhood. However, even in isolated Riguepeu there was some evidence of a growing change in attitude toward marriages among couples of grossly disproportionate ages. Several persons openly referred to the incompatibilities between a jealous old man and a young girl—which indicated some appreciation of newer ideals of companionate marriage. One witness characterized the Lacostes' relationship as more one of father and daughter than husband and wife. And a woman who kept the local inn and on whom Euphémie had called during the customary marriage visits confessed that she had told the new bride that, despite her money, she did not envy her being married to such an overbearing old man.[47]

Marie Lafarge's defenders attacked her relatives' arrangement through a marriage bureau and the trickery in hiding the fact from the young woman. Yet callous as it seems, the course of applying to an agency was probably a natural one for guardians, who had no legal obligation to share the family fortune with an orphaned niece. In the absence of a sufficient dowry, her relatives could not easily seek an eligible young man from among their own circle of wealthy friends. The marriage bureau selected, de Foy's, advertised regularly in the middle-class press and claimed to serve a large and "respectable" clientele.[48] No study has been made of this or similar establishments, but they seem to have been very active, especially during a time when so many ambitious provincials were coming to Paris in search of status and fortune. One of the lawyers at Marie's trial declared that the popular criticism of the marriage bureaus was unfounded and that he personally knew of many happy couples whose unions had been arranged through their services.[49]

Admittedly, Marie's relatives did fail to make a thorough independent investigation of the glowing reports they received on Lafarge, though in that they probably were no different from most of the bureau's clients. Still, had they troubled to question the family of Lafarge's first wife, they might have learned that the ironmaster had misrepresented his situation to them before marriage, that he had later confessed to his father-in-law a debt of thirty-eight thousand francs, and that he had even admitted that he had married in order to get the funds to pay it off.[50] There were other things as well, such as the fact that Lafarge was still involved in a lawsuit with his former father-in-law to recover money from a will he had persuaded his first wife to make to his benefit.

The testimony of Lafarge's former father-in-law was tragic evidence of the possibilities of abuse of parental power over daughters, even after marriage when their well-being could be threatened by feuds between husbands and fathers. Asked whether Lafarge had made his daughter happy, the father responded that he knew only that his daughter and Lafarge's mother often quarreled and that he had heard them doing so. He admitted that he had visited Le Glandier on just the one occasion when his son-in-law had confessed his reasons for marrying, and he stated that he had vowed then never again to set foot in the place. He acknowledged that despite having received word of her illness, he had failed to visit her before her death. Whether her mother or other relatives did visit her is not mentioned, but the pathetic story is evidence of how parents as well as guardians, without being consciously cruel, could continue to place family honor above the welfare of daughters, leaving the young women no source of appeal.[51]

In her memoirs Marie Lafarge presents a h ghly unattractive portrait of an aunt, sister to her guardian, who helped arra ge her marriage. A letter from that woman to her niece which was presenteu in court was more than blunt. Specifically, the aunt was bothered by Marie's dreaminess and also by what she suspected was a duplicitous nature.

> You flatter everyone, you coax everyone, and in a way that is not the least bit sincere. I wish your intelligence would teach you not to be false and clever, but good, friendly and simple.... Remember that people who are double-faced make themselves loved to begin with, but are detested afterwards when one gets to know them. Instead of dreaming about a whole lot of useless things, you should concentrate on correcting yourself.[52]

Her Aunt Garat's reported reaction in the episode with the young druggist was harsh too, yet that woman's own life had well taught her the futilities of dreaming about Prince Charmings. Daughter of aristocratic but not wealthy parents, she had been married at age sixteen to a rising financier more than ten years her senior.[53] Within a year she had become a mother and had assumed the social responsibilities necessary for the wife of a prospective executive of the Bank of France. Eighteen years later, when she scolded Marie for her romantic pretensions, she was still a young woman in her thirties, although by then she had a child old enough to marry. There were reasons why such a woman might feel disdain for romantic enthusiasms and reasons why she might sincerely have felt that in Charles Lafarge the marriage bureau had discovered a more than satisfactory husband for her niece.

Although Euphémie Lacoste gained fewer champions among the press and the public, there was less to be said in defense of the arrangers of her marriage, especially since they, being her own parents, might have been expected to give more consideration to her happiness. With eyes only for their future share in Euphémie's prospective inheritance, they, or at least Euphémie's father, M. Vergès, pressed ahead, despite some daunting obstacles. In a letter which he sent to the court,[54] Vergès explained that the priest in Riguepeu had told him that although he would publish the banns, a dispensation would be required from the bishop because of the couple's blood relationship. On top of this, he wrote, he, his wife, and their "poor daughter" had encountered another barrier in Lacoste's militant atheism—a view shared by many of his generation who grew up during the Revolution. In these circumstances several priests refused to marry the couple, and Vergès accused them of "failing to take enough account of the situation of my daughter." [55] Finally, he said, he arranged a compromise with an abbé in Tarbes who knew Lacoste and who agreed to ask the bishop's permission to bless the marriage. A private ceremony, which was never officially recorded, was held in the abbé's lodgings as a concession to Lacoste, who reportedly stated that he would be dishonored by entering a church. Vergès admitted that his daughter's conscience had been deeply troubled by the matter as a "child raised, thank Heaven, in the principles of our holy faith." [56] But he hastened to add that his daughter had sought and found reassurance and consolation with her confessor in Riguepeu. Vergès's letter contained more than a hint of regret for sorrows for which he had been responsible, and, as he well knew, these were less than the half of those that she was to discover.

Still, a remarkable feature of the introduction of both young women to marriages each had hoped to avoid was their early determination to make the best of things. Marie, despite her initial disillusionment, seems to have realized quickly enough that she had no options save to cope with her situation as best she could. Her first letter to her aunt did not mention the dramatic scene she had provoked upon her arrival by threatening to leave or poison herself, and while it acknowledged some discouragement, its tone was optimistic.

> In short, I was thrown into utter confusion for twenty-four hours. Then I bestirred myself, looked around me, and realized that I was married, I had adopted this situation: on the surface, it was extremely unpleasant, but with strength and patience, and with the love of my husband, I would be able to manage. . . . I have no wish to attempt the impossible, that would be to dream of creating a house which would look like one of those in Picardy; but I will exist nicely and pleasantly, and each year will give me some new source of enjoyment which will have been my handiwork.[57]

She asked her aunt, who cheerfully complied, to send her various items from Paris for which she had immediate need, including lamps, stationery, pens, and the essential imported tea which was so regrettably absent in the provinces.

To an aunt of her old friend, Mlle. de Nicolai, Marie wrote that despite her wild surroundings, she was adored by her husband and covered with caresses by her mother-in-law. That excellent woman, she said, had her intelligence smothered under the minutiae of household chores, but she would go through fire for her son. Again, acknowledging some disillusionment, Marie reiterated her new resolve.

> The misfortune of this life is that one dreams about it before living it, and nothing is so sad as being deceived in one's dreams. Yet if my arrival here

wrung my heart, I am stronger now and I have gaily set myself up as the Robinson [Crusoe] of my little domain.[58]

Indeed, the awe Marie inspired by the combination of her first explosive scene and her elevated Parisian manners had helped establish her ascendency as mistress in her new home. She gamely boasted of her regal status to her aunt in her first letter: "I am truly the most authoritative and obeyed woman in France and Navarre." [59]

Euphémie Lacoste, newly installed in the Chateau Philibert in Riguepeu two years later, would hardly have used such expressions to describe her situation, and yet she too displayed the same combination of disillusionment and plucky resolve. Publicly she insisted that she was content with her husband. She informed a neighbor that although she had wanted to get to know people better, she would not be going out much since she had learned how it upset Henri.[60] For Euphémie, of course, there was less in her new situation to compare unfavorably with her upbringing; she even enjoyed an elevation in status as the wife of the most prominent citizen of the community. But, as a comparatively well-educated young woman exposed to disappointment in love and, more recently, to the trauma of a religiously irregular wedding ceremony, she now faced adjustment to marriage in strange surroundings isolated from regular familial contacts.

The fact that both Marie Lafarge and Euphémie Lacoste managed to summon any public optimism requires some explanation. Each, of course, realized that serious pleas for a separation would have humiliated their families and themselves; pride and duty played a role for both. But more remarkable than this comprehensible acceptance of their situations is the expressed enthusiasm which went beyond resignation and which appears to have been genuine, even in two such disappointed brides. It appears that for both women the enthusiasm emerged from self-conscious play-acting adopted as a survival technique which each believed appropriate to her new surroundings. But the models selected in the two cases were different.

For Euphémie, thrust into a traditional community where a wife's chief status still resided in her humble, self-effacing performance as her husband's chief servant, the choice was clear. She would simply "out-humble" all the possible competition and earn her status in a kind of monumental wifely submission. Neighbors reported their astonishment in the first months after the Lacostes' arrival over the countless services, large and small, which Euphémie cheerfully performed for a husband they admitted was far from lovable. Afterwards, of course, there were those, including the public prosecutor, who professed to see wicked self-interested designs in this behavior, but since it was demonstrated that she had full knowledge of being her husband's sole beneficiary from the beginning, such imputed motives were obviously inadequate. In time Euphémie does appear to have lost her early resolve and retreated into a brooding, morose existence, but such reported behavior might merely confirm a growing perception of the failure of her role-playing strategy in coping with her situation.

In Marie Lafarge's case, circumstances called for an appeal to a very different model, namely the new image of the "mistress of the home." [61] This model, trumpeted in the new advice literature for women, was a rather curious amalgam. She combined some features of the aristocratic woman, in her dual roles as chatelaine and salon hostess, with those of the leisured, urban middle-class matron, with her concerns for status, domestic order, and proper appearances. For Marie, however, the combination was ideal. Drawing on the advantages of her superior birth and education and her Parisian background, the new Mme. Lafarge succeeded in summoning enthusiasm for her new situation by casting herself in the role of the civilizing missionary to what she called the barbarian Limousin inhabitants. She took undisguised pleasure in condescending to share her elevated manners and taste and recorded gaily the pathetic attempts of the "imbecilic" provincial ladies to imitate her Parisian costumes. She also inaugurated new standards of cleanliness, and accused her mother-in-law of leaving parts of the house filthy with dust, cobwebs, and the droppings of the animals who lived there.[62]

The ideal of the mistress of the home which Marie seemed consciously to emulate was a creature who enjoyed growing recognition for the performance of altered, but still exclusively domestic roles. It has been observed that the French wife consistently exercised more unchallenged authority within her sphere of the home than her English counterpart,[63] perhaps because slower economic transformation permitted French women to combine older and newer roles more successfully. Far from being traditional, the bourgeois mistress of the home in many ways was a novelty, the product of a class whose growing wealth and education permitted a redefinition of the roles of women with special emphasis on a broad sort of domestic nurturing. As one observer well describes it, the bourgeois woman came to assume "the administration of the home as a social and moral entity." [64] It is hardly surprising that this new role was first realized in the wealthier upper segments of the class and that a woman such as Marie Lafarge should have regarded this status as her right, whereas Euphémie Lacoste did not even dare to presume to it.

In embracing her new role as mistress of Le Glandier, Marie Lafarge envisioned nothing less than the transformation of the estate and its inhabitants under her benevolent control. She at first filled her Parisian correspondence with hilarious, but often cruel descriptions of her rustic in-laws and their odd habits, as well as the hopelessly bad furnishings and dreadful color schemes in her new home.[65] Indeed, her comments on the latter might have been lifted out of a popular contemporary domestic manual designed to combat provincial bad taste in interior decoration. The scorn Marie showed for the yellow wallpaper and red curtains reflected the opinion noted there that either color was bad for a main room, since yellow made blonds look faded and red made brunettes look ill.[66] Marie promptly ordered the walls redone and had simple white curtains installed.

Naturally, this activity involved her in an inescapable domestic rivalry with her resident mother-in-law, whose devotion to her Marie appears to have exaggerated for form's sake. Marie reported triumphantly in her memoirs that she had made her terms clear to Charles, who conveyed them to his mother. One afternoon, according to Marie's story, Mme. Lafarge senior came to her and silently handed over the large key ring, symbol of household authority. This was a feat which Marie's predecessor, Charles's first wife, had not managed—or so Marie said.[67] And her account was probably true. Mme. Lafarge senior complained at the trial that she had sacrificed much to please her new daughter-in-law, including her own bedroom, which she had been obliged to abandon in exchange for an inferior sitting room.[68]

In addition to her assumption of domestic command, Marie reports that she was actively involved in her husband's business, a function which far more French than English women of the period retained. Marie evidently learned a good deal about the forge itself and about metallurgy, and she even studied ironmasters' manuals. She describes her husband's new smelting process in considerable detail, explaining that she composed the actual description which Charles submitted for his patent.

But the notable aspect of Marie's involvement in her husband's business is less her alleged interest in the forge than the way she mentally transformed it into an extension of the family's "feudal" domains. The establishment was located just down the river from the house, and Marie often visited there. However, her colored and poetic descriptions of the workers' joyous receptions and the flower garlands they ceremoniously gave her suggest that she was fantasizing the part of a medieval chatelaine, with the workmen playing updated roles as happy serfs loyal to their mistress.[69] The same attempt to disguise the unpleasant reality of her connection with the new industrial world is evident in her admission that she ordered a family seal which had the hammers of the forge engraved on it and an inscription of her own invention. "This was our arms of industrial nobility," [70] she remarked, and without apparent irony.

Having begun with the establishment of her domestic authority and the launching of a physical transformation of the estate, Marie turned next to the inhabitants, and especially to Charles. She instructed her maid to make sure that her husband's personal appearance, at least, did not offend, and the maid duly saw to it that Charles's ties pleased her mistress and that he abandoned the bright-colored waistcoats Marie detested. In addition to transmitting these sartorial suggestions, the maid informed Charles that if he wished to please his wife he should shave every day, attend to his hair and shoes, and wear gloves to keep his hands clean on his visits to the forge. Marie reported, too, that by her tactful prodding through the maid, she managed to cure her husband of two habits which she pronounced to be "infallible preservatives against love" [71]: floppy slippers and dirty fingernails, or, as Marie put it, "fingernails in deep mourning." [72] Yet, despite these successes, there were limits to Marie's attempts to make her new world conform to the vision she fancied.

A special problem area was the new bride's distaste for sexual relations. In her memoirs Marie reports that Charles had once tried to break his promise to live with her as a "brother" and that he had even attempted to break down the locked door to her bedroom, an effort which appears to have led him to an epileptic seizure. Marie explains that after this episode a sympathetic friend attempted to make her husband understand that "a woman's bedroom ought to be a sanctuary where she is the all-powerful queen; he told him that love cannot exist without veils of mystery and modesty; that a great delicacy in words, thought and action would gain my confidence, my esteem, and perhaps even my affection." [73] Elsewhere, Marie describes a scene from this early period in which a wheedling Charles begs to know whether once in a while, he might "love you also a bit as my wife?" As she recalls, her reply was, "We shall see. On special days, when you have been very good, and very loving, and when you have given me great courage . . . for I confess I am afraid, terribly so!" [74] Glumly, but with alleged protestations of greatest love, Charles agreed.

In her memoirs Marie insists that she and Charles never consummated their marriage, although she states that in December 1839, four months after the wedding, she believed that she was pregnant with the girl child she wanted so badly. She explains this somewhat extraordinary situation by alleging that her mother-in-law had told her she showed signs of being pregnant and that she, in her innocence, thought that perhaps it might be so. "I believed in a miracle, and I hoped to be raised to the dignity of motherhood by the grace of God." [75]

The immaculate conception Marie desired had not occurred, nor had the more ordinary sort, but there is independent evidence that Marie had finally relented and slept with her husband, despite her official denials. His rather awkward love letters to her after his departure from Le Glandier for Paris suggest so.

> It is ten o'clock, good little Marie, and you know it is the time to think of nothing but our love for each other. I am separated from you by sixteen leagues, and this night will leave me filled with sadness when, seeking you at my side, my hand will no longer encounter the object of my dreams and thoughts.[76]

Marie herself came close to an admission of their sexual relations in the trial. When she was asked why her attitude toward her husband improved after the first bad scene, she replied that Charles had been very good to her and had given her many proofs of his affection. "That touched me. I was not able to do otherwise than (hesitation) . . . than to fulfill my duties, to make life happier for Monsieur Lafarge." [77]

Marie's obvious reticence about sex, her invocations of veils of mystery and modesty, and her admitted effort to keep her husband at arm's length, despite his recent reforms in personal hygiene, provide a fascinating case study in the effects of the romantic movement and the bourgeois cult of female purity on domestic power relationships.[78] The ideal of womanly innocence and delicacy helped establish a prolonged period of sexual initiation in marriage, with the woman setting the pace. Moreover, the "rationing" of sex by women as a reward or punishment became possible once men began to acknowledge the "legitimacy" of female claims of purity, frailty, and innocence. Charles Lafarge was apparently a slow learner, and Marie managed to make him appear a brute even to some of his closest friends, including his lawyer, simply because he wanted to sleep with his bride and was not afraid to say so.

It has been plausibly argued that a new female influence in sexual relations came to be accepted in the nineteenth century as part of middle-class wives' growing gains in domestic authority.[79] Marie Lafarge clearly already took such influence for granted, and despite exaggeration and fantasies, she did enjoy real marital authority. Hers, however, owed much to superior social status and education prior to marriage.

Her continued misery is transparent in letters of forced cheerfulness she sent to her sister late in December 1839, in which she expresses the hope that she might be pregnant. She describes her dream of having a beautiful girl child to whose "interior happiness" she declares she will devote herself. This make-believe daughter was an obvious projection of her own self-longings,[80] combined with probable jealousy of her sister, who was actually pregnant at the time. As for the sister's child, she declares her wish that it might be a boy and adds wistfully that she would like to share with him "a bit of this ambition which merely dries up in my woman's heart, but which would be a powerful motivating force in a man, who can give life to his ideas." [81] The letters to her sister also cast some doubt on the innocence Marie publicly claimed in matters involving pregnancy. At one point, she matter-of-factly tells her sister that she hopes the baby will arrive "without lacerating your poor insides too badly." [82]

For Euphémie Lacoste, as for Marie Lafarge, the first months of marriage brought erosion of initial optimistic resolve. But to all outward appearances the two women had opted for nothing so drastic as premeditated murder. Euphémie, whose expectations were more modest and who was necessarily cast in a humbler role, was unable to appeal either to romantic notions of her delicacy or to a concept of her right to greater authority in household matters. There were fewer options for her in what was arguably a more troubling situation. For example, even though her husband appears to have been far more physically unkempt, and generally repulsive, than Charles Lafarge, Euphémie could not have presumed to employ their housemaid as an intermediary to remedy the situation, as Marie had done with her personal servant. Yet Henri Lacoste was unable or unwilling to tend to his person, and as he refused to pay others to do so, his wife assumed responsibility for his daily toilette. In apparently guileless testimony Euphémie shyly informed the court that her husband's insistence upon frequent kissing made it essential for her to shave him daily to spare her complexion.[83]

Being a personal servant to her husband, however, may have been among the least of the adjustments Euphémie had to face. Even his best friends, who enjoyed his heavy-handed humor, admitted that Lacoste was overbearing, opinionated, and full of strange notions. Several acknowledged that his jealousy and stinginess made his wife's existence difficult.[84] As a retired small tradesman, Lacoste had inherited his brother's wealth when it was too late to alter ingrained miserly habits. A friend noted that although he had a cellar full of fine wine from his own vineyards, Lacoste habitually drank only the filthiest, most inferior wine.[85] He was also reported to be fond of making coarse jokes of which Euphémie was known to disapprove, and friends reported that his normal manner of greeting male acquaintances was to leap on them from behind with growling noises and mock biting sounds, a practice which amused his cronies, though its impression on Euphémie can be guessed. Witnesses also acknowledged that Lacoste upset his wife by constantly attacking priests and the church. A neighbor who came to visit him during his last illness testified that when she urged him to pray to the "good Lord" for recovery, he had ordered her out of his house with curses.[86]

Although barely literate, Henri Lacoste seems to have had intellectual pretensions. He used to spend hours with an old friend who had two pet projects: designing a revolutionary sort of barometer and solving the vexing problem of squaring the circle. Lacoste considered himself an expert in several fields, including medicine, though friends said he customarily denounced all doctors as frauds and joked that the only practitioner he trusted was his friend the veterinarian. The popular maverick health cure movements fascinated Lacoste, however, and to a few friends he confided that he had a secret medical book which was worth more than the advice of any doctor.[87]

Questioned by the prosecutor at the trial about her relationship with this eccentric husband, Euphémie offered laconic replies which only hinted at the unhappiness which she had dared to acknowledge to a few friends and which now, not unnaturally, had become part of her alleged motive for murder.

Q. It has been said that your husband was very jealous, that he did not want to let you go alone to church?

A. I knew that would not please him, and I refrained from doing anything that might displease him; but he had never forbidden me in the matter.

Q. Were you in the habit of not returning visits which were paid on you?

A. I never went anywhere.

Q. Wasn't your husband jealous?

A. Perhaps so.

Q. Did you say as much?

A. It's possible.

Q. Apart from this, wasn't he stingy?
A. He never was towards me. . . .
Q. But witnesses, even some who are favorable towards you, have said that you complained that he refused you even the bare necessities.
A. That is false: he always provided me with what I needed.[88]

In fact, it appears that her elderly husband's more traditional views and his personal idiosyncrasies denied her much of the acknowledged, but limited domestic authority already enjoyed by most of her peers. It is true that since she was better educated than her husband—a not uncommon state of affairs in middle-class marriages in this period [89]—she did manage the account books and write all her husband's letters. Nonetheless, even her rights in the kitchen were usurped when Henri, a food faddist who took to vegetarianism, began to give orders there as well. A neighbor testified that he once saw Lacoste fly into a rage upon discovering his wife roasting a chicken on a spit. Shouting that it was unfit to eat, Lacoste reportedly grabbed the bird and tossed it out the front door.[90]

In sexual matters, too, Euphémie Lacoste could hardly expect special deference of the sort Marie Lafarge commanded. Her husband, she soon learned, reveled in a local reputation as a womanizer, and Euphémie could not have presumed to attempt ploys of innocence or frailty to deflect his advances. Henri Lacoste would have been less receptive than even a Charles Lafarge.

Lacoste's sexual demands may well have been frequent too, since he was reported to have wanted a son and heir as soon as possible. And witnesses reported that when his wife failed to become pregnant, Lacoste began to proposition the housemaids to have his children. One maid alleged that her employer had even told her that if she complied, he would provide her with a pension in his will.[91] Euphémie denied any knowledge of these goings-on and declared that if she had fired one of the housemaids, it was merely because the woman's work was unsatisfactory. Of course, the accused was bound to protest ignorance, since admission of knowledge of a possible disinheritance in another woman's favor would have provided her with a plausible motive for murder.

Curiously, although a threat of losing her inheritance was accepted as a possible motive, no one suggested that Henri's actual or attempted adultery might in itself have prompted Euphémie to plot the killing of her husband. True, everyone knew that the romantic attachment required for a "passion killing" was absent, but the notion that Euphémie might have killed out of rage over the personal insult of her husband's infidelity was inconceivable. Women—and certainly women of her status—were not deemed to possess any such claims over their husbands' persons and, when men did commit adultery, were expected to ignore it. The law recognized the situation by giving husbands alone the "right" to kill a wife or her lover discovered in adultery without being subject to a charge of murder.[92]

Other evidence in the trial did shed more light on the couple's sexual relationship and suggested that Euphémie's griefs in this area involved something even more elementary than injured pride over her husband's adultery. Questioned about whether she had not kept a close watch over Henri for fear of his fathering a child with another woman and changing his will, she replied, "If I had kept an eye on him, it would have meant that I thought him capable of fathering children." [93] The court at first passed over this and other hints she dropped about their sexual relations, but the entire testimony includes enough evidence to reconstruct those relations. They appear to lie at the heart of the case.

The probable truth of Euphémie's situation was revealed when she explained that after her marriage she had been upset about her husband's health and had gone to her father to question him about a hernia and some skin eruptions, as well as "other symptoms" she had observed. Her father, she said, admitted that he had known at the time of the marriage that Lacoste had had "secret diseases," the catch-all euphemism for venereal ailments, but he tried to persuade her not to worry, since he was sure that Henri had been cured.[94] Euphémie, as she hinted, had good reason to suspect otherwise. Descriptions of her husband's symptoms pointed to a long-standing case of syphilis. She had new cause to ponder the avarice of a parent who had knowingly turned her over to a man who was not only old, atheistic, and overbearing, but syphilitic.

The conspiracy of silence concerning the secret diseases in the nineteenth century was widespread, even though as late as the turn of the century syphilis was estimated to be responsible for fifteen percent of all deaths in France. The disease was one of the main causes of madness and was also held to account for over 40,000 stillbirths each year.[95] In less virulent forms it and other venereal ailments affected millions, many of whom, like Henri Lacoste, had recourse to self-treatment. Euphémie reported that Henri habitually treated himself with ointments and a preparation he mixed with liquids and took internally. Lacoste's condition was likely sufficient explanation for the couple's failure to have children, though his embarrassment and egotism prompted him publicly to attribute that failure to Euphémie. Of course, if his wife was actually sterile, it was probably because she had had relations with him.

The testimony of a notary who was related to Lacoste's first wife bore out this likelihood. The witness, in an embarrassed quiet voice, said that in a conversation he had had with Mme. Lacoste soon after her husband's death, he had expressed sympathy for her situation since he knew how difficult Lacoste had been with his first wife. At this, he maintained, Euphémie confided her husband's indiscretions before marriage as well as his attempts to proposition the servants. The notary reported that she also admitted fears of a disinheritance. More significant, Euphémie allegedly blamed her husband for giving her a disease from which she feared she might never recover.

According to the notary, Lacoste had ordered her to take the same medicines he took for his own condition.

Disturbed by the testimony of this prosecution witness, whose statements were not only offensive to her modesty, but possibly incriminating, Euphémie firmly denied the entire story. Her lawyer argued that the tale was wildly implausible on the ground that a woman like Euphémie was hardly likely to divulge to a new acquaintance things which she might be expected to hide even from a mother or a doctor. Still, the notary was probably telling the truth. Another witness, who had known Lacoste for forty-five years, testified that he knew of another woman who had contracted secret diseases from his friend. Lacoste had been in the habit of visiting her at a rest home, the witness reported, and she had been crippled ever since he had given her some of his home cures.[96]

Particularly revolting, it seems, was Lacoste's callousness, given his past experience, in proceeding to have sexual relations with his young wife in full knowledge of his condition. Such callousness, however, can hardly have been unique. In all the sympathy which her lawyer expressed for her, he never indicated any feeling that Lacoste ought to have refrained from having intercourse with Euphémie, nor did anyone else. Venereal disease may have been so common that to propose abstinence for so many would have been thought unrealistic. A recent study describes the spread of syphilis to the French countryside in the late eighteenth century by married seasonal laborers, who reportedly contracted the disease while working in the cities and brought it back to their wives.[97] This might have been what happened in the case of young Lacoste. In his *Dictionary of Received Ideas,* Flaubert said syphilis had become nearly as common as the cold and alleged extravagantly that "more or less everybody" was affected by it.[98]

However common the affliction may have been, there remains a special poignancy in the situation of naive, religious, convent-educated brides, forced to cope not only with the effects of the disease, but also with the humiliation of concealing their condition. That a man should have a venereal disease was, in a social as distinct from physical context, unfortunate and probably embarrassing; that a "respectable" woman should have one was degrading and disgraceful, the more so since popular myth maintained that the only women thus infected were prostitutes. It was true that there were no real cures, but the shame which kept men and especially women from seeking professional advice helped forestall serious medical investigation of the problem, which did not get under way in France until the 1880s.[99]

Euphémie, it appeared, had more than sufficient motive and means for murder: an admirer she had not forgotten, a will which made her sole heir to a fortune, a domineering and diseased husband who had threatened to disinherit her, and a friend to whom she had given a pension and other gifts of money and who, Lacoste allegedly said, had offered him some foul-tasting wine on the day he took ill. Still, though the hypothesis is impossible to prove, it is improbable that Euphémie Lacoste plotted to kill her husband. The apparently strong circumstantial case against her and her codefendant was demonstrated to be deficient in several points. First, the alleged accomplice, the schoolmaster Meilhan, may have been truthful in denying serving Lacoste a fatal glass of wine. Witnesses testified that when Lacoste felt stomach pains, which was frequently, he used to blame them on a bad meal or a bad drink, possibly to deflect suspicion concerning the syphilis and hernia which embarrassed him. Indeed, he had stoutly denied having a hernia, even though a doctor testified that he had treated Lacoste for one and had prescribed baths and leechings, which Mme. Lacoste had performed.[100]

As for Euphémie's gifts of money to Meilhan, these were hardly payments for his participation in a murder (their smallness made the suggestion ridiculous anyway), but rather tokens for his having performed the service of go-between for the young widow and her admirer Bérens in Tarbes. Another witness, the priest, said as much, although Meilhan's wish to protect Euphémie prevented this admission. Perhaps aware of the weakness of its case against him, the prosecution shifted to an attack on the schoolmaster's morals, suggesting he had impregnated his landlord's daughter.[101] This young girl had in fact died after an abortion attempt partly supervised—and bungled—by Meilhan, but many character witnesses, including the girl's father, came to the defense of the seventy-year-old schoolmaster and denied he had had sexual relations with the girl. Meilhan's assumption of medical expertise in the case of the unfortunate young woman is reminiscent of Charles Bovary's witless attempt to cure the local clubfoot. But however foolish or cruel, it had nothing to do with Lacoste's death. The prosecution succeeded in showing only that Meilhan was a cantankerous, proud old man who sympathized with Euphémie and who indulged in harmless subterfuge to prevent his allegedly greedy son from learning he had a few more francs than the son thought.

There was, as the defense argued, good reason to believe that no murder had been committed at all, and some recently discovered evidence in the case bears out this view. First, a reconstruction of the events prior to his final illness suggests that Lacoste became aware that his syphilitic condition had suddenly taken a dramatic turn for the worse. A few weeks before his death several persons noted the appearance of many new sores on his upper lip and on the rest of his face. One, his friend the veterinarian, related that when he expressed concern, Lacoste told him it was nothing and that he was looking forward to a forthcoming trip with Euphémie to Bordeaux and to the health resort of Bagnères. He even announced, "I'll be hanged if in nine months there is not a little Lacoste." [102] When the veterinarian told his friend that he should first see a doctor about his sores, Lacoste fumed that he wanted to hear nothing of either doctors or priests and added that he had procured a foolproof remedy which he intended to take before leaving on his trip.

Trial evidence makes it practically certain that Lacoste's remedy was a medicine called Fowler's Solution. The special ingredient of this dangerous potion was arsenic. Dissolved in a base of oil of lavender and cinnamon, the poison was so concentrated that a coffeespoonful of the medicine was alleged to be fatal for a person unaccustomed to its use. Widely advertised and readily available in France and England, Fowler's Solution and other similar remedies containing arsenic were considered beneficial in the treatment of many conditions, including skin disorders, anemia, ague, and cardiac pain.[103] Victims of the secret diseases were known to use arsenic remedies, and since the latter were also believed to be aphrodisiacs, they were taken by many men to improve their sexual performance. Lacoste indeed once hinted that this was purpose of his "secret potion." More likely he took it chiefly to cure his syphilis, though he apparently never divulged its deadly ingredient.

His announced intention to take his cure at precisely the time of his fatal illness provides the probable explanation of his death: Lacoste most likely succumbed to an overdose of Fowler's Solution administered by his own hand. It is fairly certain that Euphémie Lacoste did not know her husband's remedy contained arsenic, for if she had, when she heard there were rumors that she had poisoned her husband, she would hardly have ordered the immediate exhumation and autopsy of his body to clear herself.

The defense did suspect that Lacoste had used Fowler's Solution. The autopsy was consistent with the hypothesis, since a build-up of arsenic was found in the liver, which would not have been the case if the substance had been administered in a single fatal dose. Moreover, Lacoste's symptoms, which were reported by witnesses and catalogued in his own message to a doctor, fit exactly with those known to be characteristic of patients using the arsenic solution, which were different from symptoms produced by larger doses of the poison. A Parisian doctor who regularly treated his patients with Fowler's Solution testified for the defense that Lacoste's reported thinness, loss of appetite, and trembling in the limbs were typical symptoms.[104]

A recent case study of Charles Darwin's medical history maintains that arsenic tonics were probably responsible for the so-called dyspeptic and hypochondriacal symptoms of many persons of the period, including Thomas and Jane Carlyle, Thomas de Quincy, George Lewes, Robert Browning, Herbert Spencer, Margaret Fuller Ossoli, Thomas Huxley, George Eliot, and, of course, Charles Darwin himself.[105] This account provides additional evidence to support the defense's theory of chronic arsenic poisoning by citing numerous symptoms identical with Lacoste's. For example, there was immobility of the arms caused by boils and swellings, a condition noted as the reason Lacoste could not shave himself. Wartlike growths on the body, which were remarked by many witnesses, were another symptom. Finally, there were dizziness, chills, nausea, vomiting, and flatulence—all reported by witnesses or by Lacoste himself and all included in the syndrome for Darwin's Victorian malady.[106]

The problem faced by the defense at the time of the trial was that it was unable to prove that Lacoste had had Fowler's Solution in his possession at his death. A druggist did testify that Lacoste had asked him for it two years before, but said that his shop did not stock the tonic since it was known to be so dangerous. Only the local shops were canvassed, however. After the trial, word was received from a druggist in Toulouse who said that he had sold Fowler's Solution recently to an Henri Lacoste of Riguepeu. This evidence, which only recently came to light, strongly suggests that the acquittal was just.[107]

If Euphémie was not prompted by her troubles to turn to poison, it is likely that Marie Lafarge was. Having coped with establishing her authority and having made it clear that sex was a privilege for which Charles would have to grovel, Marie remained discontented, despite the piano and Arabian horse which her husband had purchased in his pathetic eagerness to please her. Several reasons have been cited to explain why Marie's early resolve melted away in the fall of 1839, but most important was her growing conviction by late November of that year, after Charles had left for Paris to seek a loan for the forge, that he had married her chiefly for the ready cash of her dowry and for the possibility of influence with her wealthy relatives and friends. Incapable of love for Charles, she nonetheless shows herself in correspondence of that period unwilling to tolerate anything from him save unceasing praise and fervent declarations of devotion. What she received instead much of the time were orders to write glowing letters in his behalf to her family and acquaintances.

> Therefore, *ma chère amie,* I think that you must immediately write the best letter you have ever written to your Uncle Paul. . . . I fear that your family finds me a scatterbrained amateur who is fond of plunging headlong into schemes without deliberating over them. . . . It is essential that you write to M. Garat in a way appropriate to the circumstances to explain that I am asking neither for his guarantee nor for any commitment on his part save for his affirmation that M. Lafarge, the husband of his niece, is an industrialist capable of going far; that before his marriage he made the most thorough inquiries among notable and honorable persons, and that Lafarge's morality, his knowledge of the trade of ironmaster, and his wise business acumen were unanimously guaranteed; that the value of his property was assessed at over 200,000 francs. . . .[108]

Lafarge urged Marie to distribute flattery when necessary, in terms which she declared humiliating; and intelligent as she was, she could hardly have missed the unconscious humor in her husband's directives.

> Coax Mme. de Valence for that little cross you want for me (the Legion of Honor). Tell her I have made a magnificent and most important discovery in metallurgy, and that as mayor of my commune, I carry out my duties with distinction and have brought about many improvements over the past administration. Finally, I have the credit of having saved six persons who were drowning and another found in a chimney, lying with his face to the ground, whom I brought back to life. I have plenty of witnesses.[109]

Many new wives who were "well connected" were doubtless obliged to perform similar chores for their ambitious husbands, and most probably did so with few complaints. But Marie was unlikely to suffer the task gladly, especially given her husband's heavy-handed condescension. He noted at the end of one of his letters:

> You may simply copy many of these things directly from my letter and send them along, for it is impossible that you could understand affairs of this sort.[110]

Marie understood only too well, but to reveal her feelings directly was forbidden. Instead, incensed over business letters which neglected the references to love that she required, she used indirect means to vent her rage which were probably too subtle for Charles.

> I love you, my Charles, I tell you so because I feel it with all my heart, because my vexation in receiving this lengthy letter, empty of love and empty of you, has proved it to me.[111]

Marie was more candid in her memoirs about the letters her husband had ordered her to write.

> I spent entire days in this loathsome occupation. I do not know how to beseech, the role of supplicant, which is impossible for me to play in person, was even more difficult to fulfill with pen and paper. . . . In the midst of these affairs, I often failed to understand M. Lafarge's behavior. I disliked the way he conducted himself in negotiating his loan, his resort to petty ideas and miserable means. . . . I was obliged to pray and close my eyes whenever the revelation came to my mind of the inferiority of this man who was my guide and master. In these moments of pride-filled insight, I would say aloud, in order to numb myself: This man is good, he is above you, everything about him is serious, useful, and belongs to the real world; he is your husband, you love him. . . . It is not he, it is rather the world, society and reality that you ought to blame for these first pangs which mark the transition from your beautiful existence of dreams and illusions to your present one of deceptions and duties.[112]

Her admonitions to herself suggest received opinion about what respectable young women disillusioned with their husbands were supposed to think. But in passages such as the above, Marie was broadly hinting between the lines that if she were guilty as charged, she had performed a service. For his shady business dealings, his vulgarity, and his inability to appreciate her as she wanted to be appreciated, surely Charles "deserved" to die, or so Marie seems to say. Her romantic creed, after all, gave to elevated, uncommon beings the right to dispose of prosaic obstacles to happiness, the right to liberation from normal moral constraints. Shortly after Marie wrote to tell Charles that his "empty" letter made her realize she "loved" him, she ordered some arsenic from the local druggist, to whom she explained that Le Glandier was overrun with rats.[113]

Marie's first plan appears to have been murder by mail. In mid-December she wrote to Charles in Paris to say he would soon be receiving some cakes she had asked his mother to bake. She urged him to eat his at a fixed time when she declared she would be eating hers—a romantic notion which may have had a deadly purpose.

There was never any solid proof that Marie had arranged to add a secret ingredient to the recipe, but circumstantial evidence was strong. Her mother-in-law, who broke into sobs during her testimony, stated that after the pastry was sent, Marie had had "premonitions" of receiving an announcement edged in black. Charles's mother testified too that Marie had asked her then about local customs for the length of a widow's mourning. Upon being informed that the time was two years, the young Mme. Lafarge allegedly announced that should the misfortune of losing Charles befall her she would wear mourning only for a year, according to Parisian practice.[114]

Even more suggestive was the testimony of a disinterested witness, an employee of Charles's hotel in Paris, who stated that he had unwrapped the package Lafarge received and that it contained a single large cake rather than several small ones, as Mme. Lafarge senior and Marie had insisted.[115] Charles had reportedly eaten only a tiny piece, which he pronounced not very tasty, and soon afterwards he had become ill and vomited. It is likely that Marie had arranged the substitution of cakes and that a single cake containing arsenic was baked by her servant, a woman who had grown up with her mistress and who, having been Marie's partner in more innocent forays against the master, became her ally in a more serious matter. Just before her trial Marie was overheard complaining that despite careful coaching her maid was hopeless in reciting her testimony.

Still, the cake episode was less incriminating for Marie than what followed. Charles made the mistake of returning home to recuperate from his illness, and almost immediately after his arrival on January 3, 1840, his condition began to deteriorate. By the time of his death on the fourteenth the entire household had reason to suspect that Marie had poisoned him. One of his doctors stated that toward the end, convinced that the substance he had seen his wife stir into his drinks was not, as she said, harmless gum arabic, Charles himself turned away when Marie approached his bedside. Suspicious authorities had her arrested when analysis revealed arsenic in liquids vomited and in the stomach of the deceased, in addition to that already discovered in the eggnog Marie had administered.

Soon the press had acquired the story, as well as a copy of the dramatic letter she had written to Charles just six months before, upon her arrival at Le Glandier. Its publication drew crowds of romantic youth to her cause.

Charles, I come to you on bended knee to beg forgiveness! I have unworthily wronged you! I do not love you, I love another; my God! I have suffered so much! I admire you with all my heart, I venerate you; but customs and education have placed enormous barriers between us. . . . Don't accuse me of falseness; since Sunday, since the hour I learned that I would be something besides a sister to you, since my aunts informed me what it was to give oneself to a man, I swore I would die. I took poison, but in too small a dose . . .[116]

The charges against the new widow prompted the family of her old friend Marie de Nicolai to press inquiries in another matter, namely, the disappearance during her visit the previous summer of a diamond and pearl necklace. When a search at Le Glandier produced the jewels, Marie explained the awkward situation by alleging that her friend had arranged the "theft" with her so as to have valuables in safekeeping to give to their old flame Félix Clavé, who, according to Marie, had threatened to blackmail his former idol with her old notes to him. This implausible story was later disproved,[117] despite the will-to-believe of Marie's supporters; her aunt testified that what Marie alleged were wedding gifts of jewelry from some acquaintances had turned out to be items her niece had ordered herself, made from the stones in her friend's necklace. At the time of the theft Marie, who was still unmarried, was acutely conscious that her old friend was both newly married and very wealthy. Wearing expensive jewelry, she knew, was forbidden to a single woman, and she may have been overwhelmed by the temptation to possess something of great value which was recognized as a symbol of the married state. It is possible, too, that she convinced herself that her friend had so much jewelry that she would not be concerned over the missing necklace.

In the end Marie Lafarge provoked her former friend to bring suit for theft by being audacious enough to write her an imperious and accusing letter, demanding an acknowledgement of the blackmail scheme. By then under suspicion for murder, she appears to have believed that her old companion could not deny her this favor which would help establish her credibility.[118] But her friend, with justice, refused to spare Marie Lafarge by subscribing to self-incriminating lies.

Of course, proof that Marie Lafarge had lied about wedding gifts and diamond necklaces was no proof that she had poisoned her husband, and her defenders rightly maintained that the public prosecutor used just such tactics. The necklace affair, heard by the correctional tribunal at Brives in July 1840 and decided against Mme. Lafarge, who was sentenced to two years imprisonment, was cited by the prosecution at the subsequent murder trial that fall as the first step toward premeditated poisoning. The act of accusation, which was based on the preliminary interrogations and, according to custom in French courts, read aloud at the outset, not only rehearsed the entire story of the diamonds, but made much of the "good and generous" Charles Lafarge, who had allegedly only wanted his rights to the sweet affection of a wife and to a dowry to develop his forge.[119] It was not extraordinary for an act of accusation in France to go beyond the statement of the *prima facie* case common in the more restrained indictments of English law, but this one, which flatly asserted a long planned murder and referred to Marie as "the poisoner," was unusual.

However, the verdict of guilty, which emerged after a trial of over two weeks in Tulle, was probably the correct one, if for some of the wrong reasons. In addition to the evidence of the cakes, there was the suspicious timing of Marie's ordering of arsenic for rats, as well as the discovery of an unexplained substitution of harmless bicarbonate of soda for arsenic in the paste prepared for the rats. There was also the revelation of arsenic in the mysterious box Marie carried in her apron and which witnesses had seen her dip into in preparing Charles's drinks. Finally, there was the conclusive report of the famous chemist Mateo Orfila that arsenic was present in Lafarge's body. Orfila had been summoned after local chemists at first had found negative results with the new Marsh apparatus for detecting arsenic, and most expected that his tests would merely confirm the earlier results. During Orfila's report Marie, whose composure until then had been perfect, collapsed. Attempts were then made by her supporters to bring in Orfila's famous rival, François Raspail, but by the time he arrived [120] the jury had already found the accused guilty with extenuating circumstances and she had been sentenced to life imprisonment.

Marie was spared the customary public exposure in the town square, as well as hard labor—such were the privileges of "respectable" female criminals—and she was also permitted the favor of imprisonment in Montpellier near relatives who visited regularly. After losing her appeal of the case, she devoted much of her time to the campaign to persuade the world of her innocence, though the cult which had formed around her gradually was reduced to a handful of faithfuls. In 1851, for reasons of health, she was removed from the prison to an asylum attached to a hospital. Her illness was reportedly related to the overuse of drugs, especially opium.[121] Early in 1852, after a plea from her doctors to the Minister of the Interior, Louis-Napoleon set her free. By that time most of her family, even including her sister, had abandoned her, though a devoted great-uncle and his daughter took the ailing Marie to a spa at Ussat, where she died a few months later, swearing her innocence to the end.

That Marie Lafarge had initially succeeded in convincing so many of her innocence owed much to the care she took for her romantic image. From the time of the necklace affair she had begun to correspond faithfully with "my believers," as she called them, the young men who sent poetry and proposals of marriage and the young women who sent sympathetic notes and small gifts such as a book, some flowers, or a pair of slippers. At about this time she, too, began to refer to herself as "the poor slandered one," a phrase which reappears with monotonous frequency in her letters. Marie reportedly made conquests of all she met, including Charles Lachaud, a young lawyer on her case who later became a famous criminal defender. Lachaud, according to his biographer, was blindly convinced of his client's innocence and never got over his infatuation for her. That Marie was aware of her unofficial status as a kind of national shrine was evident from a letter to Lachaud on the eve of her trial.

Now, praise God, the end is nigh, and I can count the hours until the moment when I will either be restored in innocence to my noble friends or else transformed into a radiant martyr, worthy of heaven.[122]

Marie did inspire mistrust in most older women who knew her personally, but some younger unmarried women, at least, were selflessly devoted to her. Emma Pontier, a niece of Charles's mother, had stayed with Marie at Le Glandier prior to and during Charles's illness; she was captivated by her Parisian relative's exotic ways. It is unlikely that Emma was privy to Marie's schemes, but once suspicion was aroused, she volunteered to do away with anything Marie thought might compromise her. Emma even took it upon herself, as she later admitted, to try to hide the box of poison Marie carried about with her. The maid Clémentine Servat, for her part, was almost certainly Marie's accomplice in attempted murder. Whether she realized it at the time or not, she must have known it by the trial, and yet she remained unswervingly loyal. With only her role as confidant to reward her, she stayed and attended her mistress in prison for over a year, until the authorities forbade her. At Montpellier another cousin of Marie's, who had never met her before, then assumed the role of prison companion. This young woman, Adèle Collard, literally abandoned her chances for marriage to remain till the end with her adored Marie, who acquired an exalted reputation in prison as a kind of saint of suffering.

Religious expression was a natural outlet for Marie, though even with holy men she hardly abandoned her customary seductive epistolary idiom. An intriguing set of letters to a priest and confessor which reiterates all her favorite themes [123]—constant illness and pain, innocence, need for supporters—contains numerous statements which go beyond affection. Self-taught in Latin, Marie takes childish delight in dedicating fond love poetry to her priest in this secret language "forbidden" to women. And her enthusiastic outpourings about her correspondent's sermons, even in that age of pre-Freudian innocence, contain sexual suggestions which may have been uncomfortably explicit for the abbé.

In listening to you on Sunday morning, raising the veil on the most sublime of mysteries, it would have been impossible for me to express to you what I felt. It seemed to me that you were making my heart grow larger and that each of your words, in falling there, made it grow more profound.[124]

In a little-known letter—written in 1846 to a prison inspector whom she had met at Montpellier—Marie made an absolutely unequivocal statement of her love;[125] but it is impossible to take even that seriously, except as one more expression of her return to fantasy. The letter is written in a style which suggests that the love is returned, but there is reason to believe its recipient was more bemused than thrilled to receive it. Of greater interest, in any case, are the comments it contained on her own past.

> As a young woman, I often dreamed enchanting dreams. I was later deceived in the first serious love relationship of my life, though before that relationship had become a passion. Brought back then by my aunts to a common sense view of life, seeing around me my sister, my cousins, my friends, marrying the first man to appear and showing themselves satisfied, I believed that the same thing would happen to me. I allowed myself to be married in a daze, but when I came down to earth, I was revolted. I had abandoned my dowry, my will, my life [itself] to one who had married me in order to restore his business with my fortune, adorn his parlor with my person, and complete his life with my poor life. But I announced I would only give my love if I were loved in return, and you know the reward I received for my candor: death, dishonor and perpetual agony.[126]

These were half-truths again, but convincing at least on the disillusionment and adjustment pains of marriage which faced Marie and, it seems likely, the other women drawn to her. Aware of these problems and sensing the dangers of spouses taking the law into their hands, several male reformers used the occasion to argue for the reestablishment of divorce. One paper, the Fourierist *Phalange*, was even inspired to present a bold attack on marriage for handing men the "legal right" to rape.[127] Most other journalists contented themselves with milder pleas for Marie's innocence.[128]

Women following the case left few written reactions, but their presence is reported everywhere. They waited for hours to catch a glimpse of the accused, and they fought for tickets for seats in court in the specially constructed ladies' gallery. Some made pilgrimages to Le Glandier, while others contented themselves with purchasing engravings of their new heroine which were hawked on the streets along with special editions of newspapers with accounts of the trial. For these women, it is plausible that the romantic image Marie projected was less important than the harsh realities which she faced and with which they could identify—not to mention the delicious, but unspeakable possibility that arsenic had been her answer. Marie, a consummate actress who knew that her audience was with her, went so far as to dare in court to justify her evident scorn for her husband and his family and to demand sympathy for her early escapist impulses.

> I ask you to make allowances for me. The day after my marriage I was obliged to leave my family and all that was familiar to me. I was miserable throughout the trip. . . . I had a most unpleasant scene with my husband at Orléans. . . . Upon arriving at Le Glandier, instead of the charming chateau I had been led to expect, I found a dilapidated ruin. . . . I lost my head, I thought of departing for the East. . . . I was so unhappy, I would have given anything in the world to get away.[129]

Euphémie Lacoste, in an objectively more desperate situation, would never have dared such a defense nor would she have found a sympathetic audience. Despite the flimsiness of the case against her, she was too dull and common to become the heroine of a national *cause célèbre*. And in the small departmental capital where she was tried, most of the citizens—men and women—were convinced of her guilt. Journalists reported that the deeply religious meridional population was shocked over the irregularities in the religious ceremony at her marriage, and despite the evident fact that Euphémie had been victimized in the matter and was herself troubled by it, many of the local populace insisted that such irregularities were proof enough of her guilt.[130] And if that were not enough for them, there was the persistent accusation of the prosecution that the widow was flaunting her new freedom, seeing suitors before the period of mandatory mourning was over, and spending money lavishly.

One witness said that despite her attempts to warn the accused about the impropriety of her conduct, Euphémie had had the temerity to say, "I do not care what people think; I am my own mistress." [131] If she ever made such a statement, the young widow soon learned how little it was true in a still traditional community where even small deviances aroused fear and hostility. For her the consequences of malicious gossip included standing trial for murder. It was the persistent rumors of her allegedly scandalous new life which, six months after Henri's death, prompted the mayor of Riguepeu to inform the public prosecutor of the growing popular belief that a person who could behave as she did must have taken a life. In this way the glare of publicity was focused on an unremarkable bourgeois woman whose obscure life would otherwise have passed unnoticed.

In nearly carrying off her aggressive and probably murderous role, Marie Lafarge was not unmindful of the awe in which her new family held her and the convenience of that quality in helping her openly to carry out a poisoning literally beneath their noses. That she and not Euphémie was the one who decided on murder made some sense, too, in that there was a far wider gap between her expectations of marriage and its realities than in Euphémie's case, however more pitiful the latter's situation.

Marie was clearly an original, and her intricate and troubled psyche deserves fuller exploration for its unique qualities as well as for those stressed here, which made her a symbol for a generation. In their own ways both Marie's and Euphémie's stories confirmed the still tenacious tradition of parental influence in bourgeois marriage alliances, but they also showed the ways the system was under stress and suggested how even in France the relative bargaining position of women was slowly improving. In both cases the traumas of adjustment took their toll, but the sensitive and unbalanced Marie never recovered. In the end she identified completely with George Sand's bruised and sexually damned heroine Lélia.

> Lélia, whom society has placed on the index, whom women, in their virtuous simplicity, disown and refuse to comprehend. Poor Lélia, who is reproached for her first love, and who has a second one forced on her! Poor woman, who has

suffered all sorrows, doubts, and discouragement; who was riveted to earth by evil passions and raised to the heavens by sublime instincts; who possessed equally the power for good and for evil; who did not want to be a weak woman, and who was unable to become an angel.[132]

This was perhaps the closest Marie ever came to a confession.

2.

THE WAITING GAMES OF BRIDES-TO-BE:

The Cases of Madeleine Smith and Angélina Lemoine

Madeleine Smith

WHILE THE NEW middle-class wives coped with the contradictions between their images of married life and its realities, the daughters of the class were facing the growing competition of the marriage market. The intensified public discussion of the special role of wives within marriage and the pervasive romantic and marital themes in popular literature had the natural effect of preoccupying young women's thoughts with marriage and, for many, increasing their anxieties about it. As urban life styles widened their circle of young male acquaintances and new popular fiction urged them to think about love-matches, it is hardly surprising that young women began to show signs of impatience with remaining parental prerogatives in the selection of their husbands. Some of them precipitated open conflicts with parents; others simply took advantage of increased opportunities to evade parental control.

Still, the new spirit of independence among middle-class daughters was less marked in the early decades of the period than conformity to the elaborate rituals of a system of social sorting through marriage.[1] Taught from childhood that the marital state was the unique objective of their existence, the vast majority of young women were obliged to prepare for it by passing the years from their early teens to mid-twenties in an atmosphere in which information and experience were far more restricted than for their brothers. If the daughters of the wealthier segments of the class could indulge in the proverbial array of idle pursuits, as well as in the limited freedoms of the boarding schools, all were made aware that these waiting years were critical ones. They would determine, after all, whether the efforts invested in promoting womanly "accomplishments" and in protecting virginity—if not complete sexual innocence—would be rewarded by the appearance of a suitable candidate for marriage. And a suitable candidate, as the women well

51

knew, was a man of similar social and religious background who could muster good manners, a decent appearance and, most important, a secure income.

Most young women initially accepted the formula and outwardly, at least, presented the expected pure and demure image. But given the prevailing system of surveillance, it was obvious that a young woman's being "good" before marriage might have little to do with her choice in the matter. The author of the most popular advice manuals uneasily acknowledged as much in addressing the "Daughters of England" in the 1840s: "Perhaps you are so protected by parents, and so hemmed in by domestic regulations, that you feel it more difficult to do what is positively wrong than what is generally approved as right." [2]

Despite the odds some Victorian daughters did undertake what was "positively wrong." In flouting the rules governing the waiting years before marriage, a few young women apparently even went so far as to commit crimes. Two such were Madeleine Smith, daughter of a wealthy architect's family in Glasgow, and Angélina Lemoine, daughter of a somewhat more modest but locally prominent lawyer's family in the town of Chinon in the Loire Valley. In 1857 Miss Smith, aged twenty-one, was accused in the arsenic poisoning of a shipping clerk who, to the general astonishment, turned out to have been not only her secret fiancé, but also her lover.[3] Two years later Angélina Lemoine, aged sixteen, was accused of complicity, together with her mother, Victoire Lemoine, in the suffocation and subsequent incineration of her own newborn infant.[4] Like the case of Madeleine Smith, the Lemoine affair soon captured public attention, not only because mother and daughter were alleged to have carried out an infanticide pact made soon after Angélina's confession of her pregnancy, but also because the father of the dead child happened to be the family's coachman.

Angélina Lemoine and Madeleine Smith would probably not have found pleasure in each other's company, but they had enough in common to have understood one another. Both were highly intelligent and willful; both were bored and restless; and both had a taste for romantic literature and intrigue. Madeleine, who grew up in burgeoning, industrializing Glasgow and was sent away to boarding school, might have scorned Angélina as a country girl educated at home in a town which, despite its superficially cosmopolitan atmosphere, was essentially a wine-growing community of farmers and artisans. But, when the activities of both young women came to the attention of the press in their respective national capitals, each of the accused was treated to the epithet "provincial," and not altogether undeservedly.

The two cases present many more obvious surface parallels. Both girls had reputations for being flirts; both, while in their teens, became sexually involved with older men who were beneath their "stations"; both were apparently the initiators of sexual relations; both viewed themselves in these affairs as romantic heroines; and both, finding that their adventures were not moving according to plan, participated in criminal activity to end them. These startling similarities may reflect more than coincidence. They suggest that the fantasy lives of middle-class girls, which were acted out in these two cases, included a shared set of surprising ingredients.

Explaining the similarities, as well as differences, in the two girls' behavior is hazardous, but on some issues, at least, the records do permit some fairly confident assertions. One might wish for equally full records on the majority of young women whose lives contained less dramatic episodes, but it is worth noting at the outset of an account of their stories that exposure in both cases was avoidable. With a little more care, romantic intrigue and even criminal activity might well have escaped public notice.

Madeleine Smith was seventeen in 1853 when she returned home to Scotland from boarding school near London; she was nineteen when she met and established a secret liaison with a poor but ambitious twenty-six-year-old Jerseyman of French extraction named Emile L'Angelier. The young man had been sent to Scotland in 1842 to gain the experience to operate his family's seed business, but he decided to remain in Edinburgh, persuaded in part by a romantic attachment. He had made an extended visit to Paris in the late 1840s and even claimed to have served briefly in the National Guard which helped crush the revolution in the bloody June Days in 1848. But discovering on his return that his intended had tired of waiting for him, Emile left Edinburgh and eventually settled in Glasgow, where he took a position in 1852 as a shipping clerk in a trading firm.

By 1855 L'Angelier had established a reputation as a hard-working employee and a regular church-goer, but friends described him as restless and dissatisfied. He earned a meager salary of fifty pounds a year, a good portion of which he seems to have spent on stylish clothes. These permitted him to play the gentleman during the walks about town which were one of his few pleasures. On one of these walks he had occasion to admire Miss Smith, who was permitted unchaperoned daytime outings in the company of a younger sister. Emile soon discovered Madeleine's identity, but the gap in their positions precluded their meeting at a social function. The best Emile could arrange was an introduction on the street by a mutual acquaintance from his firm.

To L'Angelier's delight Madeleine Smith was receptive to his good looks and apparent continental charm. The attractive, dark-haired young woman accepted a flower from her admirer, and the pair soon established a regular correspondence, employing the Smiths' servants and a sympathetic woman friend of Emile's as confidential go-betweens. The letters from Madeleine were carefully saved by Emile; when they were discovered in his lodgings after his death, they brought their author before the High Court of Justiciary in Edinburgh.

These letters, over sixty of which were introduced in evidence during the nine days' trial,[5] chronicle a relationship which captivated a Victorian public with an already keen appetite for crime and illicit sexual adventure in high places. As historical documents the letters are equally captivating, not only for the doubts they raise concerning some received opinions about Victorian beliefs and behavior, but also for the puzzles they present about an individual young woman and her perceptions of herself and her society. On the most obvious level they recount the growing intimacy between Madeleine and Emile, their professed plans for marriage, their first experience of sexual intercourse, and, finally, Madeleine's increasing coolness toward her lover and her unsuccessful attempts to break off their affair.

Although L'Angelier's part of the correspondence was nearly all destroyed by Madeleine,[6] we know that he discovered independently that his intended wife had accepted another marriage proposal from a suitor with superior social credentials, a merchant named William Minnoch who was a partner in a prosperous trading firm and a friend of Madeleine's father. Enraged over this betrayal, Emile threatened to expose Madeleine's letters to her father, and Madeleine, panic-struck, begged Emile to return the letters to her. Shortly after these events, on March 22, 1857, Emile L'Angelier died suddenly; a post-mortem examination indicated arsenic poisoning. Madeleine's letters were turned over to the police, who then discovered that she had recently purchased large quantities of arsenic. The druggist reported that she wanted the substance for rats; the young lady contended she had used it in a face-wash for her complexion. Madeleine Smith was arrested and charged with murder.

In one of the most sensational trials of the century, Miss Smith, whose guilt was more than likely, was acquitted, and the decision was greeted with loud cheers in the courtroom. Admittedly, she was not entirely absolved of suspicion, even in a legal sense. Although she could not be tried again for the crime, the verdict was the peculiarly Scottish one of not proven, which did not commit the jury to the innocence of the accused. Still, the sympathy for Madeleine was overwhelming. Newspapers, pamphlets, legal reviews, and even religious publications either stoutly maintained her innocence or else defended her for taking righteous revenge against a depraved fortune-hunter and seducer.[7] Everyone, or nearly everyone, seemed to want to believe Madeleine's story.

Angélina Lemoine was also acquitted of her alleged part in a murder, although in her case the victim was not her lover, but the child of their union. Born in Chinon in 1843, Angélina was seven in 1850 when her parents were legally separated. She remained in Chinon with her mother and an older brother, and her father moved his legal practice to Paris. The records of Angélina's tragic adventure begin in the spring of 1856, before her thirteenth birthday, when her mother hired a new coachman named Jean Fétis.

The little that is known of him suggests that the twenty-five-year-old Fétis, like L'Angelier, was a restless young man with ambition, but with even fewer resources than his counterpart. Like L'Angelier, too, Fétis had lost his father, who was a small farmer, as a young boy and had helped to support his mother until her death in 1854. Then he had come to Chinon to live and work with his brother, who had a small match-manufacturing business there. Jean appears not to have got on well with his sister-in-law, however, and he soon decided to go into domestic service. According to his account he was sacked from one position after nine months, allegedly for his inability to build a proper fire; he stayed only two months at the next place because he found the work too hard. The position he then took with Madame Lemoine initially seemed to suit him better, but he soon complained to his brother that young Mlle. Lemoine made a game of teasing and tormenting him, that she pinched him, pulled his hair, and often pushed him over as he weeded in the garden. By the summer of 1858 these games had become overtly sexual, and by November of that year the fifteen-year-old Angélina knew that she was pregnant.

In late January 1859 Jean Fétis finally confronted Mme. Lemoine with her daughter's condition and announced their desire to marry. He found himself promptly ejected from the household and, despite his efforts, never succeeded in seeing Angélina alone again. Mme. Lemoine, meanwhile, set about teaching her daughter some tardy lessons on the subject of a daughter's duty to obey the codes of society.

According to Mme. Lemoine's account of subsequent events her daughter's pregnancy was a fact, but she insisted that it was the result of a single act of rape. Mme. Lemoine dismissed as ridiculous the charges of neighbors, who claimed as eyewitnesses that she had attempted to induce a miscarriage by forcing her daughter to roll down hills and take rough donkey rides. She denied, too, the allegation that Angélina had been pregnant since November 1858 and maintained instead that her daughter's condition dated from at least a month later. In support of her statement she pointed out that Angélina had never worn other than her regular garments, that she had gone out practically every day, and that her figure remained small until close to the end. What happened in August 1859, then, according to Mme. Lemoine, was not a "delivery" at all, but a miscarriage. In her words, "everything came at once," with no afterbirth. The baby was tiny, physically undeveloped, and—most important—dead.

Soon after the event two anonymous accusations of infanticide were sent to the authorities, which forced Mme. Lemoine to file a formal complaint against the authors and submit to inquiries about the truth of the charges. She acknowledged that to protect Angélina's honor she had kept the pregnancy secret and burned the little corpse after the event, but she argued that what she had done was only her duty: "I did what any mother would have done in my place."[8] The court, as things turned out, disagreed. On the basis of evidence which had been elicited from Angélina and her lover during the extensive preliminary interrogations, much of which never came out in the trial itself, the court justifiably took the stand that Mme. Lemoine was lying. It accepted the view that Angélina was guilty of complicity in murder, but maintained that her actions were excusable on the grounds that she had been coerced. Angélina Lemoine was acquitted on December 11, 1859, and her mother was found guilty with extenuating circumstances and sentenced to serve twenty years in prison.

The verdict was greeted enthusiastically in Chinon, where Mme. Lemoine was condemned and Angélina was pitied. But the local populace was bothered not by Victoire Lemoine's heartless desire to preserve reputation at any cost, even murder, but instead by her alleged Voltairean beliefs, her separation from her husband, and, most importantly, her "failure" as a mother. Locally, Fétis escaped the brands of cad and seducer which Emile had received, although reaction in Paris, for reasons which will become clear, showed antipathy toward the coachman on just these grounds and sympathy for Mme. Lemoine.

The popular partiality for both Angélina Lemoine and Madeleine Smith was not totally without basis. There was some justice in the view that Angélina was coerced by her mother and even that Madeleine, though acting alone, had been driven by near irresistible terrors. Nevertheless, there was more than sufficient evidence to show that both these young persons had neither been dupes nor innocents and that many of their actions were both self-conscious and calculated. Most organs of public opinion ignored this, however, since young women, respectable ones at least, were by definition not responsible. Gentlemen were taught, after all, that nothing was a young lady's fault and, although the notion may have stripped women of human identity, they could find it useful in times of trouble. Indeed, irresponsibility was a kind of compensation for the relative ignorance in which they were kept. Madeleine and Angélina both learned to take advantage of it.

At the outset of their respective adventures, however, both young women were apparently eager to assume responsibility for their behavior, and they even seemed determined to make that behavior outrageous. Angélina, on reaching her fifteenth birthday, boasted to her mother and to the servants that now that she had arrived at the legal age for marriage, she could marry just as soon as she found herself a lover. Madeleine, reveling in her decision to carry on a parentally unauthorized correspondence with Emile, confided to him, "I know from experience that the world is not lenient in its observations. But I don't care for the world's remarks so long as my own heart tells me I am doing nothing wrong." [9]

Neither Angélina nor Madeleine, as it turned out, sustained the bravado or the behavior which these remarks suggest, and their reputations as crusaders against restrictive social codes are undeserved.[10] The real problem in understanding them is to ascertain how these young women, whose circumstances were typical in so many ways, made the initial decision to pursue the relationships they did. A sexual liaison with a social inferior, with the declared intention of marriage, appears to be the ultimate act of defiance for a young middle-class woman. Yet, within the limited set of experiences which was their lot, both Madeleine and Angélina found ingredients which made their actions follow almost naturally.

Their educations, in different ways, contributed to their decisions. Madeleine, at the age of fourteen, was sent away to Mrs. Gorton's Academy for Young Ladies near London, an establishment similar to hundreds of girls' "finishing schools" which had sprung up since the late eighteenth century to meet the demands of the status-seeking middle classes. Its program (to call it a curriculum would be too generous) comprised a daily routine of prayers, piano lessons and practice, walking trips, discussions of current affairs, needlework, and, most important, deportment. The company of males was forbidden, save that of the clergy of the local St. James Chapel. Religion was stressed—all of Sunday was devoted to services and church-related activities. Occasional special outings were also provided; during Madeleine's tenure the seventeen pupils were privileged to be conducted to the Great Exhibition and to Wellington's funeral.

Madeleine's performance at the academy in no way singled her out from her peers. Mrs. Gorton did note that she was "diligent, attentive, and exceedingly bright"; but faithful to her responsibility as moral guardian, the head added that Madeleine "could be most provoking" and that she was "given to stubborn sulks which most alarmed us." [11] The Smiths were apparently well enough satisfied with Madeleine's "education" to send their second daughter, Bessie, to Mrs. Gorton's as well.

The miserable quality of the education available at these establishments, as well as their unfortunate moral influence, were topics which were increasingly discussed in the Victorian decades. In an "Inquiry into the State of Girls' Fashionable Schools," [12] written not long before Madeleine's stay at Mrs. Gorton's, *Fraser's Magazine* condemned both the mercenary motives as well as the deplorable preparation in "fine ladyism" so characteristic of these institutions. More important, it complained that one lesson was communicated at all times to the inmates of the fashionable ladies' academies; that they were preparing themselves for the ever more keen competition in the marriage market: "Girls learn to grasp after show and pomp; and, as women can rarely acquire these for themselves, they are taught to look at marriage as the means of making their fortune." [13]

Fraser's Magazine also decried a less well-known feature of the fashionable boarding schools—the system of conspiracy which allegedly pervaded the daily routine.

> Concealment and deception prevail at girls' schools to a degree which the uninitiated would be slow to credit. Much that goes on is never told, for very shame—girls either fearing to confess that they have been confederates, or shrinking from being supposed to have shared in the common parlance. Many school-mistresses make a rule of reading every letter written or received: by such a plan the girls are left at their mercy. . . . It leads to collusion between the pupils and the servants—a result fraught with mischief: it induces cunning and

strategem in order to evade the rule; in many cases it weakens the tie between the girls and their home.[14]

It is not known whether Mrs. Gorton or one of her staff read the letters of the pupils, but the practice was common enough. Complaints about this system of spying were noted throughout the century, both in reformist educational writings and in the memoirs of many women who survived the system.

The pervasiveness of the kind of mild police state at the boarding schools and the natural resort to secrecy by the students make it hardly necessary to postulate any peculiarly well-developed sense of cunning in Madeleine. Her letters certainly do demonstrate a sustained, though often transparent, pattern of deception—indeed, probably more so than has previously been thought. Moreover, she was capable of arranging her meetings with L'Angelier by blackmailing a servant, who was herself admitting her own fiancé into the Smith home after hours. Shocked contemporaries might refer to an "efficiency in simulation and dissimulation rarely equalled in one who has scarcely seen twenty summers," [15] but it seems more probable that Madeleine was employing techniques perfected at school which were familiar to many young women of her class.

Angélina Lemoine's formal education was conducted in the more confining atmosphere of her home, but in this her experience reflected that of many of her peers in France, where home education was more common than in England. Angélina was therefore denied the pleasures of developing skills in small intrigues with companions her own age. Her instruction was imported daily in the persons of music masters and professors of history, language, and literature. Her mother, who appears to have taken more than an ordinary interest in Angélina's education, hired teachers from the local *collège* in Chinon. These gentlemen praised their pupil for a quick, open mind and an apparently precocious intellectual development, although two of them suspected that she lacked feeling and imagination. One even cited her habitual tone as "cold and dry." [16] Since several other witnesses reported Angélina's disposition as lively and outgoing, her cool attitude during her lessons suggests the detachment and boredom which were common among young women subjected to dull rote learning.

Angélina's father, like many parents, expressed concern that his daughter might be tempted to supplement her approved lessons with the "dangerous" romantic fiction of the day. He wrote to her from Paris shortly before her sixteenth birthday to congratulate her on her educational progress and to outline his own ideas on female education:

> but you must not forget an essential thing in the education of a girl; that is a knowledge of history, which teaches one to understand men and events which can ornament memory and provide essential nourishment to the conversation of a young woman; I urge you then to read history, and to read a lot of it, both

ancient and modern; it is the most fruitful reading you can do; you can also—and this is most engaging—read travel literature, until such time as you are able to visit places for yourself, but above everything do not read these products of the imagination of our so-called modern men of letters, these novelists, the reading of whose works leaves nothing behind, either in the heart or the memory; try to apply yourself to housekeeping, for even if she does so only occasionally, a woman needs to know how to practice everything which constitutes good organization of a household; in whatever situation a woman finds herself, this knowledge is indispensable for her.[17]

Angélina dutifully perused a history of France and an illustrated volume on the Touraine, but such relentlessly uplifting advice was hard to follow. Besides, it had come too late.

Madeleine Smith was also aware that history and housekeeping were officially approved subjects, selected to equip her to serve the future husband in both her decorative and practical roles. But far from following the prescription of cultivating these skills for later use, Madeleine, and Angélina too, chafed for something more immediate. Both created for themselves dramatic roles which preserved the accepted notions about the well-educated wife, but each re-cast the paradigm to serve her purposes and to justify otherwise unacceptable behavior.

In her letters to Emile Madeleine painted herself as the ideally educated bride-to-be. She regularly regaled her lover with recitals of her serious reading in the histories of Gibbon, Hume, and Macauley, though she said almost nothing substantive about any of them. She also solemnly announced her intention to abandon Byron, who stood, she knew, for all that was unhealthy and impure. Moreover, Madeleine led Emile to believe that she was preparing for their marriage by single-handedly directing the family's household. Revealing a probable acquaintance with the recent popular literature for women on thrifty home management, Madeleine declared in a letter to their go-between:

My Dear Friend, it shall be my constant endeavor to practice economy for Emile's sake. I proposed lodgings because I thought they would be less expensive than a house, and if there should be a little discomfort attending our residing in lodgings, we must just put up with it for a time. In time Emile's income shall increase. I don't fear but what we shall get on very well—with economy. I have taken the charge of Mama's house for the last two years.[18]

Madeleine exaggerated the occasional help she provided; she also failed to mention that her home was staffed with half a dozen servants.

Since formal and informal educational accomplishments were viewed simply as stepping stones to the more important goal of marriage, it is hardly surprising that the educational experiences of Angélina and Madeleine, like those of their peers, only served to focus their attention more sharply on matrimony. All, in a real sense, were in competition for a good match, and the awareness of this competition was bound to produce tensions. Some young women, including Madeleine and Angélina, appear to have sought immediate relief from their anxieties by creating a "husband." Each began with the only means available: romantic literature, flirtation, and subterfuge. But Madeleine's relative advantage was soon obvious.

Miss Smith's situation involved a return to family life after three years of boarding school. However regimented that life had been, it had at least provided the diversions of a peer group and an opportunity for an identity apart from her family.[19] Now, back under the parental roof passing the customary final waiting period before marriage Madeleine was idle and restless, a not uncommon state of affairs. Indeed, in England the awkward situation of the young woman just beyond school age, but too young for marriage was frequently discussed by educators, moralists, and the young women themselves. Ironically, while Madeleine was in prison waiting trial for the murder of the man who had relieved her boredom, one of her favorite journals commented on the sad plight of the girl recently returned from school with "an abundance of time and nothing to occupy it; plenty of money and little use for it; pleasure without end, but not one definite object of interest or employment." [20] This young woman, the article stated, is at first filled with romantic notions; then in disillusionment she turns to matrimony, "matrimony in the abstract: not *the* man but any man—any person who will snatch her out of the dullness of her life and give her something to live for—in short, something to do." [21] For Madeleine the pattern was slightly different, but all the ingredients were there.

Not all young women of the middle classes, of course, enjoyed the mixed blessing of idleness. But the vast majority who did not have to support themselves and who might reasonably expect to marry would not have dreamed of pursuing a career, and Madeleine was no exception. Still, even some of the majority of young women who were just as happy to stay at home were showing signs of discontent and comparing their lot unfavorably with that of their more fortunate brothers. One place where this discontent was registered was in the correspondence and advice columns of the new women's and family magazines. One enterprising young woman expressed herself as follows:

> We belong to the happy middle class, whose men are mercantile or professional; while the women do not require to work for a maintenance, but are, as gentlemen express it, "young ladies with nothing to do but amuse themselves." Now I wish it to be remembered, that we are offered no choice in this matter: the men of the middle classes do not choose that their females should work for money, so we have no option but as we are born or bred to be ladies, must live as such. Ask our brothers if they would exchange places with us, taking our "happy idleness" and our allowance of pocket-money; see if you would get one to agree to it, highly favoured as they talk of us being. Again, ask a similar

number of girls if they would willingly take the toil and anxiety of a business life, with its chances of making money. I can answer for it, you would find many ready who are now pining in the monotonous round of home-pursuits—busy idleness, unremunerative employment. But do not let anyone fancy I mean to advocate women going into the business world when it can be avoided. . . .[22]

This young woman went on to suggest that unmarried girls in a household be remunerated for their work in the home. "The wholesome stimulus of gain, which is the mainspring of most of man's labours, surely cannot fail to act well with women also." [23]

Madeleine Smith was occupied neither in seeking outside employment nor in fighting for remuneration for her services at home; but the same symptoms which prompted her more exceptional sisters to do so were prompting her to seek the more usual outlet in romantic flirtation. Her opportunities for unsupervised indulgence were few, but they did include those daily walks. Whether Madeleine gave her unknown admirer any encouragement in seeking an introduction is unknown, but she obviously welcomed his attentions thereafter. To her it mattered little that in reality L'Angelier was rather dull, vain, and something of a prig. She early confided to him: "I used to say there were three things I would like to do. 1st, to run off, 2nd, to marry a Frenchman and 3, that I would not marry a man unless he had a moustache and yours is such a nice one." [24] Madeleine filled her letters with all the romantic and sentimental clichés of the period. She quoted tender little poems, told Emile she wore his notes next to her heart, and coquettishly denied him a lock of her hair, claiming to respect a promise to one who "is now in the cold grave . . . and a promise to the dead is sacred." [25]

In her flirtation, at least, Madeleine had plenty of company. The women's magazines of the 1850s spoke with growing alarm about the new generation of "fast young ladies." [26] "Fastness" covered a wide range of behavior, but it generally designated a woman who was thought brash, self-assertive, and flirtatious. Like the "Girl of the Period" of the sixties, the "fast" young woman of the fifties was a caricature, but she reflected the reality of an increasingly wealthy upper middle class which could provide well for its daughters and thus create a distinguishable group of leisured young women in search of diversion.

Madeleine Smith admitted to Emile that she had once been "fast," but after she agreed to marry him, she pretended to be a stern judge of her still-wayward sister.

I shall do all I can to prevent my sister being fast—alas Emile that was what put us in such a conspicuous place in the matter of young men. At one time we tried to make ourselves conspicuous and we liked to be talked of—by gentlemen. B[essie] and I did succeed in that and I assure you that I am sorry for it now—I never did any other thing but flirt and I do regret it much. I weep to think of my folly, weakness, and thoughtlessness.[27]

In criticizing her own flirtatious behavior, Madeleine, as usual, was mouthing the standard admonitions of the women's magazines. She may have been fast, but she also listened to the magazines' warnings. In both ways she was anything but unique.

Angélina Lemoine, in embarking on forbidden literature and flirtatious games, faced a situation with rather different ground rules. Most important, her experiences and her physical world were drastically limited, compared even to the relatively restricted world that Madeleine inhabited. The tiny community of Chinon offered few diversions for the daily stroller who wished to "see and be seen," and handsome mysterious strangers were unlikely to turn up with any regularity. Madeleine enjoyed the more extensive opportunities for entertainment offered by Glasgow, such as theater, operas, and concerts, and she also regularly visited Edinburgh and even London. Angélina's only direct acquaintance with a larger urban center was through occasional shopping and visiting in nearby Tours, but since these expeditions were always made in the company of her mother, she had had no opportunities for independent exploration. There is no indication in the extensive depositions that Angélina ever visited Paris, although when her father conceived the plan to regain custody of his children, he tried to tempt his daughter with the prospect of a convent school in the capital.[28] The only large social events Angélina could look forward to were the mayor's and prefect's balls in Tours.

Unlike Madeleine, who had numerous friends and who was even permitted to make extended visits to some schoolmates who lived outside Glasgow, Angélina appears to have had no close friends her own age. One of the local residents questioned at the trial mentioned with disapproval that Mlle. Lemoine often chatted with the local *grisettes,* the working girls in the boutiques near her home. This appears to have been her only opportunity for socializing with young women. Nearly all the girl's other acquaintances were adults: friends of her mother and father, a few artisans who had shops near her home, her teachers, and the servants. The only age peers she saw with any frequency were relatives, first cousins who lived nearby. Mme. Lemoine's separation from her husband may have prejudiced some of the local bourgeois families against the Lemoines, but the situation was probably not extraordinary. The children of French bourgeois parents were constantly reported to be more restricted to the extended family circle than their English counterparts, even in the larger cities where opportunities for contacts were greater.[29]

With her options thus restricted, Angélina nonetheless managed to gain a reputation for loose behavior by local standards. Of course the witnesses deposing on her past activities were doing so in the knowledge of her subsequent pregnancy, and their testimony also appears to have been exaggerated by the prosecution. Still, among these witnesses were persons who saw Angélina frequently, including neighbors such as the tailor and the locksmith. The latter, for one, admitted that Mlle. Lemoine amused him, even though he found her a rather shocking young woman. He recounted that in the mornings when his fires were heating, he often walked across to the tailor's shop, which was located in lodgings rented from Mme. Lemoine, where Angélina used to come to pass the time with the tailor's wife. There she carried on conversations which the locksmith described as "more than singular for a girl of her age and position." [30] He added that he enjoyed joking with her, however, especially when young men would walk by and Mlle. Lemoine would make impertinent comments about them.[31] She adored gossip, he said, and was fond of speculating about which of the local girls might be pregnant.

The same witness volunteered that for some time before the Fétis affair, Angélina had been "fully developed" as a woman and quite aware of her charms. He cited the occasion of a *Fête-Dieu* parade on which Angélina had leaned out over her balcony to wave at two young strangers passing by, exposing in the process her very ample breasts. The young men reportedly whistled and made signs for her to come down, and the locksmith, while admitting that she did not do so, professed to deplore her evident pleasure in the incident.[32] Occasions for even such tame flirtations were rare, however, and Angélina, far more than Madeleine, was obliged to resort to vicarious experience through literature.

At the trial the presiding judge, who was eager to display a deplorable moral education, stressed that numerous witnesses had reported that Mlle. Lemoine was often left alone, that her mother frequently was not present as a chaperon during her lessons, and that her religious education was sadly neglected. Most damning in his eyes, however, was the influence of the "pernicious" literature Angélina was permitted to read, and he questioned her closely about it.[33] The young woman told him that for several years she had regularly read the serialized novels in her mother's newspapers, at first scanning them furtively while her mother read the rest of the paper, and later openly. She also said she read numerous other novels, including those of George Sand and a book entitled *The Confessions of Marion Delorme,* the famous seventeenth-century courtesan who had been the subject of Hugo's controversial play. The novels she claimed to have read in secret, but she may have said this to spare her mother the further opprobrium of the court. Whether these works were procured from the local girls she met in the shops or through the servants or the tailor's wife, she did not say. But it was a fair contention that such works did more than nourish her fantasy life. In a telling phrase Angélina would refer to her pregnancy as "the only way to complete my novel." [34]

The combination which Angélina presented was explosive: a precocious mental and physical development, limited experience, and an imagination crowded by romantic adventures of women struggling to find love and transcend social barriers. Still, for her, and for Madeleine as well, there was a considerable leap from the fantasy escape shared with many of their peers to the reality of sexual relationships and marriage plans with clerks and coachmen. In making that leap, both young women had to consider the stance they would assume toward the most important potential adversaries: their parents. To their lovers Angélina and especially Madeleine declared an open defiance toward their parents; yet both young women would show how much their parents' approval ultimately mattered. Moreover, in her choice of a lover, each young woman, consciously or unconsciously, seems to have been influenced by incidents of family history which each initially chose to view as a kind of sanction for her behavior.

The information on the parent-child relationships in both cases is limited, especially for Madeleine, since the elder Smiths were protected from public testimony and the evidence of other witnesses gave few clues. Other than Madeleine's actions the only guide is her colored and often unreliable correspondence, but the picture which emerges is the not unfamiliar one of a stern, fond father and an ineffectual, semi-invalid mother. Mr. Smith reportedly presided over weekly family prayer sessions which included the servants, enjoyed giving gifts to his family, occasionally obliged Madeleine to read him the newspaper, and was vastly amused by his younger son's precocious talent for swearing. More significant was the fact that he was frequently distracted and often away from home: "Appearing in low spirits has no effect with papa[,] he never notices. We see very little of him, only in the evening—I have never seen him in the morning all the summer—he goes at 8 o'clock—I don't get up till 9 o'clock." [35] Madeleine obviously revered and feared this aloof father; she constantly portrays herself performing his will in various ways: reading books, taking walks, receiving visitors—all at his behest.

Of her other parent, Madeleine said simply, "Mother is very good, but you cannot make a confidante of her. I could not open my heart to her." [36] The only other apparently reliable information about Mrs. Smith is that she suffered from migraine headaches and was frequently ill, but this may refer at least as much to her psychological as her physical condition. Her response on learning of her daughter's possible involvement with L'Angelier's death was once again to take to her bed. On the whole, Mrs. Smith appears a shadowy, background figure, dominated by her husband and outmaneuvered by her five children.

In December 1855 Madeleine summarized her feelings about her family for Emile.

> The love I have for my family is a natural love—I love them for they have been kind to me—but I must confess I fear them—I could not confide in Father Brother Mother Sister [note her ranking]—I fancy they are the most indulgent parents—yet there is an awe which should not be.[37]

Madeleine had compelling and self-serving reasons to stress the impossibility of confiding in her parents, but the awe she felt was genuine enough and it was perfectly typical.

One atypical element in the family history which may have weighed in Madeleine's reckoning was the example of her mother, who, as the daughter of a wealthy and respected architect, had married beneath her. James Smith was the son of a mere crofter, and he was only a promising young builder when he met Elizabeth Hamilton. Madeleine Hamilton Smith may have seen something of her father in Emile, but the choice of a poor clerk was less extraordinary than it might appear in any case. It was a natural selection for one whose head was full of romantic stories in which love triumphed over differences of rank and fortune. Even the more respectable women's magazines habitually preached the wisdom of considerations of affection over fortune in matchmaking,[38] and Madeleine parroted the current platitudes: "Wealth is the ruling passion. Love is a second consideration where it should be the first, the most important."[39] As the selfless heroine, she announced to their go-between:

> It was expected that I would marry a man with money—but is my happiness not before all fortunes[?] In marrying Emile I take the man I love. I know that all my friends shall forsake me, but for that I don't care. So long as I possess the affection of Emile I shall be content.[40]

There was perhaps another reason why Madeleine selected a poor clerk as her lover and husband-to-be, and it may have been the most persuasive one. Despite her protestations to the contrary, it is arguable that she intended nothing more than a secret fling, and for that purpose an obscure clerk whom she could keep hidden and whose world never touched that of her parents was the ideal candidate. The fascinated commentators, in their eagerness to portray a young woman who broke society's rules, failed to notice the obvious: evidence that Madeleine actually did declare her love for Emile to her parents and stand up to their wrath in announcing her decision to marry him is to be found only in her letters. Naturally, those letters are eloquent testimony to Madeleine's desire to defy the codes of society. The irony is that L'Angelier, who suspected that Madeleine was a liar, and subsequent commentators, who know she was, believed that in this instance Madeleine was telling the truth.

Though it is impossible to prove conclusively the hypothesis that Madeleine was lying about her parents' knowledge of her liaison with Emile, no other explanation accounts so well for her behavior. What emerges then is not a headstrong, willful young woman, but rather a manipulative schoolgirl, consciously acting out a romantic drama with herself in the leading role. There is no need to postulate Madeleine's gradual realization that she had to obey her parents and marry a man acceptable to them; she never intended anything else. What Madeleine appears to have wanted was a temporary escape from her boring existence. Indeed, since she was already aware of her parents' approval of the drab Mr. Minnoch at the time she met L'Angelier, she may even have decided that if she was ever to taste romantic adventure before settling down to married life with Minnoch, the time had come. To make that adventure both exciting and safe, Madeleine had to convince her partner that she loved him desperately and, in the end, hopelessly and her parents that she was the model of respectability and dutiful obedience. She nearly succeeded.

The evidence that the whole affair was a charade must be read between the lines of Madeleine's letters, but it is persuasive. From their first meeting Madeleine ensured that Emile, who desperately wanted to present his suit in the proper fashion, would never so much as gain an introduction to her father. Of course to Emile she protested the contrary. In her first letter she said, "And ere long may you be a friend of Papa's is my most earnest desire." [41] But within a few days Madeleine was already pointing to the obstacles: her father had been told that she was walking with a gentleman unknown to him and he was "very angry." [42] Soon she was urging Emile not to try to get an introduction "at present," since "my dear Emile all this must remain a profound secret." [43] Not long after, in despairing tones, she wrote, "I shall never be able to introduce you to papa—It must be a stranger so how we are to manage it I don't know." [44] By July 1855 a few months later, the two were secretly engaged, and Madeleine was still postponing the much-discussed introduction.

As Emile became increasingly exasperated, Madeleine was obliged to manufacture showdowns.

> I intend to be very decided with papa. Tell him I will never marry any other one but *Mr. L'Angelier.* I shall try and bear with all the threats he will hold but I am not easily frightened. He will find out that his daughter has a mind of her own.[45]

The vaunted confrontation was a disaster; Madeleine wrote the script.

> Farewell Dear Emile,
>   A last fond farewell. My Papa will not give his consent. I have given my word of honor I shall have no more communications with you. . . . Be happy, forget me, and may she whom you call your wife be a comfort unto you. . . . Fare thee well.[46]

Emile was amazed and hurt by Madeleine's treatment. A draft of his reply, one of three of his letters to Madeleine which survive, shows that by the fall of 1855 he was already deeply suspicious of his fiancée.

> How you astonish me by writing such a note without condescending to explain the reasons why your father refuses his consent. He must have his reasons and I

am not allowed to clare [sic] myself of accusations. . . . I warned you repeatedly not to be rash in your engagement and vows to me, but you persisted in that false and deceitful flirtation, playing with affections which you knew to be pure and undivided, and knowing at the same time that at a word from your father you would break all your engagement.[47]

Puzzling over why her father should have been so peremptory, Emile for a moment permitted himself to doubt that Madeleine had ever talked to her father:

I flatter myself he can only accuse me of a want of fortune. But he must remember he too had to begin the world with dark clouds around him. *I cannot put it into my mind that you are at the bottom of all this* [italics mine].[48]

Madeleine was very likely at the bottom of it all, but Emile never found out for sure, and even her most hostile critics have since all accepted her manufactured scenes with her family at face value.

Her immunity ensured for the time being, Madeleine reestablished her relationship on the old clandestine basis and began at once to act the role of devoted wife—perhaps out of guilt for her recent betrayal, but also for the pleasure of fantasy. She addressed Emile as "dearest husband," signed her name Mimi or Mini L'Angelier, and talked about their having a "little one." Eager to have Emile act the role of stern patriarch in this familial drama, she urged him to point out all her faults and solemnly described the inferiority of her own sex.

I have a very poor opinion of my sex. There is no doubt man is a superior being and that is the reason why I think a wife should be guided and directed in all things by her husband. I get few ladies to agree with me—they all think Woman is as good and clever as man. I allow there have been many clever women, but a Book written by a woman never makes the same impression on my mind as one written by a man.[49]

Madeleine was telling Emile what he wanted to hear; and it was the standard litany of the advice literature for prospective brides.

Until the spring of 1856 Madeleine managed to maintain their intrigue without serious incident, but Emile's growing impatience with her failure to gain parental approval prompted her to stage a second phony showdown, this time with her mother. The usual defiant and tearful scene was colorfully described, complete with Madeleine's account of her mother's refusal of consent. This time, however, Madeleine may well have felt that compensation, in the form of sexual favors, was called for. In any case, their prolonged marital fantasies as well as a few stolen sessions of what Madeleine called "fondeling" had prepared them for the final act, which took place in an outdoors tryst late that spring at the Smiths' country residence. Afterwards, both pronounced that they were "truly" married, but in contrast to Madeleine's evident delight, Emile expressed some regret and even upbraided Madeleine.

> Why, Mimi, did you give way after your promises? . . . I was not angry at your allowing me [,] Mimi, but I am sad it happened. You had no resolution. We should indeed have waited till we were married, Mimi. . . . No, nothing except our marriage will efface it from my memory. Mimi, only fancy if it was known. My dear, my pet, you would be dishonoured, and that by me! [50]

Emile's letter has been cited in proof that he was a cad and social climber who seduced Madeleine and then tried to convince her that marriage alone would spare them God's wrath.[51] No doubt Emile did appreciate the advantages of a possible marriage with parental approval, but it is as certain as these things can be that his protestations were sincere and that he would willingly have postponed sexual intercourse until marriage. There was a schemer to be sure, but it was Madeleine.

Because of her parents' separation, Angélina did not have as typical a family relationship as Madeleine, but she, too, was concerned to plan her affair with her lover so as to avoid any permanent rupture with her parents. In Angélina's case, however, the script involved an announced marriage. What else it involved is not clear, nor is it certain that Angélina herself knew for sure. Lacking Madeleine's canniness and experience, she was less prepared for the responses of everyone in her drama, including her own.

Angélina's mother, Victoire Mingot Lemoine, shared with Madeleine's mother a social and financial superiority to the man she married, but little else. Hers was a highly respected family of wealthy landowners, which boasted several lawyers, a judge, and a member of the Chamber of Deputies during the Restoration. In 1838, at nineteen, Victoire might have made a "distinguished" marriage, but instead she aroused considerable surprise by gaining her parents' reluctant consent to marry Denis Jules Lemoine, a young legal clerk from an obscure local family. After twelve years of marriage which she declared to be intolerable, Victoire Lemoine was awarded a legal separation in 1850 which included the custody of Angélina and her older brother Jules. Mme. Lemoine retained the administration of four to five hundred thousand francs worth of landed property which she brought to the marriage, and she gained from her husband the right to borrow without his consent. In return, she agreed to pay him an annual pension of eighteen thousand francs.[52] Monsieur Lemoine, who moved to Paris, arranged to be able to visit his children occasionally in Chinon at the home of a friend.

By 1856, when Jean Fétis was hired, Angélina's brother had taken a clerk's position at the prefecture in Tours, where his father had found him an opportunity to train for the law. Angélina remained at home with her mother, who stated that she chose not to send her daughter away to school because she did not want to be separated from her. After her father had left, Angélina had shared her mother's bedroom, and witnesses reported that the girl imitated and idealized her mother.

Victoire Lemoine had a reputation for being both intelligent and outspoken, and according to one townsperson, she beamed with delight when her daughter began to express firm ideas on many subjects.[53] Approval of such forthrightness in a young girl was hardly typical of bourgeois parents, but Victoire Lemoine would reveal the real limits to her approval. Indeed, it seems likely that in her desire to have a companion, she may well have overestimated her daughter's maturity. Angélina, in her turn, seems to have misinterpreted her mother's intellectual flights and alleged iconoclastic enthusiasm and falsely calculated that she could maneuver her mother into accepting her behavior, even when it included an announced marriage to the coachman.

The choice of Jean Fétis was, of course, a surprise to all who commented on Angélina's case. No one noted that it was commonplace for well-situated young men to receive their sexual initiation from servants; the initiation of a young woman in this fashion seemed unthinkable. The carriage maker's wife declared that she had refused to believe the rumors since Fétis was "far from being handsome."[54] The bourgeois newspapers, however, were incredulous on class grounds. *La Presse* remarked of the young man that there was no one "more ugly, more insignificant, more rustic, in a word more a coachman. That is the irritating puzzle in this affair."[55] *Le Figaro* professed to comprehend a young girl's being carried away by someone else: "One can understand a professor of drawing or a music instructor—but the coachman!"[56]

The simple truth was that the coachman was the only available young man for Angélina's adventure, so she had to make do. A relationship with most any other townsman was impossible in tiny Chinon, where privacy was at a premium. Angélina was left with the choice of a live-in servant or a tutor, and there is some evidence that she may have had designs on the latter at first. The head of the local *collège* testified that two years before, against his recommendation, Mme. Lemoine had selected a single man from Paris to teach her daughter languages, rather than the married family man he considered more appropriate on moral grounds, if not professional ones (the married man was a mathematician). Mme. Lemoine, he reported, soon informed him that the young Parisian was unacceptable, but without giving any reasons. It is at least possible that Angélina had been entirely too pleased by her new teacher; but in any case, the hiring of the other man removed the possibility of a romance with her instructor. Fétis alone was left.

In one sense Fétis was a good choice given that Angélina intended initial concealment. Her mother was accustomed to their bantering together and would not be suspicious. Why Angélina chose the summer of 1858 to alter their relations is not clear, but there are several plausible reasons. First, she had just turned fifteen and flaunted the fact that she was now of legal age to marry. Second, it is possible that the death of the tailor's wife that June cut off her one regular source of vicarious emotional experience outside literature. Finally, her own physical development and attractiveness were becoming more obvious to her.

There is no doubt that the initiation of a sexual relationship was in both cases the work of the young women. Angélina denied it, but her initial story of rape in the cellar was hardly believable, especially when she switched the account to describe an initial "overpowering" followed by several instances of passive submission. Angélina's aggressive role was simply mentioned in the trial, but the preliminary interrogations spelled out her orchestration of the affair beyond any reasonable doubt. Those remarkable documents chronicle the systematic breakdown of the rape story on which Angélina and her mother had agreed and reveal the painful details of how the enthusiastic and headstrong young woman was brought to acknowledge the duties of a daughter.

For the account of the sexual adventure itself, the authorities relied upon Jean Fétis, who told with naive pride a story which was more credible than that of either Angélina or her mother. According to him their sexual activities had already begun in the summer of 1858: "she embraced me, I would return her kisses; she would place her hands on my sexual organs and I would similarly touch her; but things went no further than this." [57] No further, that is, until the end of September that year when the two were supposedly fetching wine from the cellar. This time, Jean said, he managed to unfasten her underpants and put his hand inside; but despite the fact that she had initiated things, she asked him to stop and he did. A few nights later, however, she detained him on their return home in the carriage after her mother had gone inside. On this occasion Fétis alleged that she aroused him by stroking his genitals and then opened her dress and invited him to kiss her breasts. He complied, but added that when he warned that her mother might discover them, she had charged: "You'll never be anything but a simpleton." [58] Next, Angélina ordered him to come to her room early the next morning after he had driven her mother to the coach for Tours. Jean recalled that her parting words to him were "I need something, and you will give it to me." [59]

Fétis said he appeared by her command the next morning, entering Angélina's ground floor bedroom from the outside to avoid detection by the cook. Angélina told him to undress and get in bed with her; but he said that before doing so he wanted her to repeat her earlier promise to marry him. Without that, he explained, it was not worth the risk of losing his position. She promised again and, according to Fétis, added, "My mother made my father happy, and I want to do the same for you. Anyhow, I am young enough and nice enough to please you and make you happy." [60] With that Fétis eagerly joined her in bed and he reported, "I slept next to her without thinking about whether she was rich or poor." [61]

Angélina's statement suggests that she was consciously appealing to her mother's example, although the references are somewhat puzzling. By her father's "happiness" she cannot have meant his personal relationship with her mother, which was a disaster. Possibly she had been told that her parents had had a good sexual relationship or perhaps had enjoyed sexual intimacy before marriage, but there is no indication of this. It seems more likely that by his "happiness" Angélina meant instead her father's social elevation. She knew that what really mattered to ambitious young men in her society was moving up. Her father's marriage may have been unhappy, but she knew that it had raised him in the world and she intended the same favor for Jean. During the preliminary interrogations, Angélina confessed to elation in her first sexual encounter, which she linked directly to this definition of happiness. "I had read the novels of George Sand and I was divided between the shame of having given myself to a servant and the joy of having raised to my level a man who, according to the social laws, was in a position inferior to my own." [62]

For Angélina the shared excitement of sexual pleasure and intrigue was heady. She entered the sexual relationship with confidence and enthusiasm as well as an evident sense of drama. She had prepared the romantic setting in which she received her lover in bed, clad in a nightdress which, according to Fétis, she had carefully unfastened at the neck. Her lover reported that thereafter it was she who watched out for further opportunities to pursue their relations. He said they never had intercourse unless they were quite sure they would not be surprised, but that even when her mother was with her, Angélina used to take pleasure in leaving her for a few moments to steal a kiss with Jean in another room. He stated that except for the interruption of the grape harvest that fall, which took him away from home, they had intercourse almost daily.[63]

Madeleine's first experience of sexual intercourse with Emile has already been described. It too was the unsurprising outcome of a series of stolen sessions of kissing and caressing, and Madeleine had been the initiator. Her letters give abundant evidence, shocking even to her sympathizers, that Madeleine thoroughly enjoyed making love. The morning after their first "criminal intimacy" she wrote: "Beloved, if we did wrong last night, it was in the excitement of our love. Yes beloved I did truly love you with my soul." [64] So scandalized was the public prosecutor by such language that he declared he was withholding the most explicit passages out of respect for decency. Even Madeleine's own counsel thought the letters most disturbing and found their only explanation in "the corrupting influence of the seducer." [65] The judge pronounced himself astonished by Madeleine's "licentious" letters and declared that one passage, in particular, was written "in terms which I will not read, for perhaps they were never previously committed to paper as having passed between a man and a woman." [66] The offending passage was doubtless Madeleine's frank admission that after their first intercourse she had not bled, although she had felt considerable discomfort.[67]

Naturally, the withholding of some parts of the letters left the eager public free to imagine much worse. Had the letters been published in their entirety, their titillation value would have been sharply reduced. Madeleine never described love-making in any but the most general terms, never referred to sex organs, never used any expressions which might have been called vulgar. She employed euphemisms for menstruation (she was "ill") and for intercourse (the word "love" underlined). Her most explicit language was merely coy and suggestive.

It was a punishment to myself to be deprived of your *loving me* for it is a pleasure, no one can deny that. It is but human nature. Is not everyone that *loves* of the same mind: Yes, I did feel so ashamed of having allowed you to see (any name you please to insert).[68]

Elsewhere she chided Emile playfully: "You are a naughty boy to go and dream of me—and get excited." [69] Still, such admissions and expressions were startling enough from one of Madeleine's station.

Indeed, in the same year that Madeleine was brought to trial, the widely read physician, William Acton, defined the "proper" female as one who lacked sexual feeling. He even suggested that women who convinced themselves that they could take pleasure in sexual intercourse courted the danger of cancer of the womb or even insanity through overindulgence.[70] Even though Acton's views are now argued to be hardly representative of a middle-class consensus,[71] belief in the "unsexed" Victorian woman dies hard. Evidence of what actually went on in respectable Victorian bedrooms is scarce, and since the women themselves almost never expressed their opinions openly, the views of some of their self-declared spokesmen have prevailed.

Madeleine Smith's letters, however, bear out recent views that the traditional picture of the unsexed Victorian woman is overdrawn. Those letters, after all, were meant to be destroyed, not to be published abroad; it would be instructive to know how many similar letters were discreetly burned. Contemporaries remarked that women were declaring a moratorium on writing love letters since Miss Smith's letters had been made public.[72] It may be that Madeleine was not alone in her effusions about sex. The fact that her language was hardly pornographic supports this view, as do her conventional ideas about the relations between the sexes. Madeleine was no believer in free love or in sexual equality; she simply wanted a romantic adventure and she discovered along the way that sex was fun.

Madeleine probably had far fewer sexual encounters than Angélina, not only because opportunities were scarcer, but also because, unlike Angélina and Jean, both Madeleine and Emile were determined not to have an "accident." Madeleine wrote, "We must not indulge again—What if anything was to occur—What would they say—But darling it is hard to resist the temptations of Love." [73] Emile wanted desperately to have Madeleine, but not at the expense of the middle-class respectability he coveted. Referring to his chagrin over their intercourse, he wrote, "Oh! why was I born, my pet? I dread lest some great obstacle prevents our marriage. If Mary [their go-between] did know it, what should you be in her eyes!" [74]

Jean Fétis, on the other hand, felt none of this "respectable" remorse. He announced that he had no regrets for his sexual adventure and added on the subject of their intimacy, "What can you expect when young men and young women are always together, it is perfectly natural that relations of that sort take place between them. I do not think that Mademoiselle could say that I took her by force." [75]

Ultimately, of course, neither Emile L'Angelier nor Jean Fétis was completely satisfactory to the young women who created their roles, even though their actual personalities had initially made little or no difference. Madeleine found first that Emile took her pious promises to reform her behavior far too seriously. It was no wonder, for Madeleine repeatedly expressed a near obsession to be dominated and L'Angelier duly complied with lists of proscribed activities: no public balls, no card playing, no riding with men friends, no flirting, and so forth. Madeleine became increasingly annoyed, and by August 1856 she drew up the following rather blunt list of resolutions.

1. I have not flirted for a long time, so don't you. 2. I shall study watercolours if I can get father to allow me. I shall study anything you please to name. 3. I shall not go to a Glasgow Ball without asking your consent. Is that fair? 4. I cannot promise to go out only twice a week. This I could not promise. 5. I shall go in Sauchiehall St. as little as I can. 6. I cannot promise not to go out with B[essie]. I must go out with her when I have no other one. Janet is at school. I do not think it fair of people to speak of B as they do, for she is not so bad. You may have heard many stories as your friends have misinformed you more than once regarding me, so they may of her. 7. I shall write to you as often as I can and as long as I can. . . . my dear husband I don't suppose you have confidence in my promises, but will do my best to please you in all things.[76]

The rules were based on the couple's fantasy that they were in fact married, and it is remarkable to observe Madeleine's ambivalence toward marriage and her presumptions about the strictures of the marital state for women. She knew well that, as for most English women of her class, her period of "freedom," such as it was, was the years before marriage; once married, she would no longer be permitted even the innocent pleasures of flirtation. At first she was compensated by visions of a romantic poverty she had never known, but even these delights began to pale.

Dear me dear Emile have you only 50 [pounds per year] from Huggins [his employer]. . . . I thought you had 100. . . . How could I make such a mistake. I wonder you stay for such a small sum—You could have much more.[77]

In rather more sadistic fashion Madeleine used Emile's low status as an excuse for treating him badly whenever she chose. She was fond of describing her flirtatious adventures in social settings he would never know; and she often deliberately cut him on the street, only to apologize thereafter, emphasizing the *noblesse oblige* quality of her real feelings toward him. Her curiosity about Emile himself was virtually nil; she had known him nearly two years before she ventured to ask, "Please to tell me love what the P. before Emile stands [for]—I must know all your names." [78] Madeleine also constantly led Emile to believe that she was a victim of her family's taunts about his being "only a clerk," and she admitted candidly, "I love you more because you are poor. Perhaps if you had been well off I would not have loved you as I do." [79] The alternation of her fond endearments with her humiliating class references hurt Emile more than she ever suspected, but in her fantasies, her class prejudice, and her oblivion she was a distinctly representative young woman of her station.

The male authority role that Madeleine urged Emile to adopt had the practical function of bridging the social gap between them and may well have involved Madeleine's unconscious effort to duplicate her father's devices for gaining ascendency over his socially superior wife. Her insistence upon her father's disapproval of Emile also suggests a fantasy of a rivalry between the two men over her. On one occasion she assured him, "Papa's opposition would only make me love you more and more." And then, in an outburst of far greater intensity than would be required merely to discourage Emile's attempts to gain an introduction, she declared, "he hates you with all his heart—he despises you." [80]

Gradually, however, Madeleine began to get glimpses of Emile's real situation and personality; and her romantic drama, with this fantasy husband cast in the queasy role of authority substitute and romantic puppet, became increasingly difficult for her to maintain. By the time her father began to press the suit of his friend, William Minnoch, Madeleine was ready to abandon her adventure and submit willingly to her father's choice. She meant the dutiful words she sent to Minnoch shortly after the two had decided on a wedding day. "That walk fixed a day on which we are to begin a new life—a life which I hope may be of happiness and long duration to us both. My aim through life shall be to please you and study you." [81]

Angélina Lemoine left behind no revealing letters to chronicle the deteriorating relations with Jean Fétis, but her testimony is fortunately far more candid than she intended, and other witnesses filled in many details. Angélina's script was different from Madeleine's in that from the very beginning it involved a promise of marriage made in good faith. Making the best of the fact that Jean Fétis was the only available vehicle for her fantasies, Angélina cast him in the most appropriate role in her "novel." Fétis was to be one of George Sand's heroes—a rustic, unspoiled youth. Like Madeleine, Angélina insisted that her lover's humble social status pleased her. Fétis announced to one of his relatives that Mlle. Lemoine had told him, "I want to marry you, I don't want a bourgeois." [82] She confided to him from at least as early as the first time they had intercourse in October 1858 that the only way to achieve the marriage they both desired, given the social barrier, was by means of her pregnancy. The young man then proudly reported their plans to his brother, adding that Angélina was probably not pregnant yet, since she had told him that "success" after only one time was doubtful.

Angélina's naiveté and excitement blinded her to obvious precautions which Madeleine had known to take. Despite their agreement to keep their relations a secret until Angélina became pregnant and her mother noticed, rumors began to spread. For one thing, Mlle. Lemoine overlooked the danger of the servants telling tales. She took no pains to remove or prevent suspicious stains on the sheets, and the laundress soon provided local scandalmongers with this telltale evidence. Angélina also neglected to win over the cook who, as the only other live-in servant besides Jean, represented a threat of exposure. That woman soon claimed to have discovered the couple in compromising situations.

Most important, however, Angélina was unaware that her new lover was totally incapable of hiding his delight over his good fortune. He admitted keeping from her the fact that he had told his brother and also a violin teacher, with whom he had begun lessons before his affair in hopes of leaving domestic service and learning to play the violin for dances. When his teacher told him he was wasting his money and would never learn, Jean boasted that he no longer needed to make a living by music anyway, since he was going to marry a rich girl. With a little prodding Jean not only revealed her identity, but boasted of conquest. Nearly every day, he said, she preceded him into the cellar, removed her underpants, and waited for him. Fétis told others as well. His brother's mother-in-law reported that when she told Jean she had a "little marriage" to propose to him, he told her to forget it, since he had a "big one simmering." [83] "I am going to marry the daughter of the biggest *bourgeoise* in Chinon," [84] he declared.

To the wife of the carriage maker he confided that he planned to exact a yearly income of at least four thousand francs—a sum which must have seemed princely to him given his annual salary of two hundred francs. He added that their household would require, to start, a nurse and a cook. Angélina's unspoiled rustic was beginning to sound very unlike a George Sand hero. He even ordered a new suit from the tailor Lieubray, which he had not paid for when Mme. Lemoine ordered him out of the house.

Emile, too, had told his friends about his engagement to Madeleine. The other clerks where he worked knew, as did his landlady, a shopkeeper, a friend in the French consulate, a few other acquaintances, and his family in Jersey. But in Glasgow, not only the larger population, but the social isolation of the classes ensured the Smiths' ignorance of the affair. In Chinon many social ties between individuals of different status groups remained, and a sense of deferential responsibility remained as well. Fétis's brother's wife, shocked by the affair, decided in October that Mme. Lemoine needed to be told and went to the local curé. The curé enlisted a respected elderly widow, who had helped to farm the Lemoines' property and who had known Angélina since she was a child, to tell Mme. Lemoine. The woman visited Victoire Lemoine before the end of October and warned her of rumors about Angélina and Jean, but she was so timid in her mission that Mme. Lemoine dismissed the story as the work of gossips. She did question her daughter closely, but Angélina denied everything and the matter was temporarily dismissed.

The greater skill Madeleine showed in producing and directing her romance with Emile doubtless owed much to her being older and more experienced. But these factors alone do not account for the differences in the original scenarios. Madeleine knew from the beginning that her success in maintaining a marriage in fantasy depended upon preventing her father's knowledge of the affair. Also, for her, a marriage in fact to Emile was out of the question, not only because she accepted the social barriers, but because marriage, any marriage, signified the end of woman's already limited independent action and the beginning of a lifetime of submission. Her mother's own pathetic example bore this out, as did the popular advice literature for women. It has been remarked that her marital fantasies involved masochistic demands to be dominated. Her actual control of the affair was her own secret, of course, but it was based on the assumption, conscious or unconscious, that women were forbidden open exercise of will. The fact that her romantic fiction was written by men and populated by passive, fainting heroines who waited for love to "happen" to them helps to explain her contortions to satisfy her desire for an active role and at the same time fulfill her need to conform to the submissive models of romantic fiction.

Angélina, on the other hand, found in her romantic reading precisely the opposite, that is, the enthusiastic endorsement of woman's active role in pursuing happiness in love and marriage. There was no need to keep secrets from Jean; she shared everything with him and gloried innocently in her power to make him happy and raise him to her level. Unlike Madeleine, who until nearly the end successfully separated the reality of her social role from the fantasy of her romantic image, Angélina was convinced she could unite the two and set about calculating the obstacles. It is hardly surprising that the failure of her mother's marriage did not deter her. Angélina, armed with George Sand, believed implicitly in her power to overcome. Her mother's example was important to her, but chiefly as a strong and decisive woman who reinforced her.

Angélina's disillusionment did not come until after Fétis's abrupt dismissal in January 1859, when she was more than three months pregnant. At his departure she pledged Jean eternal love and promised to try to join him, but she soon learned things about her lover which mortified her. The florist, who had grown up with Mme. Lemoine, confided to her friend that Jean had spread detailed accounts of his sexual adventures all over town and that he had boasted to all about his forthcoming prosperous marriage. Thereafter, Angélina was deaf to Fétis's pathetic attempts to see her and write to her. Jean tried to use the tailor Lieubray as an intermediary, but Angélina refused to accept the letter which Jean, a near-illiterate, had persuaded a friend to write.[85] Instead, she submitted willingly to what she confirmed were her mother's attempts to induce a miscarriage and to hide her pregnant condition.

By the time of the trial Angélina's sadistic remarks about her former hero easily vied with Madeleine's own. She scoffed at the idea that Fétis had used the familiar *tu* with her, and she denied that marriage had ever been one of their topics of conversation. Instead, she said that she spoke with the coachman only about "indifferent things, things one talks about with a servant." [86] When she was reminded that Fétis had testified to the contrary, she replied indignantly, "Is it possible that the word of a man such as that, a man as unworthy as Fétis, could be accepted above my own?" [87]

In the meantime Angélina had undergone considerable humiliation, not only from her mother, but from the townspeople as well. The dismissal of Fétis had started the rumors again. On the day of the mayor's ball in February a crowd consisting largely of women had gathered in the Lemoines' courtyard to see whether Angélina would be joining her mother. Several persons followed along behind the carriage to the ball, where another group had gathered to await the Lemoines' arrival.[88] This and several subsequent public appearances of the mother and daughter together temporarily quieted the rumors, but the gatherings of curious townspeople demonstrated again how traditional communities continued to enforce their codes.

Victoire Lemoine planned to tell no one about her daughter, but dealing with her husband was especially difficult. When he came to Chinon for a visit early in March, he had already heard the stories; his fears were confirmed when for the first time his wife forbade Angélina's visit, alleging that their daughter had a migraine. Jules Lemoine then visited a lawyer who advised him to try to discover the truth and who also informed him that his wife had abused her borrowing privileges and was a hundred thousand francs in debt. Lemoine decided to revoke the right to borrow and also to use his wife's bad management as grounds to gain custody of the children. He demanded that a doctor be permitted to examine Angélina, and in the case of her pregnancy, he recommended that she be sent to his parents in Montrichard. If she were not pregnant, Lemoine urged that she should be made to stay in town and go out every day to scotch the rumors.[89] His wife refused the plan, on the grounds that the rumors were false and that a doctor's visit would be psychologically dangerous for her daughter. She then enlisted both her children to persuade their father to restore her borrowing rights and drop his custody suit. Lemoine, in despair, backed down.

Unable to learn the truth from his wife, Lemoine wrote several pleading letters to his children, begging them to explain the situation. He complained to his son of being kept in doubt about Angélina's health: "I repeat to you, your sister is ill, I know it, I am sure of it, and you do not want me, your father, to look for the reason." [90] He urged Angélina "not to leave the impression, by your prolonged silence, either of being under the pressure of a constraint which would hardly recommend its author, or of having never learned the duties of a child towards its father, which is not the case." [91] Describing his suffering over being shut out and his fears of being portrayed by his wife as the real author of Angélina's suffering, he pleaded:

> for such a long time, my dear daughter, I have been apart from you; I left you when you were a child, and I see you still as such; our very short and infrequent meetings have been so constrained that neither of us is clear about the degree of mutual affection which we have; all that you have seen, all that you have learned about your father may have seemed so strange, perhaps so monstrous in your eyes that you might well not be able to appreciate cause and effect or have any idea of the admiration I feel for you and your brother.[92]

To his son in Tours, however, Jules Lemoine confided the belief that his "poor sister" had always been under her mother's domination, and he added that his wife was responsible for bringing financial disgrace on the family and—through Angélina—dishonor.[93] From Angélina, he continued to demand love and understanding, and he offered some equivocal praise.

> Love your father then, my dear daughter, assure him of your affection, console him in the midst of his privations. I do not know your character, I do not know your heart, but it is impossible that one or the other could be anything but excellent and good: that thought is my illusion, my happiness for the future.[94]

Apparently, Jules Lemoine did care for his daughter, but he stayed away from Chinon, obeying his wife, his friends, and his own mother, who convinced him that his appearance in town would only add to a scandal which he, too, dearly wanted to avoid. And despite the tender words to his children, it is worth noting that Lemoine was, at the same time, trying to use both of them as go-betweens in his financial dealings with his wife. Nearly every letter urges them to present his case to their mother. He showed a fondness and frankness which Madeleine's father may never have done, but he was blinded to his daughter's problem or, rather, he chose to interpret it as his own. It reminded him of his fears of rejection by his children, and it troubled him because it threatened to dishonor his family. In the end, he would leave his wife alone as she attempted to prevent public knowledge of Angélina's pregnancy. He was not required to give testimony at the trial.

The criminal denouements of both Angélina's and Madeleine's dramas were not part of the original scripts, and they both resulted from the characters' refusal to conform to their assigned roles. In Angélina's drama Jean Fétis was supposed to keep his mouth shut, but he betrayed his mistress.

Victoire Lemoine was expected to bow to a marriage, but she had no such intention. Angélina broke down in the preliminary interrogation and alleged that her mother had told her from the beginning that if she had the infant, it would have to be destroyed. She described how a spare bedroom was prepared well in advance of the event and explained that her mother intended to burn all evidence of the birth in the fireplace of the adjacent parlor. Angélina maintained that she herself had raised no objections because her mother's strong will and fierce temper terrified her.

On nearly all points the story which was extracted from Angélina contradicted her mother's description of a rape and stillbirth, and it also had the merit of accounting for the other known facts in the case. Her interrogators quickly seized on details which cast doubt on Victoire's account, such as the fact that a scissors and two basins—one for the baby and one for the afterbirth—had been set out in advance. This indicated, contrary to Mme. Lemoine's tale, that a normal birth was anticipated. In addition, a servant's report that Mme. Lemoine had brought firewood up to the parlor well in advance of the delivery again showed the premeditation, which the accused woman denied. This astonishing bit of stupidity ultimately accounted for the accusations which alerted the authorities, for neighbors who saw the smoke rising from the chimney pots were naturally curious as to why the Lemoines were building fires in August.

Angélina gave a harrowing account of the actual night of the birth. When the pains began, she said, her mother reminded her of the drill that they had agreed upon and warned her again that she was not to cry out during the ordeal for fear of alerting the servants. The young woman apparently succeeded in this, for servants later reported that they heard nothing. But in the most critical matter of all Angélina contradicted her mother: the baby, she confessed, was born alive. It was a boy with dark hair, whom Mme. Lemoine had pronounced "enormous," [95] and Angélina had seen him move. She did not know how his grandmother had killed him, but she assumed he had been suffocated. Angélina admitted that she had not begged for the infant's life. Less than two days later, she said, her mother persuaded her to make a public appearance at a concert in the chateau.

That Angélina should have caved in and told her story after the first questioning is hardly surprising. Her romantic illusions had been shattered; and although she had come to despise Fétis, she not unnaturally resented her mother as well. She now pictured herself as simply not responsible, the helpless victim of her mother's ruthless will; she related that when she saw her infant moving in the birth basin, it seemed to her that "all he asked was to live." [96] She added, too, that she had cried bitterly when she knew the baby was dead.

While her mother's leading role was undeniable, the court neglected to note the evidence that Angélina had come to accept Mme. Lemoine's stern solution. She had passed up opportunities to write to Fétis, which she might have done without her mother's knowledge. More important, she had made no effort to save her baby by confiding in her father, who was ready to help her. Indeed, in the trial itself she denied her allegations in the preliminary questioning and reverted to her mother's story that the child was born dead and that Fétis had forced her to have relations with him. Angélina had learned the rules of class, tardily and painfully.

It is probable that in the last months of her ordeal Angélina again turned to fictional accounts to find support for her new submissive role. This time she was no longer one of George Sand's aggressive heroines, but instead a persecuted bourgeois daughter who was featured in a serialized novel from *La Presse*, which Angélina had cited in another context as part of her reading.[97] The young unmarried heroine of this tale had become pregnant by a secret lover, and her parents were determined to hush up the affair. The girl, in the midst of labor, is depicted pleading with the midwife to protect her baby, but the midwife, uncomprehending, hands the infant over to the girl's parents, who murder it in an antechamber a few feet from its mother. The father then confides to the thunderstruck midwife, "You know, it is very embarrassing for a family when things of this sort happen."[98] The account may have provided some consolation for Angélina in her newly humbled state, though it is unlikely that it formed any part of her original script.

Mme. Lemoine's special obsession with destroying her daughter's infant was no doubt related to her own experience of marriage to a social inferior. She wished to save the family from disgrace, but she also seems to have wanted to spare her daughter a repetition of her own unhappy marriage. In accomplishing her end, she convinced Angélina that a series of tortures were necessary, and she denied that her husband had any rightful role to play. "The matter concerned myself alone. I had to safeguard the honor of my daughter. A mother never acknowledges such things; the father is only the father, the mother is the mother."[99] Such assertions, and such behavior toward a child, might be attributed to serious unbalance, but this was not the way they were interpreted in the national press, nor is it the way they were presented by Mme. Lemoine's lawyer, the famous Charles Lachaud. He naturally denied his client's guilt, but argued that even if she had been guilty, she would deserve both pity and respect as a "heroine" who had placed honor above life. Referring to the mothers everywhere who he insisted would be on her side, Lachaud said: "There are, Messieurs, sacred sorts of despair which are understood by them."[100] The Parisian press agreed and pitied Victoire Lemoine for being attacked by small town gossips for the performance of her duty.[101]

If Angélina's fantasy world came tumbling down with Fétis's betrayal and her mother's intervention, Madeleine's juggling act between fantasy and reality was disrupted by Emile's decisive action. Madeleine's fairy-tale fiancé suddenly threatened to prevent her marriage to her real fiancé by exposing her love letters to her father. Madeleine was totally unprepared for Emile's stepping out of his role in her psychodrama in this way. With any forethought she might have extricated herself from her involvement with L'Angelier long before her engagement in January 1857 to Minnoch, but doubtless the fascination of her intrigue and perhaps guilt over her treatment of Emile prevented her. More important, since so much of the affair with Emile was the product of her imagination, Madeleine may have convinced herself that the whole situation was unreal, that Emile too was consciously playing a part, and that therefore prompt action to end the engagement to him was unnecessary.

Indeed, without the assumption that Madeleine was capable of dismissing the actuality of her affair with Emile, her behavior in the last few weeks before L'Angelier's death is incomprehensible. The awkward way in which she tried to break with Emile a few days after her engagement to Minnoch is a case in point. Her letters right up through the month of January were full of the usual fond endearments and beatific descriptions of their future married life, despite her characteristic vagueness about a wedding date. Suddenly a letter in early February, in a radically different tone, announced that since her feelings had cooled, the engagement was off.[102] Madeleine might have expected Emile's furious response if she had ever pondered the possibility that he was capable of independent action, but only when that action took the form of a threat to expose her did she recognize that Emile was in a position to ruin her. In her horror she let her mask slip and told some partial truths about her games.

> Emile, I have deceived you. I have deceived my mother; . . . I deceived you by telling you she still knew of our engagement. She did not. . . . Emile write to no one, to Papa or any other. . . . I am the most guilty miserable wretch on the face of the earth. Emile do not drive me to death. When I ceased to love you, believe me, it was not to love another. I am free from all engagements at present. Emile for God's sake do not send my letters to papa. It will be an open rupture. I will leave the house. I will die. . . .[103]

In her agitated state Madeleine appears to have grasped at a dramatic solution to her dilemma. On the evening of February 19 she went with Minnoch to the opera *Lucrezia Borgia*. Later that night, after a visit to Madeleine during which she gave him some hot chocolate, Emile had a serious, but not fatal gastric attack. It will never be known whether Madeleine was inspired by Lucrezia's legendary reputation as a poisoner, but the hypothesis fits with the rest of her romantic posing.[104] The crime, in the end, bore all the marks of the bungling amateur. A second dose was again ineffective, producing only vomiting and severe weakness in the victim. On the third attempt L'Angelier was less fortunate. Doctors at the autopsy discovered that he had swallowed enough arsenic to kill fifty men.

Of course, Madeleine's decision to murder was hardly logical. As her supporters tried to argue in defense of her innocence, the crime made no sense if her object was to obtain the letters; Emile's murder practically ensured their discovery. Madeleine may have had an additional motive to dispose of L'Angelier, however. She doubtless knew that Scots law recognized the validity of a marriage contracted by simple oath in the presence of a witness and that it also accepted evidence of sexual intercourse as sufficient to constitute a legal marriage. L'Angelier had probably told Madeleine that the letters provided such evidence of their marriage,[105] but given her failure to recover them, her crime was still illogical in that her reputation, at the least, was bound to be compromised. But there is no reason to assume that Madeleine was acting rationally by this time and every reason to believe that she was panic-stricken.

> On my bended knees I write you, and ask you as you hope for mercy at the Judgment (Day) do not inform on me, do not make me a public shame. . . . I shall be undone. I shall be ruined. Who would trust me. . . . I could stand anything but my father's hot displeasure. Emile, you will not cause me death. If he is to get your letters, I cannot see him anymore. And my poor mother. I will never more kiss her—it would be a shame to them all.[106]

There is no doubt that Madeleine's solution to her dilemma, the poisoning of Emile L'Angelier, was the act of a deeply troubled personality. Still, even if Madeleine was genuinely pathologically disturbed, her act was no less obviously rooted in the middle-class code of female innocence. A young woman was constantly reminded of the absolute necessity of a pure reputation and her. fears for that reputation centered on the immediate judge whose approbation and retribution mattered most, her father. What compelled Madeleine Smith to murder was her terror that her father would discover that she was not the pure and innocent daughter she wanted him to believe in. Emile had seen clearly enough that Madeleine's fear of her father was his own strongest weapon. What he failed to fathom was the length to which Madeleine was willing to go to prevent her father's knowledge of the affair.

What hostility there was toward the two young women was marked chiefly in their home towns, where they and their families were known. In Angélina's case even those who accused her of "loose" behavior were inclined to excuse her and blame her mother. Elsewhere, assessments of Madeleine and Angélina were accommodated to the stereotype of irresponsible middle-class maidens.[107] Madeleine's tested skills in dramatic role-playing were especially useful in this respect, and she took full advantage of the courtroom stage to present the part of respectable young womanhood wronged. The *Spectator* remarked on Madeleine's "perfect self-possession," her "fashionable" clothes, and her "most attractive appearance." [108] Noting that her demeanor seemed to advocate her cause, it reported that she "stepped up the stair into the dock with all the buoyancy with which she might have entered the box of a theater." [109] Angélina was less fortunate in that the French legal system obliged her to testify in court rather than simply to create an impression by her presence; but most were still willing to ignore her provocation and to cast Fétis in the role of corrupter and seducer, the "outsider" who had dared to threaten the established social order.

Both young women had embarked on adventures which set them on a collision course with parents whose final authority they both feared and admitted; but Angélina's relative disadvantages were obvious, and they were not limited to daughters of the provincial bourgeoisie alone. Even as late as the 1880s observers frequently noted the relative sophistication of English as compared to French young women. "The English girl is more *au courant* with life than the French girl," remarked one French commentator. "She may be as pure but she is less innocent, less untouched, and as a result in a better condition to defend herself." [110]

Madeleine demonstrated that she knew how to land on her feet. Buoyed by the general public sympathy, she was capable of writing these words to the prison chaplain a few days after her release.

I trust that painful, unhappy affair may tend to do us all great good—I see a different feeling pervades our family circle already. I am so glad they all view it an affliction sent from God for past errors and crimes, and if this be the means of drawing a family to the feet of Christ, I shall not grumble at the pain that sad event cost me.[111]

In any event, the Smiths moved out of Glasgow and appear to have sought what oblivion they could. Madeleine's two sisters never married. She herself moved to London, and there found companionship in a circle of artists who were less concerned about respectability. In 1861 she married George Wardle, who became a close associate of William Morris. The couple settled in Bloomsbury, had two children, and joined the Socialist League with Morris. After her husband's death Madeleine apparently lived alone for several years and then, soon after the turn of the century, moved to the United States and remarried. Little is known of her life there save that she survived her second husband and continued to reside in Brooklyn, where she died in poverty in 1928, at the age of ninety-three.[112]

Angélina, predictably, was less fortunate. As was common in cases where a wealthy young heiress was concerned, she received many letters requesting her hand in marriage, but such a solution was considered out of the question. Angélina's father and the magistrates arranged something more discreet: the young woman was placed in a convent, where it was hoped that the "more healthy" [113] atmosphere would benefit her. This decision had the added advantage of removing from the family the presence of a most embarrassing creature.

In explaining the behavior of Madeleine and Angélina, contemporaries were quite right to point to romantic literature and ideas as critical influences, but it is curious how wrong they were in viewing these as simply creating a passive receptivity to the advances of scoundrels. The obvious fact that both young women set out actively to find a lover and to construct their own romantic novel was difficult to admit, for such an admission entailed the specter of a topsy-turvy social world in which daughters forsook sexual passivity and dependence. The few who accepted independent action by the accused young women themselves were careful to point out that the two were freaks. Miss Smith, the Glasgow *Sentinel* admitted, was probably "as much the seducer as the seduced. And when once the veil of modesty was thrown aside, from the first a very frail and flimsy one, the woman of strong passion and libidinous tendencies at once reveals herself." But, reassuringly, the paper hastened to add that Miss Smith was "one of those abnormal spirits that now and then rise up in society to startle and appall us, and to which under the extremes of depravity human nature, in some of its aberrations, may go." [114] The comfort to be taken from such pronouncements was already uncertain.

There was one response to the trials not based on stereotypical images of respectable young ladies, and that, once again, was the fascinated absorption of "real" middle-class women who flocked to the courtrooms and vied for seats on reserved benches and in public galleries. The press in both countries, but especially in England, recorded the women's curiosity with disapproval. While ignoring the men's motives, the papers hinted that those of the women were more than suspect. Noting the numerous women in the crowds of thousands at the Smith case, one paper accused them of having "dishonored their sex" by "eagerly drinking in that filthy correspondence." [115] A few women protested the charges in letters to the papers, and while women's real motives can only be guessed, it is likely that they did differ from those of the men. The explanation that the trials provided a diversion in lives which were devoid of excitement is only partly satisfactory. In a similar but more immediate way than literature, the trials seem to have supplied a vicarious outlet for frustrations. The accused young women had acted out what the female spectators, in their most secret thoughts, had hardly dared to imagine.

None of the commentators on the two cases reflected that for the majority of the "brides-to-be," romantic literature performed the useful function of a safety valve, one of the few ways to enliven the dull waiting years until marriage. Madeleine Smith and Angélina Lemoine were unwise enough to have taken such literature as a guide for life, but their societies were still willing to give them the benefit of doubt. The belief that respectable women were not responsible for their behavior remained intact, but the challenge to that consoling conviction was not far off.

3.

THE SINGULAR OUTCASTS:

The Cases of Célestine Doudet and Constance Kent

Constance Kent

IF MOST middle-class women ended their waiting years by marrying sometime in their early or mid-twenties, there were some whose waiting years stretched into a lifetime. The percentage of unmarried women in England and France remained fairly constant and significant throughout the nineteenth century. In England about fifteen percent of all women reached their fiftieth birthday without having married, as compared to twelve percent of men. In France the figures were somewhat lower, twelve percent for women and eleven percent for men.[1] Though the marriage rate for middle-class women may have been somewhat higher, there remained, in the popular condescending phrase, many "unplucked flowers." In an age which exalted marriage as woman's sole and natural vocation and which, until well past mid-century, restricted respectable female employment to some sort of ill-paid teaching, spinsterhood cannot often have been a freely chosen state.

The unmarried woman assumed the status of a recognized social problem more quickly in England than in France, probably not because there was any great increase in the percentage of single women there, but because they were more visible in a growing society which was urbanizing faster.[2] More rural France gave the appearance of a society where all women married, and single women did not exercise the greater liberty which contributed to the visibility of their English counterparts. Travelers such as Mrs. Trollope, who visited France in the 1830s, noted that Frenchmen liked to boast that in contrast to England they had "no old maids"; and Trollope, at least, concurred. She remarked that a Parisian friend had claimed to have known just one unmarried French woman, an unfortunate creature who drowned herself![3]

In England, especially, much was made of the problem of a "surplus" female population, which increased the numbers of unmarried women. It was true that women did outnumber men more significantly there than in France, chiefly because the far larger emigrations from England were predominantly male. At mid-century, when English census figures revealed that there were over half a million more women than men, a huge cry went up over what should be done with the so-called redundant woman.[4] Schemes were even proposed to deport and resettle masses of these women. Some critics, at least, recognized that the more urgent problem was not finding husbands for the women, but rather training them and providing decent opportunities for employment. But the stigma of redundancy, especially for the middle-class woman, was hard to escape. In France, where single women still could play an active and productive role within a more traditional domestic economy, talk of redundancy was less often heard.

The precise incidence of middle-class spinsterhood and any class-specific causes are admittedly not easy to pin down in the absence of class-differentiated statistics. Nonetheless, if spinsterhood was a condition arguably beyond the control of most women who experienced it, it was still subject to human decision. Too often neglected in considerations of the plight of unmarried middle-class women is the role of parents in influencing whether their daughters would marry at all. It is true that their intervention in the actual choice had lessened considerably in England by mid-century and that somewhat later in France daughters gained more active roles in selecting their husbands. But parents still retained considerable control, for their financial status and support remained a real factor. In France, where the dowry system persisted throughout the century, a woman's ability to marry depended heavily on whether her parents had put away a sum for her, and marrying "well" depended almost exclusively on a handsome dowry. In England, although formal dowries had ceased to be customary, marriage settlements were common among the wealthier middle classes. In any case the business of getting a daughter courted and married entailed considerable parental expense.

Despite growing incomes overall, middle-class families in the nineteenth century faced changing circumstances and new income insecurities as well as pressures to "keep up appearances" which could jeopardize a daughter's chances to marry. In France the law did help young women to the extent of guaranteeing fairly equal distribution of inheritance among all children in a family, a portion normally distributed to daughters at marriage as a dowry. No similar protection for daughters existed in England, and a girl normally would receive her inheritance years after marriage. Given the growing need to educate young men if they were to gain places in the new business and professional worlds, it is more than likely that a family with limited economic resources would sacrifice a daughter's portion to provide for a son's advancement. How often such sacrifices narrowed or eliminated entirely the opportunities of middle-class daughters to marry is impossible to know with certainty. But the abundant literary portraits of maiden aunts occupied in unpaid domestic chores in the homes of relatives, caring for sick parents, or acting as teachers for a brother's children are too familiar to dismiss.

Discriminatory financial decisions were not the only means by which parents might endanger the marriage prospects of their daughters. Common middle-class child-rearing practices appear to have contributed their part, although precise evidence is again hard to come by. Despite recent investigations the child-rearing practices, like the sexual habits, of the middle class in the nineteenth century are still something of a mystery. Children, we know, were the objects of increasing attention as the century progressed, and their parents, according to many indices, were ever more solicitous of them. Not surprisingly, we know a good deal more about recommended child-rearing habits than about actual ones, just as we know more about recommended sexual behavior. The middle classes, jealous of the privacy purchased by relative economic security and free from the prying of the government committees which explored working-class households, managed to guard many secrets about themselves. Recent literature on childhood, moreover, has tended to ignore or slight what evidence there is on the differences in treatment and attitudes toward girl children in particular.[5]

The cases to be discussed here have the advantage of taking two middle-class households by surprise, and each provides some glimpses of the goings-on behind the normally closed parlor and nursery doors. The accused, two unmarried women of twenty-one and thirty-seven, were themselves simultaneously the agents and victims of a system of misunderstanding, neglect, and abuse of middle-class children. Both were charged with causing the death of a child: their behavior clearly stemmed in part from circumstances which were far from typical. Nonetheless, their stories—and the stories of the children and adults around them—can be used to understand much that formed the fabric of existence for more ordinary young women whose chances to achieve the one vocation their society sanctioned for them, marriage and motherhood, were compromised by parents, well-meaning or worse.

The primary subjects of the two dramas, Constance Kent and Célestine Doudet,[6] had both been effectively consigned to celibacy long before the events which brought them to public attention. Both were regularly referred to as plain and unattractive creatures of quiet disposition; both were reputed to have had a "cruel streak" since early childhood and were considered to have displayed peculiar sexual attitudes or behavior. There were other resemblances as well. Both had lived in England and in France for an extended time, were believed to be deeply religious, and had had the misfortune to lose a parent at a critical period. Still, in many respects, perhaps the most important ones, Constance Kent and Célestine Doudet differed.

Mlle. Doudet, a former governess who ran a small day-school in the cité d'Odiot in Paris, stood trial in that capital in 1855 on charges relating to the physical abuse of four of her pupils and the death of a fifth, all of them daughters of an English doctor who had placed them in her care. The accused, a highly educated woman with impeccable credentials for her post, insisted that the deceased child had died of natural causes related to a severe case of whooping cough. She maintained, too, that the emaciated condition of the other girls was not the result of her ill treatment, but rather the product of their own peculiar habits, exacerbated by the harsh regimen prescribed by their homeopathic doctor-father. Mlle. Doudet pleaded innocent to the charges of beating and involuntary manslaughter.

Constance Kent pleaded guilty to the more heinous crime of willful murder, perpetrated in June 1860 on Francis Savile Kent, her three-and-a-half-year-old stepbrother. Suspected of the crime at the time, the sixteen-year-old Constance had been arrested by Scotland Yard investigators who were summoned to the scene of the tragedy, her family's home in Wiltshire. She had protested innocence and was released for want of evidence. Five years later she stunned her family and the country by coming forward to confess that "alone and unaided" [7] she had murdered the little boy who had been his father's favorite. Constance Kent's guilt and Célestine Doudet's innocence were and remain the subject of controversy, but their pathetic stories go far beyond mere questions of legal guilt or innocence.

The background of events which forced the two women into public scrutiny was very different. Célestine Doudet, at thirty-four, had long been earning an independent living as a governess when she was hired in 1852 by the recently widowed Dr. James Loftus Marsden of Malvern to train his three eldest daughters and tutor them in French. Highly recommended by one of his patients, Mlle. Doudet came to Malvern with the glowing reports of several upper-class English families for whom she had worked in the past ten years. More than this, she had the distinction of an endorsement from the Queen herself, whom she had briefly served as a wardrobe mistress (with special responsibility for jewelry) at a time when Victoria wished to improve her French. In April 1842 the Queen had written:

> I consider Mademoiselle Doudet an excellent person, of mild disposition and amiable character; but her education has been too good for her situation of wardrobe woman with me, and I think that that of governess would suit her better. I look on her as a person of the greatest probity and worthy of confidence.[8]

Victoria, whatever her virtues, was not an especially gifted judge of character, but her appraisal of Mlle. Doudet appeared sound. Nevertheless, there were signs that Mlle. Doudet was not fully reconciled to the station in life to which she had been assigned. Even her most vehement supporters, including one who had rushed to Paris in her defense (and announced that to arrive in time to aid such a cause she would cheerfully have "exhausted ten horses" [9]), acknowledged that Mlle. Doudet's manner and bearing were more like those of a "lady" than of a governess. This witness obviously saw these qualities as an asset and claimed that the governess had delighted her children by assuming "grand airs." But others viewed these qualities less favorably and accused Doudet of adopting the *hauteur* of an aristocratic English matron. Given her experience at Victoria's court, this evidence of feelings of status incongruence is hardly surprising.

Flore-Marguerite-Célestine Doudet had some reason to feel that life had dealt cruelly with her, though it was family circumstances rather than ill will which initially determined her fate. Born in Rouen in 1817, she was one of three daughters of a captain of a frigate in the French navy and his English wife. Her parents had met during the Napoleonic wars when M. Doudet, then attached to the Dutch navy, had been captured and imprisoned in England. The couple settled in Rouen when the officer received his commission with the French navy, but Doudet, who had lost his fortune, decided that he could not afford to provide dowries for his growing daughters. He determined instead to use what money he had to give them decent educations to become governesses and arranged to send all three to the respectable Parisian boarding school of Madame Chabaud-Latour. At the time of his death in 1839 he and his wife had been living in retirement in England, but Mme. Doudet was forced to leave her country and return to France to be eligible for payments on her husband's pension. Her daughter Célestine, then studying with Mme. Chabaud-Latour, came to live with Mme. Doudet in Paris and tutored some students to supplement their income. Soon after, her mentor launched her career by placing her with Queen Victoria. Mme. Chabaud-Latour later testified warmly in Mlle. Doudet's defense, though it was clear that she had seen little of her former pupil during the long intervening years which Célestine had spent in England.

Mme. Doudet died soon after Célestine was engaged by Dr. Marsden in March 1852. Célestine suggested to Dr. Marsden that she take all five of the girls to her mother's former apartment in Paris and set up a small school. The thirty-six-year-old widower, preoccupied with a thriving practice in the popular water-cure establishment at Malvern, agreed to the plan on a six-month trial basis. He gave the governess three thousand francs (about 120 pounds) for the girls' food, lodging, and education; it was an adequate, but hardly generous sum. In mid-June 1852, the Marsden daughters—Alice, Rosa, Mary Ann, Emily, and Lucy, aged six and a half to thirteen—departed for Paris with their new governess. Their father decided to send his one son to boarding school in England.

At first the arrangement with the governess seemed to work well. Mlle. Doudet enjoyed the unpaid help of her younger sister Zéphyrine, who cleaned and cooked while Célestine supervised the instruction of the five sisters and some occasional day students. In September the girls' maternal uncle, an Anglican minister called John Rashdall, visited his nieces and returned with good reports. In December Marsden himself paid a visit during a wedding trip to Italy with his new wife, a former patient whom he had restored to health after a fall from a horse. At this time, apparently satisfied with the situation, the doctor settled with the governess for another six months.

Upon their return from Italy in March 1853, the couple stopped again in Paris. Marsden noted then that the two older children seemed a little thin and that all ate voraciously when they were taken out. When the governess confirmed that they were very greedy, the doctor prescribed the "cure" of taking them to the pastry shop every day until they were heartily sick of sweets. Perhaps he was inspired by the homeopathic principle that the agent of a malady can also be the agent of its cure, but his apparent blindness to the possibility that his children were being starved is remarkable. He noted, too, that the manner of the girls was reserved and that they had developed the peculiar habit of repeating one another's words, but, as he later explained, he ascribed this at the time to simple social backwardness. As a remedy he instructed the governess to hire a dancing master.

In May Marsden received word from the governess that four of the girls had contracted whooping cough and that the ten-year-old Mary Ann was seriously ill. At the same time neighbors of the governess, alerted by Doudet's sister, who had reportedly quit her post in April in protest over harsh treatment of the girls, began to mobilize an effort in the children's behalf. At the end of May one of these women wrote a letter to Célestine Doudet.

Dear Mademoiselle, You expressed the desire for friendship which we genuinely welcomed; but before going further, we require a frank explanation. Such horrifying rumors are circulating about the way you are treating the poor children confined to your care, that we are both worried and scandalized. The sequestering of Lucy [the eldest child] for a month is such a serious matter that I must have an explanation before treating you again as a friend. It was not to prevent her from catching whooping cough, which you told me was the reason you shut her away by herself. It was a punishment, and it is even said that the cruel accident suffered by Poppy [Mary Ann] was in fact the result of harsh treatment. Some people have heard the children being beaten, and their faces alone proclaim that they are living under a reign of terror. . . . It is such a great and wonderful task to raise children, and especially so when it involves replacing a mother of poor little orphans! You ought to understand this mission of which you speak so well, and I leave to your conscience the responsibility of answering this question: Did your own mother treat you as you are treating these children? Well then, since you seem to miss her so much, it is in her name that I charge you to return to a mode of education more in line with the one you received from your own parents.[10]

The neighbor threatened to write to the girls' father if the governess refused to change her ways.

Another concerned neighbor sent the police an anonymous letter which described brutal treatments and even asserted that one child was being imprisoned in the cellar. The officer sent to investigate the charges said that he arrived at the governess's rooms unannounced, but there is no way of knowing whether Célestine had been warned of a police visit. The officer said that he found two children taking lessons with a tutor, two others in bed with whooping cough, and another in a ground-floor bedroom, isolated from her sick sisters but hardly incarcerated. He accepted the governess's explanation that the neighbors, several of them English women, had started the rumors after she refused to continue visiting them when they criticized her child-rearing methods. The police, however, did forward the anonymous letter to Marsden, who in mid-June sent his brother-in-law, the minister Rashdall, to investigate. Again the reports were good, for Rashdall discounted his talks with the neighbors when the girls told him that they loved Mlle. Doudet and wanted to buy presents for her. After his visit the infuriated women then designated one of their number to write a letter which would bring Marsden himself to Paris. The girls' father had previously pleaded his new wife's delicate condition and his own busy schedule as reasons for staying behind.

I perfectly understand the considerations owed to the *interesting* Mme. Marsden. I perfectly understand that as a man of the clergy, the reverend Mr. Rashdall did not believe it was his duty *to throw Mlle. Doudet out the window;* but what I fail to understand, *and what no one understands, is why he did not put her out the door.* . . . Your children are terrified, like puppies they lick the hand that strikes them in hopes of more gentle treatment. . . . Beneath their dresses of silk, your children have suffered what the children of the poor suffer: cold and hunger.[11]

The author of this angry missive later admitted that all her information was secondhand, and Marsden, who said he discounted the letters as female gossip, contented himself in the knowledge that the girls' aunt, Rashdall's sister Fanny, was then staying in Paris and visiting the children regularly. Anonymous letters continued to arrive, but it was not until the doctor received word of the death of ten-year-old Mary Ann on July 22 that he found time to go to Paris.

The day after his arrival Marsden removed his four remaining daughters. The youngest child, Alice, remained in Paris with her aunt; the others, after a brief stay with the aunt, returned to England without their father's bringing a formal charge against the governess. The dissatisfied neighbors then decided to act again and in mid-September one of them went to the police to launch a formal investigation. As the inquiries got underway, Marsden was invited by the French police to submit a doctor's report concerning the health of the three daughters who had returned with him. He declined to do so, but in late September he sent word that his eldest child, Lucy, who had been kept isolated at the governess's for over a month, had just succumbed to the combined effects of whooping cough and exhaustion. In the meantime his sister-in-law in Paris had joined forces with Mlle. Doudet's accusers, and a doctor who examined Alice confirmed that the child had numerous scars on her lower back, a wound on her head, and a deep scratch on her nose—all of which were attributed to her governess's abuse.

The police investigation turned up several startling pieces of information. The maid Léocadie Bailleux, who had replaced Zéphyrine Doudet the previous April, claimed that she had smuggled food to the children, who were systematically deprived of sufficient nourishment and rarely given anything but bread and soup. The maid also testified that Mlle. Doudet habitually tied the children's feet to their bedposts, and that on one occasion when little Alice had asked to be untied to go to the bathroom, she had been ordered to urinate in the chamber pot on the floor, which was barely possible with her legs tied. As she did so, the governess allegedly struck her, and the chamber pot, breaking at her blow, severely cut the child. The incident doubtless accounted for the observed scars.

The maid related numerous other chilling events: she had seen the governess beating the children's heads against the wall, stamping on their bare feet until blood came, pulling out their hair, striking their arms with a ruler, forcing them to remain with arms crossed for entire days, and abandoning them for hours in the locked cellar or the toilet. The maid also had her own version of an "accident" Mary Ann had had which precipitated her death and which Célestine had ascribed variously to a fall or to a whooping-cough seizure. Léocadie Bailleux explained that Mlle. Doudet had in fact struck the child, who had fallen off her chair.[12] The maid acknowledged that the sisters had described the blow to her, but insisted she had heard the thud of Mary Ann's body on the floor. She added that when she had arrived in the salon, Mary Ann was in convulsions. The child had remained partially paralyzed and semidelirious until her death two months later.

The chief of the police division which directed the investigation begun that September nonetheless determined that there were insufficient grounds for a case, and Marsden, for his own reasons, was disinclined to follow the importunings of the children's aunt and her Parisian neighbors. When Fanny Rashdall and a Mme. Hooper went ahead in November 1853 and filed a formal complaint in Marsden's name with the magistrates, the doctor swiftly informed their counsel that his solicitor had advised him against this course and ordered him to send any bills to Mme. Hooper.

In taking this action, Marsden was evidently motivated less by indifference to the girls than by fear of scandal. He was perfectly aware that if he filed suit against the governess, the real reason for his sending his daughters to Paris might become public knowledge. The police investigation had already touched upon the evidence which would later become Célestine's primary defense against charges of cruelty; she claimed that all she had done was at the express order of her employer, that she had been instructed that her chief duty was to "cure" his daughters of a vice which was believed to afflict at least one of them, namely, masturbation.

At Mlle. Doudet's request the police had already interrogated the female operator of a health establishment, who informed them that when the doctor had visited his daughters the previous January, he and his new wife had consulted with her about ways to prevent the "secret vice" of his children. The woman said she had recommended a "preservative belt" which Marsden had ordered. In addition, a Parisian doctor who saw the girls in the late spring, 1853, told police that he had been struck by their singular appearance: "sunken, rickety and emaciated faces, pinched noses, discolored eyelids, which Mlle. Doudet attributed to the bad habits in which the children indulged themselves." [13] Another doctor went further still; he claimed to have examined Alice and discovered inflamed areas on her genitals which he designated as the "local marks of passion." [14] The same man professed that while attending the half-paralyzed Mary Ann, who was on her deathbed, he had surprised the child in what he described as "frenzied" masturbation. It was understandable that Marsden wished to prevent public disclosure of such testimony and, as he wrote to his sister-in-law's lawyer, Mlle. Doudet would not fail to respond to charges by alleging "that I myself whipped my child in her presence, and that acts of . . . [masturbation] could, to a certain point, be admitted for some of my daughters." [15]

Marsden was hardly alone in his concern over the alleged vice of masturbation. His children were "afflicted" during the mid-century period when masturbational anxiety was at an all-time high. Among the conditions attributed to "self-abuse" were hysteria, asthma, epilepsy, melancholia, paralysis, and insanity.[16] Prior to this period masturbation had admittedly been thought harmful and sinful and was often believed responsible for these conditions and more, but medical and religious suggestions for controlling the habit were rather mild: diet, exercise, hydrotherapy, moral readings, and the like. However, from about 1850 doctors, participating in the general anxiety over sexuality, turned their attention from "cure" to "suppression" of any autoerotic activity. Increasingly sadistic methods were used and, until the turn of the century, at least half the recommended measures in all countries were drastic ones, including restraining devices, severe punishments, and even surgery.

At about the time of the Marsden case a well-known London surgeon introduced the operation of clitoridectomy, a cure for masturbation in females by means of the removal of the organ on which it was performed. The practice does appear to have been mercifully brief in England, where its chief proponent was expelled within ten years from the obstetrical society, and it was used in France for only a short time around the 1890s. But other surgical practices continued to be recommended in textbooks and medical literature as late as the 1930s. These included blistering the thighs or genitals, "burial" of the clitoris beneath the labia with sutures, cauterization, and infibulation of the labia majora.[17] The Marsden girls did not undergo such cures, in part because their father did not believe in any kind of surgery, but their suffering may well have been as great, if not greater, than if they had.

Not surprisingly, the subject of female masturbation was discussed less frequently than male masturbation, in part because female sexuality itself was difficult for even professional medical men to accept. Female masturbation is ignored almost entirely in Tissot's famous early treatise on onanism (1758), although "self-abuse" among females began to receive more attention in the mid-nineteenth century, with the onset of the era of sadistic cures. We do know, for example, that in 1848 a Scottish physician named John Moodie proclaimed himself distressed by the "notorious" immorality among young ladies at boarding schools in his country. He devised for women a kind of panty girdle with back laces and an ivory grill sewn into the genital area, the whole of which was fastened by belts to a pair of tight-fitting drawers and then secured by a padlock. The device sounds formidable indeed, but it must be remembered that the enemy was believed so as well. The most terrible consequence of masturbation in women was not, as for boys, the grave or the asylum, but instead the brothel, a fate considered worse than death or madness.[18] A young woman who "indulged" was in danger of becoming a nymphomaniac. Failing that, she ran the risk of being barren, having a defective child, or suffering other painful difficulties.

The Marsden case provides documented evidence of how people responded toward female children suspected of being infected by masturbatory practices. Although preventive treatment stopped short of surgery, it nonetheless involved systematic torture, both physical and psychological, and shows how heavy a price children might have to pay to appease the anxieties of adults. The testimony would show that in charging the new governess to cure his children's habits, Marsden was deeply and genuinely concerned for what he saw as their welfare, at least at the beginning. But he would ultimately come close to abandoning hope for his girls; and it was longer still before he came to the conclusion that in hiring Célestine Doudet, he had got rather more than he bargained for. In the end, when Marsden finally decided to press charges, his three surviving daughters received partial revenge for their suffering. Célestine Doudet was acquitted of causing Mary Ann Marsden's death, but she was sentenced to five years imprisonment and a fine for her attacks on the others.

Constance Kent, like Célestine Doudet, was marked for spinsterhood in her early youth, but the father who determined her fate appears to have been more open to charges of indifference and neglect, and perhaps worse, than Célestine's father. Constance, born in 1844, was the ninth of ten children born to Mary Ann and Samuel Kent. Her father, the son of a successful London carpet manufacturer, had acquired a partnership in a drysalters firm by 1829 when, at twenty-eight, he married Constance's mother Mary Ann Windus, the twenty-one-year-old daughter of a highly respected city merchant who was a fellow of the Royal Society of Antiquaries. By 1833 the young couple had had three children and had suffered the loss of one of them, the only boy. Samuel Kent had been forced to leave his partnership in London because of a respiratory ailment, but his influential father-in-law had secured for him a post which seemed ideally suited to Kent's experience and his ambitious and gregarious nature. He was named sub-inspector of factories for the West of England under the new Factory Act, a position which for the next thirty-odd years kept him constantly traveling through much of Devon, Somerset, Wiltshire, and Dorset.

Mrs. Kent, meanwhile, remained at home and much alone in a series of imposing but understaffed rented dwellings. Her husband insisted on lavish external display, complete with the best in entertainment, clothes, and horses, but, as servants later reported, this lifestyle meant a cramped domestic budget, with slighting on expenses for the children and added burdens on Mrs. Kent's already frail constitution.

Only one child, a boy called Edward, survived of the five babies Mrs. Kent had in the period from 1835 until Constance's birth in February 1844. As her health had deteriorated seriously by then, a full-time nursemaid, who styled herself a governess, was hired to care for the new infant. The following year Mrs. Kent's last child, a boy called William, was born. Her husband selected this time to move to a bedroom in another part of their house. As a family friend later described it, "Mrs. Kent was left by her husband to live in the seclusion of her own room, while the management of the household was taken over the heads of grown-up daughters by a high-spirited young governess." [19] It was true that at the time the two eldest daughters, fourteen-year-old Mary Ann and twelve-year-old Elizabeth, were not yet precisely "grown up," but there is no doubt that the new governess, twenty-one-year-old Mary Pratt who was the well-educated daughter of a local greengrocer, assumed the reins. When the three elder children were sent to boarding school, it was soon whispered that Mary Pratt had become mistress of the household, in all senses of the term.

In the sixteen years that elapsed from her birth in 1844 to 1860, when she was briefly arrested for the murder of her young half-brother, Constance Kent underwent a childhood which bore little resemblance to the period of loving and nurturing which had become fashionable in the prescriptive literature on the subject. There were domestic tensions from the beginning, when her father, instead of earning a coveted advance to the Board of Factory Commissioners, was queried by a member of that body concerning rumors over the seclusion of his wife and was urged to remember that his growing daughters needed the society of young people of their own rank. Kent explained then that Mary Ann had become an invalid who required her daughters' help, and he probably hinted that his wife was insane. When the issue was raised much later, a doctor and friend of the family asserted that Mrs. Kent had become insane as early as 1836. [20] This was most peculiar in view of the evidence that she had not gone into complete seclusion until her last child's birth in 1845 and especially in view of the fact that during the period she was allegedly insane her husband had proceeded to beget five children by her. In any case young Constance and William knew their mother only as an invalid, and it was the governess who raised them.

There is little information about Constance's early family relationships, save the indication that she and her younger brother developed into close companions and that their mother was fond of them. There are also some hints that Mrs. Kent perceived the ascendancy of the new governess, but decided to resign herself to the situation, for she had few options. A return to her family, perhaps her only alternative, would have invited embarrassment and scandal, would have required her to abandon her children, and might have been uninviting, since she had married Kent against the inclinations of her parents.

In 1851, when Constance was seven, her adored elder brother returned briefly from naval training school and their mother made him a gift of her Bible, which he promised her he would always keep.[21] At the same time Mrs. Kent made arrangements for the transfer of a thousand pounds of her inheritance to Constance, to be held in trust for her until she reached twenty-one.[22] Whether Mrs. Kent sensed the special vulnerability of this girl child is impossible to say, but the action, which she carried out through her family without her husband's knowledge, must surely have infuriated a man who had long been living beyond his means. Kent's yearly salary of eight hundred pounds was supplemented by a private annual income of three or four hundred, but the sum was barely sufficient to preserve the lifestyle he had adopted.

Mrs. Kent's ability to arrange the legacy for Constance casts further doubt on the notion that she was insane. And it is at least possible that she hoped to ensure a future for the child which was different from that of her two elder daughters. She knew that their father's dubious reputation, his refusal to devote attention or money to find marriage prospects for them, and her own physical incapacity had already doomed Mary Ann and Elizabeth to a shadowy existence as unpaid members of the governess's inadequate staff. It would have been reasonable for her to assume that her sons would have a better chance, but her husband, in an economy move which may have reflected anger over his wife's secret financial arrangements, peremptorily removed Edward from naval training school and placed the disappointed boy in a cheaper private trading establishment where he trained for merchant service. In the end, the thousand pounds which might have served to launch Constance independently or to improve her prospects for marriage failed to save her. And, less than a year after she arranged the legacy for her daughter, Mrs. Kent, who had been reported in good health, died suddenly in great agony of an ailment diagnosed by the attending physician as "an obstruction of the bowels." [23]

In August 1853, after the customary year of mourning was complete, Samuel Kent married the governess Mary Pratt. Young Constance, aged nine, was a bridesmaid. The couple soon began a new family, and it appears that the children of the first family, especially Constance and William, suffered an eclipse. Stories were circulated that their educations were neglected and that they were badly clothed and harshly disciplined. The recently elevated governess-stepmother chose to establish her authority through severity, and even friends remarked on her dubious treatment of the children. "Whether the governess possessed that experience, and tact and moral weight which fitted her for the responsibilities she had undertaken . . . are questions to which her memory and conscience alone can reply." [24] The new Mrs. Kent, it was alleged, "ruled with a severe hand all beneath her sway." [25] To punish Constance and William, she "boxed their ears" [26] and often "confined them to their rooms." [27] One friend did acknowledge that Constance, particularly, was an unruly child, with a "strong obstinate and determined" character and an "irritable and impassioned" nature.[28] The truth here is not easy to determine, for the subsequent inquest would also reveal that at her school Constance was later awarded second prize for good work and behavior.

The events of the fatal night of June 29-30, 1860, are simply described. By then the Kents had three children: five-year-old Amelia, three-and-a-half-year-old Francis Savile, and an infant daughter Eveline. Young Savile, who slept in the second-floor nursery with his baby sister and a nursemaid, was discovered missing from his cot on the morning of the thirtieth. At quarter after seven the nursemaid, having discovered Savile's bed empty, had knocked on his parents' door across the hall to inquire whether Mrs. Kent had the boy with her. When Mrs. Kent replied that she had not seen the child since he went to bed at eight the previous night, the household was alerted and a search begun. The four children of the first family, who slept on the third floor with the two other members of the live-in staff, the cook and a maid, all declared that they had not been disturbed by any noises the previous night, but the maid reported that when she went downstairs to the drawing room at six in the morning, the door was ajar and a window was open. The distraught Mr. Kent departed for Trowbridge, four miles away, to tell the police about his missing child. During his absence nearby cottagers, informed of events and thinking of a possible reward, began to search the grounds.

Shortly before Mr. Kent returned from his mission the body of Savile was discovered in a detached privy across the stable yard. The boy's throat had been cut with a slash of such violence that the head was nearly severed from the body. There was little sign of blood, which suggested that the child might have been killed elsewhere and carried to the privy. There was also a deep stab wound in the child's chest, which was believed to have been made after death in an attempt to force the body further down into the cavity of the privy.

The horror of the crime itself was matched only by the ineptitude and willful manipulation which marked the coroner's inquest and a series of subsequent judicial investigations.[29] The official inquiries ultimately came to an end without any formal indictment in the case, and only two individuals were singled out and brought before local magistrates: the nursemaid Elizabeth Gough and Constance Kent. The nursemaid Gough managed to satisfy the authorities that she had slept soundly on the night of the crime. She admitted that she had wakened briefly at five in the morning and noticed that the child was missing, but had merely assumed his mother had heard him crying and had come and picked him up. Mrs. Kent at first pointed out how unlikely this was; not only had she never come for the child before, but she was then eight months pregnant and Savile was a very large child for his age. Later, and rather oddly, Mrs. Kent acknowledged that the nursemaid might reasonably have assumed that she had fetched the boy after all, which helped to clear Miss Gough.

The suspicion which settled on Constance was prompted by a combination of her own past behavior and some apparently incriminating circumstantial evidence. Constance was known to have resented the favoritism shown to the second family over the first. When the famous Chief Inspector Jonathan Whicher from Scotland Yard was called in on the case in mid-July, after the failure of local authorities, he quickly settled upon Constance as the most likely suspect. He learned that just after the crime, a nightdress belonging to the girl which should have been in the weekly laundry was missing, and he decided to arrest the sixteen-year-old. Constance was brought to jail, unescorted by any member of her family, and imprisoned for a week. The local papers registered fury over the peremptory act of this outsider:

> any other inmate of the house having committed the murder could easily have taken the garment from the [wash] bundle for the purpose of throwing suspicion by pointing it at Miss Constance.... This latter opinion is the view very largely shared by residents in the neighborhood, who will not listen to the charge against her, but sympathize with her as one who has been put forward as a scapegoat.[30]

By the time she appeared before local magistrates on July 27, Whicher had gathered little evidence in support of his suspicion, but hoped that the proceedings would be sufficient to prompt a confession. Instead, Constance listened impassively to the testimony with black-gloved hands folded in her lap. Whicher had managed to enlist two of Constance's close friends at the boarding school near her home which she attended. One acknowledged that Constance had confided a "dislike through jealousy" of the deceased, but she added:

> I have heard her say that she disliked the child and pinched it; but it was done in fun. She liked to tease them—not this one more than the others ... she was laughing when she said it.[31]

Constance had in fact been observed "romping" with Savile on the afternoon before his death; the boy was then making a bead necklace for this older sister, and she had painted a little picture for him not long before.

Her friend recalled a conversation they had had towards the end of term.

> We were speaking about the holidays one day when we were out walking in Road, near the house [the Kent's home], and I said, "Won't it be nice to go home shortly?" She said, "It may be to your home, but mine's different." [32]

Constance had allegedly added, "My mamma [her stepmother] would not let me have what I liked; if I wanted a brown dress, she would make me have a black, just for contrary." [33]

The second school friend asserted simply that although Constance "never said anything particular about the deceased," [34] she had noted that partiality was shown to the younger children. Master William, for example, was made to wheel his baby sister in the perambulator, which he disliked, and the parents used to compare William unfavorably with Savile, saying how much finer a boy the younger son was. The lawyer hired for Constance quickly saw that this was far from being sufficient evidence, and without even summoning witnesses for the defense he won his client's release through an impassioned speech.

> Was there anything strange that, in the unlimited confidences of schoolchildren, she should speak of her stepmother and say the younger children were preferred by her? . . . Where is the stepmother who will not prefer her own children to those of a former wife? [35]

The defender insisted that the laundress had merely lost the mysterious nightdress and that Constance, in any case, hardly had the strength to have silently carried the heavy child out to the privy and to have committed the ghastly crime.

> Is it likely that the weak hand of this young girl . . . can have inflicted this dreadful blow? Is it likely that hers was the arm which nearly severed the head from the body? It is perfectly incredible! [36]

In conclusion, he warned:

> I ask you to consider the effect of dragging this young lady from her home at such a time, if she is really innocent, as I believe she is. I know that an atrocious murder has been committed, but I am afraid that it has been followed by a judicial murder of a scarcely less atrocious character. . . . If this murder never be discovered—and we know how dark are the paths of crime—it will never, never be forgotten that this young lady was dragged from her home like a common felon, a common vagrant, to Devizes Gaol. . . . The steps you have taken will be such as to ruin her life—her prospects are already blighted—every hope is gone

with regard to this young girl. If she is innocent, as I believe, it is really terrible to contemplate the result to her.[37]

The judgment of the original coroner's jury was allowed to stand as death inflicted by "person or persons unknown." Constance was released, although a two-hundred-pound bond was required to guarantee her reappearance should she need to be called upon. After the inquest Constance was placed in a convent school in France to escape the embarrassment of publicity. Three years later she was permitted to return to England. She enrolled as Emilie Kent in a High Church establishment with an affiliated hospital in Brighton where she planned to train for a career in children's nursing. But after she had pursued her work for a year and a half, shortly after her twenty-first birthday, Constance traveled to London, where she confessed the murder of her half-brother. Her brief statement suggested neither circumstances nor motive, though she publicly denied that "cruel treatment" had prompted her action.[38] The accusing Inspector Whicher of Scotland Yard was vindicated after all.

On July 21, 1865, Constance Kent, having pleaded guilty, was condemned to death in proceedings which lasted only a few minutes. Judge Willes, a man not known for sentimentality, accepted her guilt, but spoke in a voice choked with sobs as he passed sentence; it was reported that "the greater part of the assembly as well as the jury were in tears." [39] Press opinion, which had generally sympathized with Constance five years before, now largely accepted the young woman's guilt, but countless questions were raised about the unsatisfactory explanation of the crime. The only statement offered appeared a month after Miss Kent's conviction in the form of a letter to the press from Dr. John C. Bucknill, a respected authority on lunacy, who had examined Constance after her confession and declared that she was sane.

A few days before the crime she obtained possession of a razor from a green case in her father's wardrobe and secreted it. This was the sole instrument she used. . . . Soon after midnight she went downstairs and opened the drawing room door and shutters. . . . She took the child from his bed and carried him downstairs through the drawing room. . . . Having the child on one arm, she raised the drawing-room sash with the other hand, went round the house [rather than through the stable yard] and into the closet, lighted the candle and placed it on the seat of the closet, the child being wrapped in the blanket and still sleeping. While the child was in this position, she inflicted the wound in the throat. She said she thought the blood would never come . . . so she thrust the razor into the left side and put the body with the blanket round it into the vault. . . . She went back to her room, examined her dress and found only two spots of blood on it. . . . She thought the bloodstains had been effectively washed out . . . but afterwards she found the stains were still visible. . . . She eventually burned it [the dress] in her bedroom. . . . As regards the motive for her crime, it seems that although she entertained at one time a great regard for the present Mrs. Kent, yet if any remark was at any time made which in her opinion was disparaging to any member of the first family, she treasured it up and determined to revenge it. She had no ill will against the little boy except as one of the children of her stepmother. She declared that her father and her stepmother had always been kind to her personally.[40]

In all, it was a most curious sort of explanation, which raised many more questions than it answered. But whether Constance was guilty or not, the matter was settled at law. The condemned young woman had her sentence commuted to life imprisonment, and twenty years later, in 1885, she was released. A friend who knew her then during her brief residence with an Anglican sisterhood reported that Constance adopted an assumed name and emigrated to Canada, where she became a nurse. The mystery over her role in a murder remains.

Obviously, neither Constance Kent nor Célestine Doudet can be held up as representative members of nineteenth-century middle-class spinsterhood. Both were troubled and possibly seriously disturbed personalities. Their disturbances nonetheless stemmed partly from pressures of social and sex roles which were imposed on them and to which they reacted in extreme ways. Moreover, what makes their cases worth considering not merely for themselves, but for a better understanding of a middle-class domestic world are the responses of those around the two accused women: relatives, servants, neighbors, pupils, friends, acquaintances, and members of the public whose views were recorded. When these are considered, the structures which could prejudice the position of children, especially girl children, in middle-class society, are revealed. At the same time, the probable explanations of the two young women's behavior become apparent.

Although both Constance Kent and Célestine Doudet emerge as victims and as victimizers, Mlle. Doudet appears more sharply in the latter role. It is curious that in her long experience as a governess her own peculiar qualities do not seem to have surfaced until she took charge of the Marsden daughters. For the previous period and even afterward she found many persons willing to attest to her excellent qualities as well as to pay for her defense, and there were few hints that she was seen by anyone as either eccentric or strange. A male relative of her previous employer, for whom she worked after 1848, did state that on one occasion Mlle. Doudet had become upset when she saw his nephew with his arm around his sister while the pair were reading together. This witness, who added that he thought Mlle. Doudet tried to create tension between the parents of her charges, reportedly concluded that the governess was odd, even a little mad.

A more telling portent was contained in the statement of the grandmother of the girls, Henriette Marsden, who became acquainted with Mlle. Doudet at Malvern before her son arranged to send the girls to Paris. She explained that she had had misgivings about the governess, partly because she observed what she considered unfair punishment of young Rosa, but chiefly because Mlle. Doudet once told her that while she was employed by the Queen, Prince Albert had made improper advances to her.

I tried to put my son on guard against her. The way she [Doudet] spoke to me about Prince Albert, her insinuations about him and herself, convinced me of her vile machinations. If the insinuations against the children were true, I alone should have heard them. It was indecent to speak about them to a young widower. But that was part of her plan, she knew he would keep it secret. My son was fooled by the recommendations of people in high places, and by [Doudet's] modest manners and affectation of piety.[41]

The governess, then, appeared already to be preoccupied with sex and sexual impropriety when she took her position at Malvern. Half-English and raised in the austere Protestant faith of her mother, she appears to have developed the morbid fascination with sexual matters characteristic of many persons whose circumstances deny them socially sanctioned sexual expression. When she arrived at Malvern, she quickly learned that one of her charges, the eldest daughter, Lucy, had been suspected of masturbation and that the child had been beaten by her father. The nursemaid who had reported the incident to Marsden later alleged that Lucy had had a "disposition to a female ailment," [42] that is, a vaginal infection, and that she had not been masturbating, but rather just relieving itching. Whether or not this was the case, Mlle. Doudet promptly set herself up as watchdog over the girls and was soon reporting to the doctor that Emily and Alice were afflicted. Alarmed and eager to prevent scandal at the same time, Marsden readily assented to the governess's discreet solution of removing the children to Paris to effect their cure. He later stated, "I made all possible recommendations to Mlle. Doudet, who seemed to have more experience than I for detecting these habits in children, and I ordered her to do all in her power to bring the habits under control." [43]

Once they settled in the cité d'Odiot, it was clear that Mlle. Doudet became obsessed with her mission. For the first time her sexual preoccupation was given social approval in the form of Marsden's directive. She now felt free to dwell on sexual behavior, with its expression safely projected onto the girls and with herself in the trying role of their vigilant would-be savior. Doudet had no compunctions about confiding her new burden to everyone; neighbors, servants, relatives, doctors, even her concierge were all duly informed. Witness after witness testified that Mlle. Doudet had discussed the girls' masturbatory habits on first meeting and frequently in the presence of the children themselves. Later, when the presiding judge accused her of gross impropriety in this matter, she replied:

I recognize that in this I may have lacked discretion. But since it was the occupation of my whole life to break these habits, I constantly was thinking about them, and it happened that I would discuss them as a way of comforting myself.[44]

The constant accusations of moral guilt had immediate, visible effects on the girls, even before their governess began to adopt harsher treatment. It is likely that if the children had ever masturbated, they had ceased to do so out of sheer terror, so the allegations must have been all the harder to bear. One of the children later sobbed that if she masturbated, it had to be in her sleep. The girls were described by most witnesses as listless and diffident in the period after their arrival in the summer of 1852. Forbidden to talk with one another because of their guilty habits, they would sit together on outings in the park with hands folded, staring dumbly. Asked by a neighbor on one occasion if they did not play games, one child reportedly replied that they did not know any. They displayed affection only for their governess, but the neighbor women, at least, suspected that their fear of her and their isolation were sufficient explanation for this exaggerated attachment.

Others were more easily fooled. A doctor reported his astonishment at what he described as the "cynical" [45] admission of one of the girls that she masturbated regularly. It seems never to have occurred to him that Mlle. Doudet might have ordered her charges to "confess" their habits, despite his admission that he found the woman's behavior odd. Marsden, too, seems to have been taken in, for he accepted at face value the alarming letters which the girls later said the governess had ordered them to write home, letters which proclaimed that far from improving, they were actually getting worse. Mlle. Doudet, according to these communications, was making heroic efforts to cure them, but the habits were spreading and becoming uncontrollable. Their angered father replied on one occasion that he no longer knew what to do and told them he had thrown the offending letters into the fire. The girls' frustration can only be guessed, and it is obvious that the governess's tactics effectively ensured that the children would seek no rescue from their enraged father.

The girls' uncle, John Rashdall, later joined the chorus of disapproval and wrote in December to explain that he had decided not to visit them again because of all the negative reports. Upbraiding them for behaving so badly after their father had allowed them to spend the year in Paris, he stated:

> I do not know how to tell you how much all this has cooled the interest which I had in you. . . . One of the main reasons I moved to Malvern was to be closer to all of you, but since then your conduct has demonstrated that I would be better off by being far away from nieces who give me so little satisfaction. . . . Allow me the fervent hope that you will begin the new year with a humble prayer to God, to beg him for the forgiveness to commence a new way of living.[46]

Through a combination of deception, ignorance, and shame, the girls' father persisted in defending a woman who was abusing his children. The few letters he sent leave no doubt that it was his concern over their alleged habits which informed all his behavior toward them. He wrote to Mlle. Doudet as early as August 1852 to express the hope that Emily's bad habits were being conquered. If not, he said, the governess was to consult a doctor he recommended immediately. "I am pleased that they are learning to jump rope like the little *Parisiennes,* but I beg you not to forget that *morals are more important than anything else.* " [47]

To Emily, whom he considered the worst offender, Marsden sent a special letter which was even more emphatic on the subject of masturbation.

I beg you in your own interest to make every effort to follow the advice and instructions I gave you before leaving you. If you have not done so, I shall be deeply disappointed when I see you again. Neither French nor music nor in fact anything else will compensate if you neglect to do what I recommended in this matter. And physical illness—a goitrous neck, a crooked back, tender feet—as well as this moral illness, drying up all self-respect, which will destroy every good quality you have, will cause you to feel personally, and oh how bitterly when you grow older, just how you have forced the laws of nature to your own destruction, and how you have disobeyed my wishes to your own ruin. [48]

Later that fall, as the bad reports continued to roll in, Marsden hardened his position. By October he was urging the governess to let Emily sleep with her as the only means of keeping an eye on her. And in mid-November, five months after their arrival in Paris, he seemed ready to wash his hands of the whole affair.

I can only say that unless their conduct changes for the better, my conduct towards them will change for the worse. They are too old to continue behaving this way; the weight of their behavior should now fall on their own heads. As for myself, I shall not long feel disposed to make personal sacrifices of all sorts for children who seem impossible to raise. Soon, I will cease to scold them, I will place them in an ordinary cheap *pension* and I will leave them to follow their own habits and suffer the consequences. Will you please convey this to those among them who can understand it? [49]

This was the same man of medicine who three years before had written warmly about the marvelous benefits to children of his own conversion to homeopathy, the new school of medical opinion which scorned the use of large doses of drugs and harsh or painful cures. "What tears and distress, and nausea from nauseous drugs, does it spare the poor little invalids," he had exclaimed. "Thank heaven I am no longer the terror of the nursery, children no longer cry at the sight of me." [50] It was a sincere and heartfelt statement, but it was also true that in the meantime his very own children had become terrified of him.

Homeopathists were especially persuaded by the popular belief that physical signs betrayed the habitual masturbator. These doctors placed special emphasis on the alleged intimate links between mental and physical disorders, and they accepted the view that masturbation was the sign of a depraved mentality. James Marsden himself later wrote a short treatise on the influence of the mind on the body and his notions are suggestive of his feelings toward his daughters.

It has been wittily said, "The body and the mind are like a jerkin and a jerkin's lining—rumple the one, and you rumple the other." I may add, ill-use the one, and you ill-use the other. . . . I must repeat—the mind grows by what it feeds on—that impressions and images (and these include every kind of learning) are the food of the mind, is the reason of the importance that good thoughts and impressions should be received, whilst the mind is ductile, as in infancy and youth: channels of feeling and thought are then formed. . . . These channels are real, material parts of the brain, that grow in size and vigour, as a blacksmith's arm grows and increases by continual use; their outward manifestations are called Habits.[51]

Marsden's euphemism for his daughters' alleged masturbation was, of course "bad habits."

It is clear that the girls' reported behavior caused the doctor deep professional as well as personal concern. He wanted to regard his children as perhaps too young to be held accountable for their actions, but he gradually came to see them as morally repulsive and loathsome creatures who were responsible for their physical ruin and who deserved much less than the attention he lavished on them.

When the Marsdens visited the girls on their wedding trip late in 1852, the doctor's sympathies remained unaltered. He admitted ordering the preservative belts at this time, adding that he had then believed there were compelling reasons to do so: "for so terrible is the misfortune of this vice that once it has taken possession of a child, *and especially a girl child,* it too often only lets go of its prey at the brink of the tomb [italics mine]."[52] Marsden added that he had respected his daughters' own desire to extend their stay with the governess, though it is likely that he was also moved by an unspoken desire to abandon daughters who he had come to believe were hopelessly corrupted.

The statement of his new wife, Mary, hinted that she, like many of the women who testified in the case, had more clearly understood the situation, but she had obviously been reluctant to contravene her husband's wishes. She mentioned that what troubled her on their visit was that children she had known as healthy, gay, and nice had developed a "constrained manner towards me" which "formed a painful contrast to their exaggerated marks of affection towards Mlle. Doudet."[53] It was she who had urged her husband that they stop again in Paris in the spring of 1853 on their return from Italy, and her statement suggested that she tried to persuade Marsden then to bring the children back. It would seem that at first Mary Marsden viewed the children's situation only in terms of her relationship with them. She did not express concern for their safety, but rather fear that her love was being supplanted. She stated that she told Doudet that at the expiration of the remaining three months of their agreement, her services would no longer be required. She added that she had ordered the governess to stop her remarks against the children, because they made her husband so wretched.

More disturbing was Mrs. Marsden's account of the girls' return to England late that summer after their sister's death in Paris. They were withdrawn and strange, she said, and it was weeks before they gradually "assumed the manners and ways suited to their ages." [54] The eldest child, Lucy, attached herself to her stepmother and reportedly was fearful of leaving her.

> Little by little they told us all the horrors they had undergone at their governess's hands, and their statements were verified and corroborated by the states of their bodies. Rosa was black and scarred from head to foot, Emily was in the same state. Poor Lucy had not only marks on her back but large bruises on her chest, on her side, and on her bowels [stomach] which were, she told me, the result of blows given her by Mlle. Doudet, who had shut her in a dark room alone.[55]

Lucy told her stepmother that Mlle. Doudet had called her a "red-haired devil" and had pulled out her hair by the handful. The doctor's earlier references to Lucy in his letters make it clear that he considered her the least bright and found samples of her written work which were sent to him pathetically inadequate.[56] The child seems, in fact, to have been a natural scapegoat. She reportedly told her stepmother that the governess had had such power over her that if she had ordered her to "plunge a knife into your [her stepmother's] breast, I should not have dared to disobey her." [57] Lucy died soon after, crying out in her delirium that the governess was after her. As Mary Marsden later recalled:

> Not satisfied with beating her, Mlle. Doudet frightened her with ghosts and told her she had power over her soul, and if ever she [Lucy] told what was done to her, even if she [Doudet] were in her grave, she would rise again and murder her. . . . I still grieve over the early death of this child, whose pure heart was full of dignity and sweetness.[58]

Of course, there was no one who was disinterested in the case to corroborate her account, but Mrs. Marsden's statement does not seem to have been manufactured. It does make her husband's reluctance to press charges the more puzzling; he waited from the time of their return in August 1853 until the following May to file suit. His reluctance can be attributed to several sources. Filing a suit entailed a public airing of what was to him a most delicate and embarrassing issue. It also involved the admission that his previous diagnoses may have been mistaken and that he just might have permitted personal revulsion to prejudice his daughters' safety. He might also have to admit to himself and in public that his behavior did in fact contribute to the abuse of his children and not to their care as he tried to maintain. During questioning he tried to object that he had disapproved of the procedure of tying the girls' wrists and ankles to their beds, but his actions do not support this later statement of disapproval. His sister-in-law, who was no doubt acquainted with Marsden's views, had observed the girls tied and had not intervened. Indeed, this practice appears to have been fairly common as masturbation prevention.[59] Marsden himself had seen two of his girls tied together in the same bed without objecting. In recounting the incident, he unwittingly gave away that his real concern was not that the girls were tied, but that one whom he believed to be "pure" had been bound with her "corrupted" sister. He declared that he had burst out to Mlle. Doudet and in front of the girls, "You have tied a living body to a corpse!"[60]

James Marsden, then, with his good intentions, had been more than a passive agent in his daughters' mistreatment, although it was Célestine Doudet who from the beginning, and with some justice, was labeled the monster. By contrast, until her confession and even after, Constance Kent was portrayed more commonly in the role of victim than of victimizer. At the time of the crime her youth aroused sympathy, as did the servants' accounts of the Kents' mistreatment and their blatant favoritism for the children of the new family.

The Kents' favoring of the second family was not an unusual attitude at the time, although their actions may represent an extreme of the common pattern. It was taken for granted that children of a man's first marriage assumed a subordinate role to those of the second and even that a second wife might legitimately display her "natural" favoritism for their own children. Novels and new writings on child rearing were beginning to urge equal attention for stepchildren,[61] but a story such as Charlotte Yonge's *The Young Stepmother* (1860), which attempted to combat the image of the wicked stepmother, only serves to underline her continued reality.[62] During the inquest in the Kent case it was alleged that when the second Mrs. Kent wished to hurt young Constance, she would make deprecatory remarks about the girl's dead mother. Even when a stepmother's preferential treatment for her own was less open, it is obvious that the girl children of a predecessor were especially vulnerable.

There were, however, some special reasons for the sympathy which Constance received, and some of these long antedated the hasty accusation against her at the time of the crime. The Kents were evidently notorious for ill treatment of servants, who, on departure, spread tales about the parsimonious household and the meanness of the Kents toward Constance and William. One source mentioned that "from their own misconduct or from domestic mismanagement, a constant and unvarying succession of female servants prevailed at Road-Hill House."[63] One contemporary estimate stated that there were more than a hundred servants there in the space of four years,[64] which is especially remarkable since the domestic staff at any one time was not large. These servants shared the abuse meted out to the older children and appear to have identified with their suffering. Indeed, the fact that the Kents relegated Constance, along with the other three children of the first family, to the third floor with the servants made the alliance even more natural. At the time of the crime this segregation was singled out as odd, for there were three empty rooms on the second floor, where the Kents and the three children of the second family slept.

One of the family's servants appears to have been the original source of an anonymous document which was sent in 1929 from Australia to the author of a study of the case [65] and which accurately recounts so many details concerning the Kent residences that it appears genuine. This document accepts Constance's confession as valid, but reports several incidents which portray her sympathetically as a victim.

> Days were spent shut up in a room with dry bread and milk and water for tea. At other times she would be stood in a corner of the hall sobbing "I want to be good, I do, I do." [66]

Perhaps it was these punishments of standing for hours which led ultimately to what her physician later called a "painful malady of the legs" [67] when Constance was ten or eleven. She was ordered to wear "laced stockings" and for a time had to use a wheelchair. But, according to the author of the anonymous document, her stoic disposition helped her make the best of things.

> Constance did not take her punishments very seriously, but generally managed to get some amusement out of them. Once, after being particularly provocative and passionate, the governess put her down in a dark wine cellar. She fell on a heap of straw and fancied herself in the dungeon of a great castle, a prisoner taken in a battle fighting for Bonnie Prince Charlie and to be taken to the block next morning. When the governess [later the second Mrs. Kent] unlocked the door [she] . . . asked her what she was smiling over. "Oh," she said, "only the funny rats. . . . They do not hurt me. Only dance and play about."
>
> At one time at Baynton House Constance's place of punishment was in one of the empty garrets. She used to climb out of the window and up the bend on the top of the roof and slide down the other side. She tied an old fur across her chest to act the monkey and called it playing Cromwell. To return she got through the window of another garret. The governess was puzzled at always finding the door unlocked with the key left in. The servants were questioned but of course knew nothing.[68]

This remarkable document also contests the view that the first Mrs. Kent was insane and makes references to Constance's childish intimations of the relationship between the governess and her father before her mother's death.

> Why did the mother when speaking to her [Constance] often call herself "your poor Mamma," which the governess said was silly? Why was the governess taken out for drives and her mother never? . . . She remembered many little incidents which seemed strange. One was during a thunderstorm, when the

governess acted as though frightened and rushed over to her father who drew her down on his knee and kissed her. The governess exclaimed "Oh, not before the child." [69]

Children saw and heard many things, as did servants, but Kent was still able to dismiss that reality.

Better documented was another incident in Constance's past, one which occurred four years before the death of little Savile and which was instantly recalled by authorities seeking someone with a motive to murder the boy. In 1856, when Constance was twelve, she gained a certain local notoriety. At that time, during summer holidays when her stepmother had been especially harsh and soon after she had announced to Constance a decision not to send her back to school that fall, the girl conceived a plan to persuade her younger brother William to leave home with her. The youngsters apparently hoped to find a ship at Bristol which would carry them to their sympathetic elder brother Edward, who was with the merchant marine in the West Indies. They only got as far as Bath, however, where they were brought to the police as suspected runaways.

Constance's performance there startled and impressed the officers, who referred to her admiringly as a "little hero." [70] According to the local press, which carried an account of the flight, Constance had fooled the authorities into thinking she was a boy, since she had shorn her hair and was wearing her brother's clothes. The police reported that the children only had one and sixpence between them and that Constance had pleaded to be held as a hostage so that her little brother might have a bed at a hotel. The police, too, were touched by the girl's stoic bravery during an interrogation which had prompted young William to burst into tears.

Not unnaturally, Constance's performance failed to impress the Kents. They beat both children severely and locked Constance in the cellar for two days as the instigator of the scheme, instructing the family to ostracize her upon her release. Mr. Kent was especially upset, since for the second time he was called upon to explain his domestic situation before the Board of Factory Commissioners. This time he spared himself by throwing all the blame on Constance, who he alleged was an intractable child, lacking in "feminine delicacy." He added that "she had wished to be independent," [71] a quality which was laudable in a boy, but hardly considered a virtue in one of the female sex.

The runaway incident at first created sympathy in the neighborhood, and the predisposition in Constance's favor was one reason the outsider, Chief Inspector Whicher of Scotland Yard, encountered such hostility. Still, it was natural enough that Whicher found the incident suspicious, for the children's evident desperation did suggest a possible motive for the resolute Constance.

After her confession, however, the incident was popularly accepted outside the locality as proof that she was both insane and sexually peculiar.

The episode provided an escape from the dilemma that Constance, a young girl, could have committed a violent crime. The flight from home somehow demonstrated that she was tainted with madness. Moreover, the shocking fact that she had cut her hair and donned boy's clothing was then seen to have "unsexed" her; she became a male soul in a female body and thus a more plausible culprit. No one seemed to notice that adopting a boy's identity was the only way the twelve-year-old Constance might have hoped to escape from home without being immediately picked up. It was an eminently sane act. And few recalled, apparently, that the two children had divulged their plan to become cabin boys on a ship to the West Indies.

The sympathy toward Constance Kent (at least until her confession) as well as the hostility toward Célestine Doudet were affected by a growing reaction against harsh discipline and especially manual correction of children. This issue was more central in the Doudet trial, however, not only because the charges expressly involved physical abuse of the children, but also because the case was tried in France, where manual punishment was less common in the middle classes than in England.[72]

To be sure, the growing concern for children's welfare was prompting a reevaluation of corporal punishment in England. By the 1840s child-rearing manuals were urging that corporal punishment should be only a last resort.[73] Educational journals and women's magazines were recommending less corporal punishment.[74] The specific issue of manual correction for girls and young women was discussed less often, but one of the best sources for material on actual practice is the correspondence columns of the new and rapidly growing women's magazines.

The *Queen* in the mid-sixties and the *Englishwoman's Domestic Magazine* in 1870 devoted several issues of the letters column to the question.[75] Indeed, the controversy over corporal punishment of girls aroused so much interest that the *Englishwoman's Domestic Magazine* was obliged to publish several monthly supplements, and the editors were still unable to include all the letters. They are a remarkable collection. A woman principal writes to explain the correct procedure of whipping in minute detail, even to descriptions of how the tunic of the victim should be tucked up and under the lower part of the stays to facilitate the process.[76] A rector explains that on many occasions he has whipped girls aged twelve to sixteen who were brought to him by widows who could not cope with them.[77] Several parents professing to have incorrigible daughters request the names of schools "still" practicing corporal punishment. Other letters discuss the merits of rods of varying woods and thicknesses, taws (leather straps cut into strips at one end), and other devices; many give advice on where to purchase the best instruments of punishment and describe the exact bodily effects of each.

Many of the letters do object to corporal punishment of girls, although usually with qualifications. Some say it should not be public, as it was in many schools, especially earlier in the century. Others say that it should cease at a certain age, although there is wide disagreement about that age. Several men object to women being permitted to whip boys past the age of ten or so.

But most interesting for this discussion are the large numbers of young married women who write to describe their school experiences, many of which were contemporary with those of the Marsden girls. The majority of these speak of regular corporal punishment in their schools or administered by governesses, and most mention their impression of the growing infrequency of whipping in recent years. Many allege that the situation is most unfortunate, citing fond memories of some schoolmistress or governess who beat them severely but, as one confesses, "strange as it may seem, from that day to the present I have loved Miss Margaret and felt her to be a true friend." [78]

The few letters from young women still undergoing such treatment by 1870 are less rhapsodic. One from a schoolgirl in Kensington explains that parents are unaware of the tortures suffered by students. As the "show pupil" in the school, she was the one sent for when ladies came to inquire about placing their girls there, and she was required to play a piece or give a recitation. Visitors, however, had no clue that the girls were regularly beaten. The mistress, she says, "thinks we all love her to distraction, but we hate her like poison because she birches us." [79] A veneer of decorum over brutality also described the Marsden girls' situation, but they did not even have the chance to complain. It seems obvious that if corporal punishment was on the decline and that if most young English girls were spared the intense tortures of the Marsden children, many nonetheless were subjected, like their brothers, to harsh canings and psychological humiliation.

Constance Kent and the Marsden girls suffered physical punishments, withholding of food, and incarceration both for general "intractability" and for failure in performing their lessons. But in the case of the Marsden children, the main reason for punishment was masturbation or rather the suspicion of masturbation. Emily testified that if they made the slightest movement in their beds at night, their vigilant governess would order them to stand with bare feet on the cold floor and arms outstretched. The maid confirmed Emily's account, adding that the girls remained in this position until they begged for mercy or collapsed.

In the late spring of 1853, after the Marsdens' visit, Célestine Doudet reportedly advanced her tortures. In addition to continued starving she also regularly rubbed soap around the children's eyes, struck their torsos, and stamped on their feet until they were bloody and swollen. These punishments appear to have had a special purpose: Célestine Doudet was taking no chances that the physical signs attributed to masturbation should be absent. These procedures were surely employed to produce the emaciated, deformed bodies, puffy eyes, and tender feet believed characteristic of those addicted to the vice. Especially disturbing in this regard was the testimony of the girls that their governess had tied a rough cord between their legs and forced them to wear it for days at a time, thereby creating the inflamed areas which provided telltale evidence for the examining physicians. Although medical authorities now reject the notion that any physical examination can betray the habitual masturbator,[80] nineteenth-century authorities fully accepted the idea, and both sides in the Marsden case were convinced by it.

The disagreement then lay over what constituted appropriate restraint or punishment. Despite his denials Dr. Marsden clearly endorsed whipping, as well as tying the children's limbs to the bedposts. There is evidence, too, that a meat-restricted diet was part of his plan; meats, especially those cooked rare as was popular in France, were believed to excite the passions.[81] Still, Doudet's policy of starvation was not part of Marsden's ideas; he later listened in despair as the concierge told how his five daughters used to gather in the courtyard to smell the dinners cooking and stare longingly while her family took their meals.

Certainly the governess dismissed the milder remedies. A doctor complained that Doudet had ignored his own solution of gymnastics lessons for the girls, as well as the purchase of a bedtime garment which was a sort of nightgown-straitjacket. Doudet acknowledged, too, that she had not used the preventive belts which Marsden had ordered, although she claimed that this was only because the belts arrived at a time when she was treating most of them for whooping cough. Interestingly, she admitted having finally taken only three of these belts, on the ground that Rosa, the second to youngest, seemed strong and healthy and that Lucy, the eldest, was old enough to cure herself. It is possible that Doudet employed "divide and conquer" tactics to keep the children firmly under her control.

Why Célestine Doudet and Constance Kent behaved as they did requires further explanation. That each had resentments is obvious enough. But it is unclear why Célestine Doudet might have persisted in her cruelties, and even intensified them greatly in the spring of 1853, when it was apparently in her interest to demonstrate some success in her mission to cure her charges. Her behavior suggests that she was a deeply disturbed woman, but it is remarkable that the legal proceedings touched so lightly on this probability. As for Constance Kent, the real mystery surrounds the circumstances of her confession. From the time of the crime Constance enjoyed public sympathy not only as the victim of past parental abuse, but, as local papers put it at the time, as a "scapegoat." Almost immediately, another inmate of the house was singled out as the guilty party, though that person was never formally accused. Why then, five years later, when, guilty or innocent, she had the opportunity and means to escape, should Constance Kent have confessed to the crime? The final explanations of the two women's actions are imbedded in their peculiar responses to the ways their societies defined them as female creatures and identified their duties, their expectations, and their sexual natures.

In the case of Célestine Doudet the prosecution found a simple explanation, which may have been a partial truth, and looked no further. Mlle. Doudet, they said, had wished to marry her employer; when he married another, she took revenge on his children. It was true that the prosecution did not concentrate on this theory until the third occasion on which Mlle. Doudet appeared before Parisian magistrates. On the first occasion, in February 1855, Doudet was brought before the Seine assize court, accused of having voluntarily administered blows to Mary Ann Marsden which resulted in the child's unintended death. Acquitted, Doudet faced a correctional tribunal the following month and received two years for physical attacks on the other four girls. Then in April the prosecution successfully appealed the correctional case on the ground that new evidence, in the form of a remark made by the governess to one of the court doctors, suggested that her real motive was premeditated revenge and that the case thus fell under a different law requiring stiffer punishment. Allegedly, Mlle. Doudet had said, "I am innocent; but if I am condemned, I will suffer less in the thought that M. Marsden also will suffer through his children's honor." [82]

The ground of new evidence was a pretext to permit the prosecution to introduce the revenge theory it had developed after the case was filed under a lesser charge. At the outset of the appeal proceedings, the presiding judge reacted sympathetically to these opening remarks by the state's attorney.

> Mlle. Doudet is not insane; she did not think she was curing the children by means of these punishments. It remains for us to choose between two equally shameful motives: vengeance and cruelty. Some say vengeance is only a hypothesis. But what of these tears shed upon learning of the marriage, and [what of] the change in her language about M. Marsden? [83]

The prosecutor's statement attempted to shore up this theory by presenting the case, complete with Latin phrases, as one more example of woman's perfidy. The conduct of Célestine Doudet, he declared, has only "made manifest once again the *furens quid femina possit.*" [84] Simply, too simply, the case was seen as just another example of the fury of a woman scorned.

Admittedly, there was some evidence for this position. Neighbors pointed out that on her arrival in France, before she knew of Marsden's impending marriage to a patient, she had glowed with reports of him. "If only you knew how kind he is. If you could just see how good!" [85] Doudet, they said, displayed Marsden's portrait prominently on the mantelpiece and told everyone what a fine and worthy doctor he was. Later, when she learned of his marriage, her attitude allegedly changed abruptly. One neighbor reported that Célestine had burst into tears and called it disgraceful that a man with so many children should remarry. The girls reportedly announced to everyone that they would never call their new stepmother "Mamma," although

Zéphyrine Doudet confided to the neighbors that "The children do not have these feelings, my sister makes them say that." [86] At the same time the portrait of the children's father came down from the mantelpiece.

Such a response by itself might have reflected a natural disappointment, and it is not impossible that the governess, as the prosecutor said, did for a time "cherish the dream" [87] of marriage to Marsden. However, her subsequent response went far beyond simple disappointment, and not only in the previously described area of abuse of her charges. Mlle. Doudet reportedly began to denounce Marsden to everyone as a man who cared nothing for his children and spent all his time womanizing. To one doctor, she declared, "The father is a man of loose morals who enjoys much success with the ladies; he is concerned with nothing but his pleasures." [88] To the Englishwoman Hooper, who subsequently tried to file a suit against her in Marsden's name, she charged that the doctor had been living with his new bride for two years before their marriage and that he had married her only because she was pregnant. She also once confided to this woman that the real reason for Lucy's sequestration was that the child, at fourteen, had taken to flirting with the young men passing by.

Doudet's sexual allegations were not limited to the Marsden family. The girls soon were made to claim that they had acquired their "bad habits" from their "immodest" aunt, Fanny Rashdall, who had initiated them in these practices at Malvern. Their Anglican uncle was not spared either. Once when the thirteen-year-old Emily was visiting her aunt, she wrote Doudet to say that her Uncle John had entered the bedroom where she and her aunt were sleeping and that he had been "very jovial" [89] with the aunt [his sister]. By the time of the preliminary interrogations, Mlle. Doudet had transformed the innuendo, which Emily said she had inserted to please the governess, into something more explicit. Emily had told her, she said, that her uncle the minister had, in her presence, done things with her aunt "that a woman ought never to see." [90]

Any question that these reported incidents were distorted was removed by Doudet's courtroom performance. When the maid Léocadie Bailleux produced her catalogue of disciplinary horrors, the governess charged that Léocadie had been seduced by Marsden. And again, after Emily's testimony, when Doudet was asked about having compromised the "future and reputation of these young girls," [91] she replied:

He himself [Marsden] has done so, and before all of Paris! When I saw my student, a girl of fourteen, walk up the aisle with two rows of lawyers on her right, jurymen on the left, and judges in front of her, with her father right there, I was so upset that I turned my head away; it is M. Marsden who had disgraced his daughter, for at that moment he was responsible for making her abandon a woman's modesty. [92]

As it turned out, it was Célestine Doudet's attacks on Marsden himself, rather than on his children, which had finally prompted the doctor to file suit. He even told the court that he had given up the idea of any action until he learned that the governess was "defaming me. . . . She dared to call my children illegitimate. . . . Then, I swear, I decided that honor was the first among life's goods, and I came before you." [93]

In undertaking his suit, Marsden decided that his own complicity in his children's treatment required that he present himself as duped from the very beginning. He asserted that Doudet had sought him out as "a widower with a fortune," [94] and insisted that he had never had the slightest indication of his children's vice before the governess confided in him, both of which claims were demonstrated to be false. In fact, Marsden brought his case, as he stated in the act of accusation, not chiefly to punish Mlle. Doudet for physical attacks on his children, but instead to save the family honor and especially his own, by proving that his children were not and never had been masturbators.

Correspondingly, the whole thrust of Célestine Doudet's defense was not to show that she was innocent of mistreating the children, but rather to demonstrate that all the girls were guilty of vicious habits. Her lawyer, the talented Antoine Berryer, argued that once masturbation was proved, there was no need to invent bad treatment to explain the deplorable physical condition of the girls; "these habits, when they last, when they are inveterate, are sufficient to explain everything." [95]

In preparing his case, Marsden compiled a dossier with signed statements from numerous persons who swore that his daughters were "untainted." He also worked to discredit those who had already testified to the habits. He allegedly bribed a maid from Malvern to stay away from the trial. The French doctor who had previously sworn to "frenzied" masturbatory behavior and claimed to have identified the "local marks of passion" now obligingly testified that the girls' remarkable recovery since leaving their governess proved that he had been mistaken. The girls' appalling physical condition, he said, had clearly been the result of mistreatment rather than masturbation.

Mlle. Doudet engaged an English solicitor to prepare an opposing dossier, bearing witness not only to the masturbation but to other actions, such as lying, cheating, and pilfering, designed to create prejudice against the children.[96] In the ensuing battle important information about Mlle. Doudet's actual behavior toward the girls tended to be pushed aside. The postmortem on Mary Ann showed a skull fracture which the governess never had to explain fully. She was aided in this by some doctors (initially including Marsden himself in a diagnosis based on incomplete accounts sent to him) who asserted that death might have resulted from internal hemorrhaging, independent of a fall, which could have been occasioned by a coughing fit. But the "bad habits" came to Doudet's aid here, too. She made the astonishing charge that young Mary Ann, in despair over her uncontrollable masturbation, had developed suicidal tendencies. The child had once attempted to jump out the window, Doudet said, and on another occasion she had purposely bashed her head into the wall.

The pathetic result of the case was its reduction to the question of whether the Marsden girls were or were not masturbators. In the process the children were forced to be as much defendants in the proceedings as Célestine Doudet. Both sides, after all, accepted masturbation as a morally culpable act which produced recognizable physical consequences. The children, then, were literally on trial.

Newspapers reported that the crowds of women in the courtroom trained their scrutiny on the three Marsden girls, who were identically dressed in tartan outfits popularized by the Queen, with smart little black velvet caps.[97] If some spectators detected any telltale signs of vice, the recorded reaction was overwhelming sympathy for their past suffering. The three girls were pronounced "charming" and "adorable," [98] and their healthy appearance was cited to prove their father's case. Their testimony was warmly received, and they were described as very well-behaved, sitting together quietly with the maid who had taken their side and, from time to time, "phlegmatically devouring a cake or an orange drink." [99] Their former governess, by contrast, failed this "sight test," and hostility toward her was apparent from press descriptions. She was conceded a distinguished if severe appearance as a tall woman with blue eyes and tightly coiffed blond hair, but she was pronounced charmless, with a bad English accent and "the physical carriage of a schoolmarm." [100] At the outset of the first trial the presiding judge categorized Doudet as a familiar type of spinster: "she cannot see a young woman endowed with the charms of her sex without saying something bad about her." [101]

The sexual politics of the Marsden affair were brutal and cut several ways. The victim turned victimizer who was Célestine Doudet was a complex and deeply troubled woman who was recognized as such by other women who knew her well, but not by the doctor who hired her, the minister who checked on her, the physician who examined her charges, the policeman who visited her, or the male magistrates and jury who judged her. It was easier to "understand" Mlle. Doudet by forcing her into a comprehensible stereotype: the frustrated spinster. The real tyranny she exercised over the girls was trivialized by this simplification, as was the seriousness of her own psychological disturbance.

At the same time the court permitted the case to be developed as an archaic defense of patriarchal honor through a father's insistence on the sexual purity of his daughters. Time and again the combatants referred to the presence or absence of masturbatory vice as the real issue of the case, while the question of the children's physical and psychological suffering took second place. The girls, who knew their father was lying to protect himself and, he thought, them, may have considered, too, that their sisters Mary Ann and

Lucy had been sacrificed to his obsession. That Marsden remained convinced of his daughters' corruption was obvious, despite his denials. That he should then have required them to stand witness to their innocence was the more tragic, for they cannot have failed to recall that he had labeled one of them, a child who survived, a "corpse." The fact that Marsden's views on masturbation were extreme, even for this repressive period, was implicitly acknowledged by Doudet's lawyer himself, who accepted their basic validity. But his concessions can have been small comfort for the girls:

> No doubt, the fault recognized in these young girls is a moral evil, but it is still more a sickness. At the age when the daughters of M. Marsden abandoned themselves to these habits, it was much more the consequence of an irritated and irritable nervous system, an involuntary attraction. It is likely that in growing up, they will be cured of these habits through vigilance and firm resolution, that having arrived at the age of reason, they will rediscover their innocence, their purity, and their dignity in the world. They are not dishonored forever.[102]

Perhaps unsurprisingly, none of the women who testified to the girls' situation, either for prosecution or defense, made the children's alleged habits the central point of their arguments, and most never even mentioned them as relevant. For the women, the kindness or, more often, the cruelty, of the governess was the main theme. It is true that taboos on the subject may have inhibited them more than the men, but as women and as mothers, they had observed that children masturbate from infancy. While they themselves may have taken steps to discourage and restrain such behavior, they could not condemn as lost the beings who indulged in it. Still, as women, they were in a position to exert only indirect pressure. Even their best collective efforts were dismissed, and individual efforts were hopeless. The grandmother's warning, the sister's and maid's defection, the aunt's thwarted intervention, the neighbor's anonymous letter, the stepmother's hesitant intimations were all doomed attempts to spare the girls. And all give witness to the deference and powerlessness of women, who saw and heard and knew, but could not rescue.

In the case of Constance Kent the same theme of the sacrifice of children to adult obsessions emerges. Once again, new middle-class privacy provided relative isolation from outside pressures, and adult mediators ensured that what pressures there were further prejudiced the position of children. It was true that the mistreatment of Constance and her past record of resentment and calculated escape appeared to provide the girl alone with a motive to commit such a heinous crime. Nonetheless, local journalists, who were less affected by deferential niceties toward "respectable" folk than the investigating officers in the case, promptly concluded that if the affair was seen in another light, there were at least two other persons who might have been responsible for the deed. Simply, the journalists submitted that premeditated murder had not been committed, and they cited some compelling evidence in favor of their theory.

Without actually naming him, the local *Bath Chronicle* dared to propose a candidate in Mr. Kent himself, assisted by the nursemaid Elizabeth Gough.[103] Aware of Kent's previous behavior with his former governess (now his wife), the paper suggested that a similar intrigue was being carried on with the new nursemaid and that after the family retired, Kent, with "impure objects" in mind, habitually made visits to the nursery where Miss Gough and young Savile slept.

> Let us suppose him to have paid a nocturnal visit to the partner in the wrong; . . . that the dawning of a June morning revealed him to the wondering eyes of an awakened child; that the mingled feelings of the moment rushed upon him at a time when we are all prone to give way to foolish promptings. . . . What would the effect of that hour be to a man who was guilty, meanly guilty, and was convinced that in an hour or two an innocent voice that could not be silenced would proclaim him guilty. . . . A weak, bad, terrified, violent man sees a child between him and ruin—and the fearful deed is madly done.[104]

There was support for the theory, both in material evidence and in the behavior of Kent himself and others. Of course it was unlikely that a father would have dashed for a knife and slain his beloved son on the spot, but medical evidence indicated that Savile did not die by the knife. The examining doctor reported that bruised and blackened areas about the child's mouth suggested instead that the boy had been suffocated. This possibility supported the *Chronicle's* theory, for it was far more plausible that in the panic of the moment Kent might have grabbed something and pressed it over the child's mouth, perhaps only to stifle his cries. It was possible, indeed, that what he used was the breast flannel or brassiere which was found in the blanket around the body, a garment which was later discovered to fit Miss Gough and only her of the female inmates of the house. The theory suggested that when the child's face was uncovered, Savile was discovered to be dead, whether by design or not. Kent was then left to contrive a credible story.

It is at least possible that he first decided to mutilate the body to suggest that his son was another victim in a recent series of unexplained knife murders in the area. If he slashed the child's throat after death, of course, this would account for the observed small amount of blood in the outdoor privy where the deed was probably performed. Especially with the aid of Miss Gough, the whole episode could have taken place without rousing the household. A back stairs led directly to the short route to the privy, which would have protected them from any passers-by on the lane, and the vicious dog in the stable yard would have known his master. Finally, it would have been a simple matter for Kent, on returning to the house, to raise the heavy sash in the drawing room to suggest the entrance of an intruder.

This reconstruction seems to be more plausible than Constance's account after her confession in 1865. She claimed that her father's razor was the sole instrument, despite evidence that Savile died from suffocation and that the stab wound in the child's side could not have been inflicted by a razor. Her version of events required that she enter the nursery and pick up the child without rousing either him or the nurse, remake the cot (while she was holding him on one arm), make her way down darkened stairs and through the drawing room window (why not out the door?) and thence across the yard to the privy where, according to her account, she slit the child's throat as he lay cradled in her arm. She thought the blood "would never come," yet if she had done exactly what she said, blood would have been everywhere.

Samuel Kent did have a stronger motive than to prevent his family's knowledge of an indiscretion with the nursemaid. Already deep in debt, he was once again counting on being named to a seat on the Board of Factory Commissioners, a lucrative post for which he had recently troubled to collect two hundred signatures in his support.[105] Having twice been called to explain himself before that body, which he accomplished by defaming his first wife in one case and Constance in another, he knew he could not afford additional scandal. And there was little cause to be sanguine about young Savile; the child had a reputation as a "talebearer," and the nursemaid herself once remarked: "He was always running to his mother with stories of all he heard and saw." [106] To avoid the scandal and possible loss of a post, Samuel Kent may have offered up the life of his son Francis Savile and possibly that of his daughter Constance Emily as well.

The hypothesis of Kent's guilt does help to explain the extraordinary sequence of events which followed the death of Savile. Kent's sudden departure to inform the police was unnecessary, for he might have sent others; and, in any case, there were policemen closer by. As observers noted at the time, it appeared that he wished to be absent when the body was found. More incriminating was a statement he made to the turnpike-keeper on his way to Trowbridge: "I have had a child stolen and carried away in a blanket." [107] When he left his home, the coverlet on Savile's bed had been pulled up, and the missing blanket was not "discovered" by nurse Gough until sometime during Kent's absence.

Nevertheless, Mr. Kent, as the newly bereaved father and head of the household, was permitted by the awed local authorities to orchestrate all events. He succeeded in keeping them out of the house until past noon on June 30, 1860, on the grounds that "the murderer would not be found there." [108] According to a family doctor who came to the scene, Kent "suggested a succession of suppositions all equally vague and improbable and unsupported by any testimony or by the evidence of a single fact." [109] He proposed that the cottagers nearby had avenged his attacks on their fishing in his stream; he claimed that former nursemaids had sworn vengeance on his "horrid" children; and he even declared that gypsies had murdered his boy. By the time the police were finally admitted in the afternoon, Kent had gained their complete support. They later admitted that they had shared all their findings with him and failed to consider him as a suspect at all.

The search did reveal one crucial bit of evidence: a bloody "night shift" of coarse material, characterized as the sort worn by a woman of the servant class, was found jammed up inside a boiler stove. Under normal circumstances it would have been consumed when the morning fire was lit, but that day, in the excitement, the housemaid had neglected this part of her routine. Incredible as it sounds, the officers reported their discovery to Kent and entered into a compact with him to trap the murderer, who by this time was believed to be an unidentified member of the household.

The policemen were invited to return secretly later that evening, and the night shift was returned to its hiding place in the scullery. Kent then ordered the officers to keep their stake-out in the kitchen, which he bolted according to custom, as he later said, so as not to arouse the suspicion of the murderer, who he insisted would descend to retrieve the incriminating shift. What happened was that the witless officers were trapped for several hours in the kitchen, which had no access to the scullery but which was thoughtfully supplied with cheese and beer for them. By the time Kent finally released them, the night shift was missing, and they realized they had been duped. But they were not about to reveal their stupidity. When Scotland Yard was called in, the officers kept quiet, and it was not until a final investigation of the case five months later that the episode came out. By then, however, so much confusion had been sown that the missing garment was dismissed as irrelevant (it was hinted that the discarded shift belonged to a servant who had been menstruating). Five years later, after Constance's confession, the garment was recalled and became the child's missing nightdress. It is at least possible, however, that the coarse night shift was the garment Elizabeth Gough had been wearing when she aided her lover in his grisly chore.

It was not only the policemen who were obliging in their behavior toward Kent. That gentleman appears to have influenced in his favor all the weighty local opinion-makers, including doctors, lawyers, clergymen, and magistrates. His own lawyer managed to spare Kent and his wife from even appearing at the inquest. The coroner arranged to have some potentially hostile nominees removed from the jury and named a sympathetic friend of Kent's, the local minister, as foreman. This man announced that it was "their duty to spare the feelings of the family as far as possible." [110] But the stacked jury still objected to the curious haste of the procedure and demanded to be taken to the Kent home, where jury members were permitted briefly to interview two persons, William and Constance, whose protection appeared to be a matter of concern to no one. The press outrage over the affair succeeded in prolonging subsequent inquiries, which focused on Constance and then on Miss Gough, and finally on the missing night shift. But the last investigation ended and the attorney general, who applied to the Queen's Bench to quash the coroner's inquest on grounds of faulty procedure, was refused in February 1861, when all efforts to find a responsible party ended.

That Samuel Kent from the beginning worked to impede the authorities is clear, but his motives have been variously interpreted. If, despite the apparently well-founded local suspicion against him, his daughter Constance was the real culprit and he suspected it, then his behavior might well have been seen, as his friends hinted, as a desperate effort to shield the girl. Of course, Constance may have been lying about how she did it. Had she perhaps enlisted her brother William again in this more terrible scheme? Proof is impossible, but all the evidence makes it far more likely that local opinion was justified in pointing the finger at Kent himself, and that five years later an innocent young woman had her own private reasons for calling herself guilty.

Far from suggesting the attempt to shield a guilty child, Kent's behavior after the crime hints at something very different, namely, a subtle effort to implicate the sixteen-year-old girl. Indeed, if Kent's guilt is assumed instead of Constance's, then the whole sequence of events pointing to the girl's involvement assumes a terrible logic. It was quickly apparent that the authorities dismissed Kent's early insistence on an intruder and settled on the guilt of someone in the household, a theory which Kent himself promptly entertained as soon as the bloody night shift was found. But if, as seems likely, he did contrive its mysterious disappearance, he doubtless felt obliged to divert suspicion away from himself, especially when rumors about a bloody shift were heard in the general protest over the inquest. Constance, with her history of "strange" behavior, was a natural scapegoat.

In a few days Kent was heard soundly accusing the laundress of stealing *Constance's* nightgown, an item easily confused with the missing shift. Though the Kents' maid swore she had seen the garment in the basket and recorded it as usual, evidence of domestic collusion on the story that Constance then extracted the gown is strong. The intended implication then was that although the girl wished to blame the disappearance of this nightgown on the laundress, she had been obliged to destroy it since it contained the blood which proved her guilt. Nurse Gough soon was heard to declare: "You can depend on it, that nightgown will lead to the discovery of the murder." [111]

Constance, however, appears to have had no opportunity to extract the gown during the brief time before the readied basket was delivered, for she was in her room on the floor above the whole time, save once when she descended briefly to ask the maid to fetch her a glass of water. The girl, according to the maid, was out of her sight for less than a minute and returned upstairs. But her stepmother, who was in her room on that floor and could not have failed to overhear the conversation, herself had had ample opportunity to slip out and extract the nightgown which implicated Constance and later provided the core of the Scotland Yard investigator's case against the child.

Precisely when Mrs. Kent "knew" is unclear, but in mid-July she summoned the magistrates to amend her previous statement about never having taken Savile from his cot at night. Now, she declared that she might well have done so and that she had once told Gough, "Nurse, do not be frightened if I come in and take the child away." [112] This event signaled the closing of the ranks with her husband and Nurse Gough. Mrs. Kent, realizing what had happened, saw no choice but to protect the husband who killed Savile and the rival who had helped him. At about the same time the nursemaid was reportedly in a state of extreme agitation prior to renewed questioning by the magistrates. A female witness at whose home she was detained during questioning later reported overhearing her say to Mrs. Kent, "How can I bear it? I must give in—I can't hold out any longer." Mrs. Kent had allegedly replied, "Oh, don't say that! You have done so well so far—do keep it up—you must, for my sake." [113]

The trio seemed to have used the arrival of Inspector Whicher as an opportunity to cement the case against Constance. The inspector was immediately informed not only of the runaway incident, but of numerous other peculiarities about Constance, including the "fact" that her mother had gone mad. Whicher was told that one night the year before Savile, who had a cold and was wearing bedsocks, was found uncovered in his cot with the socks removed. Although there was nothing to connect the girl with the incident, it was now hinted that it might have been a kind of rehearsal for the crime.[114] With such crumbs Whicher built the case against Constance.

From the trio's point of view this solution was perfect. The suggestion of hereditary madness neatly explained both the crazed murder of Savile and the previous resentment of a stepmother—and all without prejudice to Mr. and Mrs. Kent. Moreover, the weakness of the evidence and the suspicion of madness helped ensure the discreet dropping of the affair by the authorities and permitted the Kents quickly to send the supposedly disturbed young woman off to France. They may not have counted on the persistent local suspicion, but even there friends came to their aid.

Most important among these was Dr. Joseph W. Stapleton, who promptly undertook to vindicate the maligned sub-inspector of factories by writing a ponderous work entitled *The Great Crime of 1860*,[115] a volume he published a year after the event. The obliging Stapleton had appeared on the scene on the day the crime was discovered, and from the beginning, whether from honest conviction or not, he had publicly defended the innocence of his friend Kent. While Stapleton maintained official neutrality on the issue of the real guilty party, the book's unofficial purpose was to identify Constance as the murderess and then to absolve her from further inquiry on grounds of madness.

The study opens with a lengthy, and otherwise inexplicable, general discussion on the transmissibility of personal traits from parents to children and remarks, "It is in the woman's soul that poets and moralists have sought and found the most frequent and disastrous examples of revenge." [116] Some pages later, when Stapleton introduces the Kents and lingers long on the first Mrs. Kent's alleged insanity, the attentive reader recalls his earlier remarks and thinks on Constance, although her name has not even been mentioned by the careful author. He further comments about the first Mrs. Kent that "It was not discovered that she at any time contemplated murder or suicide; and the fact of a knife having been found concealed under her bed appears to have occasioned little or no apprehension in this regard." [117] This not-so-subtle little conceit naturally prompts the reader to ponder again the transmissibility of traits which the good doctor stressed in his introduction. He gently tries to persuade that the latent tendency to murder in Mrs. Kent was realized in the next generation in Constance's terrible female revenge. Again and again, Stapleton hints strongly at Constance's guilt, only to draw back from a firm accusation. He cites Gough's alleged outburst to Mrs. Kent when the boy's body was actually discovered: "Oh, Ma'am, it's revenge!" [118] and he hints that Kent's admittedly odd behavior was explained by his realization of Constance's guilt: "the general, indistinct dawning notion that he himself was haunted by some horrible and unavowed and guarded suspicion of a heavier calamity impending over him." [119]

In an attempt to refute the strong evidence that Savile was suffocated, evidence which he saw could incriminate Kent, Stapleton asserts his authority as a doctor who examined the child: "That he died instantly by the knife is a scientific and inevitable conclusion." [120] To account for the observed small amount of blood, he offers the feeble suggestion that the terrified boy's heart "stood still" [121] when the knife was raised over him. Stapleton also lends support to the suspicion of Constance based on the missing nightdress. Police officers had testified that Stapleton himself had seen the other garment, the bloody night shift, but Stapleton dismisses that episode and points again to Constance. "Miss Constance Kent had three nightdresses. . . . Where is the third, the missing nightdress?" [122] This apparently willful distortion of evidence suggests that Stapleton at least suspected Kent, but sympathized with his plight. In the need to save a desperate friend, a child's existence was expendable, particularly since that child was evidently "peculiar."

The circumstances of Constance Kent's confession of April 1865 provide another of the arguments for her innocence. Once again, adult authorities with their own purposes to serve, this time religious ones, intervened. Having returned from France in 1863, Constance had been studying for a nursing career for eighteen months at St. Mary's Convent in Brighton. All indications were that she intended to use the legacy she would receive in February 1865 to emigrate to Canada. But when the new Lenten season arrived shortly after her twenty-first birthday, "Emilie" Kent took eight hundred pounds of her new legacy, went to the rector who founded the convent, the High Anglican A. W. Wagner, and begged him to accept the money for charities. When he refused, she adopted the course of leaving smaller amounts in alms-boxes during prayer, amounts which the rector said he quietly set aside until the total of eight hundred was retrieved. Then, on Wednesday of Holy Week, Constance, who had never been confirmed in the Church, came to see the rector "on the subject of her confirmation." [123] Miss Kent may have been hoping to take the sacraments on Easter Sunday, but Wagner, who alone knew her real identity, appears to have refused the request.

That the Reverend Mr. Wagner and subsequently the Lady Superior, Miss Greame, now took the matter of a confession in hand seems clear. That same day Constance was summoned to speak with the Superior, to whom Wagner for the first time divulged the identity of "Emilie Kent." Constance saw Miss Greame again on Thursday and on Good Friday. The following Monday, with his Easter duties performed, Mr. Wagner traveled to London for an interview with the Home Secretary, and he carried a letter from his penitent addressed to Sir George Grey: "Sir, It is my own particular request that the bearer now informs you of my guilt, which it is my desire to have publicly made known. Yours truly, Constance Emilie Kent." [124]

For Wagner it was a spectacular opportunity to gain publicity for the benefits of his own particular pet cause, the High Church confessional.[125] In delivering the document and in subsequent testimony, he affirmed that though Constance's admission of guilt was genuine and had not been extracted, he could give no details because of the confidentiality of the confessor-penitent relationship: "My duty to God forbids me to answer any question which will in any way divulge anything that has been said to me in the secrecy of the Confessional." [126] Wagner, who failed even to inform the young woman's family of the event, escorted Constance to London two weeks later in the company of Miss Greame, and the Bow Street magistrate promptly sent her to the authorities in Wiltshire, where the crime was committed. When the news broke, it was greeted with suspicion and outrage by the press, chiefly for the odor of clerical influence which surrounded it.[127]

On April 26 Samuel Kent, who had been living in seclusion since 1861 in Denbighshire, read of his daughter's confession in his morning paper.[128] Five days later, while the news was causing a general uproar and hostile crowds were still jeering outside Wagner's chapel in Brighton, Kent visited his daughter, who was once again incarcerated at the Devizes jail. Constance by then had declared her intention to plead guilty and declined legal counsel. Only the meeting and parting of father and daughter were witnessed. She "rose to her feet, staring wordlessly at him," and then "swayed as though she would fall and he caught her in his arms." [129] At his departure Constance, who had been "walking up and down and weeping," flung her arms about her father's neck and was heard to sob, "My course is due to you and to God." [130]

At the magistrates court where she was committed for trial on May 3, the Lady Superior, who could claim no immunity, insisted there had been no inducement to make Constance confess, but her evasive testimony more than suggested otherwise. Miss Greame, who had clearly allowed herself to become Wagner's instrument in his self-aggrandizing religious campaign, was deeply troubled as she responded to questions and reportedly appeared to be murmuring prayers throughout her interrogation.

Q. What did you say?
A. I said "I know about it." I asked her if she fully realized what it involved. . . .

Q.   That was before she gave herself up?

A.   Yes. I think I said I was sorry for it. . . . I had her up to speak on religious subjects. Something in the conversation made her tell me that she had carried the child downstairs; that she left the house by the drawing room window, and that she had used a razor for the purpose. . . .

Q.   Did she say anything else?

A.   She spoke of the nightdress that was lost. I think she said that she had taken it out of the basket again.

Q.   In your examination you referred to *"something* in your conversation" which you had with her—what was that something?

A.   I think I said to her that Mr. Wagner had told me of it. I never used the word "murder.". . . I cannot remember exactly what I said, but I think I said to her, "Did the child cry to you for mercy? . . ."

Q.   Did you say anything before that?

A.   Yes, I tried to point out how a sin would be aggravated in God's sight.[131]

All other testimony taken reiterated the same accounts from five years before, save that of the doctor who had previously declared his conviction that the postmortem clearly pointed to suffocation. Now he testified just the opposite: "In my opinion the incision in the throat was the immediate cause of death." [132] This obliging new statement fit Miss Kent's confession, and Dr. Stapleton hastened to write to the papers and medical journals to confirm that he had always discounted suffocation.[133] At the same time the court accepted without question the testimony of the triumphant Inspector Whicher, who now declared his conviction that Constance's missing nightdress, which he had sought, was identical with the bloody garment discovered in the boiler stove, despite all the previous testimony that the bloody shirt was a coarse servant's garment. In the interests of neatness a certain amnesia seemed called for.

The subsequent trial at the Devizes Assize Court on July 21, 1865, was brief, for Constance's guilty plea was accepted and she had been declared sane and responsible. Her air of composure was noted, but there was a troubling hesitation. The judge declared, "Constance Emilie Kent, you stand charged with having willfully murdered Francis Savile Kent at Road-Hill House on 30th June 1860. How say you; are you Guilty or Not Guilty?" [134] Constance did not answer. The question was repeated and the young woman still remained silent. Twice more the question was reframed and posed to her and finally the prisoner answered, "Guilty." It was little wonder that the normally stern judge delivered the death sentence with sobs choking his voice: "And may God have mercy on your soul." [135]

Despite their pity few papers by the end seriously questioned the guilt of the self-accused woman.[136] And when they did so, it tended to be as much if not more from hatred of the High Church confessional as from conviction of innocence. Indeed, the real controversy was waged among those who accepted her guilt for the murder, but disagreed over her motives and the extent of her responsibility. The variety of explanations offered indicated the troubled state of opinion at a time when the issue of criminal responsibility was being challenged by a multiplicity of theories on human behavior and mental illness which circumscribed or negated the individual's will.

Many commentators were deeply disturbed by any suggestion that Miss Kent should not be regarded as fully responsible. The *Law Times* showed a somewhat confused leaning toward still prevalent theories of "moral insanity," but insisted that the prisoner was accountable.

> This is not insanity, nor anything like insanity. It is a case of mental deformity. The mind of Constance Kent is defective in one or more of the moral faculties, just as some men are born with a withered arm or leg.[137]

The *Saturday Review* agreed: "her confession shows that she was not mad; only preeminently wicked, crafty, unfeeling, treacherous, vile, deceitful and hard-hearted beyond almost all human experience." [138]

The *Times* was the only major organ of public opinion to make a case for lessened responsibility on physiological grounds; it suggested that Constance was in the transitional period when her female organs were changing and that this was a time when girls tended to be especially cruel and heartless.[139] The outrage which greeted this rather timid suggestion is epitomized by this selection from the *Medical Times and Gazette.*

> But there is a kind of unctuously sentimental philosophy afloat, according to which young women about the age of puberty "cannot help" committing any wildly wicked and extravagantly cruel act that may enter their imaginations. . . . We are also told that a "bewildering sense of the new existence" of womanhood may impel young girls irresistibly to the most fiendish acts. . . . In the name of all that is sacred and manly [!] and stedfast, and on behalf of the sober and innocent part of the population, we admit no such plea as "couldn't help it.". . . Self-control must be upheld as the most sacred of duties, whether as to thought, word or deed.[140]

Sex-role arguments were enlisted on all sides of the responsibility controversy. On one hand, Constance was portrayed as a masculinized woman whose real male identity had been revealed first when she donned boy's clothing and cut off her hair and then when she committed a most "unfeminine" murder. On the other hand, she was portrayed as the eternal Eve and thus capable of crimes far more evil than any man could commit. The *Bath Express* stated:

> It was a wanton murder, not done by the hand of a man, for there is a *finesse* of cruelty about it that no man, we believe, however depraved, could have been guilty of; but it is the revengeful act of a woman—morbid, cruel, cunning—one in whom the worst of passions has received a preternatural development, overpowering and absorbing the little good that she ever had in her nature.[141]

All of this controversy over responsibility revealed much about the preoccupations of middle-class spokesmen, but the concern for the young woman was eclipsed long before it was over. Once again, as in the Marsden affair, the female became the multipurpose scapegoat for all the fears, obsessions, and anxieties of men who, whatever their motivation, professed to understand her and held power over her life.

That Constance Kent should have yielded to confession when she was so close to freedom is sadly unmysterious. Religion, the eternal consolation for suffering women, had been offered as her refuge for five long years. For the first time in her life she had known caring guardians, religious persons who accepted her. But now there was suddenly a price for that continued acceptance: confession of a sin she had not committed. It was a price she was ready to pay. Her religion, after all, taught that One who was innocent had sacrificed his life at his Father's wish for those who were guilty. And Constance had explained her own sacrifice to her father: "My course is due to you and to God."

Constance Kent and Célestine Doudet were two of the unplucked flowers, two of the redundant women. They are proof, in their different ways, of their society's ability to impose its negative stereotypes on women. They accepted the stereotypes and internalized them to form their self-images. Thus, not only did men relate to them in terms of stereotypical expectations, but their own feelings and behavior patterns were determined from within by the same expectations. Célestine Doudet, the dowryless girl without marital hopes, became the sex-obsessed spinster, who detected impurity everywhere. Constance, the neglected twelve-year-old runaway lacking in "feminine delicacy" who had "wished to be independent," unwittingly set herself up for suspicion of murder and then embraced her female outcast state in what one writer has called "a spirit of pure self-immolation." [142] Ironically, this act of confession was finely "female," just the sort of submissive, sacrificial, and self-destructive act which, in lesser forms, was explicitly demanded of all respectable creatures of her sex. And they, at least, may have understood. The courtroom in Wiltshire was full of weeping women.

Accidents brought both Célestine Doudet and Constance Kent out of obscurity. The deaths of Mary Ann Marsden and Francis Savile Kent were not premeditated acts, but they led to the exposure of many hidden female lives and a variety of tactics which worked to keep women in their place. The headship of a household permitted, if it did not endorse, the sexual exploitation of servants, the discarding and branding of wives as insane, and the special domestic seclusion of female children in the name of protection of virginal "property."

The limits of the system were reached in Samuel Kent, whose terrible catalogue of crimes against women may even have stretched to include the mysterious death of his first wife, which was so quickly ascribed by a physician to a sudden intestinal complaint.[143] But Kent, the unscrupulous and aberrant family tyrant, is finally less frightening than the legions of those whose endorsement he gained or whose authority he manipulated. The extension of sexual domination can explain the complicity of his wife and mistress, but what of the local and even national notables who ought to have been harder to convince? They readily accepted reconstructions of events and descriptions of personality which accommodated widespread prejudices about women's sexual peculiarities. Constance Kent was ultimately handed from a father driven by social and professional status to a minister of God driven by the same forces. And she finally surrendered to her female duty.

Célestine Doudet, the "monster" spinster, took more than her share of the blame for vicious acts of cruelty. Had her employer recognized what powerless women perceived at once, that Doudet was mentally unbalanced, the little victims would have been spared. Moreover, the fact that the children were girls increased their vulnerability. Had they been boys, it is unlikely that even if they were discovered to have been masturbators and sent to live with an unbalanced schoolmaster, that their suffering would have gone so long unrecognized. First, it was uncommon to deport male children to a foreign country, as was done so often with girls, a situation which automatically created isolation and increased the opportunities for paid guardians to commit all varieties of abuse and go undetected.[144] Second, since domestic sequestration was more common in raising girls and exercise (one of the most recommended "cures" for boys) less practiced, the isolation of female children in a household could persist longer without comment. The poor Marsden girls knew that their own brother James, at least, led a very different life. Forced themselves to write regular letters home, they complained of receiving none from their brother, and their stepmother wrote to take young James' part: "You know how little boys find it hard to trouble themselves about writing." They lead such active lives, she says, "they dash from study to recreation and then to bed." [145]

The girls, meanwhile, spent their own recreation hours painstakingly copying dictated letters which their father subsequently threw into the fire. Mlle. Doudet, however, submitted in her defense some of the letters the girls had sent to her, letters her lawyer argued to be genuine, but which were obviously composed by the governess. They reveal, at least, the image of herself which she constantly held before the terrorized girls, as well as her anxieties over her own role in the death of little Mary Ann.

> I am persuaded that she [the dead Mary Ann] often thinks of you, and that she would be pleased to repay you for all you did for her. . . . She is dead forever but we can hope to see her again in heaven. . . . If there is someone worthy of going to heaven, it is you. I have never seen anyone fulfill her duty more faithfully than you. . . . you have had as much patience as Job. But whereas his trial was in

the outside world, yours is wholly in the interior of the household, and the trial of Job seems to me *so* public. . . .[146]

Even in testings of faith, Doudet saw men capturing the attention and rewards. She tried to console herself that the women, hidden away, were superior in their suffering.

Imprisoned for three years until 1858, when her health began to fail, Célestine Doudet was pardoned and, after travel in Germany and England, returned to Paris. There she reportedly found mothers still willing to confide their children to her care.[147] Constance Kent, whose death sentence was commuted to life imprisonment, spent twenty years in Millbank and Fulham prisons. She was employed first in the laundry and then as a nurse in the infirmary, and she also was permitted to do mosaic work in several religious establishments. A prison inspector described her as

> a small mouse-like creature, with much of the promptitude of the mouse or lizard when surprised, in disappearing when alarmed. . . . She was a mystery in every way. It was almost impossible to believe that this insignificant, inoffensive little person could have cut her infant brother's throat under circumstances of peculiar atrocity.[148]

If after her release she did make her way to Canada, her whereabouts were never discovered. Her father, meanwhile, had remained in seclusion and died in 1872 of a disease of the liver.[149]

About the Marsden girls, who were unofficially tried for the offense of masturbation, I have been able to discover even less. If one genealogical account is correct,[150] there may well be very little to know. According to it Rosa, the second to youngest, died in 1877 at age thirty-four. The death dates of the other two girls, Emily and Alice, are not known, but the account notes that none of the three married and all of them predeceased their father. James Loftus Marsden, after a promising youthful career, died in obscurity in 1891. He had married a third time, and he left most of his estate to his adoptive daughter Ellen Welsh Marsden. He also willed a thousand-pound inheritance from his mother to a niece.[151] Of course it is impossible to know his motives in these bequests, but Marsden may have been thinking of a kind of restitution.

4.

THE NEW WOMEN:

The Cases of
Florence Bravo
and Henriette Francey

Florence Bravo

In the last decades of the nineteenth century the "respectable" accused murderesses whose cases made the greatest public sensation were neither the unmarried nor the recent brides, as had been so earlier, but instead somewhat older married women. Of the six to be discussed in the following chapters, whose cases were tried from the 1870s to the 1890s, three had been married at least ten years and two others over five years when the crimes with which they were charged took place. The shift to older and more "experienced" women may, of course, have been coincidental or explicable without reference to changing positions of or views about women. On the other hand, the shift might have reflected a change in the situations most likely to prompt respectable women to consider murder or a change in the preoccupations of the public who judged their reported behavior. Or both.

The alternatives will be explored, but there is no doubt that middle-class women in England, and to a lesser extent in France, were experiencing a heightened "visibility" in the last decades of the century which added new dimensions to their task of adjustment to changing roles. One ingredient of this visibility, especially marked in England, was the growth of a women's movement, which introduced more women of the class into the public forum than ever before. Although most women were not directly involved in the movement, the agitation for legal, educational, and political reforms in their favor elicited a barrage of comment and criticism which kept women in the public eye and which prompted many of them to reevaluate previously unquestioned assumptions about their social position.

The women's movement was itself the result of a whole set of economic and social changes whose effect was to widen women's sphere of activity and increase their social visibility. Ordinary women of the class were appearing

130

outside the home more than ever before. By the 1870s resourceless unmarried daughters of the middle classes were no longer faced with the odious alternatives of being either life-long domestic drudges, dependent upon relatives, or governesses eking out marginal existences. With improved educational opportunities and the opening up of the merchandising and service professions, they were able to take better paying positions as clerks, shop assistants, teachers, and nurses.[1] Participation in these professions brought growing numbers of middle-class women into regular contact with the public for the first time.

Even among the majority of women of the class, who were neither active feminists nor members of the labor force, visibility increased in these years. New affluence and increased leisure prompted the growth of public entertainments and activities which took them outside the sheltered circles of traditional family and church gatherings. Women began regularly to attend theaters, concerts, and museums. They visited restaurants, went on sightseeing excursions, took more active part in volunteer charity work, and even began to take up sports such as lawn tennis, golf, and bicycling. Although most women remained more faithful in religious observance than their husbands or fathers, churches were increasingly obliged to compete with a variety of attractive secular options. Church-related activities did increase, but there is evidence that the level of religious fervor among women declined.[2]

Slowly but perceptibly, the new visibility of middle-class women altered the stereotype of the ideal woman. Without abandoning her primary domestic role as family nurturer and moral guardian, the new paragon was cast in a larger role as moral purifier of the society as a whole, one who set a public example of rectitude and whose duty was not only to be personally blameless, but to exhort others, including men and women outside her class, to adopt her code of chaste, temperate, and charitable behavior. Not surprisingly, this new ideal woman was conceived as older, wiser, and more mature than the previous girlish and naive model.[3] The new stereotype, in other words, tacitly incorporated the social fact that women's enlarged spheres of activity made them less likely to be as "innocent" as before, even though it obligated them to be as "pure." Chastity in the unmarried state and fidelity in the married were still assumed, but they were recognized increasingly as matters of choice which entailed personal responsibility. Women were still thought to have special advantages bestowed by nature which helped them to resist temptation, but they were now conceived as active moral agents in doing so. The perfect woman, or "new woman" as she came to be called, was in some ways a more admirable creature than her forebear, for she had actively chosen her righteous path. Still, that path had become more treacherous, for she had lost much of the immunity which had accompanied the assumption of innocence.

Indeed, by the late 1860s in England, and somewhat later in France, the whole generation of middle-class women was coming under fire. Admittedly, especially in England, there had long been some voices raised against them for various sorts of incompetence, flightiness, and extravagance with money; the ceaseless carping of the household manuals of the 1830s and 1840s is part of the evidence.[4] Critics had already lampooned the political women, who had gained attention since mid-century, and they had also found a target in the literary women, whose allegedly pernicious ideas were believed to be leading so many otherwise pure young ladies astray. But the criticism entered a new phase in this later period and its manifesto was Eliza Lynn Linton's savage essay, "The Girl of the Period," which appeared in 1868 in the *Saturday Review*,[5] an organ with well-established credentials as an opponent of legal and social reforms for women. Linton's essay caused instant sensation and controversy.

> The Girl of the Period is a creature who dyes her hair and paints her face, as the first articles of her personal religion—a creature whose sole idea of life is fun; whose sole aim is unbounded luxury, and whose dress is the chief object of such thought and intellect as she possesses.... All men whose opinion is worth having prefer the simple and genuine girl of the past, with her tender little ways and pretty bashful modesties, to this loud and rampant modernization, with her false red hair and painted skin, talking slang as glibly as a man, and by preference leading the conversation in doubtful subjects....[6]

Similar criticism began to appear not long afterward in French popular literature. Some of it, such as Barbey d'Aurevilly's attack on "bluestockings," continued a vendetta against female writers.[7] But increasingly the jibes were aimed at the allegedly typical middle-class woman, and particularly at her role in the much decried degeneration of the family. She was blamed for many things. What was called her selfish desire for fewer children was argued to be responsible for the especially marked decline in the rate of French population growth. One typical study, like Linton's, pictured a golden age earlier in the century when French bourgeois wives were pure, decent, and dutiful. The author singled out the year 1880 as the dread year of change, when republican power was consolidated and "individualism" became the order of the day. Bemoaning the loss of the older generation, he asserted that the women since 1880, despite religious education, were no longer really religious. He complained that their ideas were changed, that they were far too money-conscious, that their old deference was gone, and that they were more susceptible to the "temptations" of infidelity.

> It is no longer true that they are formed from childhood with unceasing care to take a submissive role in marriage, a role of devotion and even sacrifice.... At the same time that they seem to demand more of marriage, they intend to give less effort to it.[8]

Although the critics in both countries hesitated at the words themselves, they came close to identifying the new generation of middle-class women with prostitutes and adulteresses. Linton remarked of the Girl of the Period that "the net result of her present manner of life is to assimilate her as nearly as possible to a class of women whom we must not call by their proper—or improper—name." [9] In France the same themes appeared. The divorce law of 1884 was bitterly attacked, partly on the ground that a woman who divorced and remarried would have "absolutely no secrets from two living men." [10] Although in fact very few women championed the divorce law, alarmed critics chose to see it as a kind of sexual license for women.

It is a truism that the new generation always fails to live up to the shining paragons of the old, but the attack on middle-class women, which intensified in these last decades of the century, was something more than simple nostalgia for an imaginary perfect past. Middle-class women were being made into scapegoats by many who were frightened or resentful of the rapid social change whose signs were everywhere. The irreligious, unsubmissive, outspoken painted creatures, the luxury-hungry imitators of the "queens of the demimonde," the so-called rampant modernizations were monsters of the mind. But like most such creatures, they had some relation to the real world.

The new woman, then, had a dual aspect in popular image. While increased visibility was argued to have expanded her theoretical opportunities to raise the moral tone of society, it had also, according to observers, made her recognizably more open to dangerous and corrupting influences. This situation worked to break down the previous nearly automatic identification of the pure woman with the middle classes and the impure with the lower classes. The new woman, in herself, was now seen as potentially either pure or impure, but her critics were coming to suspect the worst of her. The very fact that middle-class women were now added to the "common" women who had long been visible, day or night, in the streets and in public places doubtless helped to reinforce the identification of hitherto irreproachable women with their polar opposites, the adulteresses and whores. Increasingly, middle-class women in many circumstances would discover that they were no longer automatically granted the "benefit of the doubt." And those circumstances naturally included criminal investigations.

Given the preoccupation with the morality of middle-class women, it is hardly surprising that adultery figured prominently in all six of the remaining cases and that in five of these the accused woman herself was held up as a suspected adulteress. Of course, the fact that the most highly publicized cases of murder by "respectable" women in the last decades of the century involved the issue of adultery suggests the probability of shifts in behavior as well as in image, namely, that extramarital sex was a growing reality in these years for middle-class women in general. Given the increased opportunities for extramarital sex, made possible by higher standards of living, better transportation, wider circles of acquaintances, and growing leisure and privacy, it would be surprising if middle-class women had not committed more adultery. However, as all these cases suggest, it would be hasty to conclude that many women of the class were enjoying a new sexual freedom outside marriage, that they had arrived at their own versions of the masculine formula of discreet "side arrangements" which neither interfered with the other demands of their lives nor caused them undue emotional involvement or guilt. Extramarital sex may have been increasing, but discovery remained a far more serious matter for women than for men. That the women in these cases revealed an extraordinary ambivalence toward their sexual affairs was only to be expected given the new distrust of middle-class women in general and the absence of cultural reinforcement for their behavior.

The two women to be considered here, Florence Bravo and Henriette Francey, were both caught in the net of ambiguities surrounding the new women of the period. Accused of murder in 1876 and 1884, respectively, they both gained attention as much for suspected sexual improprieties as for alleged criminal offenses. It is clear now that sexual matters did prompt the critical actions of both women in these cases, but not in ways that either juries or journalists understood. And behind the highly publicized, sensational, fascinating, but often irrelevant accounts of their sex lives lay a whole set of less spectacular issues which reveal some of the anxieties which touched the lives of a larger group of women of that time.

Florence Bravo and Henriette Francey both came from eminently respectable families, and each exhibited in full measure the negative features of the stereotype of the new woman. In Florence's case, in fact, the resemblance to Lynn Linton's caricature was uncanny. Remarried at thirty in 1875, Florence Bravo was an independently wealthy young London matron who appreciated luxury and coolly indulged her taste for all the best in clothes, riding horses, jewelry, and continental travel. As she blandly admitted, "I had always been accustomed to live largely within my income." [11] Whether her conversation frequently led to "doubtful" subjects is unknown, but no one would have mistaken Florence for Mrs. Linton's "simple girl of the past." Neighbors, and even her own parents, suspected her of having had an illicit affair with a married society doctor. And to top it off, newspapers revealed that Florence Bravo was brazen enough to have dyed her hair red.

Henriette Francey, who was French, had fewer resources for self-indulgence than Florence Bravo, but she exhibited many of the same qualities. Restricted to the smaller stage of Tonnère, a subprefecture of just over ten thousand persons in the department of the Yonne not far south of Paris, Henriette nonetheless gave a plausible rendition of the new woman. Hardly the image of the docile, submissive, and pious bourgeois wife, Henriette, at twenty-five, herself acknowledged that she was not especially religious. The routine police report on her moral character, based upon comments solicited from townspeople, alleged that Mme. Francey was very free in her speech and that often "she allowed herself to initiate conversations with people by making rather fresh remarks about them." [12] Reinforcing this negative image were the facts that she often attended the theater and concerts, went on shopping excursions to Paris, and even accompanied her husband on business trips, leaving their small son behind. What was worse, Henriette Francey, like Florence Bravo, was suspected of sexual indiscretions. Some of the residents of Tonnère stated that she had kept secret rendezvous with both an architect and a priest. This was a grave charge against a respectably married wife and mother.

These matters naturally would have escaped widespread public attention had the two women not been implicated in crimes. But on April 21, 1876, when Florence Bravo's second husband, Charles, a barrister, was discovered to have died of poison, the new widow became an instant suspect and celebrity. Similarly, in late December 1884 the news that Henriette Francey was being held in custody for the fatal shooting of one of the local townsmen captured headlines throughout the country. (Among those stunned by the news was Mme. Francey's husband Paul, a would-be politician established in the iron trade who had recently been named a sales distributor for McCormick farm implements.) Both women were made aware that suspicion of illicit sexual activity could be more damaging to them than proof of premeditated murder, and both felt called upon to devote most of their defense to these charges. The interrogations revealed that these new women, at least, although hardly qualifying as moral paragons, were not, in truth, precisely the abandoned libertines of legend. Each was torn between new options and old values, and each faced conflicts which reveal a good deal more about the real lives of new women than the stereotyped caricatures to which they were made to conform.

Many aspects of the two women's roles in "unnatural" death remained a mystery, even after the formal investigations, but the backgrounds of the suspects and the events which brought them notoriety can be straightforwardly summarized. Florence Bravo, born in 1845, was the second child and eldest daughter of seven children of Robert and Ann Campbell. Her father, who had inherited a fortune from his father's sheep-raising ventures in Australia, had established his credentials in London circles. He joined the Reform Club and purchased an estate in Berkshire, where he served as a justice of the peace and later as high sheriff. The little that is known of her girlhood indicates that Florence developed a close relationship with parents who indulged their chestnut-haired, blue-eyed daughter, especially in her passion for riding horses. Like many young women of her station, she had a governess, studied French and a little German, read novels, did needlework, and grew accustomed to being waited upon. She also traveled with her family; on a visit to Canada when she was in her late teens, she met the man who would be her first husband, a young British officer in the Grenadier Guards called Alexander Ricardo.

Florence was only nineteen at her marriage in 1864, and it seems likely that her parents had abbreviated the customary period of courtship in order to promote a socially advantageous union with the twenty-one-year-old Ricardo, whose antecedents, at any rate, were impressive. Grandnephew to the famous economist, Alexander was the son of Lady Catherine, sister of the Fifth Earl of Fife, and of John L. Ricardo, an executive in several railroad companies, founder of a telegraph company, and, from 1841 until his death in 1862, a political writer and highly respected member of Parliament for Stoke-on-Trent.

Unfortunately, young Alexander either was or shortly became an alcoholic, and Florence later alleged that he was constantly ill and had several times threatened her with violence. Late in 1869 she finally confided to her mother her wish for a separation, but Mrs. Campbell, determined to avoid a scandal which she feared would reflect badly upon herself and her husband, urged instead that both Florence and Alexander visit the water-cure establishment at Malvern in Worcestershire. There, she said, her old friend Dr. James Manby Gully was achieving marvelous results with "nervous" patients. His clientele, indeed, was a kind of Victorian *Who's Who* and included Bulwer Lytton, Disraeli, Jane and Thomas Carlyle, Tennyson, Darwin, and Florence Nightingale.

Mrs. Campbell could not have anticipated that this friend, who had treated Florence as a child of twelve, would take an intense personal interest in the case and decide late in 1870 that the young Mrs. Ricardo's health depended upon a separation from her hopelessly ill and potentially dangerous husband. To the fury of her parents—and especially her father, who quite illegally suspended payments on her marriage settlement—Florence, with Dr. Gully's help, proceeded to arrange for a separation, which was signed in March 1871. Alexander, meanwhile, had divided his time between visits to the furnished home they rented in Malvern and drinking bouts in London. Before the separation papers were complete, he had vanished. Some weeks later the young man's body was discovered in lodgings in Cologne which he had shared with a "female companion." A final alcoholic spree had killed him. Since he had not altered the financial arrangements made at his marriage, his widow became mistress of a fortune of over forty thousand pounds.

In subsequent years, as Florence would inform the coroner's jury in 1876, she and Dr. Gully were "constantly in each other's company." [13] She admitted to a long-standing though not, in the contemporary legal parlance, "criminal" intimacy between herself and the doctor, who, though in his mid-sixties and over twice her age, exercised an immense personal charm. As Florence put it, he was a man of "great information and agreeable conversation." [14] Mrs. Campbell acknowledged that what she called her daughter's infatuation with Dr. Gully had met with her parents' disapproval and had produced a long estrangement. She added, however, that when Florence had announced her intention in late 1875 to marry a young barrister named Charles Bravo, all was forgiven: "In consequence of this contemplated marriage, the estrangement between us and my daughter terminated." [15]

Although Florence was never brought to admit anything more than "conversations about marriage" with the doctor, there had in fact been a prior understanding between them. The obstacle to marriage was that the doctor was already married, and although he had been separated for thirty years, his wife, who was seventeen years his senior, remained in excellent health at over eighty. Gully had married this woman, his second wife, in 1841 to help him finance the practice at Malvern; when they separated eighteen months later, he invited his two maiden sisters to live with him. They watched after their brother while his practice thrived and he became an active and beloved figure in the community, as well as the most famous of the water-cure specialists. In 1871, after the attachment with Florence had begun, the doctor retired and leased a home near one Florence had rented in London—there, presumably, to await the decease of the hardy Mrs. Gully.

During this time, the doctor and the widow traveled together on the continent and, when in London, often went on rides, shopped, and took tea and meals in one another's homes. According to the servants, however, they never spent any nights together nor did they ever travel as husband and wife. But as time passed and Gully's wife lingered on, Florence appears to have felt the strain of social ostracism and determined to end their relationship. Late in 1874 her lady's companion, Mrs. Jane Cox, introduced Florence to the handsome, ambitious Charles Bravo, stepson of Mr. Joseph Bravo, a merchant and banker who had been a business associate of Mrs. Cox's late husband. Graduated from Trinity College, Oxford in 1866, Charles had been admitted to the bar in 1870 and lived in London with his family at their very fashionable address of 2 Palace Green, Kensington.

In the fall of 1875 Florence abruptly informed Dr. Gully that their liaison had to end, and though she pleaded the desire to reestablish relations with her family, she acknowledged that a certain Charles Bravo was "approaching" her. The doctor testified that he had accepted the break and noted that Florence agreed to wait until the following spring before considering any proposal of marriage. Instead, however, she soon sent word of her forthcoming wedding, which took place on December 7, 1875. Dr. Gully reported that although he had continued to supply occasional medications for Florence on request from her lady's companion, he had informed his manservant that neither Mrs. Ricardo nor Mrs. Cox were to be admitted again to his home.

Although letters exchanged during their brief courtship do not reveal a deep romantic attachment, Florence and Charles were reported to be a happy couple by servants, friends, and family. They lived in the south London suburb of Balham in a home that Florence had rented the year before, a fifteen-room house called the Priory, done in "bastard Gothic" complete with turrets and battlements. Never one to stint on her own comfort, Florence had staffed the place with a butler, a footman, a cook, three housemaids, a gardener and assistants, a coachman, a groom and a stable boy, in addition to Mrs. Cox, who stayed on as her lady's companion. Dr. Gully, a kind of ghost from the past, resided down the road in a house he had taken when Florence had moved. The proud doctor said he was careful to avoid embarrassing encounters with Florence or Charles and added that he even began to take his walks in a different direction.

Letters the couple sent to both sets of parents describe a cheerful domestic round of riding, gardening, lawn tennis, trips to "town," visits from relatives, and entertaining of friends from London and what Charles jokingly called local "aristocrats." The letters are full of banter, with the pen passing back and forth: "My Charlie is very well," Florence tells her mother, "and equally happy." Charles protests: "[He is not. The quality of the tobacco he is smoking has been impugned, and his pipe is ordered to be extinguished.]" [16] Charles playfully casts himself in the domestic role of the long-suffering, but indulgent husband. To his mother, he writes:

> I rode both the cobs the day before yesterday, and I feel very much as if the muscles of my legs were ossifying. I have difficulty in dragging my shooting boots, which I am obliged, *par ordre supérieur*, to wear, in addition to a red flannel garment, which is a cross between a kilt, a sporran, and a pair of bathing drawers, and has as many strings as a harp. Nothing but great firmness on the part of my better half, and an assurance that "it became me," made me put it on. I feel as if I had stays on my stomach. [17]

Charles' "domestication" was not always so lighthearted, but evidence for that is understandably rare in correspondence with parents. Having made their own choice in marrying, and in Charles' case, against his mother's will, the couple naturally wanted to display the image of united bliss. And yet even these letters occasionally show barbs among the banter. Charles complains of being inundated by bills and takes mock solace in at least enjoying superintendence of the stables, if not of the house. Florence adds a chiding postscript to a letter to her mother.

> Charlie, as usual, writes tersely, as all barristers do; but you must imagine twice the amount of affection, as I had to do when he wrote me love letters, which, by-the-bye, nobody would have recognized as such, as they were as cold and undemonstrative as possible—Your loving child, Florence Bravo. [18]

That there were in fact some chill currents beneath all this appears undeniable. Charles acknowledged as much in a tantalizingly cryptic letter sent to his wife, then away at the seaside, in mid-February 1876. At the time, he had just over two months to live.

> My darling Wife . . . Looking back on the ten weeks of our marriage, I feel that many of my words to you, although kindly meant, were unnecessarily harsh. In the future my rebukes, if it be necessary to say anything, which God forbid! shall be given with the utmost gentleness. . . . I hold you to be the best of wives. We have had bitter trouble, but I trust every day to come the sweet peace of

our lives will not so much as be disturbed by memories like those. . . . I wish I could sleep away my life till your return. . . . Come back as well as you can to your devoted husband, Charles.[19]

The "bitter trouble" possibly refers to the miscarriage Florence had suffered and from which she was then recovering; there would be another miscarriage early in April. On the other hand, it might have been money trouble. At the inquest Florence's mother testified that her daughter had accused Charles of being penurious and of listening too much to his mother, who had told him to get his extravagant wife to economize. Florence found it outrageous that her mother-in-law wanted her to give up two of her favorite ponies and a maid: "My daughter did not see why she should not manage her house as she liked." [20] Mrs. Campbell also mentioned as another source of possible conflict that Charles had thought Florence drank too much and had complained that she regularly took a glass of wine before she dressed for dinner. In addition, there was possible "trouble" in an anonymous letter which Mrs. Campbell reported Charles had received a month or so after his wedding. The letter, which he had called "vile," suggested he had had financial motives for marrying Florence and referred to a previous relationship between his wife and Dr. Gully. All these undercurrents in the marriage, and more besides, were explored in lengthy proceedings. Still, it was not readily apparent why any of them should have prompted someone to do away with Charles Bravo—or why he may have wished to do away with himself.

Charles took ill on the evening of April 18, 1876, just before retiring. He had dined on eggs, lamb, and burgundy with Florence and Mrs. Cox; Florence, who was not feeling well, had gone up to her room at about quarter to nine. Charles went up about half an hour later, exhausted by an unpleasant ride he had had that afternoon when his horse bolted with him. The maid reported that five or six minutes after he entered his bedroom, he appeared at the door in his nightshirt shouting, "Florence! Florence! Hot water!" [21] Mrs. Cox, who was sitting on the bed in Florence's room next door, ordered the water fetched and went in to Charles who, having vomited out the window, was in a stupor. While she made mustard water for a footbath and urged him to swallow some mustard paste, a maid went in search of some spirits of camphor in her mistress's room and noticed that Florence had been asleep. Wakened, and alarmed at the news, Florence put on a dressing gown and went to her husband's side. Failing to rouse him, she frantically summoned help.

During Charles's two-and-a-half-day ordeal there would be six doctors summoned, including the renowned Sir William Gull. A last minute diagnosis was even sought from the neighbor, Dr. Gully, at Florence's request. But Charles finally succumbed. Poisoning was suspected, but the patient, conscious during much of his illness, doggedly insisted that he had taken nothing, that he had only rubbed a bit of laudanum on his gums for neuralgia.

When the family gathered, Charles remarked sadly that he had never been a religious man, but he prayed and recited the Lord's Prayer with them. After making a will in Florence's favor, he urged his mother: "Take care of my poor, dear wife." [22] A postmortem examination revealed that the cause of death had been a massive dose of approximately thirty grains of poisonous tartar emetic or antimony.

On the day Charles died Florence confided to a cousin on the Bravo side that she was convinced that Charles's death would "always remain a mystery," [23] and in a real sense she was right. The coroner, eager to spare the Campbell family, failed to inform the press of the inquest or even to summon Florence to appear. He accepted with minimum cross-examination the rather suspicious allegation of Mrs. Cox that in their few minutes alone together Charles had confided to her that he had intentionally taken poison. The angered jury refused to return a verdict of suicide and instead declared an open verdict, whereupon the combination of pressure from both the press and Charles Bravo's family and friends, plus a new and explosive statement from Mrs. Cox, prompted the attorney general to authorize a second inquest. Nonetheless, despite the numerous revelations of an astonishing twenty-three days of testimony in the case and despite the climax provided by Florence's appearance, no one was indicted. The jury, confused or cowed, turned in a most peculiar verdict. Charles Bravo, they said, "did not commit suicide. . . . he did not meet his death by misadventure. . . . he was willfully murdered by the administration of tartar emetic, but there is not sufficient proof to fix the guilt upon any person or persons." [24]

This ended the matter so far as the law was concerned, but the press was far from content. The popular verdict, indeed, was not so equivocal as that of the coroner's jury, and was summed up in a parody on Goldsmith which quickly made the rounds:

> When lovely lady stoops to folly, and finds her husband in the way,
> What charm can soothe her melancholy, what art can turn him into clay?
> The only means her aims to cover, and save herself from prison locks,
> And repossess her ancient lover, are burgundy and Mrs. Cox.[25]

It is true enough that evidence presented at the inquest fostered the popular view. But the failure of that investigation to follow through and identify the probable motives involved in Charles's death had less to do with the deceitful cleverness of those who knew the truth than it did with the blindness of those who sought it. The prosecution seemed to assume that discovering an adulteress would be tantamount to finding a murderess and failed to ask questions exploring any other motive. Even so, in spite of this failure, by the end of the inquest there was enough evidence to reconstruct what had probably happened with some certainty, as one recent commentator has amply demonstrated.[26] The pieces of the puzzle remained buried in a mass of testimony because the prosecution was not attuned to the significance of certain facts it did elicit and was preoccupied by issues it falsely deemed more relevant. The fact that all the truth-seekers were men did not help either, for the secrets they failed to uncover were peculiarly female ones.

The case of the French woman, Henriette Francey, is radically different in bare outline from that of Florence Bravo. There was never any question about the role Mme. Francey had played in a murder: she readily admitted having killed Hippolyte Bazard, a forty-year-old municipal architect, on December 21, 1885. Indeed, having shot her victim once in her parlor, she pursued him outside and down the street in his wounded flight and shot him twice more before he collapsed just outside the gate of the local *collège* where he lived. Immediately afterwards, two of the town's residents observed her resolutely walking back toward her home, openly carrying a revolver. One of them, her neighbor, failed to identify her in the late afternoon twilight and asked who she was. She replied, "Don't you recognize me? I am Mme. Francey. I am not going to hide myself." [27] She proceeded to name her victim and declared that she had had the right to shoot him. Asked whether Bazard was dead, she answered coolly, "I certainly hope so." [28] Indeed, according to one of the witnesses, she added that if Bazard was still alive, she would finish him off.[29] As she explained soon afterwards to the police, the architect was a former rejected suitor who had twice attempted to rape her; she had merely been defending her honor and felt neither remorse nor regret.

Madame Francey was immediately taken into custody, and while the state prosecutor began the series of closed investigations in preparation for her trial, the doctors set to work on the postmortem examination. The results of both, which are contained in the manuscript records of the preliminary investigation, were considered so sensational that many details were suppressed in the trial and some evidence included there was further censored by the press. Still, as in the Bravo case, the account of her behavior provided by the central female figure raised more questions than it answered.

Until her arrest, at least, Henriette Francey, unlike Florence Bravo, seems to have enjoyed the reputation of an "honest woman" in the eyes of most, if not all, of her acquaintances. She was the third of four children, all girls, born to the Diards, who were one of the leading commercial families of Tonnère. Press accounts described her as a rather robust but handsome young woman, with dark hair and eyes, regular, if somewhat severe, features, and a firm, self-assured manner. Her education and upbringing were labeled excellent; as an unmarried girl, it was said, she never "went out" without her mother.[30]

Seven years before the crime, at age nineteen, Henriette had married Paul Francey, a local man nine years her senior. He then assumed the prosperous iron trade business of Henriette's recently deceased father and became head of the combined home and business establishment which was located next to the subprefecture on the town's main square. Henriette's mother continued to live there with the couple, though she kept an apartment in the town where she stayed with her other married daughters when they came to Tonnère for visits. Both she and Henriette worked for the business and did much of the sales as well as the bookkeeping.

After Paul Francey received the distributorship for McCormick farm implements in 1883, he began to travel a great deal, not only to Paris, but throughout France and to England as well. The couple had a son by then, but occasionally Henriette was able to leave him with her mother and accompany her husband. She even enlisted a local woman to tutor her in English, so she would be prepared for her trips across the Channel with Paul. Mme. Francey, then, by no means lived an entirely isolated provincial life.

On the surface, at least, there was nothing especially remarkable about Henriette's daily routine at home. She kept one live-in maid and hired daytime help for heavier work, such as laundering and ironing. Part of every weekday she spent in the shop, and when her husband was in town, she often worked there in the evenings as well. Aside from travel with Paul, her diversions included the theater and concerts, shopping trips to Paris, visits to her sisters nearby, outings on the river in a small boat, and tea with the local women who, like herself, kept hours "at home" for receiving callers. Henriette enjoyed reading, kept a daily journal, and often entertained visitors by playing the piano in the parlor. Although not especially devout—she stated that she had no confessor—Henriette did observe traditional religious holidays, and neither the testimony nor the police report on her character shows evidence of any local feeling against her on account of her obviously lukewarm piety. After the shooting, however, there were those in Tonnère who openly subscribed to the view that Mme. Francey had indulged in some less innocent diversions than concerts and tea parties.

Understandably, Henriette denied any hint that she was not above reproach. It was perfectly true that her victim, Hippolyte Bazard, had had a notorious reputation, though it was acknowledged that his charm had admitted him to some of the best homes. A middle-aged bachelor with a taste for dandified clothes and pretty women, Bazard was recalled as a tall, dark-haired southerner, with piercing eyes, a florid complexion, and a heavy, brushlike mustache of which he had been vain. Eldest of three sons of a watchmaker from Besançon, Bazard had been apprenticed in architecture and, after moving to Tonnère in 1867, had become the chief municipal architect. Witnesses praised him for having provided sole support for his widowed mother, who lived in town, and colleagues pointed to his unblemished professional record. Even his friends, however, testified that Bazard had been a tireless woman chaser who was fond of confiding his theories on seduction to the lads in town. One young man reported that Bazard had told him that it was possible to succeed with any woman, married or single, as long as one was persistent. The formula was simple, he had said: follow the quarry about at all times, even if a husband is with her. She will ultimately be either compromised or flattered enough to give way. The architect had allegedly added that if this technique failed, "there were always other means." [31]

Bazard did not limit himself to seduction attempts, for apparently he wished to marry. Understandably, though, he had found it hard to persuade any of the local bourgeois to part with a daughter. One woman, who had since married, testified that her mother had denied Bazard on the grounds that her daughter was too young, but added that the tenacious suitor had refused to give up. Even after her marriage, she reported, Bazard followed her on the train into Paris one day and threatened to carry her off if her husband ever failed to make her happy. The woman insisted that the architect never laid a hand on her, but her husband pointed out that when Bazard began to sit next to her at the theater and to stare at her rather than to watch the play, it had become necessary to "discourage" him.[32]

This testimony, and more besides, lent credibility to the bizarre accounts of Henriette and her mother about this "Don Juan of the subprefecture," as one newspaper dubbed him.[33] According to Mme. Diard, Bazard, some years before, had systematically requested the hand of every one of her four daughters, beginning with the eldest, who everyone knew was fatally ill with consumption. Admitting her suspicion that Bazard was after their money, Mme. Diard said: "I could not hide from him the disgust I felt over his having asked for the hand of Albertine, my dying daughter." [34] But the architect, undeterred, allegedly proceeded to the second, who was declared already spoken for, and then to the third, Henriette, who at sixteen and a half was pronounced too young. He was reported to have said he would wait for her, but ultimately asked for the fourth daughter as well. Mme. Diard declared she would never have given him a daughter, and though there is no way of proving her story of this ludicrous sequential suit, it is compatible with the man's other reported behavior. It suggests, too, why Bazard might have continued to nurse a grudge against Henriette, the only one of the three surviving sisters who remained in town to torment.

Still, if Bazard's motive was simple revenge, it was curious that he had waited more than eight years to act on it. Paul Francey did report that soon after their marriage in 1878, his wife had complained that when he went away on business, Bazard hung about the shop and made a nuisance of himself. But Francey appears to have been unaware that the man's visits had become even more frequent in the months before the shooting. A winegrower who had worked part-time for the Franceys for six years testified that in the past eighteen months, since the summer of 1883, Bazard had begun to stop by regularly whenever Monsieur Francey was gone. This witness added that he had overheard Mme. Francey tell her mother what a bore the architect was and stated that his mistress in the end had given him orders always to say that she was out when Bazard asked for her.

According to Henriette in a deposition made on the day of the shooting,

Bazard had come to visit her earlier in the afternoon while her husband was out hunting. She explained that because of a prior attempt on her the week before, she had placed a loaded revolver at hand. Her guest had then proceeded, in her words, "to make every effort to possess me" [35] and in self-defense she had used that revolver.

Paul Francey, questioned the same night, confessed he did not know what was happening and had not been told of any previous rape attempt by Bazard. He had noticed that his wife was very tense upon his return from a business trip the week before, but she had explained that she had had difficulty sleeping while he was away. Francey added that though he had been on speaking terms with the architect, he did not "receive" him socially and remarked that he was under the impression that Bazard's attentions to Henriette had ended soon after their marriage. The only other thing he reported was that late that afternoon, upon his return from hunting, Henriette had thrown herself into his arms and exclaimed, "I have just avenged myself against Bazard for the abuses he made me suffer." [36]

Henriette Francey had some reason to believe that the accusation of rape and the plea of self-defense were sufficient under the circumstances to win an acquittal. She could rely not only upon her family's position in the community, but also on the far from exemplary reputation of her victim. Moreover, there was the precedent of a growing number of cases since the 1870s in which women were committing acts of criminal violence and successfully defending themselves by pleading revenge or honor. Although this new female "crime wave" will be considered more fully in a later chapter,[37] it may be noted that a time when middle-class wives were coming under suspicion as libertines was bound also to be a time when men had sympathy to spare for any woman who dramatized the "old-fashioned" female virtues. In principle, at least, a wife and mother who dared to strike out against a would-be rapist enjoyed new respect; she was demonstrably faithful to her husband, had protected his "property" in herself, and had preserved her child's right to a "pure" mother.

Henriette understood and shared these sentiments, or so it appeared. During her interrogation she denied any feeling of regret: "At the time, I felt instead a kind of joy—this life was owed to me. I now feel the satisfaction of having accomplished my duty." [38] But, as in the case of Florence Bravo, there soon emerged a sceptical opinion which remained unconvinced of the accused woman's story. Mrs. Bravo, without insisting on it, had tried to leave the impression that her husband had committed suicide. Mme. Francey, for her part, had painted herself as a heroine who had triumphed over infamy. Each, it is clear, had something to hide, but the end of legal proceedings, in both cases, meant that neither woman would be obliged to confess her most dangerous secrets. Florence Bravo never even came to trial; Henriette Francey, after jury deliberations which lasted no more than fifteen minutes, was set free amid cheers. However, the Parisian papers, which had at first been sympathetic to the accused (this being their customary stance in the recent affairs of wives defending their honor), by the end were dubious, subdued, and divided on the verdict.[39] In truth, the release of both Henriette Francey and Florence Bravo owed much to the vigorous defense of capable counsel. If they managed to be awarded the benefit of the doubt, they had also been obliged to "prove" that they deserved it.

Their adversaries in both these affairs set out to show first that the accused were, in the current euphemism, women who "did," and Florence Bravo, at least, was ultimately brought to a dramatic and tearful admission that her relations with the famous Dr. Gully had gone "beyond friendship." After the first inquest, which had aroused so much furor over unanswered questions and her own failure to appear, Mrs. Bravo had signed a lengthy formal statement on June 2, 1876, in the effort to exonerate herself. In it she flatly denied a "criminal intimacy" with the doctor: "This attachment was quite innocent, and nothing improper had ever passed between us." [40] But a few weeks later at the second inquest her own lady's companion, the "faithful" Mrs. Cox, practically volunteered her knowledge of the affair. Mrs. Cox was asked a leading question about how much Charles Bravo, to whom she had introduced her mistress, had known of Florence's past at the time of their marriage in December 1875.

Q. Was it your impression from his conversation that he believed her to be a perfectly chaste woman?

A. . . . He believed her to be a chaste woman and I did not create any suspicion that she was different from that. I left her to tell him what she liked. I did not keep anything back before the marriage. Well, I did, but let me fully understand what you mean.

Q. . . . What was it?

A. I kept back from him what Mrs. Ricardo told me after giving up her acquaintance with Dr. Gully.

Q. What was it she told you?

A. Of her intimacy with Dr. Gully.

Q. What do you mean by "intimacy"?

A. You may draw your own conclusions.

Q. No; I decline to do that. Tell me now, madam, was it a criminal intimacy with Dr. Gully that she told you of?

A. [After a pause.] Yes, a criminal intimacy. (Sensation.) [41]

After Mrs. Cox's statement Florence had little choice but to acknowledge the intimacy and to submit to questioning both from her own counsel, who elicited details gently to diffuse the effect of cross-examination, and from the eminent but far-from-gentle George Lewis, who represented the Bravo family. But the "triumph" of Florence's confession of the affair was short-lived, for despite the fact that it had finally been handed to them after weeks of their own insinuations, the lawyers for the Crown and for the Bravos discovered that it led them nowhere. Indeed, in the teeth of popular hostility toward her, Florence scored a small triumph by turning on Lewis for his constant badgering over Dr. Gully.

> That attachment to Dr. Gully has nothing to do with this case—of the death of Mr. Charles Bravo. As to that, I will answer any question. I have been subjected to sufficient pain and humiliation already, and I appeal to the Coroner and to the jury, as men and as Britons, to protect me. I think it is a great shame that I should be thus questioned, and I will refuse to answer any further questions with regard to Dr. Gully.[42]

There was a spontaneous movement of foot-shuffling male sympathy in the courtroom which suggested that chivalrous deference toward a female suspect was not entirely dead. The *Times,* for one, upheld the view that it was "a cruel, and even a barbarous act to subject a most unhappy woman to hours of cross-examination for the mere purpose of eliciting details of this connexion [with Gully], and even, in one instance, of endeavoring to extort the circumstances under which, nearly six years ago, this fatal passion arose."[43] Still, even the *Times* expressed the opinion that the doctor and Mrs. Bravo had "no right to complain of having been asked to explain circumstances of apparent suspicion,"[44] and it also acknowledged that "all the evidence goes to show the absence of any such depression or desperation as might tempt a vigorous and not unsuccessful young man to commit suicide."[45]

The whole development of the inquest and the timing of all the sensational revelations indeed suggested that the "person or persons" who knew what had happened had made no plans for a probing investigation and were obliged to invent a self-protective theory to explain Charles's death as they went along. In the end that theory, though full of contradictions and inconsistencies, proved effective to the extent that the legal machinery was unable to produce an indictment. It worked partly because no better alternative theory was proposed and partly because it appealed successfully to the shreds of belief in the view that women of proper social upbringing were still somehow less than responsible for any of their behavior. But no huge throngs gathered to greet Florence Bravo with wild cheers as she left the scene of the inquest at the Bedford Hotel in Balham. She remained suspect, though largely as a woman who "did." As one contemporary commentator noted wryly, "Her [Florence's] detractors proved that she dyed her hair, but they did not prove that she poisoned her husband."[46] Yet, relations with Dr. Gully aside, it was more than likely that whether she had intended murder or not, Florence Bravo had been responsible for the death of her husband.

In the case of Henriette Francey, the prosecution similarly devoted its efforts to a demonstration of the view that the accused woman had indulged in an adulterous relationship. The purpose here was not, of course, to make her a plausible suspect for murder, but rather to prove that the fatal shooting to which she confessed had been prompted by less elevated motives than the ones she proclaimed. Namely, it was charged that Henriette Francey had been carrying on an affair with none other than a local priest, a man called Jules Hernest, described as a tall, pale, bespectacled, thirty-three-year-old with a sweet and inoffensive manner.[47]

Some months before the crime, Hernest had left town for another parish under rather mysterious circumstances. His most recent visit to Tonnère, it was noted, had coincided with Paul Francey's most recent business trip. The priest had arrived in town on December 10, 1884, just twelve days before the shooting. And curiously enough, the first occasion of attempted rape by Bazard, as reported by Henriette Francey, occurred on December 13, 1884, just a day after Hernest had been alleged to have visited her. Had Bazard guessed that Hernest and Henriette had a guilty secret? To the public prosecutor, at least, it seemed plausible that he had and that Henriette, terrified over the threat of exposure, decided to rid herself of a man who knew too much and talked too much.

Evidence for the prosecution's theory was not lacking, but it was understandably difficult to find townspeople who not only had suspicions, but were willing to come forward and testify against a woman from one of the leading families, particularly when the charges involved a priest. Added to this was the awkward fact that many of those in a position to know the truth were servants and neighbors of the Franceys whose loyalties were likely to be unshakable. In spite of these difficulties the preliminary interrogations did turn up some testimony which the prosecutor decided to pursue. A local harness maker reported that a tradesman who lived across the square from the Francey home had told him, after the crime, that he had seen Hernest go into their home on several occasions in the past eighteen months. The harness maker added that he was astonished by such stories and had no opinions of his own on the moral character of Mme. Francey.[48] Similarly, a welder said he had spoken with the same tradesman on this subject while Hernest still lived in Tonnère. The welder testified that he himself could not believe a priest would behave in that way, but admitted that he had once seen Hernest walking alone past the Franceys, looking up at the house, and "making peculiar gestures with his right hand."[49] He had reported this to his informant, who told him that Mme. Francey and the abbé Hernest used an elaborate series of signals in setting up their rendezvous, including a napkin which Henriette would hang from an upstairs window.

The authorities then questioned this observant neighbor, fifty-one-year-old Jules Dupaquet, who, as a semi-invalid suffering from insomnia and asthma, seems to have spent a good portion of his time looking out the window of his apartment, which afforded an excellent view of the Franceys' establishment. It was not reported whether Dupaquet had been a friend of the victim, but his willingness to talk may have derived in part from his being a relative outsider and newcomer, despite having lived in Tonnère at least since the summer of 1883. Hernest, in his effort to discredit Dupaquet's story, had branded the man a Parisian Communard who had kept a mistress and was a known priest-hater,[50] but the prosecution not only declared the tradesman credible but made him their star witness. Some papers agreed that Dupaquet appeared honorable and gave his evidence with no sign of animosity.[51] It was true, too, that the witness had not at first volunteered his story, but had told it only when the authorities came to him.

It was easy to see why Dupaquet's account troubled and angered the accused woman. The witness began with the arrival by train of Hernest shortly before the crime the previous December. The priest had been met at the station by his friend and successor, the witness stated, and the pair had walked through the main square and past the Franceys', where Henriette and her future victim, Hippolyte Bazard, were chatting amiably. As Hernest passed them, Henriette reportedly looked surprised, blushed, and quickly went inside. Bazard, meanwhile, had seemed amused and had obviously made a sardonic remark.

On December 12, 1884, two days later, the priest turned up some time after nine in the evening and, according to Dupaquet, walked slowly down the street toward the Franceys' home. Though it was dark by then, the square was illuminated by a gas light, and Hernest was observed to look around quickly and then approach the gate "on tiptoe." He began to push the gate open, but hearing voices inside, he stepped back out, rang, and went in. Dupaquet explained that on two previous occasions, once in the spring of 1883 and again in the summer of 1884, he had actually seen Hernest leaving the Franceys' between two and three in the morning. On this occasion he had not seen the priest leave, but he had heard the Franceys' noisy gate creak open at four in the morning. On all the instances in question, Monsieur Francey, he had learned, had been out of town on business.[52] At this, Henriette could no longer maintain courtroom decorum. "That's an infamous lie!," she interrupted. "You're a coward. You have said this for a hundred francs!"[53]

Whether he had or not, the prosecution succeeded in collecting a few more corroborative tidbits from other townspeople. One of the Franceys' own servants at first denied having seen the priest Hernest the previous December, but then later admitted having let him into the house on the night in question. Another servant, who was employed at Hernest's former lodgings, was reported to have stated that before the priest left town, Henriette had for a long time visited him nearly every day, "staying an hour and a half or two hours on each visit and departing with a flushed face."[54]

This statement and several other similar ones were collected by the victim's brother, Charles Bazard, a watchmaker who had come to Tonnère to try to help the authorities get evidence from local residents against Mme. Francey.[55] But, unfortunately for him, confidences they were willing to share privately they would not divulge in the formal interrogations. In this case, when the servant was actually brought in for questioning, he acknowledged only that "like everyone else" he had heard that Mme. Francey visited Hernest.[56] However, despite the understandable reticence of townspeople, the likelihood of an affair between Mme. Francey and the priest appeared great. That pair, moreover, were less than successful in dealing with evidence which suggested that Hippolyte Bazard had in fact discovered the relationship and determined to exploit it. Nonetheless, the sworn testimony of both never swerved from the denial of all the charges, both moral and criminal.

The priest Hernest, summoned from a nearby town during the preliminary investigations, explained his presence in Tonnère by alleging he had come to order some wine and to pay for a gravestone for his mother. He admitted having visited Henriette in the daytime on December 10 to bring her news of one of her sisters, but denied all allegations of nighttime visits, including the crucial one of December 12. He also promised and later produced a letter of thanks to a fellow priest with whom he claimed to have spent the night in question, though the letter itself did not mention the actual date.[57] Henriette, meanwhile, had been confronted with Dupaquet's testimony and admitted that the priest had stopped by that evening, but only for ten minutes, to retrieve an umbrella he had left there.[58] Hernest, brought face-to-face with Dupaquet, as was customary in the pretrial procedure, acknowledged a brief visit then, but denied the account of his little ballet before the Franceys' gate.[59]

More incriminating still was the stumbling over this story which occurred during the trial some weeks later in March 1885. In retelling the account, Hernest explained that he had stopped by the Franceys' to pick up an umbrella he had left on a previous visit to Tonnère. The presiding judge, who had just questioned Mme. Francey and clearly disbelieved her, pounced on a discrepancy with the pretrial records, pointing out that Henriette had claimed the umbrella was left on a visit that same afternoon. Hernest falteringly replied, "I don't remember too well," and Henriette quickly interjected, "That detail is not important." "You are quite wrong," [60] the judge corrected her.

Indeed, other evidence presented that first day of the trial raised further questions about the veracity of Henriette's account and went a long way toward establishing the link between Bazard's knowledge of a relationship between the priest and the accused woman and Henriette's decision to murder. It was not that Henriette had failed to prepare her story carefully. Unlike Florence Bravo, Mme. Francey appears to have made elaborate plans to ensure that only one construction could be put on the action she determined to take. But she failed to reckon on the more than idle curiosity of a neighbor with odd nocturnal habits.

Henriette's own account of the events from the evening of Hernest's visit to the evening of the murder nine days later on December 21 is both fascinating and disturbing in its picture of a desperate woman. She explained that as her husband was away in London, she had attended a concert on

Saturday the thirteenth with the young woman who was tutoring her in English. The architect Bazard had sat near them, she said, and stared at them throughout. Then, shortly after midnight when she returned alone after walking this friend home, she entered the courtyard and realized that a large man was crouched down next to one of the pieces of agricultural machinery kept there on display. Realizing it was Bazard and troubled that people still in the street would overhear them and invent a scandal, she admitted the interloper. She explained that they walked through the dining room into the salon, since there was a light there. Then, to calm her nerves, she hastily poured herself some rum.

At this, she testified, the architect seized the glass, declaring he wanted to put his lips where hers had been. He then proceeded to grab her and force her down onto the couch, proclaiming the while, "I have never loved you so much, you are much more lovable when you are angry." [61] While she resisted and lost her hat in the scuffle, he managed to tear open her blouse and caress her breasts. She added some details which the press declined to print, but made it clear that Bazard had failed to achieve his end before she managed to wriggle free. She then rushed into the dining room, where she knew her husband kept a revolver, seized it, and ordered the intruder out of the house.

The next day, she kept all visitors away on the pretext of a migraine, but the following day, during a visit from her brother-in-law shortly before her husband's return, a letter from Bazard was delivered which prompted her to divulge the architect's outrages to the extent of reporting his frequent harassments and the recent episode in which he had torn her blouse. Her brother-in-law later corroborated her story, reporting that the letter, addressed to "My Beautiful Lady," contained snippets of poetry copied from Lamartine which Bazard passed off as his own, as well as clichés such as "Don't leave me to languish" and "There is nothing sweeter than having a lover, the delights are far sweeter than with a spouse." [62] Her brother-in-law persuaded her to burn the letter and agreed it was not a matter worth mentioning to her husband, but Henriette acknowledged that, despite this, she was determined to seek a guarantee in the form of a written confession from Bazard, which would be entrusted to her for safekeeping. The confession, she explained, was to outline the events of the evening of the thirteenth and would be shown to her husband only in the event that Bazard dared to insult her again. She then drafted a long letter and had her maid deliver it to Bazard. Both the letter and the copy she kept for herself were duly produced at the trial. The *Figaro* labeled it the work of a *"petite bourgeoise poseuse,"* proud of the little learning she had picked up in her boarding school.

Monsieur, the scandalous scene which took place between us has so disturbed me, and since that moment such confusion has reigned in my thoughts that I have not been able to arrive at any resolution. Today, I have a bit more *sang-froid* and I can coldly envision the situation which is before me and present it to you. Your answer will dictate my conduct. It is unnecessary to tell you that I thirst for vengeance. You have offended me so cruelly, you have behaved in such an infamous way towards me, that an unspeakable hatred has risen against you in my heart which demands your life for its satisfaction, and this is within my power; I have only to say a word to my husband, tell him about your infamous attempts [on my person], and you will be finished. Do not make the mistake of believing I exaggerate, I know him, he will kill you.[64]

Henriette announces that if she hesitates to expose him right away, it is not from pity but from fear of scandal. Despite her innocence, she argues, the world would say that she had been his lover and that her husband had killed him out of jealousy. She then explains the terms of the confession she requires.

Now that I know what sort of man you are, I require a guarantee so that I have nothing to fear from you. I see that you will stop at nothing when it comes to satisfying your bestial passions and I require protection from your future enterprises.[65]

Toward the end, she softens a bit.

Permit me to believe that you suffered a moment of madness. That is the thought that came to my mind during our struggle the other day, and it is that which spared your life, for [at that moment] I saw red and *I had the right to kill you,* yes: the undeniable right. There was an attempted rape, I was in my home and had the legal right to defend myself, the law nor God [himself] would not have punished me, nor would my husband have suspected me, and wagging tongues would not have started. Above all I would have been delivered from the sight of you.[66]

Urging him to reply promptly, she warns him not to use the mails, since all postal deliveries pass through her husband's hands and "if he discovered the slightest bit of information concerning this matter, I would confess all in order to exculpate myself and retain his esteem." [67]

Bazard's reply and subsequent events that week suggested that Henriette's letter had been carefully contrived for possible future publication. The *Figaro* was not far off the mark in commenting that George Sand might have envied Mme. Francey's literary efforts.[68] At the least, it was evident from the beginning that Henriette had been bluffing about having decided to spare Bazard's life on the first occasion, for, as the authorities quickly discovered, the revolver had not even been loaded then, if indeed the incident had occurred. Henriette herself admitted exaggerating her feelings in order to frighten Bazard, and she claimed that the flippant response he tardily sent to her ultimatum was what prompted her to make preparations in earnest. That response was received on the Wednesday before the crime, the same day that her husband reported that his poor wife had suffered a "nervous crisis" and had delivered herself of what he called a "mad laugh" which had lasted for fifteen or twenty minutes.[69] The next day, he said, she had made innocent inquiries about how to use the revolver and had urged him to teach her and to purchase cartridges in case she ever needed to protect herself during one of his long absences.

Henriette later supplied the authorities with the letter she claimed had driven her to seek revenge for her honor, unaware at the time that it contained the clue which would convince her accusers that she had had more compelling motives for wishing to rid herself of Bazard. The architect had indeed taken her somber communication lightly, and he replied in urbane fashion, affecting the conviction that she had been talking about a third party. Bazard suggests slyly that in order to offer an opinion on the "case" she presents, he would need to know more about the antecedents of the characters involved, and urges that they discuss the matter verbally since it is too difficult to treat in correspondence. Then, dropping the ruse, he confides that although many imperfections might be attributed to him, he is not a wicked man but rather an unhappy one: "I am wrong to say that, you have no interest in knowing it and there are so many people in my situation that I have no right to pity myself. . . ." [70]

Then, prompted by her description of the revolver alone having gained sway over his "infamous attacks" and his "unspeakable kisses," Bazard shifts back to his literary device.

Not being an evildoer myself, I find it hard to believe that one of my fellow creatures—what am I saying?—a monster, indeed, could have obliged a woman to point a revolver at his head, and I am even less capable of explaining his flight.

I am no hero of bravado, but I am not afraid; I do not court danger, but I have courage, sustained energy, and a will of iron. In an analogous situation, I would have acted very differently. . . . To be killed by a bullet from the revolver of a pretty woman, held in an adorable hand, aimed [couché . . . en joue] by eyes which could make an Andalusian's pale by comparison. . . . Few men can dare hope to die that way.[71]

Bazard concludes that if she knows such a woman, his door is open to her any time from five to midnight during the next few days. He volunteers to supply the revolver himself and sends her ardent kisses in advance!

The tragic irony of his setting the scenario of his own death a few days later was ignored by the prosecutor, who thought he had found something more interesting, namely, evidence that Bazard had discovered a secret about Henriette which accounted for his recent attentions to her and allegedly his death as well. The architect was too subtle to remind her bluntly in writing of the knowledge, but the reference appears unmistakable. It comes at the end of a whimsical list of things which he cites as the more typical calamities men face daily, which hardly match the declared heights of ecstasy of being blasted by a woman's revolver.

In this life, one is exposed to many things: one can be bitten by a mad dog, stung by a fly, run over by an omnibus, or be the victim of a derailing. A termite can slyly find its way into your ceiling, you can suddenly receive some bad news, you can catch cholera, you can burn your mustache, you can be blinded by a falling star, you can have a mother-in-law, you can lose your umbrella. . . .[72]

The umbrella again! But the probable sequence of events was now clear. Bazard had seen Henriette soon after Hernest's visit—probably, as she said, after the concert—and he knew the priest had been admitted to her home, either having observed for himself or having learned from Dupaquet or someone else. What seems most likely is that he then revealed this knowledge, and Henriette protested that the priest had merely come for his umbrella. But Bazard knew that Hernest had not left promptly, and it is probable that he then offered the frightened woman his silence in return for sexual favors.

From the beginning, in any case, Mme. Francey's reported behavior only fitfully suggested that of a woman terrorized by the rapist assailant she portrayed, and several episodes are much more plausible if she is imagined instead as a woman desperately trying to find a way to shield her secret. Despite evidence of coaching, her maid offered an account of the initial attempted rape scene which cast doubt on the substance of Henriette's version. The maid dutifully recorded that when she came down the next morning, everything was in disarray, with furniture turned over and "dirt" everywhere; the disturbance had been so great, she said, that the clock had been bumped and the clockwinder had had to come and reset it. The problem with this detail was the discovery that the clock had stopped at quarter to two in the morning, which meant that the "scuffle" had probably not taken place promptly, as Henriette indicated, but an hour and a half after she admitted Bazard. Again, the maid said she had extinguished the lamp in the salon before retiring, which suggested that Henriette had not, as she said, selected the distant salon on the grounds that there was a light there (to explain what appeared to be an act of hospitality toward the man she claimed was an intruder), but rather had admitted him as she would normally admit a visitor for what was initially to be a discussion.[73] Finally, of course, there was the suspicious fact that Henriette had not attempted to call the sleeping maid upstairs to her aid.

Henriette's version was further challenged by several depositions from witnesses who swore that on more than one occasion after the alleged assault and as late as a day before the crime, they had seen Mme. Francey standing at her doorway talking, and even joking, with Bazard.[74] The accused woman fiercely denied these allegations, and in the face of the judge's harsh accusation that the alleged "outrage" itself was in question and that she had literally summoned her victim into a death trap, Henriette cried:

No! I killed Monsieur Bazard because he refused me the means to save my honor and even went so far as to perpetrate a second outrage by proposing that I run away to a foreign country with him, the while showing me that he was in a condition to satisfy his passion momentarily. That is the truth.[75]

At this the accused woman was reportedly seized by a violent "nervous crisis," and the first day of her trial ended.

On the second and last day, however, in the face of all the accumulated evidence against her, the tide shifted in Mme. Francey's favor. The public prosecutor had built a more than plausible case for a link between adultery and murder, a link which was missing in Florence Bravo's case, but the image of the adulterous wife was soon countered by the portrayal of the wronged and defenseless woman. The defense used to the full the scandalous reputation of the victim. It was permitted to summon one female witness after another, many of them rounded up by Paul Francey himself, who all testified that Hippolyte Bazard had been fresh with them or made attempts on their virtue (though never successful ones). The accounts had the ring of truth, and though Francey was charged with having paid some of the women, it seems unlikely that they would have testified falsely under the circumstances.

A domestic servant, who admitted that she wanted to help Paul Francey save his wife, related the rather tame incident of having answered the door once to Bazard, who in leaving his card told her she had a pretty figure and would make an excellent wet nurse.[76] A maid at the *collège* testified that Bazard once entered a bedroom where she was working and "touched me and made indecent suggestions." [77] One of his landladies swore that she had had to slap him on four or five occasions when he tried to kiss her.[78] A baker said that his servant had complained that when she went to Bazard's rooms to deliver a cake, he had closed the door behind her and tried to kiss her.[79] The wife of a local merchant reported that when she called on him to present her bill, he had followed her downstairs and embraced her. She said she had remarked, "Doubtless you mistake me for someone else," [80] and he was amused and had not bothered her since.

There were several more women with similar accounts, including a farm worker who declared that Bazard had chased her in the fields and that she finally had to fend him off with a pitchfork.[81] The wife of the principal of the *collège* testified that while Bazard was there consulting her on the interior redecoration, he constantly followed her about and made numerous "equivocal suggestions." [82] Her husband, she said, had volunteered to intervene, but she had declined on the grounds that their business relations would be made "too difficult." She added, however, that though he had never touched her, the episode had upset her so much that she had not slept peacefully until the day he died.

The women's vigor and apparent sincerity in reporting these incidents was remarkable and demonstrated a sexual solidarity cutting across class lines which under other circumstances might have been more admirable. The women were plainly convinced that they were upholding the honor of a righteous woman, and Henriette's persuasive performance in court no doubt helped. As for Paul Francey's vigorous support, it is permitted to note that it may or may not have represented belief in his wife's version of events. Francey, a radical republican with ambitions for national office, had a reputation at stake. The Catholic paper *La Croix*, remarking that Francey was a local radical leader, noted with some amusement that even the notoriously anticlerical paper *La Lanterne* was protesting indignantly the allegations of a liaison between a priest and the accused woman.[83]

The measure of Paul Francey's concern over the case against his wife can be appreciated by the fact that he engaged for the defense no less a man than the brilliant and scrupulous Edgar Demange, the last of the great nineteenth-century rhetoricians in the style of Charles Lachaud, who had defended Marie Lafarge and the Lemoines. Already a man of towering reputation, Demange had defended Prince Napoleon in the murder of the journalist Victor Noir and would later defend Dreyfus and Mme. Caillaux.[84] He was known for his traditional views, firm patriotic attitudes, and Catholic sympathies. Concentrating almost exclusively on the incidents of outrage as Henriette had finally described them in private interrogations, Demange tastefully and dramatically recreated these scenes, challenging the jury at the end: "And you would dare to say that a woman who had suffered all that and who killed is a criminal!"[85] He alleged that an enormous packet of letters from women who had "succumbed" had been found in Bazard's rooms. Then, dismissing Dupaquet as a meddler and the umbrella episode as a farce, he warned the jury against condemning a young woman who had done what she had to for her honor. Demange was interrupted by applause on several occasions and the acquittal was a foregone conclusion.

In both the Bravo and Francey affairs the legal proceedings had featured the quest for an adulteress, but then backed away when she was exposed and accepted the accused woman's dubious version of the events. Admission or strong suspicion of adultery might, if properly used, have led the accusers to a better understanding of the women's motives and a more satisfactory explanation of their actions. But in both cases conflicting images of the new woman helped obscure the probable realities.

In the Bravo affair the fact of a criminal intimacy was fairly understood as significant if it led directly to a motive for murder. But despite the popular ditty, there was no evidence produced in the inquest that Florence had wished "to repossess her ancient lover," and the medications which Dr. Gully had had delivered to his former mistress were shown to have contained no tartar emetic. There appeared then, no direct route from revelations of an illicit passion to death by poisoning. But in their zeal to find evidence for adultery, her accusers had uncovered an indirect route to Florence's state of mind on the night of April 18, 1876. Unfortunately for them the accused woman, in the process, was made to shed her scarlet hues; she emerged, for the jury at least, as another of the favorite female creatures of Victorian imagination, the wronged woman. It was not an image easily won, especially as it was becoming passé. And Florence, forever simpleminded, was not properly grateful to her lady's companion, the quiet, unassuming, and enigmatic Mrs. Cox, who had ultimately decided that admission of an adulterous relationship was the only way to save her mistress. Florence's real motive in entering that relationship with Dr. Gully is obvious enough on a reading of the testimony. Far from being an abandoned pleasure-seeker in pursuit of sexual adventure, she was a frightened and insecure young woman, temporarily incapable of coping with the strains of marriage and responsive to the sympathetic understanding of a wise doctor. For daring to voice the desire for separation from a man who had frightened her during attacks of *delirium tremens* and terrorized her by striking out in alcoholic rage, her own formerly loving father had become angry with her and refused her permission to stay in his house. That Dr. Gully in these circumstances had assumed the role of protective father-substitute—and then lover—was comprehensible. That he might have done so with honorable intentions was a notion which stretched the credibility of nearly everyone, which was fortunate for Florence.

James Manby Gully was in fact an extraordinary doctor. His practice at Malvern, like that of many doctors in the popular water-cure establishments, served a large and predominantly upper-middle-class female clientele.[86] Staffed mainly by men and women whose views deviated from the medical orthodoxy of heavy drug medication, surgery, and harsh or painful treatments, the Malvern water-cure center had been founded in 1842 by Gully and his partner James Wilson, who had espoused treatments popularized on the continent. Gully himself had become convinced of the scientific foundation of the water-cure or hydropathy, which took advantage of natural springs and employed bathing, drinking mineral water, wrapping in wet sheets, massage, exercise, and diet reform. Early persuaded that chronic nervous disorders were related to a physical condition, namely, the gorging of the viscera or central ganglionic system with blood, he came to believe that water administered in various ways was bound to help cure or relieve such disorders by regulating circulation.

Gully's practice, which he described in several studies on nervous disease and the water-cure,[87] concentrated on what were defined as chronic functional nervous disorders. He stated that neuropathy, or in its extreme form, hypochondriasis, was a peculiar condition endemic to modern civilization and one to which women were especially susceptible. Aware that his studies of nervous disorders were controversial, he remarked with good humor, "It is no uncommon thing to hear our octogenarian parents say that in *their* youth, there were no such things as nerves." [88] Early in his practice, before turning to water-cure, Gully had defined nervous symptoms to include nausea, insomnia, disorders in the internal functions, such as digestion, strange feelings in the stomach area, and "frequent sighing, yawning and sobbing and explosions of laughter that obtain in hysterical women." [89] Such nervous symptoms, he explained, had both physical and mental causes. The physical ones included improper diet, use of spirits, strong tea, or highly seasoned or undercooked meats, irregularities of lactation or menstruation, forced sexual relations, masturbation, and the use of opiates or stimulating drugs. The mental causes, he alleged, included sudden impressions, prolonged study, corroding thoughts, religious doubts, disappointed passions, and boredom. The last, he noted, was the worst form of neuropathy and especially prevalent in England where "productive economy and good government" had produced affluence and leisure in the higher classes.[90]

In a real sense, then, Florence Bravo was a patient tailor-made for Gully's attention: a wealthy, idle, unhappily married young woman with no children to occupy her, who suffered from insomnia which she treated by the use of wine and chloral, a drug commonly used as a strong sedative. On arrival at Malvern in 1870 Florence underwent normal treatment of sitz baths, spinal washings, and wrapping in sheets; her condition was subsequently diagnosed by Gully as physical exhaustion brought on by mental stress, namely, the "morbid impressions" prompted by Ricardo's behavior. As was his custom in such cases, Gully not only treated the physical symptoms, but explored ways to remove his patient from the source of mental stress, in this instance, the harmful influence of her husband.

This concern and sympathy with a woman's entire situation was characteristic of the water-cure establishments, which have recently been described as "centers of female-oriented culture." [91] As opposed to more orthodox practitioners who treated their patients singly in an office setting or at home and who often combined harsh cures with admonitions to fulfill marital and maternal duties, the water-cure doctors offered women a supportive female atmosphere in which they openly discussed their cases with one another and in which their own versions of their ailments received a sympathetic hearing. It has also been remarked that water-cure treatment provided in this sexually repressive period an almost unique "socially-approved sensual experience for women." [92]

Proponents of the water-cure treatment also normally subscribed to a set of corollary doctrines which were of special interest or concern to women, including temperance, reform of legislation discriminatory to women, mesmerism, and spiritualism. Dr. Gully himself was fascinated by the possibilities of mesmerism in therapeutics and was also for a time president of a spiritualist society.[93] Doubtless partly because he treated many women who, like Florence, were victimized by alcoholic husbands as well as women who themselves drank heavily, Gully was a confirmed believer in the "female" cause of temperance.[94] He was also at least rumored to be a believer in a more radical female cause, namely, the right of a woman to determine whether she wishes to bear a child. It was hinted that Dr. Gully had administered abortifacient drugs and had even gone so far as to conduct abortions when he was convinced that his patient's health or well-being demanded it.[95]

The doctor also appears to have held controversial views on sexual morality, although such views were not stated specifically in his publications. He owned a copy of Drysdale's *Prostitution, Poverty and Celibacy* [96] and the language of his own case studies hints strongly that he agreed with Drysdale's opinion that "sexual morbidity and repressed sexual desires," as well as fear of sexual brutality, were the cause of many of women's nervous disorders.[97] In time Gully came to diagnose Florence Ricardo's condition as partly the result of sexual fears caused by a husband whose advanced alcoholism had made him normally impotent but occasionally brutally demanding. Gully agreed with Drysdale's view of the harmful effects of linking all "legitimate" sex to marriage, but he recognized and bowed to the social imperatives. With Florence he observed all outward proprieties, and he fully intended marriage. During questioning by Florence's counsel, George Lewis, after Florence had made her "confession," Gully provided moving evidence of his convictions. He firmly denied any actual sexual intimacy until long after Ricardo's death in the spring of 1871, but he admitted a friendship before then which had led to Florence's break with her parents.

Q. Was it during the period she was a patient of yours that the attachment between you commenced?
A. Well, it commenced after a fashion; it was a friendly understanding. She was alone a great deal and she used to have tea with me at my house. . . . I knew that she had discarded her family for me in the spring of 1871 when I returned from abroad.
Q. You know that she had given you her entire affections; given up for you her home, family and all—even to her good name?
A. I knew she had been given the choice of giving me up and had refused.
Q. You know she had given up her name for you—her good name—her honour?
A. Well, she had given up her home; but what do you mean by her honour? [98]

Very likely, then, the sexual relationship which later developed was cautiously conducted by the doctor, who understood Florence's ignorance and fear of sex and who also, like many members of his profession, appreciated female sexual response and needs better than most of his male contemporaries.[99] For some time the novelty of the doctor's charming company and the probable experience of her own sexual awakening appear to have reconciled the widow to the break with her parents and to the social ostracism which her known public companionship with Gully incurred.

The doctor, however, was remarked even in highly sympathetic portraits to have been a man of "strong will and great force of character," [100] and it is possible that the immense personal influence he easily exercised over Florence at the beginning, when she was most troubled and vulnerable, blinded him to the fact that the very recovery he had effected had brought the return of her headstrong qualities. Gully's infatuation, indeed, appears to have arrested his perceptions of his patient at an invalid state and left him unprepared for a shift in their relations. A letter Florence sent to Mrs. Cox during a trip to Germany with the doctor during the summer of 1873, reveals her as a determined young woman who understood her authority in her home, at least, and could use firm language in requiring obedience from her staff.

My dearest Mrs. Cox—Many thanks for your kind letter and parcels just received; please do not send any more flowers or forward any more letters. Will you tell Rance that I have no intention of building a greenhouse, and will have nothing ordered from Mould or elsewhere without my order.... I told McGrath that he was not to sleep in the house, and *my order is to be obeyed.* Please tell him this. Will you write to Mrs. —— for me and demand my recipe book back; it is in a green watered cover and tell her unless she returns it I will write to her mistress.... Will you in the course of next week compare Watt Pegg's price for coals with Pigott's, as I should like the cellar filled before I return.... Please see Mould for me, and tell him to take no orders from anyone but from me. I am so glad all the dogs and horses are well.[101]

The letter makes no reference to her traveling companion and, more important, Florence allows herself to confide her distaste for the baths and regimen to which she is now clearly submitting as a concession to the doctor's will. The whole tone of the letter, her solicitous references to the health of Mrs. Cox, and the love she sends her suggest a kind of conspiratorial sympathy developing between the two women and a new gentle irreverence toward the hydropathic whims of the aging doctor.

I have such horrid baths now—peat soil containing iron is mixed with mineral water, and I have to sit half-an-hour in this nasty, filthy hot bath, just like liquid manure. It is for soothing the nerves, but it is horrible, and one has to take a hot bath afterwards to get clean. Then I have three glasses of cold mineral water from seven to eight in the morning, and another glass at six p.m. I feel quite wearied out by 8:30, and am glad to get to bed.[102]

Still, the event which appears to have sharply altered her sympathies for the doctor and which cemented her relationship with Mrs. Cox was the suffering which Florence experienced upon her return from Germany during what the lady's companion delicately called an "unusual natural illness."[103] Tearfully, Florence later admitted that this illness had been a miscarriage. The more likely truth was that Florence, discovering herself to be pregnant, underwent an abortion conducted by her lover, as the only means to shield both their reputations from further and irreparable damage.[104] In any case Florence's words of gratitude for recovery from the event were reserved exclusively for her lady's companion, who she insisted had not known the actual nature of her illness until shortly before her marriage to Charles Bravo two years later.

> So far as I know, Mrs. Cox did not know what that illness was, and I did all I could to prevent her from knowing it. I owe my life then to Mrs. Cox, from her attendance upon me, and I had acute physical suffering. . . . The "improper intimacy" with Dr. Gully ceased on our return from abroad.[105]

Whether their physical "intimacy" actually did cease, there are signs that relations cooled. It was true that when Florence leased the Priory in Balham a few months later, the doctor leased a house nearby, but his influence over the widow seemed to wane as that of Mrs. Cox rose. When Florence and James traveled—and they went to Italy as late as the spring of 1875—Mrs. Cox accompanied them and slept in a bedroom with Florence. Since the time of the "miscarriage," the two women had been on a first name basis (Mrs. Ricardo affectionately called Mrs. Cox "Janie"), and Florence appears to have found comfort in the company of this discreet servant—a woman close to her age and a widow like herself, the close female friend she had not had since girlhood. Dr. Gully, doubtless at Florence's request, henceforth included the lady's companion in most of his invitations; and Mrs. Cox herself admitted that she "was on terms more friendly with Mrs. Ricardo than are usual with a companion in a lady's home." [106] At the same time, Dr. Gully's manservant remarked that his master and Mrs. Ricardo "quarreled frequently." [107]

Under these circumstances it is unlikely that Florence kept any secrets of her past from the lady's companion, but it is probable, too, that Janie, who had been a governess in the families of a solicitor and two ministers, was concerned to work for a "respectable" mistress as well as a rich one. The generosity of her starting wages, eighty pounds a year in 1872, certainly reconciled her to Mrs. Ricardo's past indiscretions, but she appears to have begun slowly to encourage a new liaison more acceptable in the world's eyes. Florence, whose own "rebellion" against convention with Dr. Gully had never been fully self-conscious, now showed that she was willing to be encouraged to recover her reputation. She did miss the parents who continued to snub her, and she learned through an aunt that her mother was seriously ill. A respectable marriage, she came to believe, would solve all her problems. It would restore her to her family, rid her of the embarrassment of her attachment to the doctor, and perhaps even permit her to reenter society as an honorably married woman. The obliging Jane Cox produced a suitable candidate in Charles Bravo, one who could not fail to take his matrimonial cues. The widow may have had a "past," but she was worth a fortune.

With resolution borrowed from her Janie, Florence broke with the doctor in October 1875 without revealing her marriage plans and then penned a careful letter to the man who had just proposed to her.

My dear Charlie—After serious and deep consideration, I have come to the conclusion that if you *still hope* and wish to gain my love we must see more of each other and be quite sure that the solemn act of marriage will be for the happiness of both. . . . All I can *say* is that you have behaved in the noblest manner, and that *I* have no doubt of being happy with you; but of course before giving up my present freedom I must be quite convinced that it would be for our mutual happiness. Need I tell you that I have written to the *Dr.* to say I *must* never see his face again; it is *the* right thing to do in every respect; whatever happens, whether we marry or whether we do not, I shall ever have a great regard for you, and take a deep interest in your welfare, for I think you are a very good man. Write and tell me what you think of this letter and with every good wish, Ever your sincere friend, Florence Ricardo.[108]

Charles's prompt response was favorable, and the results of her father's inquiries into Charles Bravo's "suitability" were satisfactory. With the decision settled, Florence wrote a penitent letter to her father at the end of October.

My dearest Father—Your kind and affectionate letter gave me great pleasure last night, and I look forward with sincere and heartfelt joy to meeting you all again. My past has been a very sad one, but it will be forever blotted out and forgotten, and believe me when I say how much I regret ever having caused you or any of my family pain with regard to the last few sad years of separation. With much love to yourself, and mamma, and all at Buscat, ever your affectionate child,
Florence Ricardo [109]

The "happiness" she said she wanted, however, was not so easily acquired, and at the arrangement of a marriage settlement the following month, Charles made it clear that if Florence was to have her respectability, she must pay dearly for it. Her solicitor reported that Charles was enraged to learn that Florence had requested that the lease of her house, plus the furnishings, her carriages, and the horses—valued at a total of three thousand pounds—be placed in trusteeship for her use. On his first visit, when the solicitor had offered his congratulations, Charles reportedly replied, "Damn your congratulations. I only want the money." [110] He added that he would rather break off the marriage than be placed in the position of "sitting down to a table which was not his, in a chair which was not his—he said he would not be master of his own house in such a case. . . ." [111] Florence's father, who was conducting the negotiations, gave way. Charles received, in addition, second life interest on Florence's fortune of forty thousand pounds from her first husband plus another twenty thousand from her father. Charles's interest in the money was explained by the fact that though he stood to inherit twenty thousand pounds himself, the money would come to him only after the death of both his parents.

In a sudden panic over these financial altercations, Florence desperately turned to the only source of help she could imagine, the doctor she had recently betrayed.

A.   . . . The last interview I had with Dr. Gully was about ten days before my marriage in the lodge of the Priory. I sent for Dr. Gully because I was unhappy. I had had a conversation with Mr. Bravo about the furniture, and he had said he would not marry me unless everything I possessed became his—I don't mean my money, but I mean my carriages, ponies, furniture, jewelry, clothes.

Q.   Do you mean to say that Mr. Bravo mentioned your clothes?

A.   No, but he said "all I possessed," and I told Dr. Gully that I was afraid Mr. Bravo would marry me for what I had got. Dr. Gully advised me to accede to Mr. Bravo's wish, and hoped that I should be happy.[112]

Dr. Gully confirmed the account and added that Mrs. Ricardo had told him she had confided their intimacy to Bravo: "I said, 'I hope that will turn out well.' I think that was at the end of the interview. I think it was the last thing spoken of before I kissed her hand and said good-bye."[113]

Having burned her bridges with the doctor, Florence clung to the ideal of respectability through marriage. There were visits to parents and efforts to gain approval from Charles's mother, who had refused to attend the wedding. There were attempts to establish a footing in local society which included, on one occasion, a dinner party for thirty-one guests. Charles complained good-naturedly that Florence even made him attend church, and he noted that he forbore to play lawn tennis one Sunday "partly from a fear lest it might shock the good people of Balham and Tooting."[114]

All this evidence that Florence was struggling to win a new identity was there in the testimony. And even if her new longing for respectability was not clear, her accusers ought in any case to have realized long before they extracted her "confession" that whatever had motivated Florence, it was futile to dwell on the dead affair with the doctor.

Those accusers might more profitably have pondered the evidence that was in hand long before Mrs. Cox's remarks caused Florence to admit her criminal intimacy. For one thing, there was the peculiarity of Mrs. Cox's failure to tell the doctors until nearly five hours after their arrival about Charles's alleged confidence that he had taken poison. Extraordinary, too, was the sensational amendment Mrs. Cox made to Charles's statement after the first inquest. The amendment had helped decide the new inquest, but it deserved an even more sceptical reception. Charles, she maintained, had actually said, "I have taken poison *for Dr. Gully.* Don't tell Florence."[115] The suggestion of suicide out of jealousy was clear, but it sat badly with much of the other testimony, including that of a barrister who had gone to Oxford with Bravo and had lived with him for two years. The friend testified that the deceased had been the "last man in the world likely to commit suicide"[116] and that Bravo understood medical jurisprudence better than any other barrister he knew.

> He was a very clear-headed man, with a great deal of common sense and very little sentiment—and no feeling for any woman would make him take [a] painful and uncertain poison with the effect of which he was thoroughly acquainted.[117]

Bravo's friend added another highly significant bit of evidence.

> I noticed that he before going to bed always took a deep draught of cold water. He used to drink it from the water bottle in his or my room, or wherever he was, without using a tumbler. This was an inveterate habit with him.[118]

The maid duly reported that as usual she had filled the water bottle that day in Charles's room. The likely container of the poison which had killed Charles was thus identified. Moreover, the same maid's description of events on the fatal night strongly implicated both Florence and Janie, long before the inconsistencies in their own testimony did so. The maid reported that after delivering some wine to her mistress, she had remained upstairs folding Florence's clothes in the dressing room and was still there when Mr. Bravo stepped out on the landing and loudly called, "Florence! Florence! Hot Water!" The two women, together in the next room, could not have failed to hear the cries, but the maid finally reported the incident she may have been too abashed to reveal on the first two occasions she told her story.

> When I ran into Mrs. Bravo's bedroom, Mrs. Cox was seated where I had left her when I asked if anything more was required, and neither she nor Mrs. Bravo had risen to take notice of Mr. Bravo's cry. I don't know if Mrs. Bravo was asleep, but I think if she had not been asleep she would have got up. She did not get up then.[119]

Mrs. Cox then did respond to Charles's cry, but the witness recalled that it was not until about ten minutes later that Florence got up. "It was when I went for the camphor to Mrs. Bravo's bedroom that I awoke her. I think she was asleep (the witness smiled at the question)—well, her eyes were shut." [120] The maid clearly believed that her mistress had been play-acting.

In order to determine motive the accusers would have done well to study more carefully a document available to them: the deposition Florence signed on June 2 after becoming aware of the suspicion against her, but before a second inquest was ordered.[121] At the time Florence appears to have been playing to the sympathies of the gentlemen who questioned her and to have had no suspicion that the statement might become public. Had the authorities not been diverted by the statement made by Mrs. Cox at that time, which introduced Dr. Gully as the alleged cause of Bravo's suicide, the extraordinary qualities of Florence's statement might have been more appreciated. She did echo the theme of jealousy, but then proceeded to describe a wildly unbalanced man: ". . . although I never saw, heard of or from, or spoke of Dr. Gully after our marriage, he [Bravo] was continually, morning, noon, and night, speaking of him, always abusing him, calling him 'that wretch,' and upbraiding me for my former acquaintance with him." [122] (At this point, as noted above, she was still denying a further "intimacy.") Florence even charged that on one occasion some weeks prior to the fatal night, Charles, in his fury, had "jumped out of bed and threatened to cut his throat." [123]

The rest of this outlandish statement is a jumbled catalogue of grievances, large and small, against the deceased, which, in view of her need to exculpate herself, can only be explained by her utterly naive and self-centered nature. She mentioned the mother-in-law who interfered with household arrangements and charged that Charles threatened to fire Mrs. Cox to save money. She noted that Charles took and read all her letters when the postman came and alleged that her husband told her he had "kept a woman before marriage at Maidenhead for four years" [124] and that he owed her or her sister five hundred pounds. (He had and he did.) On the afternoon before he took ill, she said, their carriage had passed Dr. Gully's house on the way to town, which had produced another torrent of abuse.

> He went on quarreling about him. . . . I then said it was a very cruel thing his always bringing up that name. "I am not always talking to you about that woman;" and he admitted his error and asked me to make it up and kiss him. I said in a pet "No, I won't;" and he then said "You will see what I do when I get home." [125]

Implausible in all its references to Gully and Bravo's jealousy and suicide, the statement was a mine of motives for murder. But there was more, which hinted that her immediate motive may have been something quite specific, something which explained the choice of April 18 as the day when Florence dissolved tartar emetic in the drinking water she knew Charles took before retiring. On that day, on the recommendation of her doctor that Florence needed rest after the miscarriage she had suffered two weeks before, Mrs. Cox had traveled to Worthing to rent a house for them. Charles, she said, had called this a "useless expense." Then, ostensibly to illustrate his temper, Florence recalled an incident that took place on the Good Friday before the "fatal Tuesday," which had clearly troubled her deeply and which, as with so many incidents, she described only in a partial, fragmented, and distorted way.

> On Good Friday last I had just recovered from my second miscarriage. He was very restless. He got in an awful passion because I was very weak and had only left my bed that day for ten days, and he did not like my asking to be left alone to rest, as was my habit after luncheon. [126]

It has been conjectured that Florence Bravo, newly recovered from her second miscarriage in less than four months, understood in this incident that the time was not far off when Charles would again be demanding his "marital rights." [127] The couple had slept apart in the past two weeks, but normally, according to the maid, they shared a bedroom. Florence interpreted Charles's anger over the trip to Worthing and his display of temper on Good Friday as an indication that in his mind her convalescence was over. The first opportunity to act on this interpretation came on the following Tuesday. She had returned alone from London early. Charles was still in town, Mrs. Cox was still away at Worthing, and the tartar emetic was no problem. The stableman had used it in small doses to treat the horses, and as a horsewoman she would have known this and had access to the substance.

There is a final twist to the crime. It is possible that Florence had not intended to kill Charles, but only to make him too ill to attempt to make love with her.[128] Tartar emetic was commonly used to induce heavy drinkers to give up the habit, for while it could be tolerated in small quantities dissolved in water, it reacted with alcohol to produce nausea and vomiting. This information may have been known to Florence from her experience with Ricardo. And Charles, as she knew, would have just taken his customary several glasses of burgundy at dinner. It is possible then that Florence mistakenly used a more potent dose of the substance than she intended.

Either reconstruction suggests that Mrs. Cox, newly arrived home, may have learned what Florence had done only when the pair went up to bed together. In any case, Florence's Janie quickly took over and, insofar as she could, faithfully covered for her mistress. When the suicide story failed and when whispers of an affair with Gully began to spread, it was she who determined to bring the doctor into the tale to make the suicide more plausible, failing to reckon that the question of an affair would become the centerpiece of the drama. When it did, Mrs. Cox shrewdly perceived that what began as the pursuit of the scarlet woman with the poison bottle, the "gay widow of Balham," [129] could well backfire on the accusers and shift to the pursuit of another quarry, a man, as the *Times* said, "in violation of the heavy responsibilities of his profession, and with no excuse from the passions of youth or even of middle life." [130] Janie realized by the time she testified that full admission of the "criminal" nature of the intimacy had become necessary to cement Florence's image as a victim of seduction. The lady's companion had done her work well. By the time James Gully appeared as a voluntary witness, the jury members noisily protested his lawyer's request that he be given a seat and demanded that the doctor should stand.[131]

In her obviously coached testimony Florence made some seemly, if rather tardy, compliments on the character of the deceased and lied, often to no purpose, on numerous matters. In a few instances her lies were uncovered, such as when after she claimed that Dr. Gully had not helped her get a separation from Ricardo, the document with his signature was produced.

Especially implausible was her denial of knowledge of her husband's habit of taking a draught of water before he went to bed. Other testimony showed that on the night of April 18, 1876, by the time she went upstairs after dinner, Florence had drunk nearly a bottle of sherry and had ordered more wine brought to her. In retrospect it appears she was steeling herself for that moment when Charles came up to retire for the night.

In the course of the inquest Florence Bravo can be seen to have passed from the stereotyped image of the corrupted new woman to that of her more admirable opposite, the "tried but now righteous" woman, without ever being recognized for the creature she actually was. The French woman Henriette Francey underwent a similar transition after suspicion of her adultery arose, and courtroom techniques for handling that suspicion have already been described. But Mme. Francey, as noted, had something more on her side, namely, a recent elevation in France of the "heroines" of "crimes of passion." [132] These crimes, which began to receive attention in the 1870s, involved women declaring revenge for wounded honor, often by violent attacks on an adulterous husband or his mistress. Henriette Francey was aware that the acquittal rate for such crimes was high. Moreover, her decision to resolve her own predicament of possible exposure and sexual blackmail by adopting the style of the female crime of revenge appears to have been prompted fortuitously by the national attention recently given to the celebrated affair of Mme. Clovis Hugues.[133]

Mme. Hugues, married to a prominent socialist deputy from Marseilles, had learned in 1883 that a girlhood friend who was seeking a marital separation had named her as a co-respondent. At that time, determined to kill the woman, she had set out with a loaded revolver, but her alarmed husband had pursued and disarmed her. The woman died of natural causes soon after, but Mme. Hugues had pursued her revenge by successfully suing the agent who had falsely identified her while in the employ of the woman. The agent, however, had decided to appeal the conviction and in late November 1884, when his case was being heard, Mme. Hugues, hounded by anonymous letters she claimed he had sent to her, determined to take the matter in her own hands. She intercepted him as he was leaving the Palais de Justice and shot him six times. Led off calmly to the police station (her victim died after several days of agony), she declared she felt no remorse for her action and her husband announced that he supported her completely. Public opinion in the capital was overwhelmingly on the side of Mme. Hugues. As *L'Illustration* noted, "all Paris—or practically all Paris—is for her. And especially all feminine Paris." [134] It was less than a month later, in the wake of this outpouring of sympathy for a woman who murdered for honor, that Henriette Francey took a revolver to Hippolyte Bazard. Her first remarks after the event were styled on those of her predecessor: she had no remorse, she had done her duty.

That Mme. Francey self-consciously modeled her more dubious act of revenge on the Hugues affair was clear from the beginning, and she later strove to solidify the popular identification of her case with that of Mme. Hugues. Paul Francey acknowledged that immediately upon his return home three days after Bazard's first rape attempt his wife had asked for his opinion in the Hugues affair. He declared he had said she was "not guilty," that he would acquit her, and that he could not understand how the agent could have attacked the reputation of an honest woman. He added, too, that at his reply his wife had burst into tears and exclaimed, "I am so happy to see that you are a man with a heart." [135] Mme. Francey corroborated the incident, though, curiously enough, neither mentioned it until after January, when Mme. Hugues was acquitted in triumph. Both had been questioned several times prior to that acquittal, but it appears that they decided to make public use of it only in the event that the sympathy for Mme. Hugues carried the day. Henriette Francey then deposed that her husband's opinion in the case had encouraged her resolve: "The reply of my husband was not taken lightly in making my decision. But in any case, I knew him well enough to know he would approve." [136]

Mme. Francey's first plan then appears to have been to take advantage of the Hugues affair to rid herself of a man using sexual blackmail, and her initial statements suggest that she hoped that mere allegations of rape attempts would be sufficient. Doctors who examined her the following day obligingly stated that she ought not to view her victim's body: "Mme. Francey is in a state of nervous excitation which has not abated since the crime; moreover she has had her menstrual period for two days and it is possible that a sudden cessation of her period [occasioned by seeing the body] might produce cerebral congestion, a condition which might then become serious." [137] But when rumors of the affair with the priest started soon thereafter, Henriette appears to have decided to shore up her account with details of the alleged attempted rape scenes. In questioning several days after the event, she provided an explicit description of the first visit by Bazard. She explained in testimony later censored by the press that Bazard had not only torn open her blouse, but forced open her legs, caressed her genitals, and then placed his head between her legs and begun to tongue her. She said she forced him away by pulling on his hair while he, meanwhile, unfastened his trousers and struggled to "introduce his virile member." Then, according to her, he "weakened in the struggle," having ejaculated prematurely.[138] The events may well have occurred as described, but as the prosecutor later demonstrated, the time sequence she related was wrong, for they had been together prior to the alleged event for an hour and a half.

Two weeks after giving this description of the first attempt, Henriette then provided a description of the second attempt, which she said occurred again in the salon after she summoned Bazard to give him one last chance to provide the confession letter she wanted. On that day, she reported, her victim not only refused to write the letter, but joked with her about his happy memories of their last encounter and urged her teasingly to take advantage of the new divorce law and run away with him. When she persisted in her demand for the confession, Bazard then became serious, she said, and declared that on his previous visit he had left not because of her revolver, but because he was "enervated"; this time he would be master. So saying, she alleged, he grabbed her hand and forced it between his legs. At this point Mme. Francey suffered a nervous crisis and her interrogators obligingly conducted the remainder of the interview in writing.

Q.   Did he make you hold his penis in your hand?
A.   Yes, he placed my hands on his organ and I had neither the consciousness nor the strength to realize what was happening.
Q.   And then he agitated your hand?
A.   No, it was more like a pressure which he sought to make me exercise by holding me in that position with both his hands. I was overwhelmed and I do not recall how long this lasted.
Q.   Did you feel your hand become moistened?
A.   No, at least I did not feel it or notice if this contact produced the results you indicate. I do not even know if he spoke or tried to kiss me.[139]

Then suddenly, as Henriette recalled, they were interrupted by noises of the maid in the next room and Bazard released her hand. She got up and went to the window where the revolver had been placed and, as Bazard stood by the door of the salon, she aimed and fired from across the room. Her victim reeled and ran out, struck in the neck, and—unfortunately for him—selected the longer route back to his rooms. Henriette, in pursuit, caught up with Bazard just as he was about to admit himself to the safety of the courtyard of the *college*. She shot him from behind in the jaw and then, after he fell, fired the fatal shot into the clavicle area, which filled his lungs with blood.

There were some problems with her account. For one thing, when Bazard was found, it was remarked that his trousers were fully buttoned, that his shirt was tucked in, and that he was wearing a glove on his left hand. This at least suggested that the interruption and hasty leave-taking Henriette described was dubious. On the other hand, the doctors reported that finding a large moist spot on the victim's underwear which proved to be sperm led them to conclude that he had recently had an ejaculation. More interesting still, the medical report stated that in addition to the spots of blood from his wounds on the top of his shirt, there was another spot of "reddish-brown" blood on the bottom front shirt-tail. Henriette's underclothing was also examined, and although there were no spots on her underpants, there was a dark spot of menstrual blood on the back of her slip.[140]

The doctors' statement noted that the spot on the bottom of Bazard's chemise looked like menstrual blood, but since it did not contain "uterine mucus," they dismissed the possibility that it was menstrual blood.[141] This part of their evidence was not introduced in the trial. Still, it seems likely that Bazard may actually have achieved penetration after removing Henriette's underpants and then ejaculated outside, perhaps after discovering that Mme. Francey's menstrual period had just arrived. Henriette, understandably, would not choose to recall such an event if it had happened. In any case the evidence of some sexual activity is clear enough.

What is not clear, of course, is the context in which these episodes occurred. Bazard's renewed attentions to the accused woman were known to have dated back to a year and a half before, the time when neighbors reported that her affair with the priest began. Three witnesses questioned in the preliminary interrogations had stated that Mme. Francey had been seen calling on Bazard on several occasions during this time, long before the events of December 1884.[142] Had Bazard been extracting sexual blackmail throughout the entire period? Or had recent events alone convinced him that he could now safely make his demands on his quarry? It is impossible to know, but what seems certain is that in the Mme. Hugues affair, Henriette Francey found the solution to her dilemma.

That the terror of discovery of an adulterous affair could drive Henriette Francey to plot a "practically perfect crime" of murder requires an appreciation of the horror with which her society viewed the crime of adultery in a woman, especially in the last decades of the century. The annual publication of criminal statistics revealed that the incidence of adultery cases was rising at a phenomenal rate. In the years from 1825 to 1830 the average number of reported cases was about fifty a year. By 1880 the number had climbed slowly to around four hundred. Then it jumped dramatically after the mid-1880s, from 668 in 1884 to 1657 in 1891, and continued upward.[143]

This jump was largely the result of the new divorce legislation of 1884 which made proof of adultery one of the avenues to divorce, but alarmed observers naturally saw moral decay in the statistics. Moreover, since the figures showed more cases brought against women than men (for example, in 1886, 865 women were accused, as against 822 men [144]), the moralists jumped to the ludicrous conclusion that more women than men committed adultery.[145] The judicial process was partly responsible for this statistical distortion. Men accused of adultery could be pursued legally only if they kept a mistress in their conjugal home, and conviction could result only in a fine. A woman, by contrast, could be convicted on the grounds of compromising letters alone and, if found guilty, could be sent to prison up to two years.[146] This totally different definition of the crime combined with women's greater reluctance to bring a suit in the first place accounted for the apparent superiority of women. The rising statistics were nonetheless grist for the mills of the new social critics who focused on female adultery as the evil of the modern age. In France this new hostility toward women had not been countered as it was in England by a growing and vocal movement against the double sexual standard. The fear of discovery of an illicit sexual liaison was real enough for the respectable English woman, but as a motive for murder it appears to have vanished in England by the last decades of the century.[147]

The motives which led Henriette to the probable affair with the priest in the first place can only be guessed. It is unlikely that she had been one of those "fair penitents" pouring out her secret sins, who had been seduced by her confessor.[148] The image made vivid by Michelet, who attacked priests' power over women only to deliver them to the "rightful" authority of husbands,[149] retained its anticlerical force in this period. But here, at least, the accused woman seems to have adopted a more active role. Hernest claimed he met the Franceys when his bishop, despite knowledge of their cool religious sentiments, sent him to collect money from the couple to help restore the church. (One paper mentions that Bazard had done the restoration, which may have been another opportunity for the architect to observe the couple together.)

It is clear that Paul Francey's role as a modern man of affairs—his business trips and political avocation—left his wife much alone and that she and her husband had different interests. Mme. Francey loved literature and the theater, which her husband disliked. She kept a journal, which she burned during the week before the crime, and was noted by her husband to have a highly sensitive, dramatic nature. The priest, closer to her age and likely to be more interested in literature, was also available during the daytime hours when most men of other professions were hard at work. He had, too, the advantage of being "safe" company, should they be observed together on occasion.

The priest's reported "sweet and inoffensive" manner also suggests that Henriette, with her evident firm resolve, had been the initiator. Her obvious restlessness in a provincial world where her husband intended to establish a political base appears to have made her explore some new opportunities for freedom. Exposed to a wider world through reading and a little travel, she appears to have resented the obligations which kept her too often at home. Admittedly, the only hint of other prior tension with her husband is the revelation that she elected not to attend his sister's wedding, although the fact that she and Paul had had only one child after eight years of marriage may be relevant here. Her husband's support, which included blowing her kisses in the courtroom, may be dismissed as part of the drama they both now had to play. In private correspondence with the investigating authorities Paul Francey showed less enthusiasm for his wife's action and referred sadly to "my unhappy affair." [150]

Henriette's assurance to Bazard in her ultimatum that her husband would surely kill him if he knew of the attempted rape appears in this light to have been a kind of fantasy wish-fulfillment. It is more likely that had he known, his response would have been far less impetuously romantic. A modern professional, he would probably instead have acted discreetly to ensure his own reputation. And had he known of his wife's plans, it is more plausible that like Clovis Hugues, a public figure conscious of guarding a respectable image, he would have attempted to prevent her from carrying out those plans.

Indeed, the fact that the same woman who composed the arch, stylized, and threatening ultimatum was seen joking with its recipient a few days later, together with the tongue-in-cheek response of Bazard himself, demonstrate the extent to which Henriette was self-consciously employing an idiom of stock romantic responses which on one level, she knew, had become laughable. But aware that these still held meaning in a world where men needed more than ever to be assured that their women were righteous and pure, she counted desperately on their being seen as the explanation for her behavior. The same applied, needless to say, to her carefully timed "nervous crises" and "mad laughs."

Yet the fact that Henriette Francey was driven to contrive and carry out a murder as the only escape from discovery and sexual blackmail is a sad measure of the stake she had in preserving reputation and identity. Being an honest woman in the world's eyes was the only glory of a bourgeois wife, and Henriette knew the danger of the "wagging tongues." Moreover, the prospect of secrecy at the price of sexual "favors" became abhorrent to her. If it hardly excused a cold-blooded killing, it made that killing more comprehensible.

Florence Bravo lacked the sense of public identity which ultimately made Henriette Francey see her course so clearly. Still, at age thirty, signing her letters to her parents, "your loving child," Florence was an immature young woman who spent her entire life acting out the role of the helpless charge of parents or parent-substitutes—some cruel, some kind. That she was a victim in many ways is evident enough: manipulated into a hopeless first marriage which she was too terrorized to defy on her own, rescued by a sympathetic "father-doctor" incapable of viewing her as an adult, and then nudged into respectability by a quietly domineering "mother-companion," who persuaded her to marry the only sort of man who by then would have her, someone who was after her fortune. When she was considering remarriage, Florence did at least inform Bravo of the "friendship" with Gully, but doubtless only because he would not have failed to learn of it on his own, given the customary background investigations. The apparent resolve to accept a mature and sober relationship quickly crumbled in the face of problems with which Florence had never had occasion to cope.

That the effort to recover lost respectability foundered on the personal relationship with Charles is unsurprising, for Florence, having already known happiness in the liaison with her doctor, clearly wanted to find happiness in this new relationship which had society's approval, even though she half-expected she would not. She was conscious enough of this desire to mention the words "happy" or "happiness" three times in the brief letter she sent to Bravo in which she weighed his proposal of marriage.[151] Still, despite the compensation of the renewed ties with her family, she realized promptly after committing herself to Charles that mutual happiness was not uppermost in his mind. From the occasion of his scene with her solicitor over the marriage settlement, money and "economy" were constant themes. Bills, investment schemes, and saving money are mentioned in nearly all Charles's letters. Even in his warm reply to Florence's letter about their proposed marriage, he makes disparaging reference to his small income as a barrister. And his friends, too, reported that after marriage he constantly talked about ways to save money.[152] That his tone in references to this and other subjects was not always temperate is also well-established. His stepfather, who was concerned to show Charles in the best light, acknowledged that he had a "quick temper" and "had a rough edge to his tongue when he was put out." [153]

More serious than money matters and temper, however, was the issue of the quality of the couple's personal and sexual relations. In resuming an active sex life, Florence no doubt anticipated or hoped that she would find in Charles as devoted and considerate a lover as she had known in Dr. Gully before her troubles over the abortion or miscarriage. That she still had deep affection for the doctor is evident from her testimony, despite her occasional willingness to participate in the crass insinuations against him which allowed her to emerge as a wronged woman. These remaining feelings toward Gully are most evident in her assertion that she had determined to break with the doctor "long before" she decided to marry Bravo.

> I had not in the slightest grown tired of his [Gully's] society. No one could grow tired of his society, he is so intellectual. . . . I say "carefully and solemnly" that my only motive for this course [breaking with Gully] was to see my mother again, and to make her happy. I was prepared to sacrifice all my happiness to hers. (Here the witness burst into tears.) [154]

The tears for the doctor with whom she had known love were real enough, even though her statement was not precisely true. Florence wanted both happiness and her mother's approval, that is, respectability. She had in fact tired of the doctor somewhat, but largely because the happiness she had possessed with him did not include respectability. With Charles, on the other hand, she discovered too late that she had exchanged a compassionate man for one whose capacity for intimacy was, at best, undeveloped. And it was far from clear that she had got her respectability in the bargain.

That sex lay at the bottom of the motives leading to Charles's death seems clear, though Florence's accusers were so busy looking for the sex outside marriage that they never troubled to consider the sex inside. Had they done so, they might have perceived the fear of the resumption of sexual relations implied in Florence's statement. At the least, they might have pondered the timing of Charles's death, which followed so closely on Florence's recovery from a second miscarriage, along with her evident revulsion toward the "miscarriage" with Gully and her expressions concerning her great pain and suffering at that time.

Indeed, the first miscarriage in January, less than two months after their marriage, was curious in itself and might have prompted them to consider in a different context Mrs. Cox's remark that "Mr. Charles Bravo dined at the Priory before marriage and stopped there all night—his mother objecting to his going home late as he took cold." [155] Was it possible that Bravo, unknown to Mrs. Cox who slept alone on the third floor, had slept with Florence before the marriage? The lady's companion stated that for propriety's sake she had urged the couple to wait until spring to marry, to permit Florence to shore up her respectable credentials with the "ladies" in the neighborhood who, she stated, had gossiped about her mistress and the doctor. Instead, she said, the couple had set a wedding date of December 14 and then, inexplicably, had moved the date up to December 7.[156] It is more than possible that Charles, aware of her affair with Gully, had let Florence know before their marriage that she had no right to withhold from him what she had given to another man in the absence of legal sanction. It is possible, too, that this first "miscarriage" was self-induced; after all she had been through, Florence appreciated the ability of the neighborhood "ladies" to count to nine.

Florence clearly perceived the injustice of Charles's mother's presuming to disapprove of her; she knew that Charles himself had kept a mistress for several years before their marriage. But for a while, at least, she accepted that the rules of society were different for men. By the time of the second miscarriage, however, Florence had come to the decision that she could no longer play by the rules. Tired, disillusioned, frightened, and impulsive, she determined to use tartar emetic. Whether inebriation caused her to use an overdose or whether she intended to kill is impossible to say with certainty. There was in any case enough cause for resentment to make a naive and self-centered woman entertain the belief, at least for the moment, that Charles Bravo "deserved" to die. But Florence, at all events, never found her happiness. She died only two years later in a villa at Southsea, which she had taken under an assumed name. There the "gay widow of Balham," who was not yet thirty-three years of age, drank herself to death; and the press reported in the euphemistic idiom that she had long been "suffering from the effects of an undue amount of stimulants." [157]

Curiously, Florence Bravo's behavior, in its own dark way, was part of the evidence that the women of her day were demanding more from marriage than before, that they were resisting forced sexual relations and seeking closer personal bonds with husbands, that they were asking to be "happy" as well as provided for. Henriette Francey's drama, too, suggests new dissatisfactions with marriages which failed to meet rising expectations for personal satisfaction. But in her case, the turning back was sooner and the transgression of social rules more clandestine and terror-filled. Release of the two women had depended on their ability to satisfy harsh inquiries about moral rather than criminal behavior, and each had been lifted from whore to heroine long enough to escape the charges. In truth, of course, neither Florence Bravo nor Henriette Francey were new women—either scarlet or pure. They were real persons, caught between old imperatives and new options and pathetically unequipped to follow their best impulses.

5.

SEX AND
SHOPKEEPING:

The Cases of
Gabrielle Fenayrou
and Adelaide Bartlett

Gabrielle Fenayrou

ADMITTED OR SUSPECTED adultery on the part of respectable middle-class women was once again the chief popular attraction in two widely publicized murder trials of the 1880s, the trials of Gabrielle Fenayrou and Adelaide Bartlett. The subjects of these cases emerged from considerably more modest circumstances than a Florence Bravo or even an Henriette Francey. Mme. Fenayrou was married to a druggist in Paris who had run into financial difficulties in operating the pharmacy he had purchased from his wife's mother. Mrs. Bartlett was the wife of a somewhat more prosperous tradesman, a grocer who came to enjoy a reported annual income of about three hundred pounds from a chain of six shops which he managed in south London. Each couple had been married over ten years when the women were accused of masterminding bizarre crimes which brought them to trial for murder.[1]

It appeared to be sexual rather than financial matters which prompted the two women's actions. Each was shown to have harbored a deep sexual aversion for her spouse and each admitted spending long hours in the solitary company of men who were not their husbands. Notwithstanding the undeniable interest of the courtroom exploration of extramarital sexual affairs, the cases are most remarkable for the gulf between the views which informed both the legal and popular verdicts on the one side, and the likely facts about the two women's actual sexual motives, as well as their roles in murder on the other. In addition, many of the less spectacular circumstances involved suggest much about the lives of masses of anonymous women of the "middling" middle classes by the end of the century.

On the most obvious level, the sagas of Gabrielle Fenayrou and Adelaide Bartlett as "adulteresses" confirm the view that for the vast majority of the

174

less affluent middle-class wives an extramarital affair was simply out of the question. It entailed nearly insuperable difficulties, which ranged from the psychological to the logistical. Yet aberrant as they may have been in their actual behavior, and obviously in regard to criminal charges as well, the two women exhibited motives which suggest that in their own ways they appreciated the gains in status already achieved by some of the women of their class and sought themselves to assert some of these declared new "rights" in contexts in which the odds were hopelessly against them.

Both women came to resent the fact that they had not seriously been consulted in the choice of their husbands, for by the 1880s, even in France, the approval of the young woman in cases of arranged marriage was standard. Each then felt deprived of the more affectionate companionate marital relationship which was increasingly touted in women's literature and which was becoming more of a reality among their peers.[2] And both women were evidently groping toward ways to assert their authority in sexual relationships, to control their husbands' desires, and to limit their own pregnancies. The facts of their lives which were uncovered in criminal investigations reveal some intriguing national and class differences in coping with these problems and suggest that despite a more timid, indirect, and undoctrinaire approach, women of the less vocal middle-class majority were self-consciously seeking ways to improve their bargaining positions. For these two women, as it turned out, the effort led to death, notoriety, and, in one of the cases, pathetic personal tragedy.

Of the two accused women, Adelaide Bartlett was in several ways the more favored, although the social status she acquired by her marriage was hardly prominent. Her family origins remain mysterious, but the best guess is that she was the illegitimate daughter of a wealthy Englishman and well-born French woman. Born in Orleans in 1856, Adelaide was apparently raised in France by the family of her mother, but all that is known of her early years is that she spent them in a convent. It has been suggested that her father might have been in the entourage of Victoria and Albert during their state visit to France in 1855,[3] but his identity was never revealed. However, his intervention seemed to be signaled by the fact that early in 1886, as soon as Adelaide was suspected of murdering her husband, she had the best legal help available; Edward Clarke was not the sort of counsel normally employed by a person with an annual income of three hundred pounds. In Clarke's autobiography he noted simply that Adelaide was the "unacknowledged daughter of an Englishman in good social position."[4]

In the early 1870s the pretty, dark-eyed Adelaide had been brought to England to complete her education, and she was established modestly with a guardian outside London in Kingston. There she lived in the same rented house as the family of Charles Bartlett, son of a respectable but hardly prosperous cabinetmaker, who had married a widow with a small fortune which he had invested in a real estate business. Living with Charles Bartlett was his youngest brother, Frederick, who was unmarried and as yet unestablished. Adelaide was also introduced to a married sister who lived in Croyden and, in February 1875, to the middle brother, Edwin, who was destined to be her husband.

Ten years older than Adelaide, Edwin was a handsome, rather shy man who had recently entered a partnership in the grocery trade and was coproprietor of two shops. He was known to be a good-humored, healthy outdoorsman, an avid breeder of St. Bernard dogs, a faithful member of a Wesleyan congregation, and a generous man with coins for the needy. Like many persons with ambition and little higher education, Edwin had a reverential regard for learning and, reportedly, an awe for persons who had acquired university degrees. His own talents, however, lay in the more practical affairs of the provisions trade, and he was regarded as a diligent businessman with good prospects.

Adelaide's subsequent lament that she had met her husband "only once before my wedding day" [5] was perhaps less than the truth, for she was prone to self-dramatization, but there can be no question that her marriage was arranged by her guardian before she knew Edwin well. Yet at first a union seemed a bargain for all, or nearly so. For Adelaide's father and the agents who worked for him, it was an opportunity to place the young woman in a respectable situation which would nonetheless be modest enough to guarantee against possible embarrassing revelations of her real identity. For the somewhat diffident Edwin, there was the advantage of an attractive young bride whose French convent upbringing may have made her seem more complaisant, and possibly less threatening, than her English counterparts. More important, there was Adelaide's dowry, which would help Edwin in the next few years to purchase four more grocery shops. As for Adelaide herself, in addition to being "provided for," there was an agreement which guaranteed her continued education. After their marriage in the spring of 1875 she spent a year at a school, Miss Dodd's, in Stoke Newington and at her own request another eighteen months in the Protestant part of a convent school in Belgium. While she was away, she wrote Edwin long devotional letters which delighted him both for their piety and for what he deemed to be their learning.

In 1878, when she returned at age twenty-two to set up housekeeping for good, Adelaide discovered that to be the wife of a hard-working merchant was to spend much of one's time alone. For economy and convenience the couple lived over one of Edwin's shops in south London, and Edwin devoted himself to overseeing his small chain. Six days a week he rose at six-thirty, took a cold bath, breakfasted, and left home by eight. He normally did not return until six, and since the shops remained open in the evenings, he often went back to work after supper until ten o'clock or so. Adelaide, meanwhile, remained at home doing household chores, needlework, or reading, and she seems to have made few friends. Although her English was perfect, Edwin worried that people found her "foreign" and thought her manner off-putting. Adelaide, for her part, once complained to a woman friend that Edwin did not appreciate her embroidery or her musical talents, and she added that her husband left her alone far more than she liked.

Always a cautious man with his money, Edwin spent little on display or entertainment. The couple lived in modest rooms above three different shops in the first seven years, and they only took one extended holiday, a trip to Scotland. Little else is known of their activities in this period, save for the rather curious fact that one or both of them apparently developed what were labeled "strange ideas" about sex. What those ideas were, however, was far from clear, as was the precise nature of the couple's sexual relationship. Since these issues came to be regarded as central to the case, the court was obliged to deal with them, but revelations about the Bartletts' sex life failed to enlighten the court. Numerous witnesses did report that the couple were "living together as husband and wife," though, as the judge rightly observed, such testimony reveals "nothing of what passes in the bedroom." 6

If what happened in the Bartlett bedroom was far from clear, other features of the case seemed less opaque. Most obvious among these was a ripening friendship in the summer of 1885 between the Bartletts and a handsome, but not overly bright twenty-seven-year-old Wesleyan clergyman, the Reverend Mr. George Dyson. The Bartletts first became acquainted with the young man early in 1885 when he came to preach in a chapel near Wimbledon not far from a cottage they had rented. When Dyson made a pastoral call and informed the Bartletts that he was about to go to Trinity College, Dublin, to collect his bachelor's degree, they were impressed and urged the clergyman to visit them frequently. Edwin even engaged him as a tutor for Adelaide in Latin, history, and geography, and thereafter Dyson became a fixture in their household. As the son of a Methodist preacher from a small town, he seems to have been as intrigued by the successful London grocer as Edwin was enchanted to have his own "man of letters." Dyson said he soon came to feel like a brother toward Edwin.

How he came to feel toward Adelaide may have been a different matter. The Bartletts' maid reported that Dyson visited the cottage frequently that summer and stated that by August he dined there three times a week. He continued these visits when the Bartletts took a two-room flat in Pimlico that fall, and the maid who cleaned there did not remember that Dyson carried any books with him on these supposed pedagogical calls. She did state, however, that on one occasion after the preacher's visit she discovered that the curtains in the front room had been pinned together. Another time she entered the room to find Adelaide seated at Dyson's feet with her head on his knee. The clergyman, she recalled, often arrived in the morning and stayed all day, sometimes awaiting Edwin's arrival in the evening. The Bartletts obligingly supplied him with slippers and a comfortable lounging jacket so that he could change out of his clerical garb. It was natural enough to assume that on these visits Dyson shed his clerical manner as well. But he—and Adelaide, too—always denied that their relations had ever been "criminal," that is, adulterous, and perhaps it was so.

Whatever was going on between Adelaide and George that fall was interrupted in early December when Edwin Bartlett suddenly became ill and took to his bed with a most confusing set of symptoms. According to the young physician Adelaide summoned, the patient initially showed signs of mercurial poisoning, though he admitted that Bartlett hotly denied his discreet suggestion that the substance had been taken intentionally as a cure for a venereal infection.[7] Nonetheless, as the symptoms of poisoning receded, Bartlett reportedly developed a peculiar lethargy and even confided his conviction that he was about to die. The doctor was perplexed in view of the fact that Bartlett's only apparent remaining physical complaint was a painful set of gums. These proved to be at least in part the result of the work of an incompetent dentist, who had prepared the grocer for a set of plates by sawing off his teeth at the jaw line, without removing the roots. The doctor promptly arranged for the needed extractions.

By December 31, 1885, the last day of his life, eighteen of the diseased teeth had been extracted and Bartlett, according to his doctor, was showing remarkable progress. His normally robust appetite was back; despite his tender gums, he managed to consume a prodigious dinner and tea which included a jugged hare, a dozen oysters, bread, butter cakes, and a chutney dish. His spirits had obviously returned as well, for he announced his eagerness to get back to work and informed the landlady that now that the days were beginning to get longer, he would want to be called an hour earlier—a remarkable display of zeal given that it had only been just over a week since the shortest day of the year. But Edwin Bartlett did not live to enjoy the large haddock which the landlady said he had ordered with such relish for his breakfast on the first day of the new year.

Adelaide reported that she sat up alone with her husband that New Year's eve and shortly after hearing the celebrations downstairs fell asleep in a chair next to the bed, with her hand on Edwin's foot. Several hours later she awakened, noted a cramp in her hand, and—more to the point—remarked that her husband's foot was cold. Realizing that he was not breathing, she attempted to revive him by pouring brandy down his throat; failing in that, she alerted the landlord and sent for the doctor, who pronounced himself "staggered" to discover that his patient was dead.[8]

The preliminary postmortem revealed a strong odor of chloroform when the deceased's stomach was opened, a fact which appears to have unhinged the Reverend Mr. Dyson when Bartlett's doctor indiscreetly revealed the information to him. The distraught clergyman then confessed to a couple who had known the Bartletts that a few days before Edwin's death, Adelaide had persuaded him to buy a large quantity of liquid chloroform, which she claimed helped her husband ease the pain during the "bad spells" in what she allegedly described as a terminal illness. Dyson declared himself to have been "duped by a wicked woman," [9] and for this ungallant, although ultimately successful attempt to clear himself, he soon became the popular villain of the piece.

Adelaide, meanwhile, emerged as the heroine after confiding to the doctor and later to her lawyer that the real purpose of the chloroform had been to sprinkle on her handkerchief to ward off her husband's sexual advances. Edwin, she explained, was a man with peculiar ideas about sex; he had effectively handed her over to his friend, the Reverend Mr. Dyson, with promises of future physical possession. Then toward the end Edwin had allegedly changed his mind and, abandoning a prior "platonic compact," begun to demand his sexual rights. Adelaide's story was reported at the inquest by her confidant, the doctor. Peculiar as her long account seemed, it gained credibility through partial support from other witnesses. Later in the trial her lawyer, Edward Clarke, made a compelling case for his client's innocence and outdid himself with the suggestion that the deceased, who had emerged as a man of apparently extraordinary personal tastes and behavior, had obligingly swallowed deadly chloroform with the aim of hastening the united bliss of Adelaide and George by removing his superfluous presence.

The jury and public, in this first recorded trial in which liquid chloroform was the agent of death, may have chosen to accept the judge's more plausible theory that Edwin had downed the substance in the belief that it would dull the pain in his jaw and help put him to sleep. At all events, the sympathy for the thirty-year-old accused woman was near universal. Her lawyer was mobbed by enthusiastic crowds when he emerged from the Old Bailey that afternoon in mid-April 1886, and he received a standing ovation that evening when he attended the Lyceum Theater.[10] Adelaide herself was not ungrateful: "Your kind looks [in the courtroom] cheered me very much," she gushed, "for I felt you believed me innocent. I have heard many eloquent Jesuits preach, but I never listened to anything finer than your speech." [11] The irony in her remarks was surely unconscious.

Far less fortunate was Gabrielle Fenayrou, the Parisian druggist's wife, who four years before in August 1882 had been brought to trial as a codefendant charged with murdering a man who was alleged to have been her lover. The state maintained that out of the jealous hatred of abandonment, the thirty-year-old Gabrielle had confessed the love affair to her husband and begged him to kill the man who had been his rival. Then, according to the prosecutor's reconstruction, she had lured the unwitting victim to a deserted rendezvous on the promise of some money, helped her husband kill him, and finally, with the aid of her husband's brother, participated in disposing of the body.

The account of the business was especially grisly, though in some ways the prosecution's case, on the face, was less damaging to Gabrielle Fenayrou than the corresponding case against Adelaide Bartlett. The grocer's wife, after all, had been alone with her husband on the fateful night. And in George

Dyson she had had a plausible motive for willing Edwin's death. Nonetheless, jury and public chose to accept the defendant's view in Adelaide's case, but to side with the prosecution in Gabrielle's, ignoring the plea of the accused that she had been threatened and coerced throughout. It does not appear that the difference lay in Gabrielle's lack of charm. No less a confidant than the Parisian chief of police, Gustave Macé, was evidently smitten with her. The chief, who in his memoirs confessed himself convinced by Gabrielle's story, described the accused as a tall brunette with regular features, a shy manner, eyes which, though ordinarily dull, could "light up like diamonds," and "a smile like that of a child." [12] In her own demure way, then, Mme. Fenayrou appears to have been a *femme fatale*. A photograph of herself which she sent to Macé with an affectionate letter bears out his description.[13]

Born Gabrielle Gibon in 1852, the accused was the younger of two children of a pharmacist who, with his wife, ran a moderately prosperous shop near the Madeleine in the old rue Vignon. Partly because her elder sister had a mental ailment and was placed for a time in an asylum, attention was lavished on the bright young Gabrielle, who received an excellent education which the *Figaro* snootily described as "superior to her condition." [14] Her classmates in the boarding school reportedly "adored" her. The headmistress testified that Gabrielle had been a charming child and a model student; her character may have been a bit weak, but she was incapable of planning the crime with which she was charged.

Mlle. Gibon was only nineteen in 1869 when her father died and her mother assumed temporary proprietorship of the pharmacy. Without a son to take over and with only six months in which to find a legally certified pharmacist, Mme. Gibon naturally thought of their eager shop assistant, a thirty-year-old man from the southern department of Aveyron named Marin Fenayrou, who was completing the obligatory six-year apprenticeship to become a second-class pharmacist. Himself a pharmacist's son, Marin had followed the more traditional and less prestigious route to his vocation, which entailed less formal training and a longer apprenticeship than first-class certification.[15] Though he was reportedly neither handsome nor especially bright, the widow appreciated the advantages of keeping the shop in the family and decided that Fenayrou would be not only an ideal manager, but a fine son-in-law as well. Gabrielle confided to a friend that she found Fenayrou repulsive, but she accepted her mother's decision. As she explained at the trial, "It was a marriage of convenience. My mother was a widow and the shop needed to be run. That was what made me accept the choice that was offered to me." [16] Obviously, there had been no choice involved.

Like Edwin Bartlett, Marin Fenayrou received a dowry, though a more modest one of ten thousand francs. Mme. Gibon also sold him the pharmacy on credit for thirty thousand francs, and he was required only to pay the interest on his debt. He agreed to permit his mother-in-law to live with them on the premises and to continue working in the shop with Gabrielle, but once the marriage contract and bill of sale were complete, he began to fear her influence over her daughter and forced her out. Mme. Gibon took rooms not far away and the estrangement did not last long, since Gabrielle's advancing pregnancy prompted Marin to permit her to spend more time with her mother. Nine months after the marriage Gabrielle had their first child, a boy; a year later she had another son.

At about that time Marin reportedly began to lose interest in the pharmacy, which until then had done well. He drank more, slept late, frequented the cafes, and took money out of the receipts to bet on the horse races. The pharmacy did not go under, however, for in 1873 it acquired a new assistant in the twenty-one-year-old Louis Aubert. Son of a grocer and dry goods merchant from Normandy, Aubert had left seminary to move to Paris and train for pharmacy. According to friends he was far from handsome, and his difficulties in passing the three examinations necessary for second-class certification suggest that he was not very bright either. But the young man had a kind of brash charm. The decision to abandon training for the priesthood recommended him to the outspokenly anticlerical Marin, who urged Aubert to consider himself a member of the family. The new assistant was soon affectionately referring to the Fenayrous as "little mother" and "little father." [17] He was aware that he captivated Gabrielle and he knew how to use her weakness for him to get money from her whenever he needed it. Moreover, since as an apprentice he lived at the shop and took his meals there, Louis spent many hours alone with Gabrielle. Neighbors later claimed that the developing relationship between them was obvious.

By 1878 Marin had apparently at last begun to harbor some suspicion of the pair. He also seems to have detected a plot between Aubert and his mother-in-law to try to sell the pharmacy to the young assistant, who complained that Fenayrou's refusal to advertise and modernize the shop with new sales techniques was ruining business. After a series of fights Aubert was fired late in 1879. Marin later claimed the disagreements were over purely professional matters, but at the same time he fired Aubert he also forbade Gabrielle to go out without his permission or to visit her friend, Aubert's sister, who allegedly had offered her apartment for the couple's rendezvous.

Aubert reportedly continued to see Gabrielle until as late as the summer of 1881, but he ultimately seems to have followed the advice of friends, who warned him that he must end his liaison with Mme. Fenayrou if he wished to establish both credit and respectability. In the meantime he had used a modest inheritance and loans from his sister to purchase a small, run-down pharmacy on the Boulevard Malesherbes. By late 1881, after he had begun to get established, he started the search for a wealthy bride and placed the following notice in the *Petit Journal:* "Pharmacist, thirty years old, would marry young woman twenty to twenty-five years old with fortune." [18] Aubert's assistant reported that he received over thirty replies, many from rich widows, but the ambitious young man never had the opportunity to make his choice. In late

May 1882 a fisherman discovered his body floating in the Seine; the skull had been crushed and there were stab wounds in the chest.

Aubert's grief-stricken sister identified the body and told the police what she knew about her brother and the Fenayrous. The police called on the couple, who at first presented a plausible picture of innocence. However, suspicion was aroused when Marin's brother, who had also moved to Paris and was a building laborer, confirmed that Marin had learned recently of his wife's infidelity with Aubert. The authorities decided to arrest the couple and Gabrielle, who was escorted separately by the chief of police, confessed that she had had a part in the crime: "I am in fact a criminal; since [your arrival] this morning I have done nothing but lie.... I have had enough.... I am suffering too much." [19]

Neither Adelaide Bartlett nor Gabrielle Fenayrou entered marriage with illusions about their husbands and both accepted their situations with outward resignation. Adelaide professed that her entire youth had been one of repression and frustration, which is not unlikely given the secrecy over her illegitimate status, so her initial acceptance of Edwin Bartlett was unsurprising. She was to announce later, "I was a consenting party to this marriage contract and felt bound by it and never complained, although when I agreed to the terms it proposed, I did not understand what they meant." [20] Gabrielle, for her part, had allegedly admitted to a girl friend before her marriage, "No, he is not the husband I dreamed of. I will be unhappy for the rest of my life." [21] The absence of options was clear enough in both cases. It was also clear that the two women found additional grievance in their own evident social superiority to their husbands, a superiority only partially compensated for by the ten-year age advantage the men possessed in each marriage.

The picture of Marin Fenayrou which emerges from the trial accounts is naturally fuller and more consistent than that of Edwin Bartlett, since Marin himself was a defendant. It is easy to see why the pharmacist was hardly the sort to appeal to a well-educated Parisian *bourgeoise*. The *Figaro* described him unkindly as a rude and unattractive peasant type with an unkempt beard and outlandish clothes which instantly gave him away, despite his claim to the title of "monsieur." [22] Another journalist, with characteristic French flair for finding the literary character in life, announced that Fenayrou was a new Homais, straight out of *Madame Bovary*.[23] But this comparison gave the man both too much and too little credit. Like Homais, Fenayrou was a provincial druggist and an anticlerical, but he had little of Homais's pretentiousness and nothing of his enthusiastic but uncomprehending faith in modernity. Marin was a man who was accustomed to the slower provincial life and who, transplanted to Paris, never quite adjusted.

To his younger brother Lucien, who had followed him to the capital, taken unskilled laborer's work, and married a working-class woman, Marin was a kind of demigod who had won bourgeois respectability. But in fact he was a rather lost and pathetic man, whose compensations included betting, beer-drinking, and bullying his new wife. Like most males of the Parisian shopkeeping classes, he had supported the uprising of the city's Commune in the wake of the Franco-Prussian war of 1870, but this in no way implied a progressively tinged spirit. Moreover, it had had the effect at the outset of his marriage of alienating him further from his still pious and conservative wife and mother-in-law, the latter of whom confessed that she had enraged Marin by shutting herself away for the duration of the upheaval. The pharmacist nonetheless displayed a simple and touching fondness for his family; and in court he would sob that he had loved Aubert, the assistant who betrayed him, as he would have his own son. In his way, too, he seems to have loved Gabrielle, although he sensed that she regarded him with distaste. Friends found him proud, naive, and emotional. One complained that he cheated at cards, another that he had a violent temper.

Edwin Bartlett also appears to have been a naive sort, at least in his relations with Adelaide, whose background and education clearly impressed him. Yet in professional matters Edwin, unlike Marin, was without question the model of the rising modern business manager: he was thrifty, attended chapel regularly, and was concerned about getting ahead. An incredibly hard worker, Bartlett had almost no social life and reportedly was an extremely moderate drinker. He conscientiously read trade journals and sought to adapt new sales techniques to his business. To all appearances Edwin was the embodiment of that pious, temperate, and industrious masculine paragon described by Samuel Smiles in his popular success manual, *Self-Help*. But that paragon, while considerably removed from the artless, provincial bumpkin, was no more calculated to inspire romantic flutterings in the breast of a young convent-educated woman.

To be sure, far from bullying his new wife, Bartlett cheerfully encouraged her intellectual and musical interests. He even bought her a piano, which was extravagant for one with his economical habits, but he seems to have appreciated the potential business advantage of an "accomplished" woman. Adelaide herself later complained that Edwin wished her to become "very learned in all subjects," [24] so that she could impress his friends. She had the requisite leisure, for the Bartletts, unlike the Fenayrous, were able to adopt the newer middle-class lifestyle enjoyed by more affluent tradesmen, whose wives no longer worked in the shops but remained at home. For Adelaide, however, this arrangement provided a very cramped stage, especially since their living accommodations throughout their marriage were mostly rented quarters above Edwin's shops. Whether she was ever content to follow her husband's scheme for occupying her time is unclear, but the trial records suggest that from the beginning she had some plans of her own.

It was true that Adelaide did not meet George Dyson until 1885, ten years after her marriage, but the testimony of Edwin's father raised the possibility of a prior liaison of some sort with a man she had known before she met Edwin—none other than Edwin's younger brother, Frederick. Adelaide and Frederick were closer in age, but when they first met Frederick was not yet "established." Mr. Bartlett senior explained that suspicions had arisen back in 1878, soon after her return from boarding school in Belgium. Adelaide reportedly had been enraged with Edwin for failing to consult her before inviting his father, then newly widowed, to live with them. According to the father Adelaide, upon learning the news, suddenly left home without saying where she was going. Edwin then checked with his elder brother, Charles, in Kingston, who reported the disturbing news that her absence coincided with the mysterious disappearance of their younger brother Frederick. To make matters worse, Adelaide had made a previous visit to an "aunt" which, it was realized, coincided with another of Frederick's odd disappearances.

Adelaide finally reported her whereabouts, which were never revealed in the inquiry, but she held out a while before returning home. She agreed to a truce with her resident father-in-law, but a few months later, when he accused her of having run off with Frederick, she insisted that he sign a formal apology for his charges. Bartlett senior did so in the presence of Edwin's solicitor, but when the document was produced in court, he admitted that he remained convinced of her infidelity and that he signed only to make peace in the family. His reasons may have been more self-interested, in that signing was likely to have been Adelaide's condition for his remaining with them. He did continue to live with Edwin and Adelaide for five years, although his relations with his daughter-in-law were never cordial. As for Frederick Bartlett, he was alleged to have taken a boat for America upon learning of the suspicions about his absences. Whether the agents for Adelaide's father had a hand in setting these things straight is unknown, but likely. Adelaide, for her part, never tried to run away again.

Startling as this surprise revelation appeared, it was unproved, and it came early enough in proceedings that were full of surprises for Adelaide's lawyer to divert attention from it. Yet if, contrary to all the plans made for her, she had managed such a liaison with Frederick, she must have realized that the risk of eventual discovery was monumental. That Adelaide was willing to undertake that risk suggested both considerable sangfroid and a strongly developed sense of righteous indignation over the forced marriage, which owed much to her sense of her own socially superior origins. Yet even given these "assets" in her struggle against that marriage, what is evident is the restriction of her options. First, the choice of Frederick was itself dictated by Adelaide's very narrow world; he was literally the only single man other than Edwin that she had had the occasion to get to know. Second, after running away on impulse, she was bound to give herself up, since neither she nor Frederick had an independent source of funds. If she had been permitting the young man to visit her in their flat during the daytime, her furious outburst at the prospect of her father-in-law's moving in and cramping their style might be explained.

Inquiries about her activities in the interim of seven years before the meeting with Dyson, gave no hint that Adelaide undertook further extramarital adventures. What did emerge from questioning about these years was the image of a peculiar sexual regimen in the Bartlett household which, if true, went far to explain the reported odd goings-on there, including the alleged affair with Frederick which Adelaide always denied. When a detailed account came out after Edwin's death, it began to seem plausible that the apparently humdrum grocer had had some very strange notions indeed. Adelaide confided the main outlines of the disturbing story to the physician who had tended Edwin in his last illness, and this man, the young Doctor Leach, repeated the account at the inquest.

The most intriguing feature of Leach's testimony was Adelaide's alleged statement that she had lived ten years of married life under a platonic compact, according to her husband's wishes. That compact, moreover, reportedly had been broken on only one occasion when, as Adelaide had romantically put it, "there came into my heart the wish that I too might be a mother, and have a child at my knee to love me. And on my entreaty, my husband broke the compact that had been made, once and once only." [25] The alleged single occasion of sexual intercourse had resulted in a pregnancy, but unfortunately the child, delivered late in 1881, was stillborn.

Adelaide had further explained to the doctor that Edwin believed every man really ought to have two wives: one for companionship and the other for the more mundane business of running his home and bearing his children. Her husband had chosen her for the role of platonic companion, she said, and outlandish as it seemed, the story was at least partly corroborated by two other witnesses. His own father and the clergyman Dyson both admitted that Edwin had discussed with them the idea that a man might have two wives and divide their roles as Adelaide indicated. His father, to be sure, insisted that Edwin had merely been joking, but the clergyman stated that on one occasion Bartlett was serious enough to inquire whether the Bible strictly forbade polygamy.

In addition to this testimony, much was made of the discovery in the Bartletts' rooms of a copy of a book called *Esoteric Anthropology (The Mysteries of Man): A Comprehensive and Confidential Treatise on the Structure, Functions, Passional Attractions and Perversions, True and False Physical and Social Conditions, and the Most Intimate Relations of Men and Women.* [26] The judge called it "garbage" which "under the garb of ostentatious purity, obtains entrance, probably, into many a household from which it would be otherwise certain to be banished." He suggested that Edwin, as the book's owner, had been incautious enough to leave the book where Adelaide would find it, and that reading it caused her so far to abandon a "woman's natural instincts" [27] as to pass it on to a friend—who reportedly had promptly returned it upon discovering the contents. But despite such tantalizing references, which the *Times* and most other papers saw fit to excise from their accounts of the case, *Esoteric Anthropology* is no pornographic thriller. First published in 1853 by an American doctor, Thomas Low Nichols, the book is a rambling tract on health, harmony, and the relations between the sexes. Like many of the publications in the free-love movement, it is far from prescribing unlimited sexual relations, despite its approval for some liaisons outside monogamous marriage.[28] It recommends that ideally a couple should have intercourse only when they want children and that at other times they should practice abstinence, which it claims is "easily done by most women and by many men." [29] Nichols provides detailed, but hardly titillating descriptions of the birth control methods and devices he condemns, but he seems to have been quite sincere in declaring that the use of means other than abstinence to prevent conception is not morally justifiable, except in situations in which a woman is "compelled to submit to the embrace of her husband while her health or other conditions for[bid] her to have children." [30] Just how the Bartletts adopted these precepts, if indeed they did, was far from obvious, but the presence of the book appeared to corroborate Adelaide's narrative to the doctor.

Most importantly, Edwin's peculiar tastes were held to account for the known details in the strange business of the preacher George Dyson. Adelaide, as her doctor-confidant explained, had related that in the last weeks of his life Edwin had shown signs of a desire to abandon their platonic compact. By then Adelaide was prepared to object, she said, though her explanation was nearly as astonishing as the alleged compact itself. She reported that she refused her husband's new sexual demands since by then he himself had already abandoned his rights to her and turned her over to the Methodist minister. And, as the sympathetic Doctor Leach stated:

> Mrs. Bartlett felt it her duty to her womanhood and to the man to whom practically she was affianced at her husband's wish to resist this change of manner in her husband, and she told him that as he had encouraged her to look with affection and expectation to another man, it was right that things should remain as for years they had been.[31]

Curious as it all seemed, the evident coziness between the minister and the grocer's wife toward the end of 1885 apparently had the grocer's blessing. In September the Bartletts had taken a holiday in Dover and young "Georgius Rex," as Dyson was known in their household, visited them twice at their expense. He admitted that in the meantime he wrote to Adelaide, and she to him, as often as two or three times daily. Unfortunately none of this correspondence survives, save for a poem which George composed and dedicated to Adelaide. The verses hardly suggest an undiscovered poetical genius, but they do indicate the quality of Dyson's attachment.

> Who is it that hath burst the door
> Unclosed the heart that shut before
> And set her queenlike on its throne
> And made its homage all her own—My Birdie.[32]

Dyson was uncomfortably aware that some low-minded persons might be less than willing to believe that Edwin endorsed these exchanges of sentiment, so he supplied a rather remarkable letter which Edwin had sent to him from Dover during that time, which at least suggested that it was so.

14 St. James St., Dover
Monday, 22 September 1885

Dear George,

Permit me to say I feel great pleasure in thus addressing you for the first time. To me it is a privilege to think that I am allowed to feel toward you as a brother, and I hope our friendship may ripen as time goes on, without anything to mar its future brightness. Would that I could find words to express my thankfulness to you for the very loving letter you sent Adelaide to-day. It would have done anybody good to see her overflowing with joy as she read it while walking along the street, and afterwards as she read it to me. I felt my heart going out to you. I long to tell you how proud I feel at the thought I should soon be able to clasp the hand of the man who from his heart could pen such noble thoughts. Who can help loving you? I felt that I must say two words, "thank you," and my desire to do so is my excuse for troubling you with this. Looking towards the future with joyfulness, I am, yours affectionately, Edwin.[33]

In his own defense Dyson admitted that he confessed to Edwin that there was, in his words, "no denying the fact that I was growing attracted to her [Adelaide], and that I wished to let him know it, that it was disturbing me in my work, and I asked whether it would not be better for me to discontinue my friendship with them." [34] According to the minister Edwin had assured him that he was a benefit to Adelaide, that she was "a better and nobler woman" [35] since she had known him.

Still, the accounts of Dyson and Mrs. Bartlett were not identical on all points. Dyson emphatically denied any knowledge of the platonic compact and said that Adelaide had never been "given" to him by Edwin. He also contested Adelaide's statement that Edwin had often requested the pair to kiss or embrace before him, though he did admit that he actually had kissed Mrs. Bartlett in her husband's presence. He also acknowledged that there was a general understanding that if anything happened to Edwin, he and Adelaide might, as he put it, "come together." [36] To demonstrate the nature of this understanding, Dyson recalled that on one occasion when Edwin had been finding fault with Adelaide over some small matter, he, Dyson, had said half-seriously, "If ever she comes under my care, I shall have to teach her differently." [37] Edwin had allegedly replied that no doubt George would take good care of Adelaide.

There was a more serious discrepancy between the accounts of George and Adelaide in the matter of Edwin's health. Dyson reported that when he had asked Mrs. Bartlett why Edwin seemed so interested in their being together, she had replied that her husband wanted a guardian for her who would protect her after he was gone, since he knew that he was a dying man. She explained that Edwin had been suffering from an "internal complaint" for five or six years and had received a written diagnosis from Dr. Nichols, author of *Esoteric Anthropology*, which predicted that he had no more than a year to live. Several witnesses confirmed that Edwin occasionally made oblique references to his imminent death. Curiously, though, Adelaide later denied that she had ever told Dyson her husband was dying. One of them was clearly not telling the truth, and both of them had motives not to do so. However, what stood out in each of their accounts were not the discrepancies, but instead the remarkable picture of Edwin Bartlett as a most peculiar man.

The catalogue of Edwin's alleged oddities would not be complete without reference to the strange behavior recorded by his physician during his illness in December 1885. In addition to the morbid references to his own death, Edwin showed an extraordinary reluctance to get out of bed or to contemplate going out, even when the doctor assured him that his recovery was nearly complete. He had long fits of despondency and cried a great deal; Adelaide maintained that on one occasion he cried for an hour and then explained that it was because he was so happy. The doctor finally became convinced that he was dealing with a victim of hysteria.[38]

Edwin also seems to have been attracted to popular notions of animal magnetism. On one occasion, when the doctor inquired whether he had slept well, Edwin replied:

I could not sleep; I was nervous and restless when I saw my wife asleep in the easy chair, so I got up and went and stood over her like this [holding up his hands] . . . for two hours, I felt the magnetic fluid being drawn from her to me, through my fingertips, and after that I lay down and slept.[39]

Another time Edwin confided to the doctor his belief that both he and his wife were under mesmeric influence, but Leach reported that he persuaded his patient that it could not be so. Still, Leach himself confessed that Edwin was so impressionable that he could not resist trying hypnosis on him for some tooth extractions. He reported that on the way to the dentist's he kept repeating to the patient that there would be no pain, that the sensation would be almost pleasurable. Edwin, who under normal circumstances refused to let anyone but his wife touch him, allegedly settled back and relaxed during the visit, and the teeth "flew out."[40]

As detail upon strange detail was added to the portrait of the deceased, it began to appear that Edwin, and not Adelaide, was on trial. The grocer's wife commanded sympathy as the helpless victim of a husband who had corrupted her mind by forcing her to read filthy literature and then compromised her respectability by throwing her into the arms of another man. This was the line of defense followed by her counsel Clarke and it worked. Of course part of the reason it worked was that it helped explain the curious mode of death. Only a very strange man, it was thought, would ever swallow caustic liquid chloroform under any circumstances. But more important, the defense worked because everyone, or practically everyone, wanted very much to believe it, including Edward Clarke himself. Evidence to the contrary was hardly absent; indeed, in the course of their investigations many agents of the law stumbled over that evidence, only to pick themselves up briskly and totter on. But not until recent years, when the spell of Victorian explanation has finally broken, has the case been reconstructed in close to the way it probably happened. In the process the grocer Edwin Bartlett has lost his exotic tinge and recovered most of his original drab hues. As will be seen, he was probably not so peculiar after all.

Although Gabrielle Fenayrou may have had a less eventful introduction to married life than Adelaide Bartlett, she soon made up for lost time. It was true that she maintained that her affair with the shop assistant Louis Aubert did not begin until 1879, nine years after her marriage, but numerous witnesses, with justification, dated it much earlier, some as far back as 1873, the year Aubert was hired and her second child was still an infant. Unlike Adelaide then, Gabrielle readily admitted the existence of a lover; she even gratuitously volunteered the fact that for a time there had been a second lover as well.

Of course, in the case of Aubert denial would have been pointless. The Fenayrous' world, unlike the Bartletts', was a close-knit one of interlocking business and family relationships, one in which Gabrielle's activities were bound to be more public. The area in the Madeleine *quartier* where they lived was noted to be one of those which retained much of the traditional style of urban life, a stable neighborhood in which the tradesmen's families saw one another both professionally and socially and where shops regularly passed down from father to son.[41] The Fenayrous' neighbors, with perhaps pardonable exaggeration, reported that Gabrielle's relations with Aubert were known throughout the entire *quartier*. Adelaide Bartlett, by contrast, knew few of her husband's associates, never worked in any of his shops, and moved four times in ten years of marriage—all of which made her better placed to hide an adulterous affair and, if required, to claim a pure reputation, which in her case was even grudgingly acknowledged by the prosecution. The clients' neighbors, relatives, and other shop assistants crowded into Gabrielle's daily life made it not merely difficult to conduct a discreet affair, as it was in Adelaide's case, but well nigh impossible. Privacy was always at a premium; her brother-in-law testified that on one occasion he had discovered her kissing Aubert in the back of the pharmacy. Clearly, the anonymity upon which Adelaide Bartlett could rely was not yet a reality for women such as Gabrielle Fenayrou.

These circumstances of a more public life doubtless ordinarily worked to ensure the marital fidelity of shopkeepers' wives, but in Gabrielle's case there were unusual conditions. Most obvious were the extraordinary absences of her husband, who normally would have been on the premises. In addition there were the admitted guilt feelings of her mother, who came to share her daughter's repugnance for Marin and who later pleaded that Gabrielle had committed "mistakes she would never have done, as daughter of her father and as my daughter, had I not myself arranged her marriage for her." [42] Mme. Gibon was probably as concerned for the pharmacy's well-being as she was for her daughter's happiness, but she did facilitate matters for Gabrielle by condoning the relationship with Aubert, approving his innovations in the pharmacy, and even babysitting for her grandsons so that Gabrielle and the young man could be alone.

Gabrielle's other confidant, her only close female friend, was Aubert's sister, Mme. Barbey, who had married a bank employee and lived not far away. It was natural that the two women became friendly and natural too that Gabrielle should share with Mme. Barbey her dissatisfaction with Marin and her affair with Aubert. In 1877 Aubert invited the Fenayrous to join him and the Barbeys on a visit to his mother in Normandy. Madame Aubert reportedly noticed the way things were between Gabrielle and her son and was so disturbed that she cut the visit short. Mme. Barbey, however, was more understanding. She not only approved the liaison, but also made her apartment in Paris available to the pair.

In Gabrielle's case, as in Adelaide's, the court never managed to solve the puzzle of the probable motives, either sexual or criminal, of the accused. And, as with Adelaide, the defense appealed to the husband's allegedly peculiar sexual tastes, although here too their precise nature, if less exotic, was unclear. To the judge the pharmacist's wife complained vaguely that she and Marin "did not understand one another" and added, "I was loving and affectionate, whereas he was cold." [43] Other witnesses, however, testified that it was Marin who labeled Gabrielle "cold," that he even alleged that this temperament of hers was what had made him disbelieve earlier stories that his wife had a lover.[44] Acquaintances, however, suggested that Marin knew of Aubert's attraction to Gabrielle and was willing to exploit it to get Aubert's labor in the shop as cheaply as possible. Toward the end, indeed, Aubert's salary was discontinued, and although Gabrielle managed to give him small sums on the side, as far as Marin knew he was only receiving room and board.

While Gabrielle did not directly accuse her husband of "giving" her to another man, as Adelaide had done, she suggested that Marin's behavior showed that he effectively did so. Her lawyer, like Adelaide's, argued initially that his client had been a mere passive agent. Aubert was painted as the "angel of darkness who insinuated himself into the household of respectable people," [45] and Gabrielle was pictured as the disappointed but still loyal young wife, who was taken suddenly and, according to the account, in a state of semiconsciousness.

Aubert did not possess her without a fight: one day he surprised her before she had finished dressing. Still damp with moisture of sleep, she defended herself; but he overcame her; and when she recovered, Gabrielle did not know what had happened.[46]

Pushing her seducer away, she then allegedly rushed to her husband, pleaded with him never to leave her alone again, and begged him to take her with him to the theater every night. Marin callously replied that she could go along by herself if she wished, that his only interest was in the horse races. It was an account worthy of sensational popular fiction, and Gabrielle may indeed have found her inspiration for the tale in such literature. But the large numbers of women in the chamber were reported visibly moved when Gabrielle's counsel invited his listeners to imagine the bitterness in his client's heart over her husband's cruel response.

Arguing that Gabrielle had initially revered her husband, her lawyer related that she used to try to encourage him to "more noble ambitions" [47] by putting a little red rosette like that worn by members of the Academy into the lapel of his frock coat. He said she even tried to learn Latin, so that she could read prescriptions as well as her husband and "raise herself to the heights of what she called, in her naivete, the genius of Fenayrou." [48] As he said this, he smiled indulgently at his client, who nodded vigorously in assent. "Ah, poor woman!" [49] he intoned.

All this was obviously a crude effort to discount the impression that Gabrielle had from the beginning flaunted her social and intellectual superiority to her husband, a trait not inclined to win her sympathy with an all-male jury. But the impression was probably justified. Marin's younger brother explained in an interview after the trial that Gabrielle had been too proud to associate with them, since his wife, Amélie, was only a working woman. (He added proudly that Amélie had "more worth in her little finger than his sister-in-law had in her whole body." [50]) The alleged Latin study, too, was sheer nonsense. The Latin required of pharmacists was minimal, and Gabrielle, who had studied not only that language but English and German as well, was doubtless more competent in it than Marin.

The defense ploy is intriguing in that while it underlines the need to present the defendant acknowledging her own inferiority to her husband, it also admits the justice in the plea of women that husbands should entertain themselves in their wives' and families' company and not in that of other men at such places as racetracks and bars. The pressure to persuade husbands to abandon old patterns of socializing without their women may well have come largely from the women themselves, imbued with the message of domesticity and their own new self-confidence. But this bourgeois lifestyle was beyond Marin.

At the trial, where he was faced with accounting for Gabrielle's continuing affair after the seduction, her lawyer produced an argument which again fell wide of the probable truth, but which was remarkable for its expression of medical arguments about female sexuality. Though reported to be obviously ill at ease, the lawyer revealed the fact that at the time Gabrielle had had her second child ten years before in 1872, she was told by her doctor that a third pregnancy might well kill her. Her husband, he said, had "spared" Gabrielle to protect her life, but he added:

> deprived of certain pleasures, she suffered, and the mind becomes troubled when the senses have not been satisfied. It is a well-known fact in medicine: how many women have gone mad because they could no longer be "wives" in the fullest sense of the term.[51]

Unable then to be a mother again, Gabrielle, in this account, became mystical and strange. Her "moral level" sank, though through no fault of her own, and she had an adulterous love affair. Then, when her husband found out, Gabrielle felt utterly bound to obey his orders to help him take revenge against her lover. She could have resisted her husband's demands, said her lawyer, only if she were "pure."

It was not a coherent defense, but it was remarkable for undertaking to argue that women both enjoy and need sex, even if that argument was mixed together, doubtless intentionally, with the more traditional statement of women's need for maternity. Arguments for women's sexual enjoyment had in fact been appearing in health literature and in marriage manuals since mid-century and before.[52] At least one handbook which stressed this need in women had gone through over a hundred and seventy printings since it first appeared in 1848.[53] Still, such views continued to meet overwhelming prejudices in both sexes, and the fact that they were presented in her behalf does not appear to have helped Gabrielle's cause. Nonetheless, that they should have been raised at all does suggest that the climate of opinion was slowly changing.

In Gabrielle's particular case, however, sexual deprivation was an unlikely explanation for her behavior, one which her lawyer appears to have constructed on the basis of some partial truths which she supplied. It was no doubt true that her second pregnancy, following so close on the first, was a difficult one and also that a decision was made not to have any more children. Gabrielle, in conveying this information to her lawyer, may well have led him to believe that their sexual relations then stopped altogether, since, as a practicing Catholic, she would have felt obliged not to admit the more likely situation, namely, that she and Marin began to use some form of birth control.

Some confirmation that sexual relations did continue, as well as further clues to her own sexual attitudes, appear in the memoirs of Gustave Macé, the police chief who was Gabrielle's confidant, although these memoirs were not published until years after the trial. As one who got to know her fairly well,

Macé provides information which is trustworthy, and he reports that Gabrielle told him that once in 1881 when Marin contracted a venereal ailment, he for a time suspected that he had got it from her via Aubert.[54] Whether he had or not, the story bears out the view that Marin and Gabrielle had continued to have sexual relations. Indeed, Macé makes a convincing case that it was not sexual deprivation which troubled Gabrielle, but instead the brutal coupling which passed for love-making on her husband's part. She alleged that Marin constantly demanded "the husband's rights" and that he had forced her to commit acts which, in Macé's words, "were only practiced by degraded prostitutes." [55] At the least, it is likely that Marin, a rather rough and unsophisticated sort, was incapable of responding to Gabrielle's need for some subtlety in sexual relations. Macé acknowledged that Gabrielle had dreamed of more "poetry and tenderness," and he included Gabrielle's surprising confidence that even Aubert had been far from "ideal," that he had been "almost as carnal as Fenayrou." [56]

Although Macé did not testify in the case, the proceedings alone contained more than sufficient evidence against the simple view that Gabrielle had turned to Aubert because she was a licentious and base woman. Nonetheless, the prosecution's case for her having masterminded Aubert's murder proceeded from this view, and it did not help her that she had volunteered the name of a second lover who, when summoned, duly admitted that he had had sexual relations with the accused woman. Still, the testimony of that man made it obvious that far from being enthusiastic about sex, Gabrielle may well have had an aversion to it.

The young man in question was a handsome twenty-seven-year-old blond journalist named Grousteau, who, as one paper noted, may have appealed to Gabrielle because he had about him no pharmaceutical odors. Secretary of the racing sheet *Le Jockey,* Grousteau had met Fenayrou at the track and was invited to the druggist's for dinner on several occasions. Grousteau reported that he soon came to pity Gabrielle, who poured out to him the story of her unhappy marriage. She complained, he said, that Marin was a gross man who had never understood her and whom she had never loved. Grousteau described Gabrielle as "a woman without material needs who had a loving, expansive and idealistic nature." [57] According to the young man, she had "suffered a good deal and was looking elsewhere for the happiness which her husband had failed to give her." [58] In November 1880 they became lovers, Grousteau said, but sexually she was "extremely cold" and they did not often make love. What she wanted from him, he stated, was "affection, consolation and encouragement." [59] She knew that he had another mistress, but this did not bother her.

> She came to me chiefly in order to abandon herself to the emotional outpourings she needed, and which she was unable to have with her husband. . . . She often said to me, "I wish so much that you could be my brother, so that you might be my supporter." [60]

Grousteau and Gabrielle exchanged letters (Gabrielle used a general delivery address at a nearby post office). Occasionally she visited her lover early in the morning, while Marin was sleeping off the effects of the previous night's drinking. At other times meetings were facilitated by the unsuspecting Marin, who used to send Gabrielle to Grousteau for information on the day's betting odds at the track. The journalist admitted that after a time he found Gabrielle's behavior "embarrassing" and that late in 1881 he picked a quarrel with Marin in order to disengage himself from her. The description of the break underlined the dependency of Gabrielle's emotional attachments upon her lover's ties with her husband. Grousteau knew that if he stopped seeing Marin, Gabrielle would no longer be able to visit him so easily and would draw the appropriate conclusions.

Grousteau's credible testimony did not change the state's conviction that Gabrielle was "coquettish, provocative and debauched," [61] and the public prosecutor was undeterred in his attempts to find proof for this conviction. However, witnesses' statements proved disappointing. The prosecutor did manage to find a pharmacist's assistant employed by Fenayrou who stated in preliminary questioning that Gabrielle had appeared in his bedroom on more than one occasion in a nightdress with her breasts partly exposed. At the trial, however, this star witness, perhaps stung in conscience by Gabrielle's presence in the courtroom, felt obliged to amend his testimony. It was only fair to add, he said, that on the occasions in question Gabrielle had been on her way to the bathroom, which could be reached only through his bedroom! Gabrielle interjected that the young man had in fact tried to take advantage of her when he lived with them. Acknowledging as much, the witness replied, "Well after all, one has to seize opportunities whenever possible." [62] The general hilarity which greeted this remark underlined the hardiness of the double standard. A man was awarded with approving laughter for acknowledging behavior which in the case of a woman was being sought as *prima facie* evidence of guilt for murder.

The government succeeded in demonstrating only that Gabrielle was a woman who liked attention, enjoyed pretty clothes, and appreciated the sympathy of men. No one could be found to say that she was not a loving and attentive mother, although two persons charged that she encouraged the boys to scorn their father, and it was duly recorded that one of these had seen the children thumbing their noses at Marin behind his back. None of the testimony proved the contention that Gabrielle was "debauched," but such testimony was not needed since jury, press, and public were content to accept her licentiousness on faith.

The suggestion that Gabrielle was behind the plot and that she had confessed to adultery in order to incite Marin to kill her ungrateful lover emerged long before the trial as the most popular explanation and gained credence thereafter, even though not one witness was able to provide supportive evidence. French opinion appeared as eager to convict Gabrielle

Fenayrou as English opinion, four years later, was to release Adelaide Bartlett. Clearly, the fact that Gabrielle had confessed to adultery, while Adelaide had not, explained much of this response. But that both courts seemed willfully blind to counterevidence for Gabrielle's leading role in murder, on the one hand, and Adelaide's complete innocence, on the other, can be explained only by first considering the probable action and motives of the accused women.

It will be recalled that the thrust of Adelaide's defense was the demonstration of the apparent peculiarities of the deceased grocer: his penchant for platonic compacts, his fits of despondency and crying, his dabbling in animal magnetism, and his taste for free-love literature. Here, if anywhere, was a man who would drink liquid chloroform. Still, in the course of the coroner's inquest and the trial there developed a set of discrepancies and loose ends, as well as some more substantial items, which ought to have strained credibility more than they did.

Among the obvious items was the implausibility of Adelaide's contention that her pregnancy was the result of a single act of sexual intercourse, an act which she also advertised as the only occasion of copulation in eleven years of marriage. Then, too, there was the oddity of the double personality of Edwin. The eccentric domestic image hardly matched the sober, stereotypical business one. If Adelaide, George, and the young Dr. Leach found the grocer a rather vague man with strange ideas, others did not. His father, admittedly a biased witness, insisted that Edwin was normally "bright" and "sharp," that he rarely read books, cared nothing for mesmerism, and was "wrapped up in his business." [63] His partner of more than a dozen years agreed that Edwin was devoted to the business. A former neighbor who had known the Bartletts for more than three years testified that he "did not notice anything peculiar about his [Edwin's] ideas." [64] Adelaide herself once remarked to Dr. Leach during one of her husband's lethargic periods, "You would not think seeing him that he rules a staff of employees, kindly and conscientiously, but with unequalled firmness." [65] It was a statement worth pondering.

More sinister, but practically ignored, was the matter of Edwin's will. According to the nurse who had tended her in her delivery in 1881 and subsequently remained on friendly terms with her, Adelaide had complained late in 1884 that her husband's will permitted her to enjoy rights as heir only if she never remarried. She reportedly added that since her marriage had been arranged before the Married Women's Property Act of 1882, which gave wives some control over their property, all she possessed had been lost to Edwin. Curiously, in the fall of 1885, just four months before his death, Edwin appears to have made out a new will. It did not go unnoticed that this one was in Adelaide's favor, with no strings attached, and that a certain George Dyson was named as executor.[66] If Adelaide had testified in the coroner's inquest, more information might have emerged, but her lawyer, perhaps wisely, advised against it.

The clergyman insisted that he had been informed of the will only after it was drawn up, but since the document had been prepared without the aid of Edwin's solicitor and cosigned by two of his employees who stated that Bartlett had not permitted them to see the contents, its origins remained obscure. The curious might have wondered whether the will was part of Edwin Bartlett's generous plan to prepare the way for George and Adelaide or whether it had resulted from a less altruistic sort of pact between the clergyman and the grocer's wife. Might not George, convinced that Edwin was dying, have agreed to help Adelaide persuade Edwin to change his will, especially if he were led to believe he would soon share the proceeds? Or had George Dyson been an even more active partner from the beginning in what was the first step in a plan for murder?

No one knows the answers to these questions, but Dyson's behavior after Edwin's death strongly suggested that he was more dupe than villain. On being informed that chloroform had been detected on preliminary postmortem investigation, he reacted convincingly as one who had suddenly realized the dangerous folly of his agreeing to purchase the drug for Adelaide, and he went to her to demand an explanation. The friend with whom she was staying overheard the conversation and testified that Adelaide flatly denied having told Dyson that Edwin required the substance to ease the pain of his fatal complaint. The friend added that Mrs. Bartlett became very angry, stamped her foot, and at one point declared, "Oh, damn the chloroform!" [67] (The *Times* duly deleted the expletive in its report.[68])

As the friend's husband later testified, the twenty-seven-year-old clergyman was distraught, but less over the danger of being charged with a crime than over the possibility of being defrocked. He earnestly asked Adelaide what would happen if it could be proved that she had given Edwin chloroform: "What would be the opinion of the world?" he moaned. "How should I come out in such a case?" [69] The Reverend Mr. Dyson's behavior was still seen by the coroner's jury as suspicious enough to charge him for being an accessory after the fact, but the attorney-general, in a surprise move at the outset of the trial, announced that the government had found no case against Dyson. The unpopular decision was very likely correct, for the minister was discovered to have purchased the bottles of chloroform openly in shops where he was known, even though he had lied about the purpose, alleging he wanted the substance to "remove stains."

Dyson clearly did have something to hide, but his terror appears to have been for his good name, not for his neck. He subsequently refrained from volunteering what he knew to the authorities, and it was not until nearly a month after Edwin's death that word of the official autopsy report finally prompted Adelaide to admit that she had had liquid chloroform in her possession. It was then that she chose to divulge to Dr. Leach the remarkable details of her married life, including the revival of Edwin's sexual passion, which she alleged had inspired her real purpose for obtaining the chloroform.

Adelaide did insist that she never actually tried the technique on Edwin.

Instead, she explained, she confessed to him on the night of his death that she had intended to use the chloroform to ward off his sexual advances, whereupon he developed a fit of sulks. She then placed the bottle on the mantelpiece and presumed that nothing was missing from it when she threw the contents away several days later. Dr. Leach, and later her counsel, Clarke, were left to draw the conclusion that Edwin Bartlett committed suicide, and they lost no time in doing so.

The *Times* was to remark that "whether on the theory of guilt or innocence, the whole story is marvelous;" [70] and in truth the story was so marvelous that even the most dramatic demonstration of its falsity failed to budge its numerous adherents. That demonstration occurred after the closing statements of both defense and prosecution, when Clarke became worried that the jury might suspect that his client's account of her platonic marriage was concocted after Bartlett's death. Clarke summoned the nurse who had attended Adelaide in her confinement back to the stand just before the judge's charge to the jury. He asked her if during her stay with the Bartletts, she had become aware that Adelaide's pregnancy was "the result of a single act." [71] Nurse Walker replied in the affirmative and Clarke was satisfied, but unfortunately for him the judge spoke up and inquired about precisely what the nurse had been told. The interrogation proceeded as follows:

A. That it happened only once—on a Sunday afternoon.
Q. She said so?
A. Both of them; that there was always some preventive used.[72]

With these few words, uttered at nearly the last possible moment, the whole story of the sexless Bartlett marriage collapsed—or rather, it ought to have collapsed. Judge Wills, in his charge to the jury, urged the gentlemen to be aware of the gravity of the nurse's testimony and reminded them of the curious police report that several "French letters," the English designation for condoms, had been found in the pockets of the deceased.

> what becomes of this morbid romance about the nonsexual connection, and what becomes of the man with such exalted ideas about matrimony that he thought the wife whom he elected for his companion too sacred to be touched? The whole foundation for that baseless illusion is swept away by the one sentence which you heard in the witness-box today.... And if the one little grain of truth which is generally to be found in any romance, in any story of falsehood, be found in these articles and in the use habitually made of them between husband and wife, what becomes of the whole story of the use for which chloroform was wanted? [73]

The probable truth about the sexual relations between Adelaide and Edwin was out at last—the "marvelous story" no longer made any sense. But fortunately for Adelaide the operative principle was not logic, but sympathy;

practically no one wanted to abandon her story, even the judge who had been so harsh in exposing the sham of its central feature, the platonic compact. The judge in fact held to the view that Adelaide had been wronged by a husband with odd notions, who was low enough to expose her to literature which was demonstrably dangerous to women and which helped to "unsex" them.[74]

It has recently been suggested that the entire sequence of perplexing events in the Bartlett affair comes unscrambled if one simple proposition is upheld, namely, that it was Adelaide, and not Edwin, who had adopted what were called strange ideas.[75] The evidence will be seen to confirm this view. But the admirable cleverness of Adelaide's account, so completely tailored to the prejudices of her audience, understandably forestalled the shift of perspective required to solve the mystery of how and why Edwin Bartlett was murdered. When her tale is abandoned, the conclusion that Adelaide Bartlett willed and carried out her husband's death is unavoidable. But after the acquittal, only a few skeptics still voiced some suspicion. One, the famous surgeon Sir James Paget, was said to have remarked that now that she was free, she ought to reveal how she did it in the interests of science![76] But the lady was not such a fool.

From the beginning Adelaide showed a flash of brilliance in selecting the young Dr. Leach as her confidant. As the attending physician, his word commanded belief, and Adelaide ensured his sympathy by turning on her charm. Leach's attentiveness—two and even three daily visits to a patient who, by the doctor's admission, was recovering nicely—is perhaps explained by the appeal of the lovely Adelaide. In any case, Leach acknowledged in an article to the *Lancet* that "a kinder, more tender, more patient or more self-sacrificing nurse could not have been wished for."[77] The doctor's favor helped ensure that any discrepancies between her account and others would be resolved in the lady's favor.

By linking her alleged need for chloroform with delicate sexual matters, the accused woman gained further guarantees against persistent inquiries. Leach himself acknowledged that the proposed tactic of dousing a hand-kerchief with chloroform to ward off a man's sexual attentions "only exists in penny novels."[78] Her credulous counsel could argue that she had not confided her reasons for wanting chloroform to the clergyman because she could not bring herself "to tell Mr. Dyson what no woman with any delicacy would have mentioned to a man."[79] In similar fashion Adelaide was excused by Clarke for the suspicious failure to testify at the inquest, since to have done so, after all, would have been "to expose herself to a trial as severe and terrible as any woman had ever undergone."[80]

Adelaide Bartlett's lies were obviously purposive: they served to over-whelm suspicions about her past reputation which might have prejudiced a jury against her and they also "explained" the rest of her behavior, thereby helping to spare her from the gallows. But the lies were not developed to serve these purposes alone. They were part of a larger manipulative strategy, which in its origins was not criminal, but rather was designed to give her a kind of autonomy in her relations with a husband whom she had resented from the beginning. The elaborate set of lies, moreover, can be demonstrated to follow a characteristic pattern. As with the other notorious liars here, such as Madeleine Smith and Marie Lafarge, Adelaide's lies were anchored at almost every point in some fragment of a truth which they served to misrepresent.[81]

For example, Adelaide's assertion that she had had intercourse with her husband on only one occasion was at once a kind of wish-fulfilling, dreamlike denial of normal marital relations and a tacit or coded admission of the truth that she had had sex with her husband only that once (or thereabouts) without contraception. Similarly, the contention that Edwin had given her to the minister and that therefore she had the right to resist his sexual demands appears to have rested partly on the truth, admitted by Dyson, that in the fall of 1885 Edwin had sought him as a companion for Adelaide, since, in Dyson's words, the grocer was worried that his wife was straying from that "frame of mind and disposition of heart" [82] which she had shown in her devotional letters as a schoolgirl bride. This entreaty to "lead her back" [83] actually suggests an alternative construction on the apparently odd letter of gratitude from Edwin to George, cited above, which was used by the defense with devastating effect to "prove" the grocer's peculiar attraction for a kind of chaste *ménage à trois*. In reality, the letter in its context more plausibly expresses a desperately naive conviction that this young man of God was fulfilling his hired mission to restore Adelaide to her former righteous ways. Admittedly, we are obliged to guess about what specific behavior on his wife's part might have disturbed Edwin in these last months of his life, but he appears to have had supreme confidence in his new friend George. And it is possible that his confidence was misplaced.

The central "lie," to be sure, was Adelaide's projection upon Edwin of her own deeply felt aversion to marital relations and her active efforts to prevent or curb these relations. Whether through the so-called platonic compact or the assertion of her right to withhold sex as one given by her husband to another man, Adelaide cast herself in the socially acceptable, passive, and dependent role. She was a woman who, far from resisting her marital duties, had been obliged to beg to fulfill them in the name of motherhood and who came subsequently to refuse sex to her husband only on the grounds that she was obeying his prior command that she become the property of another man. In truth, of course, she appears to have worked hard to avoid sex with Edwin from the beginning, when she may have hit upon education away from home as a solution compatible with Edwin's ambitions for her. Upon her return, moreover, through reading in such works as *Esoteric Anthropology*—which, contrary to the judge's assumption, was no doubt her own property rather than Edwin's—Adelaide took the step which led ultimately to a trial for murder. Harmless enough in itself, that step was a visit sometime in 1879 to one Mary Gove Nichols, the wife of the author of *Esoteric Anthropology*, who practiced as a "medical consultant" in London and who specialized in the sexual problems of married women. The fact that Adelaide saw Mrs. Nichols was merely mentioned at the trial, but if the prosecution had investigated the outlines of Mrs. Nichols' long career, many more clues would have turned up about the behavior of Mrs. Bartlett and the death of Mr. Bartlett.

A self-taught "prophetess of health," [84] Mary Gove Nichols was an American who had found salvation from her own forced marriage through involvement in the hygienic, hydropathic, and dietetic reform movements of the 1830s and 1840s. She became widely known in America as a writer and lecturer, and her speaking topics ranged from the evils of the "solitary vice" and tight-lacing to the virtues of vegetarianism, the water-cure, women's rights, and true-love marriage.

After divorce and remarriage in 1848 to a more like-minded partner, Thomas Low Nichols, Mary Nichols founded a hydropathic institute with her husband and lectured to women on midwifery, physiology, and other health topics. She increasingly devoted her time to counseling unhappily married women, and by the 1850s came to preach the free-love gospel that sexual union without love, inside or outside marriage, was prostitution. Her husband argued this doctrine in theoretical terms in *Esoteric Anthropology* (1853), but Mary put it in more personal terms in her autobiographical novel *Mary Lyndon* [85] (1854), which describes her desperate and loveless first marriage and condemns the marital laws and customs which subject women to the complete control of their husbands.

Convinced that wives were too often obliged by their husbands to overindulge in debilitating acts of sexual intercourse, Mrs. Nichols encouraged them to take a stand against sexual tyranny, while acknowledging the desperation of their position, and likening them to slaves.

> Martyrs are all about us, known or unknown. I am constantly receiving letters from true-hearted, noble women, who would escape from their adulterous lives if any way of escape [were] offered. Alas! There is no Canada for them—no place where they can earn an honest living; and then many of them have children, and their children have owners. Oh, what a bottomless pit is digged for women in the indissoluble marriage of our boasted civilization.[86]

Mrs. Nichols believed that part of the solution for the female victims of loveless marriage was insistence upon sexual abstinence: a pure, platonic relationship. For a time at least she also appears to have counseled that in some cases love unions which the world labeled adulterous might be called for.[87] In the late 1850s, however, she and her husband shifted away from earlier individualism and converted to Roman Catholicism, which at least provided institutional endorsement for the stand Mary had previously urged women to take alone—that sexual intercourse should be reserved exclusively for procreation.

Precisely what Mary Gove Nichols told Adelaide Bartlett can only be guessed, of course, but it is more than likely that when Adelaide poured out her grief over the forced marriage and her obligation to perform the wifely duties, Mrs. Nichols, paradoxical as it sounds, advised having a baby. In a book on marriage (1854), she had argued against the "amative excess" of husbands who forced their wives to have intercourse during pregnancy and lactation, and she alleged that such "destroying sensualism" produced masturbation and other serious disorders in offspring, as well as ovarian tumors in the mothers.[88] The message to women was clear: if they "submitted" to becoming pregnant, they would be "rewarded" by at least two years without sex, with the sanction of recognized medical authority. Adelaide knew that Edwin was just the sort to be impressed by such learned-sounding doctrine, and when she became pregnant, Mrs. Nichols personally recommended one of her own protegées as attendant midwife for the confinement.

In her case, though, the tragedy of stillbirth in late 1881 left Adelaide without the rationale against intercourse for which she doubtless hoped. She did declare immediately that the pain had been so intense that she would never become pregnant again.[89] It is logical to assume that for some time a sympathetic Edwin suspended sexual relations. But Adelaide did continue to visit Mrs. Nichols as well as the nurse, and there are indications that at home she launched a propaganda campaign directed at Edwin on the beauties of a "pure" and sexless relationship. Given such a campaign, Edwin's reported inquiries about polygamy and sexless marriage seem far less peculiar, for they represent the efforts of a sincere and no doubt confused man for another opinion on the subject. Edwin's stolid ways and somewhat simple-minded Wesleyan faith had just not equipped him to cope with such subtleties.

Up to this point, and before any hints that Adelaide intended to move on to higher stakes, the inquest and trial records provide a remarkable case study of the decision-making process over birth control in a middle-class marriage. It has recently been convincingly argued, contrary to prevailing views, that the adoption of birth control was already widespread in the middle classes by mid-century, that women commonly played an active role in the decisions, and moreover that contraception rather than abstinence or *coitus interruptus* was probably the most favored means, despite the recognized taboos on discussions of the subject.[90] The Bartlett marriage in this sense then was not unusual, at least on the surface. The couple agreed that at first there should be no children—Edwin for economy's sake and Adelaide, doubtless, for unspoken reasons of limiting sexual encounters she found repulsive. Condoms were apparently the preferred device, rather than the newer, and probably more common, "feminine" articles—the sponge, douche, and diaphragm. Possibly, Adelaide had religious scruples about using such devices herself. As a girl she was at least exposed to Roman Catholicism, and she was recorded as Anglican at her marriage. Both churches, of course, took a dim view of contraceptive devices.

However, the special interest of the case is in Adelaide's discovery of the free-love and reformist literature and the inventive uses to which she put it. It is not generally realized that the so-called free-love movements of the nineteenth century did not advocate sexual pleasure for itself, that they held contraceptive devices to be unnatural and recommended periodic or even permanent abstinence for birth control, and that they placed continued emphasis on woman's alleged maternal instinct. However, for their recognition of female sexuality, for their endorsement of woman's rights to her body, and also for their approval of sexual relations based upon nonexploitative mutual love, these movements have been singled out for their "modern" feminist content.[91] Mary Gove Nichols herself often linked the notions of independence and motherhood, arguing that a free and healthy woman needs no laws to protect her virtue and that hers is the "Heaven-conferred right to choose the father of her babe." [92] The literature of free love then may have helped some women gain extended freedom of person, though most likely within the confines of traditional domestic power relationships, for example, by giving them greater veto rights over sexual intercourse in marriage. The efforts of women to apply the precepts outside these limits in societies which still controlled their social options, including to a large extent their choice of husbands, were bound to have mixed results at best. This is one reason why Adelaide's case is both so pathetic and so frightening.

The case does provide evidence that women were reading the hygienic and free-love literature; numerous commentators acknowledged as much, including the alarmed judge, Mr. Wills, who pronounced that "the women of the present day are used to strange things—things which would have shocked us in the time of my boyhood." [93] But, of course, few women took what they read as seriously as Adelaide. Whether she had discovered free-love ideas before or after her affair with her brother-in-law in 1878, she resented her arranged marriage from the beginning and set out in deadly earnest to repair the wrong which was done her. Less determined women, trapped in loveless marriages, might have read the Nichols's books for escape, as they might have read a novel. More typical women might have become pregnant again or found volunteer work or church activities. But Adelaide, after failing in the effort to "play within the rules" by having Edwin's baby, appears to have developed some plans which even the forgiving and rather unobservant Edwin noted with growing concern.

It is probable that Adelaide decided on murder at least as early as September 1885, and perhaps a good deal before then. The death of Mary Nichols, her guide and counselor, in the spring of 1884, may have removed a restraining force. But whenever that decision was made, there are earlier signs Adelaide was moving to a closer identification with this woman and her varied crusades. Late in 1884, for example, Adelaide's reported frequent complaints about her husband's will and her property having been unfairly placed in Edwin's shops suggest probable acquaintance with Mary Nichols' campaigns against property laws discriminatory to women. By this time, too, Adelaide was an infrequent companion of her husband at chapel.[94] Having switched from Anglicanism to the Wesleyan faith at marriage, she appears to have turned to Roman Catholicism under her counselor's inspiration. At the time of her trial she identified herself as a member of that faith. Aside from the talk at this time about a man having "two wives," talk which can now be seen to have originated with Adelaide, there is another suggestion of her evident new seriousness about the sexual abstinence preached by Nichols. In the early fall of 1885 when she was making arrangements for their flat in Pimlico, Adelaide informed the landlady that a separate bed would be required for her husband. As several witnesses testified, this was the first occasion in their married lives that the Bartletts had not slept in the same bed. These changes in his wife were in themselves enough to have prompted Edwin's urgent visit begging Dyson to restore his wife to her earlier "frame of mind." Adelaide, however, would soon be confiding to this infatuated young man the "secret" that her husband suffered from an "internal complaint" diagnosed as fatal by the famous Dr. Thomas Low Nichols and that he had less than a year to live. The doctor, who testified at the trial, flatly denied he had ever made any such diagnosis.[95]

Whether Adelaide killed for the love of George Dyson is now less certain than that she did kill. Yseult Bridges, who has minutely examined the medical evidence in the case, has provided an explanation which accounts more successfully than any other for all the odd details and which abides by the hypothesis that all the "strange ideas" attributed to Edwin belonged to Adelaide. The puzzle of how she actually administered the poison, which obviously contributed to the jury's reluctance to find her guilty, was not solved convincingly by the prosecution. Russell's best effort was the belated suggestion that Adelaide had labeled the chloroform "medicine" and urged Edwin to bolt it down, which would account for its failure to have burned his mouth or esophagus. The problem there, however, was that as a dog trainer who owned manuals on medicine and was familiar with the properties of the poison, it was most implausible that in full possession of his faculties, he would have followed her orders. The same of course went for the judge's thesis that Edwin had swallowed the stuff to put himself to sleep. And Clarke's notion that the grocer had thoughtfully committed suicide to hasten the wedding day of George and Adelaide fails to account for dozens of details which show that Bartlett fully intended to wake up the next morning. Clarke's hypothesis, in the words of one commentator, "had a distinct air of desperation."[96]

The answer—at least the best answer available—is that at the time Edwin was not in full possession of his faculties. As Bridges argues, the secret was probably mesmerism; Edwin was under the hypnotic influence of his wife.[97] Admittedly, Adelaide's and Leach's stories suggested that animal magnetism was Edwin's indulgence, but the evidence indicates otherwise.

First, Edwin was known to be highly suggestible; Leach himself had mesmerized him for tooth extractions. Several visitors—including Leach, his business partner, and his own father—noted that Edwin behaved oddly during his last illness. The doctor even testified that Edwin declared his belief that he was under a mesmeric spell which he claimed had been cast by a friend through his wife; Leach reported that he had talked Edwin out of this belief, but he did remark that during this conversation Adelaide had several times tried to change the topic of discussion, pointing out that her husband's supposition was "absurd." [98] Still, Leach acknowledged that Edwin had behaved as though he were hypnotized. Then there were the other reported symptoms—the crying, despondency, fear of leaving his bed, fear of death—all of which were consistent with the hypnotic state and suggestion. And if Edwin were mesmerized, murder by means of liquid chloroform presented no serious difficulties. In an appropriate solvent the poison might be downed with some ease by a suitably prepared victim. As it turned out, the Bartletts owned a pharmaceutical manual which mentioned that brandy was a suitable solvent for chloroform. And brandy happened to have been among the items ordered by Adelaide a few days before for a "holiday celebration." [99]

More suggestive still was the testimony of the landlady that on the night of Edwin's death she had spoken with the couple when they returned from the dentist, and Adelaide had inquired whether she had ever taken chloroform. On her reply that she had, Adelaide asked if the sensation had not been "nice" or "pleasant." [100] This apparently innocent episode takes on sinister overtones given the possibility that Edwin, standing at his wife's side in a hypnotic state, was being prepared to accept as "nice" and "pleasant" the poisonous brew which killed him.

That Adelaide had developed skill in mesmeric techniques is impossible to prove. Yseult Bridges proposes that she had learned hypnosis from Dyson, but gives no convincing evidence. There was, however, another possible source, someone Adelaide knew well who was fascinated by mesmerism, belonged to mesmeric societies, and had even lectured on the subject. That person was Mary Gove Nichols.[101]

Mesmerism, the last of Mrs. Nichols' enthusiasms which Adelaide appears to have turned to her purposes, was a macabre and grimly apt finale to the script. Throughout, Adelaide had contrived to emerge as the innocent victim she had felt herself to be on her wedding day. Systematically attributing to Edwin the authorship of the whole set of survival techniques she herself had adopted from the beginning, she committed the ultimate passive-aggressive act by implanting the suggestion that Edwin should swallow the substance which killed him. The technique of mesmerism was ideal for maintaining her fantasy of being a mere victim, long after Adelaide had become an active victimizer. It permitted her to kill Edwin as surely as if she had pulled the trigger of a gun, but it left her free to deny responsibility. Edwin, after all, had raised the glass to his own lips.

Hypnotism, as Bridges suggests, may also explain how Edwin was persuaded to change his will the previous September, though it does not explain the grocer's earlier condition, the alleged symptoms of mercury poisoning which had first led to the summoning of Dr. Leach. Bridges convincingly argues on the basis of the autopsy discovery of minute quantities of lead, which were never explained, that Adelaide was poisoning Edwin slowly with lead acetate, a substance in the canine medical kit which she herself had used to doctor their dogs.[102] On this theory, when her father-in-law insisted on summoning a doctor, Adelaide was obliged to discontinue dosage and her husband's condition, unsurprisingly, improved almost at once. The chloroform then may have been improvised in order to meet a deadline of some sort, but unfortunately the materials for a precise reconstruction of the immediate motive are lacking.

Although the theory that Adelaide murdered in order to be united with Dyson was not implausible, the clear presumption that Adelaide tricked the minister into purchasing the chloroform and his evident revulsion upon discovering the trick at least suggest that she may have been attempting to set him up as a primary suspect in case a crime were suspected. Edwin's prior eagerness to get Dyson to spend time with his wife and his obvious unconcern over their long hours together suggest that he may have had reason to believe her heart was still elsewhere, namely, with his younger brother Frederick in America. It is known that Adelaide and Frederick did maintain a correspondence after Frederick left the country.[103] Had Edwin's unspoken reason in "hiring" Dyson been to keep Adelaide out of mischief during his long absences? Had Adelaide agreed with Frederick to have done away with Edwin by a prearranged date, when Frederick planned to sail from America? We do know that Frederick did return and that the first occasion he called on his sister-in-law was just two days after Edwin's death. Unfortunately, there is no other information about Frederick save the assertion by old Bartlett senior that Edwin had recently written to offer him management of one of the shops. Such generosity to the brother who probably betrayed him is remarkable, although Adelaide's mesmeric talents cannot be ruled out here either. We know that after the trial Adelaide simply disappeared. Perhaps she escaped with her first love to America, the homeland of that Mrs. Nichols who had so inspired her. Whatever happened, her fate was almost certainly better than she deserved.

By contrast, in the Fenayrou affair every effort was made to uncover for Gabrielle a directing role which she probably never played. By acknowledging adultery, Gabrielle had stepped outside the charmed circle of legal immunity which respectable women, if they were clever enough, might still enjoy. She had, moreover, confessed to being her husband's active, if unwilling, accomplice in a ghastly and premeditated crime. Her explanation for her role in the event was far more plausible than Adelaide's "marvelous story," but unfortunately practically no one believed it. Had Gabrielle been English, it is likely (for reasons that will be suggested) that her pitiful story would have had a more favorable reception.

Unlike the Bartlett case the Fenayrou affair raised few questions about how the murder was done, which was straightforward enough. Several witnesses said Gabrielle had finally confessed her relations with Aubert some weeks before May 18, 1882, when the crime took place. During the time between the confession and the act careful preparations were made. Gabrielle agreed to reestablish relations with Aubert, promising him a loan of money. Marin rented a house in Versailles which fronted on the Seine and equipped it with hammer, shovel, cords, weights, and a small cart. The body was supposed to be buried inside the house beneath the floor, but if that proved impossible, it was to be tied, weighted, and dropped into the Seine. Realizing help might be needed with the body, the couple enlisted Marin's younger brother Lucien, who later told reporters that he had tried to warn Marin about Gabrielle and Aubert, but that Marin, who adored Gabrielle, had refused to listen.[104]

Gabrielle arranged a rendezvous with Aubert. On the designated evening the three conspirators met for dinner in a restaurant near the Gare du Nord. After an expensive and heavy meal, at which they consumed a bottle and a half of wine, the two men departed for Versailles. Gabrielle, who reported that she first went to the nearby church of St. Louis d'Antin to pray, said she then met Aubert and accompanied him on the train to Versailles. Accustomed to paying Aubert's way, Gabrielle purchased the tickets. The young pharmacist did not notice that she had bought a roundtrip ticket for herself and a one-way for him.

The crime itself took place according to plan with no serious complications. When Aubert and Gabrielle arrived at the house, Marin, hidden behind the door, fell on his victim with hammer blows. Lucien, who was waiting in back, later alleged that Marin told him that without Gabrielle's help in fending off Aubert, he might not have succeeded. The story may have been true, for Marin, at five feet six inches tall, was both shorter and lighter than his adversary. Perhaps in order to protect her, Marin later denied Gabrielle had helped him. In any case, if there was a struggle, it was probably over quickly. The autopsy report stated that the hammer blows to the victim's skull had allowed him little or no opportunity to resist. Since efforts to dig up the kitchen floor proved too time consuming, the body was wheeled down to the Seine in the cart and lowered into the water. As a precaution against the corpse's floating, Marin weighted it and even pinned the lips together. As it turned out, these measures were insufficient, but they later provided a good deal of macabre interest. A waxworks which recreated the scene of the discovery of the body did a brisk business in tickets to view a terrified fisherman beholding the bloated corpse.

If the mechanics of Aubert's death pose few mysteries, the motives involved are more difficult. Both Marin and Gabrielle claimed that the crime was one of "passion," but given that Marin had been warned of his wife's relationship as early as 1879, at which time he reportedly had set down new rules for her which included confinement to the house, it was difficult to see why he had waited until May 1882 to act. The prosecution toyed with the notion that Aubert was blackmailing his former employer about some past deed, perhaps knowledge of an abortion performed on Gabrielle. But the favorite explanation of the prosecution pointed the finger directly at Gabrielle; jealous of the success of a lover who was ignoring her, she confessed all to get Marin to kill her ungrateful lover. As the public prosecutor charged:

> In leading Aubert to death, you were obeying a personal desire.... You were the abandoned mistress, you were in misery while your former lover was happy. Those were your feelings, and you armed your husband [by confessing the affair]; all your actions in the matter bear this out—your sangfroid, one might even say your gaiety.[105]

Gabrielle denied the charge and continued to insist that she had acted out of fear for her children's lives and guilt toward the husband she had wronged.

In all probability the explanation of the time lapse in the decision to murder Aubert was simple. Marin had dismissed the rumors on the ground that Gabrielle, with her cold temperament, was, as he alleged, "incapable of betraying me." [106] One of his friends testified that Marin once wagered that his wife had never been unfaithful to him, and it appears that his reasons involved more than bravado. Gabrielle, who found physical relations with him revolting, doubtless permitted this rather simple and volatile man to believe that her unresponsiveness was not his fault. Her relations with Aubert and Grousteau show her passions as far less physical than "ideal."

Both Gabrielle Fenayrou and Adelaide Bartlett, then, had in common not only their hostility over arranged marriages and their probable adultery, but also a revulsion toward "wifely duties," which prompted them to devise means of escape. Gabrielle's painful experience in pregnancy, like Adelaide's, doubtless reinforced her sexual aversion, but unlike Adelaide she did not have the option of recourse to arguments about nonsexual, platonic love being purer. She seems, however, to have contrived some less extraordinary means than Adelaide to limit intercourse and unwanted pregnancies. After the difficult birth of her second child, she obtained a written statement from her doctor that her health forbade her having any more children. While it is possible that this was the case, the public scepticism which greeted the news is suggestive. The *Petit Journal,* one of the largest of the popular dailies, remarked that increasingly women were seeking such certificates from "complaisant doctors." [107] This evidence of a new willingness to look for relief from sexual "duties" suggests that within a more traditional context, which already made room for appeals to religious injunctions against sex without desire for procreation,[108] French women too were taking greater initiative in limiting the frequency of sexual relations within marriage. Such action doubtless increased male resentment, which helped fuel the popular hostility toward Gabrielle. And in her case the combination of the doctor's certificate and the evidence of her extramarital affairs placed undue stress upon her apparent sexual dissatisfaction with Marin, a fact unlikely to help her with the jury.

There is strong evidence then that things were as the Fenayrous both reported, that is, that Marin did not in fact become convinced of Gabrielle's infidelity until 1882, whereupon he decided to kill Aubert. But it is also true that by the time that happened, Marin's fortunes had declined badly, and he was prepared to find in Aubert a scapegoat for all his troubles. After the assistant's dismissal in 1879 Marin had decided to recoup his gambling losses by setting up a side business in counterfeiting a well-known mineral water. But late in 1881 before he had even paid off his initial investment in bottles, corks, and labels, the police visited the deserted warehouse he had sublet and confiscated the equipment. Obliged to sell the shop to meet debts, the couple then moved for the first time in their marriage. Jobless, but with funds remaining from the sixty-thousand-franc sale of the pharmacy, Marin promptly invested much of it in a scheme for the development of copper mines. The organizer, a M. Valette who was his sons' language tutor, persuaded him early in 1882 to join the new *société;* Gabrielle, who confessed that she regained sympathy for Marin after the counterfeit episode, even persuaded her mother to allow Marin to invest the twenty thousand francs he still owed her.

The whole pathetic account makes it clear that the poor country boy was being played for a dupe. The headquarters of the *société* turned out to be merely Valette's private rooms in the rue Laffitte, and the personnel of the operation consisted of only two clerks. Fenayrou was told he was to be a partner, and it was his august duty to prepare the monthly statement of the clerks' wages. The rest of his time was occupied in improving his penmanship by copying sample business letters. When police later searched the premises, they found notebooks filled with Fenayrou's painstaking, schoolboy exercises in calligraphy. Valette, who had become Marin's employer, told the court that once Fenayrou's "literary education" was complete, he was to have been sent off to negotiate with the foreign contacts of the establishment, but it is doubtful that such contacts ever existed. Valette himself was not, as he claimed, an engineer, and there was no evidence that his company was exploiting a mine in Spain, as he had told Fenayrou. Valette instead appears to have been an ordinary confidence man, who hoped to set up a bogus investment scheme with Fenayrou's money.

By the time events suddenly came to a head in the spring of 1882, Gabrielle was no longer seeing either lover. According to neighbors, she had managed until then to persuade Marin of her innocence in the matter of Aubert, and it was not to be until the trial that he learned that Grousteau had also been her lover. But Marin apparently decided that his past assaults on religion had had a harmful effect on Gabrielle. At his order she began to attend mass and confession again after a lapse of nearly ten years. It is a curious element of both the Fenayrou and Bartlett cases that the suspicious husbands' first thought was to turn their wives back to the faith. But events would show that Marin's style was hardly limited to the gentle persuasion to which Edwin subscribed.

The Fenayrous' relatively new domestic equilibrium lasted only until March, when a correctional tribunal handed Marin a sentence of two months and a two-thousand-franc fine for counterfeiting. Stung, disgraced, and suspicious that Aubert might have informed on him to the police, Marin returned mechanically to the former assistant as the author of his troubles. According to Gabrielle, he took her aside and begged her to tell him once and for all whether she had slept with Aubert. Gabrielle said that since he promised to forgive her, she confessed, but Marin instead went off to the police and attempted to persuade them to seize his wife's letters to Aubert, which would have permitted him to prove an adultery charge. When the police refused, Marin then deposited Gabrielle at his mother-in-law's, with the announcement that he was returning her for her infidelity. Gabrielle testified that she was terrified of what Marin might do and decided to go home a few days later. Her husband agreed to take her back, she said, but he told her that unless she helped him, he would kill their two sons.

Marin Fenayrou acknowledged at least that he had decided to force Gabrielle to be his accomplice in order to expiate her guilt. From this point the fascination of his behavior is in the pattern of ritual revenge which emerges from the details scattered throughout the records. Marin methodically set out to perform the classic crime of the outraged husband, and he informed Gabrielle that until she paid for her infidelity, she was no longer his wife. In symbolic expression of the fact he made Gabrielle return his wedding band, and he had the maid remove his wife's picture from its frame and her bridal wreath from its display case.[109]

His first schemes, too, underlined the primitive quality of his vengeance. He told Gabrielle he intended to make Aubert a present of a pair of binoculars fitted with specially designed blades which would literally scoop out the eyes of an unwitting victim. She reported that she talked Marin out of this scheme, but was unable to dissuade him from a second plan to catch Aubert and slowly torture him to death. For this Marin went so far as to rent an immense wild boar trap, but he eventually abandoned the idea and settled on the hammer and house arrangement. And Gabrielle, for her part, admitted an active role in the plans. Curiously, police reported that the account book they found at their home showed that Mme. Fenayrou, in the typical fashion of the orderly French bourgeois wife, had recorded all the household expenditures, including the shovel, hammer, and boar trap!

Ritual was imbedded in the crime to the end. It was there in the formal dinner to which Gabrielle invited her brother-in-law Lucien, so that Marin could enlist him into a small-scale vendetta against Aubert. Ritual was present, too, after the crime, when Marin performed a little ceremony of matrimonial reinstatement. As Gabrielle told Macé, her husband fetched the wedding band and wreath and declared:

> Now that the past is dead, I want to create a second virginity for you. Here are your wedding band and wreath. Return the one to your finger and the other to its glass display case. Then let us walk hand in hand and be happy again. Let us seal our conjugal reconciliation with kisses.[110]

Finally, at the trial itself Marin recounted in stylized formula the statement he claimed to have made to his victim as he stabbed him in the chest: "It was by the heart that you made me suffer, and it is by the heart that you will die." [111]

The jury at Versailles gave Marin the death penalty, Gabrielle life imprisonment, and Lucien, a slow-witted tool, seven years. Marin had failed to persuade the jury that revenge alone was involved, but Gabrielle was still seen by most as primarily responsible. She was spared death and given a lighter punishment because of the traditional reluctance of the courts to give the death penalty to women, especially women above the working classes. As it happened, the Versailles decision was overturned on a technical point, and the following October a Parisian jury acquitted Lucien and reduced Marin's sentence to life imprisonment without changing Gabrielle's sentence. Opinion in the capital was only slightly mollified; the presiding judge had expressed the popular pitiless view of Gabrielle: "A more complete and horrible monster has never been seated on the bench of the assize court." [112]

The near total absence of public sympathy was remarkable in view of the numerous details, repeated in both trials, which supported Gabrielle's story of coercion by an obsessed and violent husband. Among others there were accounts by reliable witnesses that in 1881, when Marin became suspicious of Gabrielle's behavior, he not only restricted her to the home, but bought a gun with which he threatened her publicly on at least two occasions. In desperation she had visited the police, who refused to intervene. Even more pathetic was a visit she made a few weeks before the crime to her husband's employer, the opportunist Valette. She said she begged him to send Marin away so that he would not commit a horrible crime of vengeance. Valette acknowledged the visit and the request to send Marin off. He added that she had called herself a "very guilty woman," [113] but said that he had cut her off when she tried to reveal more about her personal life. Valette protested that if she had mentioned a planned crime, he would have gone to the police, but given his legally dubious operations, of which she was ignorant, that was unlikely.

Papers all across the political spectrum nonetheless agreed with the verdict of the popular *Petit Journal* that there was "nothing human" about Gabrielle.[114] Henri Rochefort voiced the general hostility to women, which was so close to the surface in many accounts, stating that although the pathetic Marin believed himself in control, it was Gabrielle who had provoked all.

What we wish to make clear is that eleven-twelfths of men believe that they are acting according to their own wills, when in fact they are speaking, writing and acting on the sole impulse of the creatures whom they think they possess and who actually possess them. The moral of the Fenayrou trial, and of many others like it, is that if we men escape from women's control at age seven, it is only to return again at nineteen.[115]

The facts that Marin had brandished a revolver at Gabrielle, had sworn to kill her children, had confessed planning brutal tortures, and had bludgeoned a man to death were of no consequence. Marin's lawyer still managed to move an all-male jury to tears and sobs by painting him as the wronged husband.

Gabrielle did manage to recruit some sympathy from one audience, the women—for whom a special, separate gallery was constructed in the Versailles courtroom. They responded warmly to her lawyer's portrayal of Gabrielle's plight, and they showed considerable sympathy in listening to the story of her decision to visit a church before meeting Aubert. The press generally greeted that story as a bald attempt to elicit sympathy, as it may have been, but the authorities did receive several unsigned letters from women who claimed to have been witnesses to the scene. One letter, sent to the presiding judge, went as follows:

> Finding myself at the aforementioned church on 18 May at about eight o'clock in the evening, I saw a woman dressed in mourning who was near me; I noticed her give a deep sigh, almost a sob, then I listened and heard these words: Dear God, don't let him come, spare us this crime, appease the anger. . . .[116]

The woman concluded the letter, which contained several spelling errors, with the statement that she hoped her information would be useful, but that she dared not sign her name "for fear it would be published, and I know I would be reproached by my husband." [117] Timid as they were, the women's letters marked a hesitant new feminine solidarity in the face of masculine hostility.

Gabrielle, of course, might have warned Aubert to get out of town until Marin went to prison to serve his term for counterfeiting, or she might have alleged that Aubert never showed up for their meeting. But by then Marin seems to have convinced her that she was obliged to expiate her infidelity. Her mother, Mme. Gibon, wrote in 1884, two years after the trial, that Gabrielle still reproached herself more for her adultery than for her participation in the murder itself.[118]

A sympathetic friend had drawn laughter from the courtroom by declaring that Gabrielle was a soft-headed thing, who might as easily have followed the road to crime as that to virtue.[119] It may have been so. Like many of her peers, Gabrielle had been taught that it was her duty to please, and she apparently succeeded in this at the expense of any consistency of ideas or principles. Some fascinating insight into her character is provided in a letter she sent to the police chief Macé. After the trial, she had been given the option to accompany Marin to New Caledonia or remain in prison in France, and though she still held out hopes to Marin, she wrote to assure Macé, who had expressed concern, that she would never leave her children.

> I do not know, Monsieur, if it is by hearsay or false reports that you believed me capable of going away and leaving my mother and children. It is true that I read you a letter I wrote to my husband in which I did not wish to refuse absolutely to accompany him; but believe me, Monsieur, that after having done what I did for my poor mother, in marrying without thinking about my future happiness, I am not going to throw her into utter despair now by my own free will. . . . I believed that by my marriage I was pleasing those who were left to me, and I became guilty by fate. Obedient, threatened, I believed I was performing a duty; I went along as though blindfolded, unconscious of the crime that I was going to commit in leading this unfortunate man [to his death]. I therefore have done more for my husband than I ought to have done. Today I believe I owe myself entirely to my children, the poor victims, and if my life one day again should become useful to someone, may it be for my children and for my mother's last days. God alone will do whatever He wills with me for anything I still owe my unhappy husband.[120]

Not until she had served nearly twenty years was Gabrielle released; Marin, in the meantime, had died in New Caledonia.

The popular Parisian view of Gabrielle's greater guilt in the affair was not accepted by the English press, which showed surprise over the outburst of hostility toward Gabrielle. Nor did the English press join the popular sympathy for Marin in the belief he had acted chiefly from motives of revenge. Instead it joined the court in suspecting other motives such as professional jealousy or fear of blackmail.[121] It is possible that such a raw and "primitive" crime of passion, carried on, as it was, in the stylized fashion of the rural vendetta, seemed incomprehensible for a man of the urban middle classes. And it was true that the evident premeditation clouded the issue from the outside: had Marin simply walked into Aubert's pharmacy and shot him in cold blood, he might well have been acquitted by a Parisian jury. But Marin cared enough about his new identity as an investment officer to avoid that. In a sense, Marin was convicted for wanting both his revenge and his respectability.

It may seem curious that there should have been more sympathy for Marin's act in Paris, where the death penalty was lifted, than in Versailles, where the case was first tried. But it must be recalled that it was in the urban centers, especially, that hostility toward the "new women" was most acute and where suspicion of middle-class women as "closet prostitutes" was greatest. The Fenayrou affair took place, moreover, in the midst of preparatory discussions of a divorce bill, which finally passed two years later in 1884, and which inflamed critics who chose to view divorce as a kind of legitimation of adultery for women.

In England there was also enough residual hostility toward the immoral "new women" to make the possibility of adultery the centerpiece of the Bartlett affair. Adelaide knew well that she could not rely on an innocent demeanor and the popular belief in female irresponsibility, as Madeleine Smith had done; she needed her "marvelous story."

Nonetheless, by this time she—unlike Gabrielle—could rely on a public opinion which was showing signs of greater unwillingness to permit the woman alone to bear the opprobrium for "illicit" sexual relations. The same year Adelaide was tried, the forces mobilized by Josephine Butler had succeeded in repealing the Contagious Diseases Acts, which subjected suspected prostitutes to periodic examination and possible incarceration. Butler conducted her campaign on the ground that the Acts were blatant examples of the double standard, and her argument was admitted by numerous men in the repeal campaign.

Adelaide's lawyer, Edward Clarke, featured the complicity of Dyson as a man suspected as her lover, but one who had been released from charges. As Clarke himself remarked, he had opted for friendly sympathy rather than hostility in questioning Dyson, for "the more closely I could associate his actions with those of Mrs. Bartlett, the more I could strengthen the instinctive reluctance of the jury to send her to the hangman's cord while he passed unrebuked to freedom." [122] The evidence of popular hostility toward Dyson, and the clear presumption that his involvement in the case rested on an "improper" relationship with Adelaide, indicated a willingness to let men share the blame in cases of suspected adultery, as did the successful tactic of pointing the finger at the husband for encouraging a wife's straying. Gabrielle Fenayrou was not so lucky.

Marital "happiness" was something both Adelaide Bartlett and Gabrielle Fenayrou felt cheated of, and each sought relief from unhappiness within the limited options of the two societies which shaped their personal choices. Adelaide demonstrated a kind of genius in manipulating a lawyer, a doctor, and a minister, representatives of three hallowed professions of her society. With more latitude, she found some solutions among "modern" medical and reformist movements. She was clever enough to take advantage of the efforts of more admirable women who had fought for a single sexual standard and for the recognition of a woman's right within marriage to be free from the physical coercion of her husband. Her astonishing defense could only have succeeded in a society which was coming to acknowledge real limits on the domestic authority of husbands.

French public opinion was as yet unwilling to accept the illegitimacy of a far more extensive catalogue of wife-abuse, which in this case included not only psychological coercion and physical "forcing" in sexual intercourse but threat of bodily harm. Gabrielle was obliged to find what justification she could for limiting sexual relations with her husband and for seeking happiness with a lover through more familiar authorities of family and church. The pattern of dependency built into her more traditional life style placed limits on her very will to betray, which Adelaide never felt. In the end, Gabrielle was punished less for her role in a murder than for her crime against her husband, just as the terrible Adelaide was acquitted not because she was shown to be innocent but because she was able to convince a prepared audience that she had been victimized by a perverted husband.

6.

POISON, REVOLVERS, AND THE DOUBLE STANDARD:

The Cases of Florence Maybrick and Claire Reymond

Florence Maybrick

FLORENCE MAYBRICK, a suspected poisoner, and Claire Reymond, charged with a revolver killing, are the final subjects in this gallery of accused women.[1] Mrs. Maybrick, an American and a "Southern belle," created a sensation greater than all the rest, with the possible exception of Marie Lafarge. Mme. Reymond, on the other hand, was arrested for a "crime of passion" which, save for the social status of the principals involved, struck the public as a rather trite episode. Seen from a twentieth-century perspective, however, the Reymond case, as part of what seemed to be a new minor crime wave among French women, is at least as intriguing as the Maybrick affair.

Florence Maybrick and Claire Reymond, in different ways, were barometers of shifting pressures that confronted women at the end of the century. By then, real social gains had created a new set of expectations among married women of the middle classes, but these women were in no position to organize successful collective strategies against criticism and personal disappointments that accompanied their achievement.[2] Despite growing public roles and the active movement for women's rights, most women were still engaged in a more private effort to improve their positions on the domestic front. Each of the two women here faced marital problems with which they were unprepared to deal. Certainly one, and perhaps both, of the women devised solutions that entailed murder. In each case, once again, accusations of adultery were central, but in both the women's behavior and public reactions to that behavior pointed in new directions.

Florence Maybrick was twenty-seven in August 1889, when she was tried in Liverpool for the arsenic poisoning of her fifty-year-old husband, James, a cotton merchant to whom she had been married more than eight years. James had died the previous May after an intestinal illness of two weeks, during most of which his wife had nursed him. Her suspicious in-laws had dissuaded attending physicians from signing a death certificate, and a subsequent autopsy disclosed traces of arsenic in the deceased's liver, kidneys, and intestines. Mrs. Maybrick was taken into custody and found guilty by a coroner's jury, a verdict endorsed by the magistrate's court that had her committed for trial.

"Florie," as her friends called her, was fragile and appealing, with soft curls ringing her small face. An American woman, the daughter of a cotton-broker who did business with James Maybrick, spent some weeks in the Maybrick home as a child of eight and recalled Florence as a beautiful woman who was the center of attraction at the numerous parties the couple gave for Liverpool society.

> She was about five feet, four or five inches in heigth [sic], rounded figure, well-developed bust and hips, slender waist, tapering arms and legs, small wrists and ankles, small feet and hands, with rather long tapering fingers. Her figure would be considered a little too plump now for the present day style [1942]. [She] had a fair, clear complexion with rosy cheeks, [to] which I think the English climate is conducive. The crowning glory of her person was her hair. It was a blonde, but not the dead, faded out type of yellow, [it] had just enough tinge of red in it to make a glossy, rich deep golden. It was inclined to be curly and always arranged in a very becoming style. [She had a] straight nose, rather high forehead, small mouth, thin lips. . . . Mrs. Maybrick's eyes were the most beautiful blue I have ever seen. They were a large round eye and such a deep blue that at times they were violet. . . . At no time was there any expression of intellectuality, either in eyes or face; yet there was a magnetic charm about her countenance that greatly attracted one, and seemed irresistible.[3]

Hers was the kind of prettiness that summoned masculine protectiveness, which may have been why her lawyer arranged for Florence to make a courtroom statement in her own defense. She chose to explain two rather suspicious items: the purchase of arsenic-impregnated flypaper shortly before her husband's death and the report of a nurse who had tended him in his fatal illness that the mistress appeared to have been tampering with her husband's food. Florence also referred obliquely to a third item that weighed more heavily than the other two in the minds of many, namely, the charge that she had been having adulterous relations with one of their cotton-broker friends.

> The flypapers were bought with the intention of using as a cosmetic. Before my marriage, and since, for many years, I have been in the habit of using a face-wash prescribed by Dr. Greggs, of Brooklyn. It consisted principally of arsenic, tincture of benzoin, elderflower water, and some other ingredients. This prescription I lost last April, and, as at that time I was suffering from slight eruption of the face, I thought I should like to try to make a substitute myself. I was anxious to get rid of this eruption before I went to a ball on the 30th of that

month. . . . My lord, I now wish to refer to the bottle of meat essence. On Thursday night, the 9th of May [two days before Maybrick's death], after Nurse Gore had given my husband beef tea, I went and sat on the bed beside him. He complained to me of being very sick and very depressed, and he implored me then to give him this powder which he had referred to early in the evening, and which I had declined to give him. I was overwrought, terribly anxious, miserably unhappy, and his evident distress utterly unnerved me. He had told me that the powder would not harm him, and that I could put it in his food. I then consented. My lord, I had not one true or honest friend in that house. I had no one to consult, and no one to advise me. I was deposed from my position as mistress in my own house, and from the position of attending upon my husband, notwithstanding that he was so ill. . . . In conclusion I have only to add that for the love of our children, and for the sake of their future, a perfect reconciliation had taken place between us, and that on the day before his death I made a full and free confession to him, and received his entire forgiveness for the fearful wrong I had done him.[4]

Mrs. Maybrick's counsel, Sir Charles Russell, perhaps the most gifted advocate of his day, ought to have realized the folly of permitting his client to make such a feeble and self-incriminating statement, especially since he strongly believed she deserved an acquittal. Mrs. Maybrick did deny that the doctored meat juice had ever been given to her husband, but what mattered was her admission that she had prepared it and, not incidentally, the fact that the powder for which her husband had allegedly pleaded had been analyzed as pure arsenic. Even at that, however, other evidence might have told in her favor with the jury had not the judge, the eminent Sir James Fitzjames Stephen, charged them to weigh heavily in their decision the admitted adultery of the accused:

> you must not consider the case as a mere medical case, in which you are to decide whether the man did or did not die of arsenic according to the medical evidence . . . you must decide it as a great and highly important case . . . involving in itself a most highly important moral question. . . . For a person to go on deliberately administering poison to a poor, helpless, sick man upon whom she has already inflicted a dreadful injury—an injury fatal to married life—the person who could do such a thing as that must indeed be destitute of the least trace of human feeling. . . . Then you have to consider . . . the question of motives which might act upon this woman's mind. When you consider that, you must remember the intrigue which she carried on with this man Brierley, and the feelings—it seems horrible to comparatively ordinary innocent people—a horrible and incredible thought that a woman should be plotting the death of her husband in order that she might be left at liberty to follow her own degrading vices.[5]

The jury deliberated a mere twenty-five minutes before returning a guilty verdict, and the accused woman was sentenced to hang.

Florence Bravo and Adelaide Bartlett had understood the seriousness of charges of sexual misconduct, and each had managed to contrive defenses against such accusations. Whether or not she was guilty of murder, Florence Maybrick had a far better case than either Mrs. Bravo or Mrs. Bartlett, but she lacked the manipulative skill, wise counsel, and luck of those ladies. Her own mother admitted sadly, "My daughter is not a woman of very much penetration," [6] and the evidence bears out her judgment.

Still, the guilty verdict was unexpected. Even the *Saturday Review*, which devoted most of its space to deploring the "folly and occasional depravity of Mrs. Maybrick's supporters," admitted that the jury's action, while "thought out and courageous," was nonetheless "based on belief not proof." [7] The *Times* claimed that "not one in three" of the hundreds of thousands following the case had been prepared for the verdict. Though it denounced her "treachery as a wife," the paper remarked that the massive public outburst against the verdict came not only from "prejudice against capital punishment in the case of a woman, and especially an educated woman," [8] but also from real doubt over her guilt. The variety of the reactions to the case will be considered in more detail later, but the immediate effect of the hostile outburst was to prompt the Home Office to commute the sentence to life imprisonment. This decision, however, was conveyed to the condemned woman only after she had endured, in solitary confinement, the sounds of the construction of her gallows in the courtyard outside her cell.

Like most of the dissenting newspapers, the *Times* was satisfied by the home secretary's peculiar explanation that although the prosecution had demonstrated that Florence had administered arsenic with intent to murder her husband (it had not), there was reasonable doubt that arsenic had in fact killed him (there was). Thereafter, though the battle to free her was far from abandoned, all but the most ardent opponents of the verdict dropped away. Because of numerous fruitless efforts to clear her name in subsequent years, the case became known as the "English Dreyfus Affair." This label was hyperbolic, but there was no question that it was proof of adultery, not proof of murder, that convicted Florence Maybrick. The jury's verdict, as one observer aptly put it, had been handed down by Mrs. Grundy.[9]

In all the public furor over Mrs. Maybrick's admitted adultery, few, even among her supporters, noted that her actions, whether they involved murder or simply sexual improprieties, had been set off by her discovery of her husband's infidelity. In the Parisian case of Claire Reymond, tried three years later in 1892, discovery of a husband's infidelity was central, since it led more directly to a confessed slaying.

Mme. Reymond, the twenty-five-year-old wife of a Parisian businessman engaged in international commerce, had been married for three and a half years when she began to suspect that her husband Paul was having an affair with her best friend. An intelligent, volatile, and attractive woman, Claire Reymond had renewed her acquaintance in 1891 with Yvonne Lassimone, a former classmate from boarding school days. Yvonne was a blond beauty and a talented musician. Like Claire, she came from a wealthy upper-middle-class family; she had married a young lawyer a few years before and had an infant daughter. The two couples soon became close friends and—in the case of Paul Reymond and Yvonne Lassimone—intimate ones. Paul, however, carelessly left about some incriminating telegrams as well as the description and jeweler's bill for a ring that Claire had noticed on her friend's finger. Claire testified that she had confronted the pair in February 1892 and that after confessing to a single indiscretion, they had promised to end their relations. For her part, Claire agreed to forgive.

But, according to Claire, her suspicions were rekindled a few months later when, disappointed over Paul's canceling a luncheon date at the fashionable Ledoyen's, she gave in to curiosity over a mysterious valise her husband kept in their bedroom and summoned a locksmith to open it. In it she discovered sixty-odd letters from Yvonne to her husband, many written since the promised break, which made it clear that parting was hardly uppermost in their minds. She also found, in addition to a corset and a veil (whose presence was suggestive if nothing else), the receipt for a recently let apartment. She took the letters upstairs to her father's apartment with instructions to her parents to read them and guard them well.

Claire described what happened next as "instinctive." She armed herself with her husband's revolver and a knife and ordered a cab to take her to the address on the receipt. The concierge directed her to a third-floor apartment; when her husband came to the door but refused to admit her, Claire slipped a note through the door stating that Yvonne's husband had discovered them and was on his way. She assured Paul that she had only come to warn them and he opened the door to her. Then, as she had anticipated, her husband dashed downstairs to instruct the concierge not to let anyone up, which left her free to make her way into the bedroom of the apartment. There she found Yvonne seated on the edge of the bed, beginning to put on her stockings. Claire described the scene to the judge:

> Finding them together there . . . I was strangled with emotion. . . . I did not really expect to see her in the bed . . . she was almost naked. . . . I reproached her: "How could you be so shameless. It was I who was so good to you, who forgave you." [10]

Yvonne reportedly dismissed Claire's charges with sarcasm: "Your husband, and is he really *yours?*" [11] At that, Claire testified, "I lost my head, I fired." [12]

Three of five bullets went into the wall, the fourth grazed Yvonne's thumb, and the fifth and fatal one hit her in the stomach. The pair also apparently struggled briefly; Yvonne, who managed only to scratch her assailant, received superficial knife wounds on her breasts and arms. Leaving her victim bleeding to death, Claire hastened from the apartment, passing on the stairs her by-now distraught and suspicious husband. She urged him to get to Yvonne quickly.

Later that afternoon Claire turned herself in to the police and made a statement that the shooting was not premeditated, that she had never intended to kill or even to wound. She argued that she always carried a gun and a knife in her purse, a practice that dated back to years spent in Port-au-Prince, Haiti, where her father had a trading business. The statement was true enough, but it failed to explain why on this occasion she had chosen her husband's revolver rather than the small pistol she normally carried.

Failing to gain indictment on a lesser charge, Claire Reymond was tried in July 1892 for premeditated murder. Though opinion was initially against her, largely for the calculated way she had trapped her husband and her rival, sympathy swung to her side when her lawyer began to read passages from Yvonne's letters to her lover. The jury, after only a few minutes' deliberation, acquitted the accused.

That knowledge of her husband's adultery appears to have prompted an Englishman's wife to commit adultery herself and then possibly to murder her husband, whereas the same knowledge prompted a Frenchman's wife to murder the mistress may be insignificant in itself. But considered in the context in which these events occurred and in view of available evidence on middle-class adultery and "crimes of passion" in the two societies, these responses to a husband's adultery suggest much about late nineteenth-century attitudes of and about women.

What is known of the backgrounds of the two accused women and of the events surrounding their unhappy discoveries reveals first that their past experiences and social milieus were bound to make their responses quite different. There were similarities. Each had been raised in relative wealth and luxury, neither had any preparation for facing personal misfortune, and each, coincidentally, had had an ill-starred shipboard romance with an older man, whom she later married. But there the similarities stopped.

Mrs. Maybrick had been born Florence Elizabeth Chandler in 1862 in Mobile, Alabama, second child of William Chandler, a cotton merchant who was nephew to Associate Justice John Campbell of the Supreme Court and later secretary of war for the Confederacy. Florence's mother, Caroline Holbrook Chandler, was a daughter of Dennis Holbrook, a flamboyant Boston Yankee who promoted the Illinois Central Railroad, founded the town of Cairo, and gained dubious immortality in the unscrupulous character of Zephaniah Scadder in Dickens's *Martin Chuzzlewit.*

Florence's father died in 1863, and her mother, who had a reputation as a high-spirited and indiscreet young woman, was remarried briefly to a Confederate officer before he died of tuberculosis. She then took her two children to France, returning to New York after the war to visit her cousin, the second Mrs. Cornelius Vanderbilt. On another trip to Europe in the early 1870s, she was married again, this time to a Prussian cavalry officer, the Baron

Adolph von Roques, with whom she reportedly led a dizzy and financially reckless existence. The children, meanwhile, were farmed out to various friends, relatives, and institutions. It was a peculiar and chaotic existence which Florence elected to gloss over years later.

> I was educated partly in Europe and partly in America under the instruction of masters and governesses. . . . I was too delicate for a college life. I lived partly with my maternal grandmother and partly with my mother, whose home was abroad.[13]

Her few retrospective comments suggest that Florence wanted it to be assumed that she had experienced a more typical childhood than she actually had.

> My life was much the same as that of any other girl who enjoyed the pleasures of youth with a happy heart. I was very fond of tracing intricate designs and copying the old time churches and cathedrals.[14]

Florence Chandler was only eighteen in 1880 when, on a transatlantic crossing from New York to London, she met her future husband, James Maybrick, twenty-three years her senior. It was reported that the vivacious and voluptuous Florence seemed rather child-like and naive to be her mother's daughter. Whether or not this was so, she was to marry younger and with more direct parental intervention in her choice than most of her peers. Indeed Florence appears to have been a pawn in a game of mutual deception between her mother and Maybrick.

The Baroness, whose money supply was dwindling and who envisioned a comfortable old age through the generosity of a rich son-in-law, painted an exaggerated picture of Florie's prospective land inheritance in Alabama. Maybrick, in his turn, discreetly neglected to mention that his cotton business, a partnership with one of his brothers, was in difficulties. When the pair married the following May 1881, Maybrick made no marriage settlement and only took out an insurance policy for two thousand pounds, naming Florence as beneficiary. Florence brought only a hundred and twenty-five pounds a year, revenues from her grandmother's mortgaged home in New York.[15] Caution in financial matters was beyond Florence and James had business motives for wishing to disguise his pecuniary problems. When they moved to Liverpool in 1882 after spending a year in Norfolk, Virginia, they rented substantial, elaborately furnished dwellings and hired a staff well beyond their means.

In spite of such financial difficulties the first six years of their marriage gave the appearance of being fairly contented ones. James, in his typical manner, kept their deteriorating financial situation from Florence as long as he could. The couple led an active social life, entertained frequently, danced, played whist, and shared a passion for horseracing. Maybrick belonged to several clubs, which he often frequented after his day's work at the Exchange; he also made trips to the Continent as well as to America. Florence oversaw the household and the raising of the children, a boy born in 1882 and a girl in 1886. She found time, too, for teas, afternoon card parties, and numerous shopping trips. An American visitor reported his impression that though the Maybricks were welcomed in Liverpool's best circles, Florence, either because she was a foreigner or because she too evidently enjoyed the attentions of their male friends, had few close women companions.[16]

The upper-middle-class lifestyle of Florence and her husband was later described by the American woman who had been a young visitor in their home in 1888.

> She [Mrs. Maybrick] was extremely conscious of her beauty and attractiveness; and courted admiration, preference and compliments, especially from the male sex. She was very fond of dress, and Mr. Maybrick gave her beautiful, handsome clothes. She had clothes for every occasion—both indoors and out. . . . If Mrs. Maybrick had not been up late the night before, she would eat breakfast with Mr. Maybrick about nine o'clock. . . . If she had been up late the night before, she would get up about eleven or eleven thirty [and] eat her breakfast either in her room or the dining room. When the weather was good, the nurse would take the children out on the grounds, as soon as they finished breakfast. Mrs. Maybrick would come out, take the baby in her arms, play with her and pet the boy. When she became tired of the children she would read some light literature. In the afternoon she would dress and go in the carriage to Liverpool. Mr. Maybrick would usually come back with her. They rarely ever spent one or two nights a week at home alone. Two or three times a week they would have company for dinner, or company would come in after dinner. They would go out for dinner or after dinner or spend the evening. Every Sunday morning they would take a long horse-back ride together. . . . The relations with Mr. Maybrick always seemed very amicable. He called her Bunny. . . . They would often walk around the grounds with arms around each other and she would often sit in his lap and tell him how many gray hairs he had and how gray he was getting.[17]

As it turned out, the Maybricks were engaged on all fronts in the Victorian ritual of "keeping up appearances."

In 1887 Florence had made several discoveries that shattered whatever illusions she had about her husband. First, James finally confessed his near-total financial ruin. He attempted to place Florence on a strict budget, with only seven pounds a week to cover all food for the family, household needs, and servants' wages. Florence was desperate, not only because the amount was insufficient, but because she had secretly been borrowing money on her jewels and on the dubious claims of a land inheritance in America to pay for clothes and to place bets on horses. She was terrified to admit her accumulated debt of six hundred pounds, and late in 1887 she wrote frantically to her mother, who by then was living alone in Paris. She said James had disclosed that his assets were reduced to fifteen hundred pounds and that the business was making almost no profit.

> I am utterly worn out, and in such a state of overstrained nervousness I am hardly fit for anything. Whenever the doorbell rings I feel ready to faint for fear it is someone coming to have an account paid, and when Jim comes home at night it is with fear and trembling that I look into his face to see whether anyone has been to the office about my bills ... my life is a continual state of fear of something or somebody.... Is life worth living? I would gladly give up the house tomorrow and move somewhere else but Jim says it would ruin him outright. For one must keep up appearances until he has more capital to fall back on to meet his liabilities since the least suspicion aroused[,] all claims would pour in at once, and how could Jim settle with what he has now.[18]

Admittedly, Florence may have exaggerated a bit to dissuade her mother from requesting money from them. The Baroness had complained to her lawyer in New York that a few years after their marriage Maybrick had cut off her "allowance" and that her "poor little girl" was "completely in the power of her husband, and he does not prove a son to me." [19]

Not only financial problems preoccupied Florence about this time. Her son contracted scarlet fever and had to be nursed through a long illness, while her baby daughter was sent away to avoid catching the disease. Her brother Holbrook, a young doctor, died in Paris, reportedly of consumption. She noticed, too, that her husband's health seemed to be deteriorating. Worried that his condition was being affected by a mysterious white powder she had seen him taking, she confided her concern to her husband's doctor as well as to one of James' brothers. Some months later, not long before her husband's death, she told her own doctor about the powder and stated her fear that the substance was strychnine. She added that when she had asked James about it, he had been "irritable" and "touchy" and had told her to mind her own business.[20] The doctor cheerfully told her then that if her husband ever died suddenly, she could count on him to mention their conversation.[21] Florence's motives here are of course susceptible of more than one interpretation.

Finally, some time in 1887 when she was facing all these other difficulties, Florence learned that her husband was seeing a mistress he had kept for nearly twenty years. The woman, who had been a sales clerk in a jewelry shop, had had five children by Maybrick and continued to receive a hundred pounds a year from him. Florence was mortified that James showed little remorse when confronted with his delinquencies. The fact of his own adulterous relationship was barely mentioned in the trial itself, but its influence on Florence's behavior appears undeniable. A doctor who testified in the case mentioned in an article soon afterwards that since two years before Maybrick's death, which is to say from the time Florence learned of James's infidelity, the pair had slept in separate bedrooms.[22]

At about the same time Florence's name began to be linked with the names of one of her brothers-in-law and with a lawyer friend.[23] She had apparently decided to take revenge in kind, and late in 1888 she set her cap for one Alfred Brierley, a cotton broker and a bachelor fifteen years her husband's junior. Whether James suspected an affair or whether his anger was roused by something else is unclear, but in December 1888 Florence wrote to her mother to complain how their relations had deteriorated. Her husband, she said, "in his fury," had torn up the will that made her sole legatee and trustee, and he planned to settle as much as possible on the children. "A pleasant way of commencing the new year!" [24] was Florence's comment.

The striking aspect of Florence's retaliation with Brierley was its openness. In March 1889, less than two months before James' death, acting either from monumental stupidity or blatant calculation, Florence telegraphed a London hotel known to be frequented by cotton men her husband knew and reserved rooms for Brierley and herself under the name of Mr. and Mrs. Thomas Maybrick, her brother- and sister-in-law. The clumsiness of the whole arrangement suggests that Florence may have intended to provoke an outraged husband to sue for divorce. But if so, the plan did not work. Brierley, mortified at being recognized by some acquaintances, decided to cut the visit short after only one night. Soon after, he purchased a ticket for a two-month cruise on the Mediterranean, which he was holding when the news of Maybrick's death broke.

Florence's apparent "shamelessness" in the affair may have owed something to her American background and her status as a foreigner, as well as to her mother's less-than-puritanical views on extramarital sex. American women were generally branded as having more "advanced" sexual views, even though their English critics often failed to note that such advanced views frequently had originated in England and simply found a more congenial climate in the more diverse, less tradition-bound American society. In Florence's case, however, the decision to pursue extramarital affairs seems to have owed less to any free-love principles than it did to an outraged sense of justice, which her more "liberal" American background may have prompted her to act out in this way. In her explanation of the Brierley episode to her solicitor after her arrest (which he wisely refrained from circulating) Florence revealed both her own active role and a startling attitude toward behavior officially regarded as ruinous for a woman.

He [Brierley] piqued my vanity and resisted my efforts to please him. I told him I was going to London [she told her husband she was visiting a sick aunt] and taunted him with being a coward and afraid to meet me and willing to let such a chance slip by. I was, however, momentarily infatuated. Before we parted he gave me to understand that he cared for somebody else and could not marry me, and that rather than face the disgrace of discovery he would blow his brains out. I then had such a revulsion of feeling I said we must end our intimacy at once.[25]

While her "revulsion" did not prevent her from further entreating a cooling Brierley, the rest of her statement invites belief, if only for its reckless self-incrimination. She appears not to have realized that her admission of infatuation and hint of the hopes she had to use Brierley in ridding herself of Maybrick provided an obvious motive for murder. Especially remarkable for her time was her open and matter-of-fact description of her feelings and manipulative techniques. Admittedly her subsequent statements for public consumption were more circumspect, and her memoirs do not even mention the escapade with Brierley.

Evidence on the events from the hotel incident in mid-March to the onset of Maybrick's fatal illness in late April is conclusive only on the issue of a growing strain in relations between James and Florence. In late March Maybrick, who at the least was suspicious about his wife and Brierley, made a scene at the Grand National steeplechase when Florence briefly walked off alone with her lover. Afterwards Florence confided to a woman friend who had joined them, "I will give it to him hot and heavy for speaking to me like that in public." [26] Apparently she did just that, for servants reported that the Maybricks quarreled violently that evening, each accusing the other of unfaithfulness. James's concern was clearly not infidelity per se, but the threat of social and subsequent economic ruin. "This scandal will be all over town tomorrow," [27] he declared, at which point Florence ordered a servant to summon a cab for her. The enraged James then attacked his wife, tore her clothing, and gave her a black eye, threatening that if she dared to leave, he would never permit her to return or see the children again. A maid then intervened, comforted Florence, and persuaded her to stay for the sake of the children.

The next day Florence described the fight to her neighbor Mrs. Briggs, an old friend who herself had been divorced. The woman urged Florence to see her doctor for advice and to consult a lawyer about an immediate separation. She accompanied Florence on her visit to the doctor. This man, a family friend, testified later that she had confided about her husband that she had "a strong feeling against him, and could not bear him to come near her." [28] Florence saw a lawyer as well, but what transpired in their conversations was not reported.

What Florence failed to understand was that both her "friends" would side with her husband in the end. Mrs. Briggs had long known the Maybrick family and resented Florence for taking the place she thought rightfully belonged to one of her own younger sisters. The doctor was soon enlisted by James Maybrick to mediate a reconciliation between himself and his wife. Maybrick agreed to pay Florence's accumulated debts in exchange for her promise to break off her liaison. Brierley did report receiving two vindictive letters from her "at the instigation" [29] of the doctor, but other letters both exchanged later suggest that neither wanted a complete rupture of relations, despite mutual protestations to the contrary at the time of the trial.[30] Brierley, however, did tell Florence in a letter which arrived during Maybrick's illness that it would be best for them not to meet again until late autumn. He added that his forthcoming cruise would buy time and make any identification of him by the London hotel man the more doubtful because of the intervening months. Ostensibly then, as Maybrick lay dying, Brierley was totally preoccupied with preserving his reputation and keeping his mistress at least temporarily at arm's length.

Florence, outmaneuvered by friends, husband, lover, and even servants, may have concluded that all the more obvious options for escape for her marriage were used up. But her precise course of action in these anxious weeks remains a mystery. She did buy some flypapers containing arsenic at the end of April, just about the time her husband first took seriously ill, but she openly soaked them in a wash basin for all to see, a curious procedure for a would-be poisoner and one which loaned credibility to her face-wash explanation. Moreover, James's symptoms appeared about two weeks before the first flypaper purchase, when he had gone to London to settle Florence's debts. At that time he was already suffering from pains in his head and numbness of limbs which prompted him to visit a doctor. He also appears to have had a premonition of death, for he drew up a new will to be treated as his last testament "in case I die before having made a proper will in legal form." By its terms Florence was cut off completely, and all James possessed was to be held in trust by his brothers for the children. Florence was to be permitted use of the house furnishings and was expected to live with the children "as long as she remains my widow." [31]

If Florence had seized on her husband's illness as an opportunity to rid herself of him, she displayed remarkable sangfroid. And whether or not her "eruption of the face" had been cleared up by the arsenic wash, she did attend the ball to which she referred in her courtroom statement, even though her husband by then was ill on what would be his deathbed. Her escort that evening, her brother-in-law Edwin Maybrick, had earlier been rumored to be her lover, but within eight days he had joined his brother Michael Maybrick in implicating Florence in the poisoning of James.

In the case of Claire Reymond the train of events leading from discovery of infidelity to murder was more straightforward and the background of the accused was rather less remarkable. Daughter of a merchant and banker with homes in Nice, Port-au-Prince, and Paris, Claire enjoyed traditionally close family ties and appears to have seriously upset her doting parents on only one occasion when, in 1887 at age nineteen, she fell in love with the handsome thirty-four-year-old Paul Reymond, a businessman who had trading interests in South America and who appears to have been an acquaintance of her father's. Claire's mother later reported that she and her husband had disapproved a match and had taken Claire on a cruise to Port-au-Prince, evidently to get her away from Reymond. Once they set sail, however, her parents discovered that Paul Reymond was a fellow passenger; they soon gave in to the couple's desire to marry in order, as Claire's mother put it, "not to break our daughter's heart." [32] The wedding took place in the summer of 1888, and after spending over a year in Port-au-Prince and Buenos Aires, the couple returned to Paris in 1890.

Claire insisted that until she encountered her friend Yvonne Lassimone early the next year, she and Paul had been "very happy," though she acknowledged their regret over not having had a child by then. Claire even admitted that she felt special pleasure when her friend asked her to be godmother for her baby daughter, since, as she put it, "our own marriage had remained sterile." [33] Conceivably, her delight in fantasy motherhood made her oblivious to the growing intimacy between her friend and her husband on the numerous occasions they spent time together.

For her part Yvonne Lassimone seemed to be tiring of her husband, the elegant but rather timid son of a famous couturière who was enjoying little success in a new business career. Younger than Yvonne by two years, Lassimone, who was twenty-four in 1892, appears to have been a passing fancy of his rather spoiled and self-centered wife. Since her recently divorced parents were well placed—her father was a lawyer and journalist and her uncle was in the Senate—Yvonne was able to use their influence in propping up her husband's career, but in the process she appears to have lost whatever respect she had had for him. The older, self-assured, and highly successful Paul Reymond was all that her husband was not, and she well knew her own powers to attract. One paper referred to her solemnly as being "perhaps too striking." [34]

Claire's initial reaction to learning of the intimacy of her husband and her friend was superficially the resignation expected of French bourgeois wives.[35] Questioned by the judge about whether she had not earlier noted anything between Paul and Yvonne, she replied that she had, but not until January 1892, nearly a year after the probable beginning of the affair. As Claire said, "One day when my husband, Yvonne and I were returning home from the theater in a cab, I thought I glimpsed them holding hands in the momentary illumination as we passed under a gas lamp." [36] Claire explained that when she found the incriminating telegrams which led her to confront the pair a month later, she cried all night and even contemplated jumping out a window.[37] However, she apparently accepted the apologies of both for an alleged single indiscretion, partly, as she contended, because Yvonne invoked the name of the goddaughter she wanted to continue seeing. Claire also reported that Yvonne begged her to keep visiting her, since a break in their relationship might seem suspicious to her husband. Claire agreed, but remained constantly on her guard.

One obvious cause for suspicion was that though Lassimone in December 1891 had been named a counselor at the prefecture at Blois, Yvonne had managed to postpone joining him there. Lassimone remarked in an interview that first it had been the excuse of the long chore of packing and then it was that she was too "ill" to undergo the move.[38] After a time the pattern was established that Yvonne remained in Paris with the child, and Lassimone visited on Sundays. The arrangement was ideal for continued rendezvous with Paul, as Claire realized, even though she was simply informed that her friend "adored" Paris and could not bear to be exiled to Blois.

Once she was convinced that the affair had not in fact been terminated, Claire attempted to make Lassimone assume the classic role of outraged husband and remove his wife from Paris. Lassimone reported receiving two anonymous letters about his wife and Reymond at about the same time Claire made her discovery in February, and her denials notwithstanding, she probably had sent them. But Lassimone was not lacking for informants. His maid in Paris, he said, had warned him of certain "scenes" between Reymond and his wife.[39] He also learned from his mother-in-law's maid that his mother-in-law was making her apartment available for the lovers' meetings. Claire, who seems to have felt Lassimone was moving far too slowly, confided in her mother who took it upon herself to send the following telegram to Lassimone's mother: "If you wish to have proof of the misconduct of Mme. Yvonne, post someone outside her door tomorrow, early in the morning, and order that person to follow her all day without losing sight of her. . . . Your charming son deserves a happier fate." [40] Mme. Lassimone was later reported too ill to follow up on the plan, though it is likely her son forbade her intervention.

Although he later maintained that he was merely waiting for enough proof against the pair to "jump on his [rival's] neck," [41] in reality Lassimone seems to have been goaded into what little action he did take by women who tried to shame him into what they considered a proper retaliatory role. Lassimone told reporters that in March he did attempt a surprise visit to his mother-in-law's, where he hoped to catch the pair and recover some of Paul's letters to his wife, which would have provided all the evidence he needed either for an adultery conviction or a divorce suit if he had wished. But he confessed weakly that he arrived "too late" and that his mother-in-law managed to destroy the letters when he was "momentarily called out." [42]

The precise narrative of subsequent events leading to the shooting is difficult to reconstruct, in part because Lassimone, as the wronged and aggrieved husband, was spared from testifying, and Paul Reymond was only questioned briefly. In spite of some disagreement of detail in the newspaper interviews with the two men, the general outline of events is clear enough.

The illness which Yvonne had claimed prevented her move to Blois was a pregnancy, which her husband knew about, but of which Claire probably remained ignorant until the first week in April, when Yvonne announced that she had had a miscarriage. The likelihood that the father was Reymond was great, not only because Yvonne and her husband had been so little together since the previous December, but also because her letters to her lover insistently demanded that Paul not even touch Claire, a demand she could hardly have made had she herself not been avoiding relations with Lassimone. The announced miscarriage, then, was most likely an abortion, for Yvonne and Paul, who intended ultimately to marry, knew that the law forbade divorced persons from marrying anyone with whom previous sexual relations could be proved.

Lassimone, apparently suspecting that his wife planned an abortion, hoped to intervene in some way. But for whatever reason he did not discover the doctor she had hired until after the event, and when he visited him, the doctor simply confirmed the story of the miscarriage. This was only to be expected, especially as the doctor was likely to have been well paid for his services.[43] The doctor, in any event, was not summoned to testify.

In his statements to the press Lassimone never directly mentioned his suspicion that his wife had had an abortion, but his remarks were transparent. He noted with sarcasm that on several occasions prior to the event his wife had mentioned her "fears" of a miscarriage.[44] He remarked also that he had come to Paris during his wife's convalescence only because he had received an anonymous letter informing him of the miscarriage, whereas Paul Reymond, according to the maid, had visited Yvonne during this time as often as two or three times a day.

Still, whatever Lassimone had planned, he continued to do nothing. During his visit in early April he and Yvonne quarreled; he admitted hitting her and alleged that she had scratched him. But Yvonne, on the grounds that her husband was violent and had threatened her, proceeded to engage rooms for herself and daughter in a convent in Paris and filed suit for divorce. Meanwhile Claire, who was growing desperate, took to Lassimone's mother two letters from Yvonne to Paul which she had discovered, hoping to get her to use her influence with her son to force Yvonne to leave Paris. Mme. Lassimone, however, declared her suspicions about the authenticity of the letters and Claire finally agreed to take them to a handwriting expert. At the same time she informed Mme. Lassimone that she intended to try to surprise the couple together. As she excitedly told the judge later, "It was essential! Once their adultery was proved, my husband would not have the right to marry Mme. Lassimone after the double divorce he dreamed of. I still loved him, despite everything, and I was determined to prevent them from marrying one another!" [45]

These events of early April cast real doubt on Claire's basic defense that on May 21, when she discovered the letters in Paul's valise, she had set out impulsively, armed to the teeth, to surprise the couple. It appears instead that she resolved upon murder when the failure of others to act convinced her that the matter was up to her. Lassimone admitted to having had two conversations with Claire in early April before his return to Blois, and her decision may well have dated from that time.

Lassimone's own reasons for inaction were obvious enough. He owed his new position as an important functionary at Blois to his mother-in-law's intervention; public exposure, especially without violence against Reymond, could only have made him appear ridiculous. Yvonne's pregnancy reinforced his reluctance to act, since doubts about the child's paternity would become public knowledge. He declared that he had loved his wife "passionately," and the desire to win her back also restrained his actions.

In one interview he complained bitterly that his mother-in-law had been the cause of all his unhappiness;[46] whether she had gone so far as to facilitate her daughter's dalliance by securing a position outside Paris for her son-in-law, her all-too-evident accommodation of Yvonne and Paul was a judgment on him which doubtless stung. Altogether, Lassimone saw clearly that he had too much to lose by taking direct action. After Claire took revenge her own way, the young man quietly turned in his resignation. He reportedly had the "sympathy" of his fellow functionaries at Blois.

Claire Reymond, unlike Lassimone, appears to have decided that she had little to lose by acting. She knew that hers would not be the first case in recent years in France in which women of her station in society had taken up arms to defend what they called outraged honor. But if she planned murder sometime before the event, as is likely, there remained the logistical problem of opportunity. As long as the pair continued to meet at Yvonne's mother's, the risks were too great. However, Paul's decision to rent an apartment after Yvonne went to the convent gave Claire the chance she needed. The apartment was rented on May 13, only a week before the shooting. Claire may well have discovered the lease promptly afterwards—her story about summoning a locksmith to open Paul's valise on the day of the crime was never verified in court. Certainly, given what she already knew, it is unlikely that she would have awaited the rather trivial occasion of a broken lunch date to conduct a search in the mysterious locked valise. Instead it is more probable that the broken lunch date was a signal to her that Paul and Yvonne were together in the apartment, a signal, in other words, of her first opportunity to commit premeditated murder.

Claire knew that in order to benefit from the notorious leniency of juries toward women in her situation, she had to make her act appear spontaneous and uncalculated. During the questioning immediately after she turned herself in, she declared that if only her rival had thrown herself into her arms instead of mocking her, all would have been forgiven again. But Yvonne had not done so and, as Claire would have had her listeners believe, passion and impetuosity took over. "I am a madwoman and a lover," she declared, "and all my troubles stem from that." [47]

By the time of the trial the following July, the judicial authorities, in deference to the feelings of Yvonne's well-connected family, had done all possible to spare those concerned from painful exposure. Paul Reymond was summoned only to recount the events of the afternoon of the crime.

Described as tall, thin, and well-dressed, with carefully coiffed and pomaded hair, full mustache, and rather cold eyes, Reymond added to the account the single observation that due to her habit of carrying a gun about, his wife was known in their circle as "the little savage." [48] One journal noted that the common agreement among the presiding judge, the public prosecutor, and the defense lawyer for minimum questioning of Reymond caused considerable unhappiness among the "pretty ladies" in court, who were avidly following the debates.[49] Aside from a doctor who had examined Claire after the shooting and reported the scratches which suggested a struggle, no other witnesses were called.

The public prosecutor made a spirited, but bumbling call for conviction, arguing that the case was not a "drama of the heart," but a "drama of hatred." He bitterly recognized, however, that sentiment was swinging in the defendant's favor and urged that juries had a duty to end what he labeled the "epidemic of murder."

The outraged spouse has no right to substitute death for the few months imprisonment by which the law punishes adultery. There are no "crimes of passion," there are merely crimes. Mme. Lassimone was more beautiful than Mme. Reymond. There you have the secret of this woman's hatred.[50]

The defense could not have ordered an attack more inclined to confirm sympathy for the accused. Even leaving aside the counterproductive suggestion about Claire Reymond's real motive, the prosecutor failed to mention that the defendant herself had had no legal recourse in this situation save through Lassimone, who had stood back. As we have noted, in France a husband's adultery was punishable only if he was foolish enough to maintain a lover in the conjugal home, and even then he could only be obliged to pay a small fine. Wives did not enjoy such solicitous protection, however; a husband was permitted to have an adulterous wife imprisoned for a period of three months to two years on the evidence of letters alone, which were deemed insufficient evidence in the case of a husband's alleged adultery.[51] Lassimone had such evidence, but chose not to act.

Claire Reymond's lawyer, rather than point out this fact, which might have prejudiced an all-male jury interested in preserving its rights, confined his defense to reading selected passages from Yvonne's letters to her lover. On March 29, just before her alleged miscarriage, Yvonne had written:

I am yours forever, and I am so exasperated by this false situation that I am ready to fly off the handle or do something rash. I am still able to reason, but God knows how long that will last. Is your better half [*douce moitié*] going to Nice? I am convinced she will use all possible means to bring you to her side, and it enrages me just to think of it.[52]

On April 15 she was imperious.

> You tell me, my dear, that you cannot avoid certain expressions of affection when you are together. I consider that a profanation of my property, of what henceforth belongs to me alone.[53]

On May 2 she continued in this vein.

> It is already too much that you persist in using the familiar form of address [*tutoiement*] with her. Stop sleeping in her bed, she disgusts me! [54]

Yvonne habitually signed herself "your wife" in these missives, and in the letter of May 2 she remarked how easy things would be for their future marriage plans if only they could interest their spouses in one another and then surprise them in adultery. All this, needless to say, was more than enough for the jury, which promptly released the accused.

Several features of the Reymond affair indicate the ways traditional patterns remained entrenched in bourgeois households, despite some evidence of change. The tightness of family ties throughout all phases of the case and especially the extraordinarily active roles played by women within the structure of the family provide instances of the persistent strength of female kinship networks in urban settings, especially in critical matters of family interest and honor. On both sides mothers assumed what were accepted as their "natural" roles as protectors of their children, and especially their daughters, even long after the children had reached adulthood.

The greater closeness of French as compared to English middle-class families, which still continues today, originally owed much to lower standards of living in the class and less social mobility. These factors meant that the literal proximity of family members, as well as their mutual dependency, remained greater. Governesses and boarding schools, which separated children from parents, were more common in England, and though it is true that the privileged Claire Reymond and Yvonne Lassimone had attended boarding schools, it is also true that they conformed to the class pattern in living near their parents after marriage and continuing to see them regularly. Claire even stayed with her parents when Paul took business trips.

The sorts of psychological intimacy promoted by physical closeness are not easy to explore historically, though most observers did report that both mother-daughter and mother-son relationships were stronger in France than in England.[55] However, in the Reymond case adultery was an issue which divided the loyalties of the mothers of the men. Lassimone's mother, despite evident reluctance to intervene, seems to have felt her son ought to have acted more decisively against Reymond, as witnessed by her willingness to receive Claire and at least partially to cooperate with her. Reymond's mother, when informed of her son's behavior, sided with her daughter-in-law. Whether she remonstrated with Paul is unknown, but Claire reported that she called on her mother-in-law before turning herself in just after the crime and the elder woman reassured her by saying, "You have done well." [56] Such evidence suggests that women may have been increasingly willing to contest the double sexual standard in private, even in cases involving the adulterous behavior of their own sons.

Female solidarity was naturally greater among blood relatives, and it has been argued that mother-daughter relationships remained especially strong in France, even after marriage.[57] Still, the precise quality of these intimacies has never been explored. The Reymond case suggests that their dimensions included sexual problems; Claire and Yvonne, at least, considered it perfectly natural to share these problems with their mothers. Claire did acknowledge that she waited a while after learning that her suspicions of Paul were founded, but offered the "excuse" that she had married somewhat against her parents' wishes and at first did not dare to reveal her unhappiness to them. Though Yvonne's sexual problems were of a different sort, the noteworthy common features are the sharing of feelings, the solicitation of help by daughters, and the supportive response of mothers. In more ordinary circumstances this primary support network doubtless helped many young women of the class to cope with the new experiences of married life. At the same time, however, it probably inhibited or retarded their emotional maturity as well as their ability to develop effective independent responses to their changing circumstances.

As a transplanted foreigner, Florence Maybrick had neither her mother nor other close relatives to turn to in need, but the situation of many of her English counterparts was probably closer to her own than to that of young French married women. In a society of greater mobility the likelihood that daughters and mothers would remain in constant touch was much reduced. Intimate confidences between them were bound to occur less frequently. In the absence of demographic studies the popular health and marriage manuals provide indirect evidence for this probable greater isolation of married English women. The manuals assumed that mother would not always be at hand to give advice and even in discussions of such traditional familial events as giving birth, women were urged to consult a neighbor woman for guidance.[58]

Florence Maybrick did write to her mother about money concerns, but she appears not to have mentioned more personal marital problems or, as Yvonne did, extramarital affairs. The Baroness did claim she knew nothing of these, and in view of an estrangement prompted by her son-in-law's cutting off her allowance, she was probably telling the truth. She complained that her daughter had even sided with James against her on money matters,[59] a natural response considering that James represented not only Florence's sole financial support, but her most immediate, if questionable, emotional support as well. The trend toward greater isolation of single family units was bound to make wives side more regularly with husbands and against their parents, even when, as in Florence's case, neither choice offered much.

Thus relatively greater removal from parents and extended family makes it likely that middle-class English women—and American women as well—had to face many of their more intimate problems alone or else seek the support of persons outside the family circle: female friends, doctors, lovers, and others whose loyalty was more contingent. While the long-run effects were no doubt greater independence and capacity to cope, the immediate effects involved greater insecurity and anxiety as more women were obliged to strike out on their own and adopt standards and behavior which differed from their mothers'.

Another aspect of these cases which suggests how traditional institutions in France worked to cushion the shocks of transition to modernity for women is the evidence that convents continued to provide a refuge for them in troubled periods of their lives. In Yvonne Lassimone's case taking rooms in a convent was doubtless a ploy to buttress her divorce suit. She intended to argue that her husband's violence had necessitated this course. For others, such as spinsters and widows in modest circumstances, the urge for sanctuary was more than a temporary expedient. Interestingly, even Florence May-brick's mother, who was living alone in Paris, reported that her daughter and son-in-law were urging her to move into a convent in order to save expenses. "I have suffered so much this winter the torture of uncertainty and the fear of each tomorrow that I will not risk it again. It is a martyrdom. I shall feel better if I know that the refuge of a convent is open to me." [60] The Baroness did ultimately take rooms in a convent.

In France, unlike England where only a few High Church establishments served such needs, convents appear to have been readily available to women,[61] and it would be useful to know more about the numbers of women who took advantage of them, their situations, and their lifestyles in the convent. Religious establishments in France may well have served a female clientele similar to the water-cure and health establishments which were more popular in England. They, too, may have fostered female subcultures which provided security and opportunities for mutual sharing of problems. The fact that convents were decidedly more conservative in tone than the water-cure establishments underlines again the more traditional framework in which French women experienced their transition to modern lifestyles.

These cases also offer some glimpses of the changing relations between servants and employers. New strains in these relations were appearing in both countries as servants began to exhibit growing signs of independence and as middle-class lifestyles underwent change. In Yvonne's case maids could not be relied upon to guard the secret of the affair with Paul. Yvonne's mother's maid confided to Lassimone the rendezvous there with Reymond, and Yvonne's own maid earlier told him about Reymond's visits there. Indeed, the untrustworthiness of her maid may actually have prompted Yvonne to solicit the use of her mother's apartment in the first place.

In Florence Maybrick's case, extra-marital relations appear to have been common knowledge among the servants, and the mistress's own transparent nature clearly did not help matters. The young American visitor recalled that, during her stay in 1888, the servants were in the habit of conversing together in low tones and that the household had an "air of secrecy" and a "current of mystery" which were "uncanny." She recounts several episodes of servants in tête-à-têtes who scattered whenever a member of the family approached and suggests, in retrospect, that these little conspiracies may have been related to the mistress's sexual indiscretions. Her memories of Mrs. Maybrick's behavior in any case provide some indications of how Florence may have arranged meetings with her lover(s), and how her arrangements may have aroused the servants' suspicions.

> There was an incident that occurred while I was at Battlecrease [the Maybricks' home] which, in my mature years, I consider very significant of Mrs. Maybrick's affair with Edwin [her brother-in-law]. She ordered the trapp one morning at a certain hour. She got herself ready before the appointed time for the trapp to be at the door; and was very restless, impatient and ill-tempered because the trapp was not there. This was an example of Mrs. Maybrick's spoiled, childish disposition. However the trapp came up in a short time and she was off to Liverpool. The next day the same act was repeated.... The evening of the next day after her last trip Mr. and Mrs. Edwin came out to Battlecrease and ate dinner, or as they expressed it "twilight meal." Only that morning Mrs. Edwin had returned from a visit to her mother, and she and the James Maybricks were discussing her visit.[62]

Obviously, the servants who waited tables on such occasions overheard conversations and were capable of putting events together. Some months later, when Mrs. Maybrick took up with Alfred Brierley, collusion against her among the servants was obvious.

Servant "betrayal" proved a serious matter to Florence Maybrick, since it led directly to conviction for murder. Four days before Maybrick's death the children's nurse, a young woman appropriately named Alice Yapp, opened a letter from Florence to her lover Alfred Brierley, which her mistress had naively trusted her to mail. According to Yapp's predecessor, who was interviewed after the trial, the nurse had a habit of snooping about her mistress's room and steaming her letters open.[63] But by the time this one was opened, gossip of Florence's relations with Brierley was rife, and servants, who had spied the soaking flypapers, had developed their own theories about the master's illness. The letter was incriminating enough, though largely in the matter of proof of Florence's recent adventure with Brierley in London and of her own desire to continue the relationship.

> I cannot answer your letter fully my darling but relieve your mind of all fear of discovery now and in the future. M.[aybrick] has been delerious since Sunday [he had not, but Florence was fond of dramatic effect] and I know now that he is perfectly ignorant of everything, even of the name of the street, and also that

he has not been making any inquiries whatsoever. The tale he told me was a pure fabrication and only intended to frighten the truth out of me. In fact he *believes* my story, although he will not admit it.[64]

Miss Yapp, upon reading this startling communication, thought it her duty to take it directly to her master's brother, who was visiting, and to the neighbor Mrs. Briggs, who had become a fixture in the household since Maybrick's illness. Mrs. Briggs then summoned Michael Maybrick, the youngest brother, while brother Edwin took charge and ordered the servants to forbid Florence any further ministrations to her husband.

The nurse did have an explanation of sorts for the opened letter incident. She said that on the trip to the post office she had given the letter to the three-year-old Maybrick daughter to carry, but the child had dropped it in the mud, so that she had to open it to place it in a fresh envelope. In doing so, she said, she could not help but notice the contents. Yapp's story later drew clucks of disbelief from Florence's sympathizers in the courtroom, and papers noted that women attending the trial were saying that Yapp would find it impossible to get another position.[65]

In both cases, then, female servants showed a willingness to betray mistresses in matters involving sexual infidelities, though it is impossible to know if there was a general rise in such instances. Given that sexual jealousy was built into the mistress-servant relationship, it is possible that more of it came into the open as the century progressed, not only because class inhibitions were lessening, but also because servants were aware that new suspicions were being aroused about the morality of their mistresses. Then, too, as the middle class's "cult of respectability" crept downward on the social scale, the new lower-class adherents may have taken it more seriously than their "betters."

Whatever the explanation, it is argued that in general servants were becoming less loyal toward the end of the century.[66] Popular literature on servant problems in both countries was full of the theme; and commentary on several of the later cases discussed here, including this one, deplored servants' alleged new untrustworthiness.[67] It is true that by the end of the century domestic service was losing ground as other more remunerative positions were opening up. And it is also true that habits of deference were fading as extended education and new legislation popularized notions of equal citizenship and as rising standards of living increased the leisure and experiences of the servant class.

These cases, however, suggest another factor operating in the observed percentage decline of entrants into servanthood, namely, an increased desire for privacy on the part of the employers. These women, at least, had more to hide than before, and it is possible that some of the new criticism of servants may simply have reflected changes in the middle-classes' own behavior patterns. Not only were new "labor-saving" devices beginning to lighten the work in middle-class households, middle-class families were experiencing new urges for privacy and new desires to keep their lifestyles—and their secrets—to themselves.

For women such as Florence Maybrick, who were insecure in authority relationships and who did engage in activities best kept secret, the problems of managing household staffs and "keeping up appearances" were acute. With Florence's additional disadvantages of foreignness, feelings of inadequacy prompted by her youth, and the twenty-three-year age gap between herself and her husband, it was especially natural that she should have taken the course recommended in the manuals for her English counterparts and sought the counsel of an experienced neighbor. Unfortunately for her, that neighbor, Mrs. Briggs, bore Florence no real affection, and her "advice," such as it was, not only undermined the young wife's authority in managing the servants, but ultimately, and perhaps unjustly, helped to close the net of suspicion around her for murder.

Florence's mother, who knew the domestic situation from visits to her daughter, later charged that Mrs. Briggs had effectively governed her daughter's household through Nurse Yapp,[68] and it is clear from newspaper interviews with other servants employed by the Maybricks that Yapp managed to place at least two of her friends on the housemaid's staff and that she ruled them with an iron hand.[69] An article on Miss Yapp in the London edition of the *New York Herald* mentioned that the nurse had recently been abandoned by a clockwinder she was engaged to marry.[70] It is more than conceivable that her own difficulties in love helped to fuel jealousy of her mistress, but Florence appears to have been either too dim or too kind to notice. As early as 1887 Florence did remark to her mother on Yapp's indifference to the new baby, but without attributing any sinister motives to the woman.

> Nurse is quite changed since baby's birth, poor little mite. It gets neither petting nor coaxing when I am not with it, and yet it is such a loving little thing and ready with a smile for every cross word that nurse says to her. I cannot understand why she [Yapp] does not take to the child. . . . I am afraid she is getting too old for a young babe [Yapp was twenty-eight at the time] and has not the forbearance and patience to look after Gladys.[71]

Among the five members of the household staff, the cook alone, an older woman perhaps less liable to resentments shared by the others, proved openly sympathetic to her mistress. The cook testified that toward the end, Florence had come to her in the servants' hall crying that she was "blamed for all this," [72] and that it was the fault of Michael Maybrick, who had had a "spite" against her since her marriage. Florence declared that if she could, she would turn everyone out of the house, but when the cook asked if that included herself, Florence reportedly said no, thanked the woman for her kindness, and kissed her.

Q.   Did it seem to you that she was attending her husband?
A.   She seemed very kind to him and spent all her time with him.
Q.   And when she told you she had been blamed, you took her part, you sided with her?
A.   Yes I did, because I thought she was doing her best under the circumstances.
Q.   You sympathized with her in fact?
A.   I did certainly.
Q.   And she was in great distress?
A.   She was very much grieved over it and very sorry. She was crying. . . .
Q.   At the time you were aware that what particularly distressed her was that she was no longer recognized as mistress of her house?
A.   Yes and I told her I would rather be in my own shoes than hers.[73]

Florence's grief over her lost status as mistress of her home was the more pathetic in that recent events had merely confirmed her own unadmitted fears that she had never really held the reins. But by then the events set in motion by the nurse's insubordination had nearly completed Florence's isolation and paved the way for the accusation against her.

The anxiety of both Florence Maybrick and Claire Reymond over their threatened status as wives and "mistresses of their homes" raises issues which go beyond the demonstration of different familial patterns and domestic power relationships which had evolved by the end of the century. Both women initially responded in extreme, though very different ways to the knowledge of their husbands' extramarital affairs, and the real interest of the cases lies in the expression of shifts in attitudes toward the prevailing double standard of sexual morality, both on the part of the women themselves and of the middle-class societies to which they belonged.

Although traditional views that a married man's sexual infidelity was less serious a matter than his wife's doubtless remained dominant, since mid-century a "new morality" had made inroads in both societies. This was less because avant-garde writers had successfully argued the case for free love or women's equality than because the middle classes by then had created a world in which some contradictions in their creeds could begin to be seriously challenged. However, the expression of this change was different in the two countries because of their different historical traditions and stages of economic and social development. Not surprisingly, public attacks on the double standard came to be more widespread in England than in France, though what protest there was in France appears to have been more extreme. Early in the century a few radical critics, especially in France, were intrepid enough to argue for free sexual unions for both sexes, but they were chiefly men in the communitarian movements.[74] The real strength of the attack on the double standard came later in the century and mainly in England from "social purity" reformers, many of them women, who were troubled by what they saw as the immorality of the new urban world. Their protests, rather than advocating free sexual unions, demanded that the same strict sexual morality expected of women be required of men as well. The feminists, who overlapped the purity reformers to an extent, also tended to endorse the single sexual standard. Their pronouncements have been called antisexual, since they frequently held up the ideal of abstinence from intercourse as the purest marital relationship, but they do suggest that middle-class women who had acquired a new self-assertiveness largely within the domestic context were beginning to demand the extension of some of their private gains into the public realm.[75]

Pronouncements of any sort against the double standard, especially by middle-class women, were rare in France. True, there was a persistent, radical feminist critique imbedded in the revolutionary heritage, and there was also a stronger literary tradition of protest. Still, the near absence of an open demand for even a single sexual standard, as well as the weakness and derivative quality of the woman's movement in France, owed much to the slower formation of a new middle-class society. This did not mean, though, that attitudes toward the double standard were not changing at all.

Indeed, the "silent protest" in the form of a probable rise in clandestine extramarital sex among women did indicate that for some, theory aside, social and religious taboos were becoming insufficient restraints in the face of growing opportunities. Still, despite the attention paid to the new "adulteresses," their numbers, as well as those of the public protesters, were doubtless small. The largely private and unrecorded views and real feelings of the vast majority of women who remained silent and faithful to their husbands are hard to discover. Some clues to their feelings, however, can be found in the circumstances of the Reymond and Maybrick affairs.

If the Reymond affair had been an isolated instance of a woman indulging in an act of vengeance, it would demonstrate little, but it was far from that. Claire Reymond's reaction was part of an outbreak of violent attacks by French women which appeared in the last decades of the century and which, labeled as "crimes of passion," received tremendous attention in the press and in popular literature.[76] Curiously, at a time when bourgeois men were abandoning their legally recognized right to kill an unfaithful wife or her lover without being liable to a murder charge, many women, including bourgeois women, were successfully claiming that right, developing new variations on it, and declaring themselves in the process the administrators of a higher justice.

As contemporaries realized, the new "crime wave" among women was easier to document than to explain. Most agreed that it had appeared in the 1870s and that initially it was characterized less by murder than by a peculiar variety of assault called *vitriolage,* that is, the throwing of sulfuric acid at a victim. Curiously, too, the usual victim in such cases appears to have been a successful female rival rather than the husband or lover of the accused. Some women, then, appear to have been registering a kind of public protest against the double sexual standard after all.

Several writers acknowledge that *vitriolage* in crimes of passion was not a new phenomenon, but that popular awareness of it was heightened in the 1870s and that there was an actual increase in incidence. In Bouches-du-Rhône, admittedly one of the departments highest in crimes of violence, though not previously in women's violent crimes, sixteen such cases involving women came before the assize court in 1879 alone.[77] The new public awareness was stimulated in part by the fact that more middle-class women began to take up acid throwing. In his study *The Contagion of Murder* (1894), the criminal writer Paul Aubry devoted an entire chapter to the new *vitrioleuses*. Though he suggests that the majority were poor, young single women who were seduced, abandoned, and often pregnant, he cites several middle-class cases. He notes, too, that there developed in the crimes a kind of dramatic ritual in which most of the accused women participated, whatever their class status.[78]

In most instances, for example, the accused gave themselves up and issued statements of sorrow, but not of repentance. They normally maintained that the interloper deserved disfigurement for having alienated the affections of an either married or "promised" man. Women asserted that in turning to violence they had acted correctly and indeed often referred to fulfilling a duty. One bourgeois *vitrioleuse* was aggrieved by her husband's affair with her dressmaker involving the unsubtle device of his changing the family dinner hour so that he could spend time with his mistress after her day's work.[79] In presenting her case in 1881, the wife knew that the insult of even such blatant infidelity was not likely to summon much support for her, so she contended instead that since she herself was ill, she feared her husband's mistress might shortly become her children's stepmother: "I had resigned myself to the adultery, but I had no right to leave the name and future of my children to the mercies of a prostitute." [80] The dressmaker she called a prostitute had been disfigured and blinded in one eye by her, but this accused woman, like most other *vitrioleuses,* was acquitted.

Contemporaries in these years commented that this form of assault was beginning to be replaced by more serious and "classic" crimes of passion. They pointed to a "contagious" spread of such crimes among women and noted a progression from acid to revolvers.[81] Again, though commentators often failed to remark the fact, it was the appearance of respectable woman in these ranks which drew the real publicity. In Paris, especially, where the Seine assizes gained a reputation for being extraordinarily kind to the female avengers, the trials became a major attraction for women spectators. Moreover, juries proved obliging in applying a broad definition to the crimes. It will be recalled that Mme. Clovis Hugues and Mme. Paul Francey were both elevated as popular heroines for taking what each stoutly maintained to be just revenge for outraged honor. Despite obvious premeditation, both cases were generally accepted as crimes of passion and their perpetrators treated respectfully by complaisant, acquitting juries.

Claire Reymond's revenge against Yvonne Lassimone took place then against a familiar backdrop, and the script was known to all participants, including judges, jury, and public. By the 1890s, however, women dared to be somewhat more open about their real motives. One bourgeois woman who had surprised her husband in bed with their cook confessed to an obsession which drove her to stalk the former servant, who had taken a new position, and finally to shoot her six months later.[82] Claire herself, shortly after her arrest, made an exalted statement which showed that despite her disclaimers, she had not intended to spare Yvonne. "If, like many another woman," she declared, "I had been an indifferent creature without a heart, I could have gone on living, outwardly honored and respected but knowingly betrayed. I was not able to resign myself to this role."[83] Such an unequivocal public protest against the husband's acknowledged right to infidelity and against the wife's duty to be silent was a novelty among the accused women, but again the silent but sympathetic presence of women spectators at the trial provided a kind of endorsement. It is true, however, that masculine opinion did not shift in Claire's favor until the revelation of Yvonne's letters spelled out the cynicism and duplicity of Claire's erstwhile best friend.

It is unproved whether the increasing percentage of acquittals of all women in French assize courts owed something to gallantry toward women whose acts of violence were construed as crimes of passion, but observers clearly believed it was so, and the figures do coincide with the new female crime wave. Of course, acquittals of women throughout the earlier part of the century were already consistently higher than those of men. In the years from 1856 to 1860, before the crimes of passion captivated public attention, thirty-three percent of all women tried in French assize courts were acquitted, as compared to only twenty-three percent of men.[84] By the late 1870s, at the beginning of the phase of crimes and passion, the average figures for 1876 to 1880 were nineteen percent for men and thirty-five percent for women. And by the period 1888 to 1892 acquittals reached nearly forty-nine percent for women, as compared to twenty-three percent again for men. In 1892 itself, the year Claire Reymond took a revolver to Yvonne Lassimone, the female acquittal rate reached an impressive peak of fifty-two percent.[85]

New alarm over the crimes showed that their novelty was beginning to wear off, and the newspaper responses to the Reymond affair underlined the growing masculine disenchantment. Several insisted that the recent divorce law of 1884 removed any excuse for such crimes.[86] Under the banner headline *"Passionels!"* the conservative *Figaro* disparagingly referred to the "abominable acts which are excused by the banal and idiotic expression 'crimes of passion.' "[87] Acknowledging the continued legal right of a husband to kill wife or lover in the special circumstances of *flagrant délit* prescribed by the Code, the paper reminded its readers that women had no similar right in law and urged readers to save their pity instead for the unfortunate family and friends of the victim. A more philosophical piece which appeared after sympathy for Claire Reymond had begun to form argued that adultery had become "more than ever before, one of the features of our civilization," [88] but added that whereas men were driven chiefly by the taste for sexual pleasure, women's motives tended to be monetary. The observation may have been prompted by evidence that Yvonne appreciated the lavish presents her lover provided, but expressed as a generalization, it both excused the male behavior as more natural and indicted the adulterous woman as the modern female predator, a prostitute by another name whose only passions were pecuniary.

The spate of violent crimes among French women during these years poses several problems, especially why they appeared at that particular time and why the women were able to commit them with relative impunity. The concerned writers who discussed these issues had numerous, but hardly satisfactory explanations. It is perhaps unsurprising that the new crime wave was noted more by journalists and legal personnel than by theoretical practitioners in the new fields of sociology and criminal anthropology. The latter were more concerned with broader explanations of crime and still tended to treat all delinquent acts monolithically, as instances of either individual or social aberrance. Crimes of passion admittedly accounted for only a small proportion of crime in general and even of "crimes against the person," and insofar as the behavior of women in such crimes interested the theorists, it was as instances of specifically female biological or psychological peculiarities, largely divorced from the context of historical setting or social class. The fashionable exploration of female hysteria was extended to provide a catch-all category of female criminal hysterics, a label which did not begin to explain either these women's individual or collective behavior. The task of interpreting that behavior in the crimes of passion was left then to more eclectic nonprofessional students who began with their knowledge of specific cases to seek whatever theoretical or commonsense explanations seemed appropriate. [89]

The most ambitious among the writers was Louis Proal, a former president of the appeals court at Riom, who in 1900 produced a massive study of nearly seven hundred pages entitled *Le Crime et le suicide passionels*. [90] Proal identified the rising incidence of these crimes of passion in the modern perversion of love relationships and cited several factors he believed responsible: the new indulgence of juries, the precocious attraction of youth for debauchery and alcoholism, the spread of "nervous disorders," insufficient legal protection for seduced and abandoned women, and the corrupting influence of contemporary novels and theater. Most important, he believed, was the nefarious modern literary output; his chapter titles are sufficiently revealing here: "The Contagion of Crimes of Passion Through the Novel of Passion," "The Contagion of Crimes of Passion Through the Theater," and so forth.

Behind this indictment of modern literature, with its themes of immorality and violence, lay the familiar conservative indictment of a modern urban lifestyle which was allegedly producing delinquent children and unfaithful wives. The solution, for Proal and for most other commentators, lay in increased censorship of popular literature and dramatic works, renewed emphasis upon discipline of children, and greater religious training for women, who were by nature especially susceptible to the corrupting literature.

> The physiological functions to which women are submitted, menstrual periods, pregnancies, nursing and menopause, often cause mental problems. There is a tight link between the condition of the reproductive organs and the state of the brain. The physical and psychic life of the women gravitate around maternity.[91]

All this, needless to say, did not go far toward explaining the new female crime wave and the participation of bourgeois women.

The case studies here suggest some limited hypotheses to account for a phenomenon which deserves more attention. It appears that although French bourgeois women may have initially been inspired by types of violence such as acid throwing which were more prevalent among the poorer classes, it was they who both popularized the new crimes of passion and gave a female definition to their ritual quality. Moreover, the fact that there was no observed parallel English wave of women's crimes makes it probable that differences in the situations and expectations of middle-class women in France must be considered to explain the crimes.

Conceivably, these acts were one response to an actual rise in marital infidelity among French bourgeois husbands. In England infidelity among respectable married men had long been regarded as officially more blameworthy than in France; though it does appear to have been open and widespread at mid-century.[92] But by the 1870s a campaign against unofficial toleration of extramarital liaisons for men began to create a new, more explicit guilt for these relations and may even have inhibited husbands' indulgence in them.[93] Frenchmen were aware that a strict sexual code for men was more institutionalized in the English social system than in France. Taine joked that "an Englishman in a state of adultery is miserable; even at the supreme moment his conscience torments him." [94] Such pangs of conscience seem to have troubled Frenchmen rather less. It is possible that, as in England somewhat earlier, rising living standards, growing urban anonymity, and increased physical and psychological separation between the spheres of husbands and wives worked to raise the incidence of adultery among French husbands in the last decades of the century. However, demonstration of a rise in male marital infidelity does not in itself explain the rise in crimes of passion and does not provide an explanation for the modes adopted by the women, especially their preference for female victims.

A more satisfactory explanation for the female crime wave can be sought in the special features of the French bourgeois woman's social position by the 1870s. During the previous fifty years they, like their English counterparts, had experienced a steady improvement in living conditions and a new concentration on domestic management and child rearing. Like English women, they too had come to expect more from marriage, both materially and emotionally, than their mothers and grandmothers. Yet unlike the English, French bourgeois women did not simultaneously experience the effects of a strong and vocal public movement to extend their educational, legal, and professional rights. Throughout French society there was a far greater consensus on woman's ideal role as home manager, family nurturer, and guardian of religious values. In the near absence of conflict over other options, French women appear to have pursued their domestic duties with greater self-confidence and even to have exercised more actual authority in running the home than English women. By the end of the century, English women were already evolving toward a more companionate marriage relationship, which reduced the segregation of the sexual spheres by emphasizing mutual decision-making.[95]

At the same time, however, French women's greater domestic insulation provided them with fewer resources against individual threats to their new status, as well as against the general barrage of "antimodernity" literature after 1870, which singled out bourgeois women for their alleged luxury-loving, child-abandoning, and adulterous behavior. Even though they doubt-less deserved such criticism even less than the freer English women, they were less capable of defending themselves in the public arena.

Given these differences, it is possible that the new wave of women's crimes of passion was a peculiar response of frustration leading to aggression at a time when a gap appeared between the increased expectations attached to marriage and its perceived realities. Even if there was no absolute rise in adultery among French husbands, women's improved domestic status could have prompted them to question the male's continued right to extramarital sex. At a time when women themselves were being attacked for alleged infidelity, the wives of some adulterers may have felt more justified than ever in seeking revenge, just as larger numbers of women were prompted to show more open approval of such retaliatory behavior.

The idea of relative deprivation,[96] already familiar in explanations of collective violence and other criminal behavior, may explain how despite improved absolute conditions (indeed partly because of them), discontent increased and sought new outlets. Obviously, criminal behavior, and violent behavior at that, is hardly the only available response in such circumstances. English women, too, appear to have experienced some similar frustrations attributable to gaps between expectations and attainments in this period, but since English society already offered them options other than aggression or resignation, they may have been able to channel their hostilities more peaceably. Even when aggression was the chosen means to express frustration, the English woman's greater exposure to educational, legal, and social ideals arguably allowed that aggression to be channeled into political rather than personal violence. The militant, even violent suffragist activities can be seen as a counterpart to the French crime of passion.

Some evidence for the appearance of new resentment among bourgeois wives over their husband's sexual infidelities can be traced in the most popular French marriage manuals of the period. For the first time writers felt it necessary to stress the wife's all-important obligation of acceptance and resignation in the face of discovery of a husband's infidelity. This new emphasis implies a recognition that growing numbers of wives were disinclined to such generosity and required some prodding. Discussions of the wife's role, which had previously glowed with pronouncements about new freedom and hopes for happiness, now spoke of little but duty and obligation. Women were warned against appearance in public with any man save a husband, father, or brother. They were informed that marriage was unlikely to fulfill romantic expectations and that husbands were likely to be unfaithful.

One manual, which went through a hundred printings in ten years after publication in 1889, devoted nearly the entire section on the young wife to the disappointments of marriage (the husband, mainly) and the compensations (security and children).

> Perhaps you are unhappy; perhaps your heart is bursting. But do not look for consolation, even in the realm of ideas, if these are dangerous or if they can become sinful. Resign yourself. Lose yourself completely in your children.[97]

The manual proceeded to advise women that if husbands were unfaithful, they should be forgiven, for then they would be more likely to return to share old age with their wives.[98]

Although the appearance of female resentment over the prevailing double standard is arguably modern, the crimes of passion themselves, as public protest, were clearly cast in a traditional and ritualistic mode. Students of trends in crime during the nineteenth century have argued persuasively that serious crimes of personal violence, and particularly homicidal attacks originating in sexual jealousies, are a more characteristically premodern means of dealing with interpersonal tensions.[99] These women's crimes then may have involved the borrowing and adaptation of earlier male styles of revenge within a transitional setting, a setting which had not yet prepared them for the more modern middle-class approaches which English women, who had experienced a more rapid and complete transition, had already begun to adopt.

As previously observed, French middle-class men had already largely abandoned the crime of passion.[100] If the above analysis is correct, this would simply support the general thesis that men "modernized" sooner than their more isolated women, and for them the concept of defense of honor over sexual infidelity in both a public and violent way became anachronistic. In the Reymond affair Lassimone's evident restraint had a purely personal aspect in his sense of social inferiority and obligation to his wife's family, but it also reflected the fact that the new bureaucratic structures to which middle-class men belonged placed a premium on the prevention of public scandal which endangered careers rather than on the preservation of honor in the older sense. With their newly aroused sense of honor and without positions in the new structures, the women who turned to acid and revolvers had nothing to lose.

The leniency which juries accorded to women accused in the crimes of passion appears to have involved little appreciation of the women's implicit attack on sexual license for men. The offense which was recognized was instead the sexual transgression of another woman. The accused women themselves, in selecting female rivals as victims more often than husbands, participated to an extent in this view. But they also knew that there was greater social approval of an attack on an adulterous woman than one on an adulterous man. The accused then were pardoned less as "wronged" women than as destroyers of "scarlet" women.

The fact that the acquittal rate for these crimes was higher in Paris is more comprehensible in this view, since distrust of the new women as potential adulteresses had gone further in the capital. The accused women themselves, wisely and at least partly sincerely, chose to underplay their personal humiliation and picture their acts as desperate measures to preserve the sanctity of marriage and the family. Even Claire Reymond, who openly acknowledged the blow to her personal status, clearly participated in this feeling. When confronted by her husband at the police station shortly after her crime, she burst out, "Wretch! I did it for you!" [101]

If the Reymond affair had its chief interest as a case study in a peculiar new genre of women's crimes, the Maybrick affair in many ways was in a class by itself. Whether it even involved a crime is unclear, since the motives of the accused woman remain hidden. However, the circumstances of James Maybrick's death make it likely that if Florence did act to end her husband's life, she impulsively took advantage of an already established illness rather than premeditating his murder. Condemned largely on the basis of proved adultery, Florence Maybrick became the subject of an unprecedented outburst of public indignation. Whereas the Reymond case revealed an as yet timid and, in execution, "primitive" form of protest against the sexual license of husbands, the Maybrick affair summoned a frontal attack on the double standard. The case was unique, too, in that for the first time, women spoke out directly against the sexual prejudice of the verdict, signed petitions, wrote letters, and even formed organizations in Florence Maybrick's defense.

The Maybrick trial, which opened in late July 1889 in the wake of another of the "Ripper" murders, quickly absorbed the country's interest. Since pretrial coverage had already extensively dealt with the adultery with Brierley, the most startling new information was the indisputable evidence that James Maybrick had for years been an arsenic-eater. A black servant whom Maybrick had employed in America testified that for several years before Maybrick's marriage, he had regularly been sent out to purchase arsenic by his master and had observed him taking small amounts of the substance in his beef tea.[102] Some more recent evidence came from a druggist who stated that until he had sold his business a year before, Maybrick had been a regular customer for ten years. He reported that Maybrick had stopped by his shop as often as five times a day for a "pick-me-up" in the form of an arsenic-laced tonic and added that toward the end the customer had increased his dosage to as much as a third of a grain of arsenic a day.[103] The tolerance Maybrick had developed for the substance can be appreciated by the fact that two grains were considered to be a lethal dose. Still, Maybrick's habit was not, according to the druggist, unique. He reported that as many as sixteen "gentlemen" from the cotton exchange would line up in his shop every morning for their arsenic tonics.

Q. Was it towards the end that he [Maybrick] got it most frequently?
A. Yes, about twelve months before I gave up in Exchange Street East he told me why he was taking the liquor arsenicalis.
Q. Do you know that liquor arsenicalis has aphrodisiacal qualities? Do you know that word?
A. I do not.
Q. Did it excite passion?
A. Yes, it had that effect.[104]

This exchange was the only suggestion that Maybrick may have believed, like many others, that the tonic would improve his sexual potency. Several other witnesses, including a doctor, pointed out that the deceased had been a notorious hypochondriac who constantly dosed himself with all sorts of medicines and who had complained for years of symptoms characteristic of the arsenic-eater.[105]

The evidence of James' habits ought to have provided a satisfactory explanation for one of the most curious features of the case, namely, the discovery the day after his death by Mrs. Briggs and the Maybrick brothers of a supply of a hundred grains of arsenic in the Maybrick home. Their search, conducted without police authority or supervision, had turned up the poison, along with numerous other bottles of various medicines, in many places throughout the house, including drawers, hatboxes, and cupboards, all of which were open and accessible to anyone in the house. Florence claimed that she had tried to explain at the time about James's habit, but that her brothers-in-law had refused to listen and regarded their discovery as evidence against her, especially since arsenic was also found in the pocket of one of her aprons.[106] The prosecution was able to argue, too, that there was no evidence Maybrick himself had obtained the poison. As it turned out, the gentleman who was the source of this final supply had in fact given it to Maybrick as part of an informal business arrangement. This man stated that Maybrick had acknowledged his habit openly and was very grateful to receive the substance, which was left over from an industrial experiment. This evidence obviously would have helped Florence's case, but the gentleman did not come forward until four years after the trial.[107]

Ironically, though the greatest portion of the trial testimony was consumed with medical evidence, the eminent experts summoned from London failed to agree on the basic question of whether arsenic had been the cause of death.[108] Since the traces of the substance found in the autopsy were so small and since Maybrick had never exhibited the usual symptoms of a massive dose of arsenic, the expert for the defense contended that severe gastroenteritis was responsible for death and that small doses of poison had merely provided an irritant. Russell, in questioning the experts, tried to present the case that death resulted not from the administration of arsenic, but rather from the withdrawal of the substance from an habitual user. The experts denied experience of any cases of that sort, but several laymen who later sent letters to the press claimed they knew of instances of death following sudden withdrawal among arsenic "addicts." [109]

Under the circumstances, of course, the presence of arsenic in any case could not alone prove foul play, and the prosecution was obliged to rely more than it might have done on the possible motive provided by Florence's adultery. Much was made of a statement by Florence in the famous letter which nurse Yapp had opened that her husband was "sick unto death." [110] At the time it was written, James was merely ill and the doctors were not yet even considering his case serious. Florence's use of the phrase suggested to the prosecution that she alone, being the poisoner, knew James would die. In vain did her defenders point to other instances of her habit of dramatic exaggeration. In vain did numerous Americans write to newspapers to protest that the phrase "sick unto death" was commonly employed by Southern Americans in a less-than-literal sense to suggest merely that someone was very ill.[111]

Florence's admitted fall from virtue was handled by Russell as a matter of "grave moral guilt," but one which hardly proved the criminal charge. The fact that Russell was even willing to offer a mild attack on the double sexual standard indicated that he believed that by then an all male jury might be receptive.

> Ah, gentlemen, for faults of this nature, the judgments of the world are indeed unequal. In a man such faults are too often regarded with toleration, and they bring him often but a few penal consequences. But in the case of a wife, in the case of a woman, it is with her sex the unforgivable sin. Those who should well consider throw stones at her from unworthy hands.[112]

True, Russell did not mention James Maybrick's own extramarital sex life or its effects on Florence in this closing speech, despite the fact that Florence's only proved liaison involved a single sexual encounter, whereas Maybrick had kept a mistress for years after his marriage. It was later reported that Russell was unwilling to press the issue further, not only because he was convinced it might backfire, but because Florence herself had wished to avoid the matter for the children's sake.[113]

The jury, however, took to heart the final charge from Justice Stephen.

> she, while her husband lived and, according to her own account, while his life was trembling in the balance—even at that awful moment there arose in her heart and flowed from her pen various terms of endearment to the man with whom she behaved so disgracefully. That was an awful thing to think of, and a thing you will have to consider in asking yourselves whether she is guilty or not guilty.[114]

Sadly enough, the brilliant judge's evident bias was probably exaggerated by the effects of a recent stroke, from which he had not fully recovered. At several points in his summing up, and throughout the trial, Stephen gave evidence of losing grip on the discussion and frequently had to be corrected by Russell and others. After the verdict was delivered, Florence was asked if she had anything to say before sentence was pronounced. Her reply was a perhaps unintentional judgment on the methods of the court: "Although I have been found guilty, with the exception of my intimacy with Mr. Brierley, I am not guilty of this crime." [115]

Although the press was divided on the verdict, petitions to the Home Office for commutation of punishment were signed by almost half a million persons, including over ninety members of Parliament and seventy thousand Liverpudlians as well as a thousand members of the Liverpool Exchange.[116] Mass meetings were organized in London, Liverpool, and other cities.[117] Doctors and lawyers circulated separate petitions, although more doctors were inclined to accept the verdict, perhaps being eager to end an affair which had made fools of so many of their profession.[118] Numerous lawyers, on the other hand, felt there was insufficient evidence for the conviction and used the case as an argument for a court of criminal appeal. But such a court was not to be established until 1907.

The familiar commercializing and sensationalism were everywhere. Street hawkers sold ballads both for and against the condemned woman. Madame Tussaud's, in the fortnight's interval between sentence and commutation, displayed in a room by itself a hastily fabricated wax effigy of Florence.[119] Entering into the spirit, Sadlers Wells Theater threw together a production of a melodrama based on the case called *The Poisoner*.[120]

Surprisingly enough, the Maybrick affair initially got little coverage in the American press, partly because cable tolls were so expensive that only a few papers could afford extensive coverage.[121] Some American papers did argue that the trial was unfair, but there was no immediate outburst of sympathy such as Florence had summoned in England. This owed something to the

Baroness's association with Cornelius Vanderbilt, who had played sponsor to the scandalous and "socialistic" Victoria Woodhull.[122] But it owed more to unfounded stories which first appeared in papers in Mobile, Alabama, Florence's birthplace, which suggested strongly that the Baroness had poisoned her first and second husbands. Fearful of the effects of these stories after they were reproduced in some Liverpool papers, the defense had even decided not to summon Florence's mother as a witness.[123]

Sympathy ultimately did come from America, but it was not until 1904, nearly fifteen years after she had been imprisoned, that remission of her remaining sentence was granted by Edward VII. Florence went to America and wrote her memoirs, [124] a somewhat disjointed and rather disingenuous volume devoted largely to her ordeals in prison. In the only extended remarks about her accusation for murder, she skirted the adultery issue entirely and argued implausibly that her courtroom reference to a "confession" to her husband for her "fearful wrong" had merely concerned a confession of her having contemplated legal action in a divorce suit. "The 'motive,' " she argued, "however regarded, was surely no incentive to murder as inasmuch if [sic] I wanted to be free there was sufficient evidence in my possession (in the nature of infidelity and cruelty) to secure a divorce, and it was with regard to steps in that direction that I had already taken that I made confession to my husband after our reconciliation, and to which I referred to as the 'wrong' I had done him, because of the publicity and ruin to his business it involved." [125] As was usual with Florence, fact and fiction were inseparably intertwined.

For several years thereafter Florence Maybrick went on the lecture circuit appealing for prison reform, but gradually friends and money deserted her. Her mother, whom she had been supporting, died in 1910, and she was never reunited with her children, who had been raised to believe in her guilt. By 1917, having decided to adopt anonymity, she applied for a position as housekeeper on a Connecticut farm. The job did not last, but she apparently acquired a small sum from a benefactor which enabled her to build a cottage on a tiny plot in nearby South Kent. Neighbors who learned her identity kept her secret, and old "Mrs. Chandler," who gained the reputation of an eccentric recluse who befriended stray dogs and cats, ended her days in poverty and obscurity. She died of a stroke in the fall of 1941 at seventy-nine years of age.[126]

The neighbors reported that the old woman was renowned for her "tall tales," so her reputation for untruthfulness, which was not undeserved, dogged her to the end. But whether she was a liar, and even whether she was a murderess, had early been recognized as irrelevant to the issue of whether she was convicted on the basis of insufficient evidence, namely, the evidence that she was an adulteress. That that issue was seized by a hostile and vocal cross-section of the public was as important, if not more so, than the actual fact that the verdict iself was delivered, especially as the jury's decision owed so much to the peculiarities of a mentally impaired judge. It is true, of course, that not all the public support for the condemned woman rested on this ground. Popular enthusiasm for Mrs. Maybrick among Irish working classes in Liverpool, for example, can be attributed largely to Russell's known stand in defense of Home Rule, which was currently being debated.[127] Still, the outraged middle-class opinion which was voiced in the press in countless editorials and letters, as well as through other forms of public expression, unveiled a new consciousness of the injustice of the double standard which extended much further than the circles of the previously vocal feminists and social purity reformers who had taken public stands.[128]

Most remarkable of all was the emergence of women among that silent set of spectators, inside and outside the courtroom, from their previously subdued roles to new articulate and active ones. The process was visible in the course of the trial, though as the proceedings began, the behavior of women in the court seemed much as before. It was reported that they were present in large numbers, they showed sympathy for the accused, and that they included many respectable women. A gesture near the end of the proceedings also suggested their traditional style. Anticipating the acquittal of Mrs. Maybrick, a delegation of "well-dressed" women petitioned the court clerk for the right to present her with a bouquet of flowers after the verdict.[129] They were refused. Upon delivery of the verdict, three women reportedly fainted and had to be carried out, while many others wept. This again was nothing new.

Still, the women appear to have communicated a new spirit of partisanship from the beginning. The usual press reports deploring their presence were more hostile than ever before and pleaded for the exclusion of the women from all cases involving murder. One especially virulent Liverpool paper decried the "creatures called ladies" with their opera glasses.

> Fancy women with pretensions to purity, education, and refinement scrambling and struggling to hear the public revelations concerning an admitted adulteress and an alleged murderess! What filth they must have in their hearts! What greed of lustful curiosity! What smug hypocrisy in their offenseless faces! What a dunghill of dirt seething and stinking behind their modest eyes and placid brows! For the women there is no excuse! Nothing but a prurient thirst for beastliness can account for their being there at all! In a place that every true woman should shrink from and abhor as she would a gaol or a brothel! [130]

Another paper labeled the women spectators the "ghouls of modern society," [131] and many others reiterated these themes. The new violence of language pointed to an increased sense of threat over the women's presence, but there was also a new confusion over why women who were arguably better off than ever before could act this way.

> Our modern women have no excuse for this behavior. They have no wrongs to avenge, no remembrance of tyranny, violence and privation to blunt their

feelings; they have been brought up in luxury, or at least in comfort, sheltered from hardship and taught from their earliest years that charity is the first of Christian virtues.[132]

Yet, all these advantages were apparently not enough. The author proceeded to plead for the exclusion of "the female element" from murder trials and offered the opinion that "the most ardent devotee of women's rights could hardly object to this." [133]

He was clearly wrong, for when the allegedly spoiled women with their prurient tastes began to voice their opinions after the trial, they argued not only for a place in the courtroom for women, but for seats on the jury.[134] And most of these were not ardent supporters of the newly revived women's rights movement, but instead quite ordinary but outraged women. Of the seventy thousand persons from Liverpool who had signed petitions, a substantial majority were women.[135] A sampling of their letters to newspapers demonstrates the new comments these women were daring to make in public.

If the sentence is carried out, immorality and murder will be synonymous terms.[136]

I do not believe but what many a woman's heart today has thrilled with a feeling of indignation and sympathy upon reading the jury's verdict.[137]

I do not by any means condone adultery, but from a close observation of poor frail human nature I fear there are numbers who would have shown no more strength in practically similar circumstances.[138]

Of course the jurors decided for their sex. Doubtless each one was a husband and became bitter on the dishonoring wife.[139]

But the sin forgiven by Christ in heaven by men is cursed away.[140]

Occasionally the letters from women were more bold, such as this one which openly touched the subject of women's sexuality.

Is this fair play in the big game of life? Crime is crime irrespective of sex. But to "stone" a weak woman for the same crime a man is allowed to commit with impunity is not by any means fair play.... Infidelity in both sexes is often a merely temporary yielding to the most powerful of human passions. The error of judgment commonly made is to assume that women are less susceptible than men to the great passion.[141]

A small number of women did write letters in support of the verdict, but the overwhelming number of the respondents, both men and women, hoped to be able to quash that verdict. How many women joined the committees for her support or attended the mass rallies is unknown, but ordinary women were clearly becoming both visible and vocal.

Less unusual was the willingness of long-established reformers, men and women, to enlist themselves among Mrs. Maybrick's supporters. It was men who organized the mass rallies, and it was a male journalist, the flamboyant William Stead, who came around to championing the prisoner, though not until 1892.[142] Josephine Butler, leader of the successful drive against sexually discriminatory legislation on prostitution, wrote:

> Nothing can exceed the strictures of Judge Stephens' language in condemning the lady's infidelity to her husband. . . . Feeling as I do the sin in such, probably more keenly than most people, I yet must express my surprise that such strong expressions should be reiterated *ad nauseum* when dealing with a woman, while they are not made use of at all in the case of men of high rank, who have been notoriously unfaithful to their wives.[143]

The long campaign to free Florence Maybrick ultimately enlisted many American women, including professional groups such as newspaperwomen who petitioned the Home Secretary for a review of the case in 1894. Three years before, an International Maybrick Society was founded under the leadership of Florence's chief American champion, the journalist Mary Dodge.[144] The executive committee included Julia Ward Howe, Elizabeth Cady Stanton, and Ida Tarford Bell, a formidable women's rights group. But American efforts to free the prisoner were complicated by the fact that they had to be unofficial, since in marrying Maybrick, Florence had lost her United States citizenship. Pressure and petitions were tried, including letters to the Home Office and even to the Queen. White House officials attempted arrangements through ambassadors and also sought informal understandings with the Home Office. But as the years passed and as all failed, despite the renewed efforts of the now Lord Chief Justice Russell, who believed in his former client's innocence, the suspicion gradually developed that the Home Office had a secret dossier with hard evidence of Florence's guilt.[145]

There was no such dossier, but there was a force which was powerful enough to prevent the crusaders from having their way, and that force was the will of the Queen. Victoria's dim view of women's rightists, who had spoken for Florence, was well known, and more well known still was her attitude toward women's sexual transgressions. It had only been in the year of the trial, 1889, that the Queen had unbent to the degree of abolishing the rule preventing women who sued their husbands for divorce from appearing at court, since the "wrongdoing" was acknowledged to be the husbands' and not theirs.[146] In the case of Florence Maybrick guilt of the charges seemed obvious to the Queen, who was most upset that the Home Office felt obliged to commute the punishment. At the time she wrote that she regretted that "so wicked a woman should escape by a mere legal quibble. . . . But her sentence must never be further commuted." [147] As long as the Queen lived, her ministers were too squeamish to stand up to her in her self-bestowed role of guardian of the public morals. But within six months of her death the Home Secretary had promised to make arrangements for the prisoner's release.

That by 1889 a woman could be convicted for murder in England chiefly on the grounds of adultery required some special circumstances—an anxiety about female morality, a very persuasive judge, and an awed and obliging jury. That the decision stuck depended largely on the absence of an appeal mechanism and on the personal power of a superannuated monarch. The women who had discovered their voices in the campaign to free Florence Maybrick had at least helped to spare her life, which may have been the life of an innocent woman. They had also dared to make the Maybrick affair a forum for their own indictment of a system of social hypocrisy. Most of the women of the campaigns returned to the security of the homes their husbands or fathers provided. But they had gone on record.

CONCLUSION:
THE LADY KILLERS

In their own time the lady killers of the Victorian era, whether excused or vilified, were almost never presented as the women they were. They assumed multiple identities fashioned both by themselves and by others. In legal proceedings the masks they wore proved useful to them in some cases and detrimental in others, but in all they served to shield contemporaries from the disturbing countenances of real women.

Subsequent tellers of their tales have usually been content to portray the accused murderesses as freaks. This rather more sympathetic survey might be mistaken as an attempt to view all the women as victims in their own right, creatures subjected to various forms of male domination. But while elements of victimization are clear enough in many of the cases, such a view is far too restrictive. The label of victim both trivializes and distorts the rich and varied stuff of these women's lives and, not incidentally, ignores their own homicidal activities. In this instance, as in most other considerations of women's roles, the charge of male oppression, however emotionally satisfying and even true, leaves much to be desired.

Equally inadequate is the related notion that the women were social rebels, even proto-feminists, using murderous schemes to challenge outmoded codes of behavior. True, it is possible to identify among them some women whose more "positive" motives suggest a growing consciousness of struggle against constricting social roles. Especially in the later period, women murder not merely to escape what they perceive as hopeless or desperate circumstances, but also to achieve or retrieve some imagined happier state. Nonetheless, the designation proto-feminist is hardly appropriate to women who were anything but crusaders, who were neither reformers nor public defenders of their sex. It is clear that by the end of the century many middle-

255

class women were unwilling to accept the same sorts of legal and social inferiority as they had earlier, but it would be rash to regard the criminal behavior of some of these women as a self-conscious feminist expression.

The accused women were not, then, simply freaks or victims or rebels; rather, they were women who were especially vulnerable to the same pressures experienced by the majority of their peers. Those pressures emerged from two sources: the actual changes which were transforming society and which encouraged women to take advantage of new options in their roles as daughters, wives, and mothers and the public efforts to interpret these changes, many of which attempted to redefine women's nature and function as well as to assign them both praise and blame for the way things were. Most women survived the upheaval by adapting; a good number—how many is unclear—never did manage the adjustments required of them.[1] Among these were the handful whose lives were exposed through investigations for murder.

All these women's dramas began on a domestic stage which was normally reserved for private audiences; the women cannot be understood unless this narrow stage is kept in focus. And the theatrical image is apt, for role playing became for them, and for their less notorious middle-class sisters, more of a way of life than ever before or since. Yet if they were obliged often enough to deliver the lines others had written for them, they demonstrated that they were more than capable of composing some of their own. For the women in this study, of course, the scene was suddenly changed; when the curtain was raised again, the whole world was watching.

Despite their varied stations within the middle class, the subjects' shared domestic environment produced similarities in their approaches to problems. Unsurprisingly, their efforts to widen the boundaries of their experience and authority were often conducted indirectly, for none of them—including Florence Bravo, who boasted of her "freedom" as a wealthy widow—was truly independent. The stratagems they devised and the goals they set were bounded by dependent relationships which invited manipulation.

It is tempting, of course, to regard the murderesses as extraordinarily gifted in deceit, but nineteenth-century middle-class conditions were so favorable for developing female skills in mendacity that the judgment would be hasty. The reputation for lying has admittedly always belonged to women, and it is deserved to the extent that, like any other group with limited control over decisions which affect their lives, they have resorted to deceit as a survival technique. But in the Victorian age, deceit, in matters large and small, was elevated as a socially prescribed form of female behavior. Women were encouraged to hide their affections, conceal their bodies (as well as the bodily functions of menstruation and pregnancy), and, depending on the advice they followed, either hide or feign sexual pleasure with their husbands. Beyond this, new boarding schools, such as the one Madeleine Smith attended, provided informal training grounds in lying. And perhaps most important, the new institutionalizing of separate sexual spheres helped make the woman's world a mysterious new place for the men who visited there and doubtless permitted women to be far more readily believed when they told tales which now seem transparent. This is perhaps the only way to account for such oddities as the acceptance by the brilliant Edward Clarke of Adelaide Bartlett's "marvelous story" of a single act of sexual intercourse in eleven years of marriage.

All the women here lied. Among them Marie Lafarge, Madeleine Smith, and Adelaide Bartlett stand out, and Henriette Francey and Florence Bravo deserve at least honorable mention. Their lies, which were ultimately used to cover illicit sexual behavior or criminal acts, originally served less shocking but still forbidden ends: a secret tryst, an opportunity to read forbidden literature, an escape from unwanted marital sex. For most women, of course, the new opportunities for dissimulation were restricted to goals within the domestic sphere which could be achieved through lying; and it does appear that by the last decades of the century, as the separate spheres began to move a bit closer together, a new distrust of women whose social lives were less restricted did reduce the level of masculine gullibility somewhat. But for those intrepid enough to take advantage of new occasions to break the social rules, residual credulity was available, even though more elaborate sorts of lies seem to have been required.

For some of the accused women the lies themselves became a kind of game, carried on partly for itself as escapist fantasy and partly as a means to allow them to integrate socially expected behavior with their own contradictory feelings and urges. This may account for their creation of elaborate and intricate tales which became a kind of secret code, identified as such only by other women. Other women could recognize themselves in the romantic fabrications of Marie Lafarge's diary or in the pious mouthings of Madeleine Smith's letters or in the exalted prose of Henriette Francey's ultimatum to her victim-to-be. And the women could be trusted not to tell.

Another feature of the accused women's domestic experience which may have been more widespread in their class was the system of alliances they formed with servants. Most servants were women, of course, and a remarkable number in these cases entered into conspiratorial and even criminal understandings with their mistresses. Marie Lafarge's Clémentine baked Charles a poisoned cake; Madeleine Smith and a young maid arranged a trade-off which permitted each to entertain her young man in the privacy of the maid's room; Henriette Francey confided to her maid her plans to murder Bazard. The obliging Mrs. Cox became her mistress's sole confidant and dear friend and ultimately created the lies which protected her. Of course the cases show, too, the less surprising fact that servants did not always take the mistress's part.

The cases are graphic reminders that middle-class women spent more of their lives in the company of, or under the same roof with, servants than any other people, including their children and certainly their husbands. While exploitation on the part of employers is a theme which is frequently, and no doubt rightfully, stressed, the cases show the complexity of the servant-employer relationship, which offered occasion for exploitation by servants as well, but which also could lead to deep friendships among women of different classes who shared confinement in the same household. By the end of the period, as noted earlier, it appears that for both parties the disadvantages were beginning to outweigh the advantages in such relationships, but further examination of similar testimonial evidence might help delineate the changing relationships between servants and mistresses and add a more personal dimension to the understanding of the middle-class domestic sphere.[2]

Another feature of these criminal investigations relating to women's domestic experience is the evidence that women were eagerly searching for authorities to guide them through the new upheavals in their lives. We already know a good deal about the rise in prescriptive literature for women, such as household manuals, health books, magazines with advice columns, and the like, but we know much less about how real women responded to these and to other sorts of authorities available to them. Obviously the women here faced—or created for themselves—some rather unusual problems. Still, the guidance they sought along the way did not in all cases set them apart; the need for looking more closely at women's "advice seeking" is evident.

The traditional authorities for women were clear enough: the family (especially the mother), the church, local custom, and the husband. But in different ways these cases all reveal women's perceptions of the growing inadequacy of these authorities. All were telling women things they no longer wanted to hear or things they found irrelevant to their own changing experience.

Not all the women were in positions to seek new sources of authority. When one traditional source, their parents, failed them, Euphémie Lacoste, Constance Kent, and Célestine Doudet turned to another traditional authority, religion. Mme. Lacoste confided her troubles to a sympathetic priest who urged forebearance; Célestine Doudet sought a fantasy religious martyrdom through obedience to the female virtues of piety and sexual purity; and Constance Kent did the same through embracing female self-sacrifice. In less dramatic ways other women sought both authority and approval in religious sanctions, though the burgeoning of secular authorities, especially after midcentury, gave them some new options.

Literature provided a critical transitional authority, especially at the beginning of the period when women's experience was so limited. Scorning her family's advice, Marie Lafarge turned first to romantic literature and then to the model of the "mistress of the home." Angélina Lemoine, too, took novels as a guide, and Madeleine Smith sought her advice from peers and from both romantic literature and practical treatises on domestic economy. All three young women adapted the literature to suit their purposes. Madeleine's performance was a parody of the prescriptive ideal of the wife: bragging to her clerk-lover of her little savings and begging this "husband" to give her rules for her life.

The women of the later period here branched out in their search for advice. For the English women especially, mother and family were called upon less, partly because they were less accessible, and friends, secular literature, and professional persons, such as lawyers and doctors, assumed a new importance. Of considerable significance is the evidence that women were using these authorities from outside the domestic sphere to argue their cases before husbands. Florence Bravo obtained release from her first husband by overruling him and her parents with the aid of a doctor and a lawyer. Both Edwin Bartlett and Marin Fenayrou bowed to the "scientific" wisdom of medical consultants and relinquished some sexual rights, though both attempted recourse to the traditional prescriptions of religion. In time the newer authorities came to include some of the principles of equality being preached in the public sphere which the women saw occasion to apply at home, as when Florence Bravo contended that her husband, who had kept a mistress, had no right to criticize her about Dr. Gully.

As the most visible dispensers of advice vying for women's allegiance, clergymen and doctors, who represented traditional and newer authority systems, were singled out for male suspicion as women turned to them for help. The most prominent theme, of course, was sexual jealousy. In commenting on the Bravo case, the *Daily News* noted, "Physicians and priests are in relations to women which no other men occupy, and conduct which might be condemned as profligate or condoned as gallant, in others, is a worse sin in members of privileged professions." [3] It is true that in the cases studied six of the subjects developed intense relationships with men of the "privileged professions," three of which led to probable physical intimacies (Mrs. Bravo admitted it; Adelaide Bartlett and Henriette Francey did not). But as all the cases suggest, these relationships were, from the women's point of view, by-products of domestic conflicts which prompted them to find either solace or justification in outside authority. Doctors and clerics recognized their delicate position and sought to mediate among the interests of jealous husbands, troubled wives, and their own ambitions for professional advancement. For the women the results were mixed: Constance Kent was sacrificed by a clergyman; Florence Maybrick was abandoned by the doctor whose help she desperately sought; but Adelaide Bartlett effected a kind of grand slam by enlisting the unwitting aid of a doctor, a clergyman, and a lawyer to serve her ends.

The changing and sometimes conflicting sources of advice and authority demonstrate another distinctive pattern which emerged even among the small number of cases here. It has been pointed out that the six cases of the earlier period from 1840 to 1870 all involved either unmarried or recently married women. Five of the six were dominated by related issues of courtship, marriageability, and women's marital vocation. The sixth, that of Constance Kent, indirectly touched upon these issues and was also concerned, as were all the others, with the roles of parents or guardians in decisions which affected the marital chances and choices of their daughters. All six cases underline the increased tensions in domestic power relationships as both French and English society moved toward somewhat greater recognition of children's rights and especially the right of daughters to a voice in selecting their husbands.

The early cases all featured the retention of strong positions by parental or familial authorities. These figures might force the choice of a husband, as in the cases of Marie Lafarge, Euphémie Lacoste, and even Madeleine Smith. Alternatively, they might veto the daughter's choice, as in the case of Angélina Lemoine, or through alleged economic motives foreclose the possibility of marriage altogether, as with Constance Kent and Célestine Doudet. The young women, however, demonstrated a consciousness of their tenuous new rights and attempted some resistance long before murder became an issue. Lafarge, Lacoste, Smith, and Lemoine justified their behavior in seeking romantic relationships by appeals to personal conscience or popular literature or both and all argued for considerations of affection over issues of fortune and status.

More significantly, though, none of the women could elect open defiance and all were deeply ambivalent about their actions. Euphémie Lacoste's was a very timid new self-assertion and the other three young women sooner or later had more than second thoughts about the brave things they confided to their admirers and lovers. Constance Kent and Célestine Doudet, of course, had little occasion even for secret defiance; their stories exposed some of the grimmer sorts of domestic tyranny which could still weigh on single women and female children. But even these pathetic cases, and especially the others, suggest why and in what ways daughters were attempting to carve out some autonomy.

Of these early accused women only Marie Lafarge and Madeleine Smith appear to have premeditated a murder and carried it out alone. In Angélina Lemoine's case, murder was conceived by a mother, who persuaded the girl that it was her only option. But in all three instances, the young women themselves murdered for status, not for romance. Both Angélina Lemoine and Madeleine Smith saw the imperative of social respectability. And Marie Lafarge poisoned Charles not because he was insufficiently romantic, but because he wounded her social pride. The personal relationship with her husband, bad as it was, mattered far less to her than the figure he cut in the world. That Charles was irretrievably bourgeois could have been borne, but only if he had been a success. The bourgeois man was obliged, unlike the aristocrat, not merely to be but to do.

Angélina Lemoine and Madeleine Smith were similarly reckless on account of their social disdain, even though both, like Marie, had toyed with the new views on the primacy of love over the barriers of class. The surprise and disgust each felt upon discovering that a coachman and a clerk were capable of acting for themselves must be seen in the context of the prevalent middle-class perception of the "lower orders" as another race. Their victims appear to have been conceived in the end as less than human, which helped provide a rationale for these women's actions.

Euphémie Lacoste, on the other hand, felt none of the reinforcing social superiority which gave assurance to Mme. Lafarge, the Lemoines, and Miss Smith. Nor did she sense that there could be any public excuse or approval for an act of murder on her part, as did the other three. For the latter, even the ultimate deviancy of murder could be condoned, in part because it was seen to provide a guarantee against more dangerous sorts of deviants: the social upstarts who masqueraded as worthy entrants into a society where they did not belong.

Another remarkable feature of the six early cases is the illustration of how prevailing images of women not only were internalized and acted upon by the accused murderesses themselves, but also how their judges, both inside and outside the courtrooms, were mesmerized by the popular stereotypes. The new image of the blameless and pure middle-class maiden was accessible to Marie, Madeleine, and Angélina, who were almost automatically accorded popular approval as irresponsible young ladies victimized by male inferiors. Having mustered the required appearance and demeanor, they gained public immunity.

True, legal decisions did go against both Mmes. Lafarge and Lemoine, which showed that popular verdicts did not always determine courtroom proceedings. In fact, French procedure, with its questioning of the accused and its more socially restricted juries, may have provided greater resistance against the impact of popular prejudice in this early period. The vindication of the unpopular but probably innocent Mme. Lacoste supports this view as well. Still, the French courts were not immune to such influences. The famous case of the sixteen-year-old Marie de Morell in 1834, though not a murder case, illustrated many of the same themes as the cases here.[4]

Mlle. de Morell, the daughter of the commander of the military school at Saumur, charged that a handsome young officer there was sending her scurrilous anonymous letters and that he had finally broken into her room one night and attempted to rape her. Legal investigations showed that Marie, jealous of her attractive mother and worried that her mother was about to arrange a marriage for her to one of the duller officers, had forged the letters and, under some provocation, lied about the rape as a means of drawing attention to herself and undoing her mother's plans for her.

The court, however, refused to believe that a "pure" young woman could have concocted such a plot. The accused officer served ten years before being exonerated, and charges were never brought against Mlle. de Morell. So solicitous was the court of the young lady's alleged "nervous condition" that she was even spared the usual examination by the judge and proceedings were obligingly conducted after midnight when the girl reportedly enjoyed her only "calm" periods.[5] The case again displayed the devious means young women were adopting to combat parental influence in courtship, as well as the same almost reflexive assumptions of immunity which were accorded to several of the accused murderesses here.

By the same token, however, accused women who failed to reflect the prevailing positive stereotypes lost their immunity. Euphémie Lacoste's case received more attention than it might have for its superficial resemblance to the Lafarge affair, but the young woman's provincial background and prosaic, petty bourgeois character placed her beyond popular redemption by the new urban ideal of middle-class maidens. Instead, and despite her acquittal, she paid in a humiliating public trial for her failure to conform to the more traditional image of the pious and subservient wife who abided by local social and religious conventions. Both Constance Kent and Célestine Doudet, too, fell outside the sacred circle of immunity. Constance, of course, was self-accused, but her peculiar and "unfeminine" past behavior helped ensure against serious inquiry into the truth of her strange confession. Mlle. Doudet, for her part, was conveniently guilty as the typical frustrated spinster, despite her far from typical behavior. Of "unmarried and unprotected females," it was often remarked that they were by definition less than full members of their sex. As a popular contemporary magazine advised, "It should be remembered that of women these are the least truly women . . ."[6] and their societies too often succeeded in making them so.

By the 1870s, as noted, the stereotypes which protected some of the accused women and left others more exposed were beginning to shift in response to the changing circumstances and new social visibility of middle-class women. The image of the new woman which accompanied this shift was, in its positive form, that of a more mature, less innocent female who accepted a larger social responsibility to purify the conditions and conduct of all. At the same time there emerged a negative view, fed by popular fears of social change, which singled out the new women as selfish, luxury-conscious, and sexually promiscuous. It has been remarked that after the 1870s a shift also occurred among the accused murderesses themselves, who were now somewhat older married women with a greater variety of problems. This shift appears to be related to the changing stereotypes in several ways; and interestingly enough, the issues of courtship and marriageability, so prominent among the younger women of the earlier period, lose their centrality or do not appear at all.

In the early years the major decision-making area in their lives in which women were making some recognized gains was that of the still contested right to a voice in the selection of a husband. This new right did remain limited in ways that women themselves perceived and acknowledged, but it is possible that by midcentury, as parental control lessened somewhat in the urban middle classes, the conflicts which remained were less likely to lead to criminal resolutions. Even in France, where arranged marriages persisted longer, it became commonplace to advise that the girl's inclinations be considered, and young women came to expect it.

Provincial custom lagged behind urban, and evidence after 1870 of a few provincial cases following the earlier pattern bears out the view that such a shift was occurring. In one case from 1891 a reportedly beautiful bourgeois bride of three months from Le Mans attempted to poison her new, unloved, and reportedly unattractive husband with strychnine to escape a parentally enforced marriage designed to replenish her family's funds. The young woman might have succeeded had she not confided intimations of her husband's imminent death to a fortune-teller. The suspicious woman's warnings led to the removal of the ailing young man from his wife's care, and the would-be poisoner was subsequently sentenced to five years' imprisonment.[7] The papers devoted little attention to the case. It appears that earlier sympathy in such affairs had dried up in the face of growing suspicion of all middle-class women and the alleged expansion of noncriminal avenues of escape from arranged marriages.

In the later years, then, among the situations which led to the accusation of women for murder, conflicts with parents over courtship gave way to a variety of problems of the mature married woman. The most dramatic feature of the last set of cases is the issue of adultery; but contrary to expectations, only one of the five women suspected of that act, Adelaide Bartlett, may have murdered on her lover's account. The rest, and perhaps Mrs. Bartlett as well, were driven by motives which were, in the end, more bound up with the experience of ordinary women who were neither adulteresses nor murderesses.

Especially notable in these later cases is evidence that the women's deepest concerns now centered upon new—and disappointed—expectations about their status and rights within marriage itself. Most expressed resentment both against their husbands' absences and against their behavior when they were around, and their complaints ranged from petty to vast. Adelaide Bartlett complained that Edwin did not appreciate her accomplishments in music and needlework, Gabrielle Fenayrou that Marin did not take her to the theater, and Florence Bravo that Charles opened her mail. Such apparent trivia did matter to the women, but it also stood for deeper discontents which they found difficult or impossible to express directly. Florence Maybrick, the child bride, dared not demand to be mistress of her own home, though she keenly felt her deprivation. Florence Bravo held out a goal of happiness through respectability which she was sadly ill-equipped to realize. Claire Reymond resented her husband's constant travel and appears to have felt that if he devoted more attention to her, they might have increased their chances to have the child she wanted so badly.

Beyond this, most of the women had specific discontents over sexual issues. Several intimated that they expected more tenderness and romance in their physical relationships and were unwilling to submit dutifully to their husbands' desires. Florence Maybrick could not bear her husband to come near her; Adelaide Bartlett experienced physical revulsion against her grocer-husband; and Henriette Francey's husband seems to have been little capable of meeting his wife's emotional and sexual needs. Both Gabrielle Fenayrou and Florence Bravo complained of being obliged to sleep with men who were inconsiderate, alcoholic, and brutal. Mme. Fenayrou even went so far as to confide her needs for affection and romance to total strangers.

Several women, too, expressed new resentments over discoveries about their husbands' sex lives. Mme. Reymond confronted Paul with evidence of his infidelity. Florence Bravo was initially pleased that she and Charles began marriage with shared knowledge of their "pasts," but she was made to realize that a husband's prior sexual indiscretions were as nothing compared to those of a wife, and the struggle to regain her own respectability embittered her. Florence Maybrick's first reaction to knowledge of James's continued liaison with a shopgirl was to take a separate bedroom. Obviously, the accused women's responses were conditioned by other features which were not introduced in evidence at the investigations, but these later cases all support the view that married women's expectations for personal fulfillment were rising in this period. They also show that women were developing some means to cope with their plights when expectations were disappointed.

The initial reactions of the accused to these discontents violated neither moral nor criminal codes, though they were mainly evasions rather than confrontations. The English women were able to take advantage of somewhat less confined circumstances and access to new ideas. Florence Bravo escaped to the sympathetic environment of the water-cure and later used extended convalescences at the seaside to keep Charles at arm's length. Adelaide Bartlett found in free-love literature a way to keep undesired sexual encounters to a minimum. Florence Maybrick took refuge in countless shopping trips and indulged in a frenetic social life which permitted her to gratify a narcissistic need for admiration while permitting her husband to show her off. At home, in conventional fashion, she shut out unpleasant scenes by absorbing herself in cheap romantic novels.

The French women, though more domestically constrained, also found some outlets for unhappiness. Henriette Francey developed a coterie of female friends, improved her literary and musical talents, and studied English in anticipation of travel. Gabrielle Fenayrou, with fewer resources, poured out her troubles to anyone who would listen and escaped marital duties through the apparently popular device of a doctor's excuse. Claire Reymond, crushed by Paul's infidelity, at first sought solace in the traditional support of family and in her role as godmother.

For all the women, these initial solutions failed in the long run. Five of the six took advantage of relative domestic isolation and somewhat freer circumstances to move on to illicit sexual relationships. They justified their decisions to themselves and their friends either as retaliation against forced marriages or as revenge for a husband's indifference, brutality, or infidelity. But all the women knew that there was no socially acceptable defense for their behavior, that husbands were not advised, as wives were, to tolerate adultery. Florence Bravo desperately tried to "undo" her act through a proper marriage; Adelaide Bartlett brazened it out by self-righteously making her father-in-law deny his allegations of her adultery before a solicitor; Henriette Francey and Gabrielle Fenayrou took considerable pains to conceal their affairs. Florence Maybrick alone was incautious enough to flaunt her liaisons, but she did so as a flighty, stupid, and childish creature, not as a liberated new woman. And it finally cost her fifteen years of her life.

The women then displayed their allegiance to the code which bound them even as they were breaking it, and the intensity of their efforts to cover their tracks once again shows their deep ambivalence over their choices. But evidence for their typicality of response, if not action, does not stop with their reactions to sexual misbehavior. Even those who moved on to murder can be seen to have taken courses which, in their troubled ways, reflected the concerns and aspirations of their more prosaic peers. Moreover, an observable divergence between the motives and actions of the English and French subjects replicates the divergence between English and French women of the class as a whole, as English women pressed more rapidly for autonomy and developed new goals for personal fulfillment.

For the English women, Florence Bravo, Adelaide Bartlett, and Florence Maybrick (if indeed she made her husband a lethal brew), the decision to use poison represented a further extension of previous noncriminal attempts to gain "rights" to individual happiness by removing the perceived obstacles to that happiness. In this sense the women were acknowledging the "modern" goal of an affectionate, companionate marital relationship, while obviously adopting socially illegitimate means to free themselves to pursue that goal. Of the three women, however, only Adelaide Bartlett appears to have worked out this rationale completely. The two Florences had both known more self-fulfilling relationships with men and deeply resented their own husbands, but both lacked the steely resolution, conditioned by fewer noncriminal options, which marked Adelaide's behavior. Their decisions to murder, if taken at all, were a matter of impulse, while Adelaide's deed was done with long premeditation.

Mrs. Bartlett's selfish pursuit of happiness introduced the darker face of a calculating, future-oriented modernity. As personal fulfillment in the marriage relationship began to assume paramount importance over older marital goals of respectability, achievement of social status, and continuation of family lines, the way was open to a more individualistic drive to achieve happiness at any price. The twentieth century has facilitated this drive through eased divorce laws and gradual removal of the stigma of divorce, which allows a pattern of serial monogamy in marriage.[8] But in the nineteenth century, if marriages were not made in heaven, they nonetheless were made to last.

By contrast with the English cases, the crimes of the French women

Henriette Francey, Gabrielle Fenayrou, and Claire Reymond, while underscoring new marital expectations, were all designed to confirm or restore a previous and conventional situation and reflected the slower pace of change in French bourgeois society. For Mme. Francey both the ostensible and real purposes of a revolver killing were conservative: to preserve her purity as a wife and mother from alleged sexual outrage and to prevent public knowledge of her infidelity with the priest. Gabrielle Fenayrou, of course, had already been exposed in her infidelity, but her motive for participating in the vendetta against her former lover was a traditional one: to restore her status in her husband's eyes by paying for her sin of adultery. Claire Reymond was in the more typical situation of being "sinned against," but she, too, turned to violent means as a hoped-for way of restoring her marriage and recreating a prior status quo.

It has been argued that the action of Mme. Reymond, like that of several bourgeois women who turned to the traditionally male passion-killing, was representative of a new female wave of criminal protest over male infidelity. In a context of hostility toward the illicit sexual behavior of women, against whom the violence was often directed, the radical novelty of the protest of the "wronged" women against the sexual double standard was often overlooked by contemporaries. Nonetheless, the crimes themselves emerged from the desire to restore established relationships, and in the case of middle-class wives they were conducted under the banner of the sacred institutions of marriage and motherhood.

In the twentieth century, the "crime of passion" has come to be popularly seen not as a revenge killing for infidelity but as a means to free oneself of a spouse in favor of a lover. If, as suggested above, such a motive represents a more "modern" form of of passion killing, then it would seem likely that it would have appeared sooner among men, who were quicker to abandon traditional attitudes. Several English cases, such as that of Dr. Edward Pritchard, who in 1857 poisoned his wife for his house-maid lover, appear to bear out that hypothesis, but more research concerning male murderers is clearly required. There seem to have been few such cases in France until the twentieth century, although it is possible that the continued greater toleration of infidelity among husbands there made the expedient of murder less attractive to Frenchmen.

The public responses to the later crimes in the two countries diverged, despite some common themes, as English women in general moved faster toward realizing personal autonomy. The new distrust of women in both countries was in itself evidence of their overall gains, but the special virulence of the popular antifemale theme in France, as seen most clearly here in the reaction to the Fenayrou affair, demonstrated how a slower rate of change in women's roles served to reinforce and harden hostility and suspicion of women. In England, by contrast, the distrust of women was countered by a new endorsement of their growing public roles as "purifiers" concerned to alleviate the alleged evils caused by male authority structures and specifically by male sexual promiscuity. For every woman who "fell," there was a fallen man who deserved to share her guilt.

The influence of this new sentiment was most apparent in the angry outburst against the surprise verdict in the Maybrick affair, but it was evident as well in the Bartlett case, where it served to free a guilty woman on the ground of her husband's abuse of his marital authority. And Florence Bravo, too, was able to turn initial hostility to advantage by appealing to the growing sentiment in favor of a single sexual standard for both men and women. If the earlier automatic assumption of women's sexual innocence and immunity was disappearing, then, it was possible for English women, at least, to appeal to the argument that men must share their disgrace with respect to sexual impropriety. But as all three English cases showed, this did not mean that the cause of justice, or truth, was necessarily served.

The evidence of a shift from the problems of the younger woman over courtship and marriage to the problems of the mature married woman suggests the need to explore the stages of women's lives more systematically in different historical periods. Historians have begun to look at youth, but have generally interpreted it as a male event and have used male models and sources. These cases suggest that young women, especially early in the century, may have undergone a special crisis period in a time when the ground rules of courtship were changing. They also indicate that later on, the responses of women to similar trends in their societies, such as the shoring up of their authority in the domestic sphere, might have been very different.

If the argument presented here is correct, the striking and singular adoption of the crime of passion by women in France was one such response, reflecting improved status and raised expectations as well as comparatively more limited options. The crimes of passion were interconnected ritual events, which featured public appeals to shared traditional roles of wife and mother as opposed to the more modern individualistic appeals being made by the English women. In adapting to their own purposes the legalized violence of sexual revenge reserved for men in the Napoleonic Code, the accused French women reverted to primitive (but, for them, untried) modes to express their new resentments. Their crimes emerged in one phase of a more gradual French modernization pattern, in which improvements in women's status and options had been realized more exclusively within the domestic context, leaving French women still unequipped to translate their rage into effective nonviolent public protest. In a sense, the crimes of passion, and the female sympathy they evoked, are part of the evidence that French middle-class women went through a stage which English women, more rapidly modernized, simply skipped.

In all the cases here in which murder became the answer, the precise ingredients of the final terrible decisions must retain some mystery. And many things remain unsaid about the women as individual personalities.

However, these areas would be the object of a different sort of investigation. The object here has been to uncover the links of experience which bound the notorious women to their more obscure sisters. Some of the things we are beginning to learn about the anonymous majority have helped us to understand the ways in which the accused women perceived and dealt with their problems, and the exposed lives of this handful offer some clues in turn about the private frustrations and terrors which, for most women of the class, will remain hidden forever behind closed parlor and bedroom doors.

In the end the argument that the lady killers here were more typical than common sense would hold must come back to the ways in which other women, their peers and contemporaries, perceived them. This study is not the first to single out the extraordinary interest which well-bred and fashionable women lavished on trials. The phenomenon was remarked at the time and has been observed since. A recent student of the Victorian fascination with murder quotes a novelist of 1864 on the subject:

> . . . that women of family and position, women who have been brought up in refined society, women who pride themselves upon the delicacy of their sensibilities, who would faint at the sight of a cut finger and go into hysterics if the drowning of a litter of kittens were mentioned in their hearing—such women can sit for hours listening to the details of a cold-blooded murder.[9]

But what did it mean? One observer has suggested that it was "among the most striking of the innumerable Victorian paradoxes,"[10] but the closer one approaches the phenomenon the less paradoxical it becomes. Despite our indirect access to the women, filtered as it is through highly colored accounts of their unseemly behavior, their real preoccupations are visible enough and hardly strange. The general female absorption in the cases was not an isolated and aberrant development, but rather an integral part of the fantasy experience of women of the class. And in the end, the trials gave women an occasion to voice their concerns and discontents.

In her recent study *A Literature of Their Own: British Women Novelists from Brontë to Lessing,*[11] Elaine Showalter discusses the immense popularity of the English sensation-fiction writers of the 1860s. She describes the ways in which the women who wrote these novels, such as Mary Braddon in *Lady Audley's Secret,* were actually "inverting the stereotypes of the domestic novel, and parodying the conventions of their male contemporaries."[12] Showalter demonstrates that the immense success of the novels rested on their willingness to display "female anger, frustration and sexual energy"[13] and to show women in self-assertive roles. "In many sensation novels, the death of a husband comes as a welcome release, and women escape from their families through illness, madness, divorce, flight, and ultimately, murder."[14] The shreds of convention are maintained, however, and Showalter indicates that these aggressive heroines who plot and murder are brought up in the end for form's sake. The "secret" of Lady Audley, who attempted to murder her husband, is revealed to be that she is the victim of hereditary madness. This device, as Showalter points out, allows the reader not to feel quite so guilty for identifying with a most attractive heroine, while suspecting, as the author clearly intends, that Lady Audley's *real* secret is that she is perfectly sane. Such literature, which was identified as subversive by male critics, served the same purposes as the trials; and the taste for it could be indulged less publicly.

The women who attended the trials did not, as we have seen, get off easily in the eyes of their masculine judges. Without acknowledging their real alarm over what the women's behavior meant, the men's remarks often display that they understood precisely what was happening, namely, that the "female element" was showing a supportive identification with women accused of adultery and murder. Covertly at first, and then openly, female onlookers were sympathizing with the plights of the accused, if not with the solutions. Their endorsement appears on occasion to have been only partly conscious. The woman who came forward and fainted as Mme. Lacoste's lawyer described his client's anguish over small-town gossip may not have been able to explain her action, even to herself. In ways that women were only gradually beginning to articulate, the trials were touching them.

These spectacles, to be sure, gave everybody an obvious occasion to wallow in the morbid details of murderous intrigue, but more importantly, as their behavior demonstrates, women found in the trials an opportunity for release of frustrations and for vicarious fulfillment of unrealized desires. Some of them found, too, that courtroom displays of blatant sexual prejudice could obliterate all differences between the prisoners in the dock and themselves, leaving only the sense of their shared and persecuted womanhood. The fascination that the trials held for the female audience bespoke an affinity of feeling and experience which is unmistakable. These women could understand the frustrations and terrors that drove the accused, for they had traveled some of the same dark paths themselves.

NOTES

INTRODUCTION

1. For the cases here, at least, the English murderesses have been written about more regularly than their French counterparts, with the exception of Marie Lafarge. See chapter notes and bibliography for references to some of the better studies.

2. R. P. Utter and G. P. Needham, *Pamela's Daughters* (New York: Macmillan, 1936), p. 384.

3. For a discussion of the modernization pattern applied to women, see Patricia Branca and Peter N. Stearns, *Modernization of Women in the Nineteenth Century* (St. Charles, Mo.: Forum, 1973). For England see Branca's *Silent Sisterhood: Middle-Class Women in the Victorian Home* (Pittsburgh: Carnegie-Mellon University Press, 1975). There is no similar study for French middle-class women as a whole, although Bonnie Smith has provided an excellent study of the upper-middle-class woman in her Ph.D. dissertation "The Bourgeois Women of Lille, 1860–1910" (University of Rochester, 1975).

4. A few French cases (of which there were more, for reasons which will be discussed) have not received full treatment, but these will be mentioned.

5. The French statistics are more complete. From 1825 the Ministry of the Interior published an annual *Compte générale de l'administration de la Justice criminelle*. The Home Office did not begin to issue annual volumes of Judicial Statistics for England until

1856–1857, though earlier collections are available. Even for those attempting a comparative study of all murders, these statistics pose serious problems, such as arbitrary classification or the lumping together of attempted and actual homicides in many of the French statistics. They have been used here along with some general works on murder and female crime simply to give a preliminary idea of how these respectable murderesses fit into the general pattern of female murder.

6. William A. Guy, "On the Executions for Murder That Have Taken Place in England and Wales During the Last Seventy Years," *Journal of the Statistical Society*, 38 (1875): 480, and Henri Joly, *Le Crime* (Paris: Cerf, 1888), pp. 250–276. Joly gives comparative figures for different countries on all serious crimes committed by women. Guy provides a year-by-year table of persons committed to trial for murder.

7. In the annual volumes of the *Compte générale*, murders and attempted murders are divided into the categories of voluntary homicide *(meurtre)*, murder with premeditation *(assassinat)*, infanticide, and poisoning. Women predominate in infanticides and poisonings, overwhelmingly so in infanticides. Their representation is small in the categories of *meurtre* and *assassinat*. For example, in 1850 11 women were tried for *meurtre* and 31 for *assassinat*, as compared with 273 and 299 men for each category. Of the 190 persons tried for infanticide that year, 172 were women and 18 were men. Of the total of 43 poisonings, 24

were charged to women. (These figures include both attempted and actual murders for all categories.)

8. A study which discusses several of these factors in a comparative context is Otto Pollak, *The Criminality of Women* (Philadelphia: University of Pennsylvania Press, 1950).

9. See A. Lacassagne, "Notes Statistiques sur l'empoisonnement criminel en France," *Archives d'Anthropologie criminelles et des Sciences pénales*, I (1886): 260-264. In the five-year period from 1850 to 1855 in France poison accusations reached a high of 294, with roughly equal participation by men and women, a pattern which had held since the mid-1830s. Thereafter, the number of poisonings steadily declined to 78 in the five years from 1875 to 1880, but, interestingly, women's representation increased; in these years there were 41 accused women and only 19 men.

10. Patrick Wilson, *Murderess* (London: Michael Joseph, 1971).

11. My survey was based on the volumes of the *Central Criminal Court Sessions Papers* (1835-1913). David Pierce, in "Crime and Society in London, 1700-1900: A Bibliographical Survey" *Harvard Library Bulletin*, 20 (October 1972): 430-435, notes that these nearly five hundred bound volumes are a source "virtually untapped by historians" (p. 432). Of the 117 cases in this sample, 83 were women who murdered infants or children.

CHAPTER 1

1. The chief source for the account here is the published transcript *Le Procès de Madame Lafarge* (Paris: Pagnerre, 1840). This double volume contains the full record of both trials in which Marie Lafarge was the principal subject: a trial for stealing diamonds and a trial for murder.

The account of the Lacoste affair is based chiefly on the testimony recorded in *La Gazette des Tribunaux;* the materials in Armand Fouquier, *Les Causes célèbres de tous les peuples*, 9 vols. (Paris: Lebrun, 1858-1874), vol. 2, cahier, 9; and correspondence with M. Henri Polge, Director of the Department Archives of Gers. *La Gazette des Tribunaux*, a daily founded in 1825, was devoted exclusively to trial coverage and provided writers from Stendhal to Zola with source material for their novels. The Fouquier collection, which is useful for several of the French cases in this study, provides extensive verbatim testimony and often supplements the accounts with eye-

witness impressions and summaries of events before and after the trials. Unless otherwise indicated, all translations from the French in this and subsequent chapters are my own.

2. The Lafarge case has had more book-length studies devoted to it than all the other cases here combined, though nearly all are simple retellings of the tale. A large bibliography appears in E. Gril, *Madame Lafarge devant ses juges* (Paris: Gallimard, 1958). Although dated in style and approach, one of the better accounts is a partly fictionalized study in English called *The Mystery of Marie Lafarge* by Edith Saunders (London: Clarke & Cockeran, 1951). Another survey in English, also a fictional rendering, is well documented: Joseph Shearing, *The Lady and the Arsenic* (London: Heinemann, 1937).

3. (Marie Lafarge), *Mémoires de Marie Cappelle*, 2 vols. (Bruxelles: Jamar, 1841).

4. *Procès*. 2:54.

5. Fouquier, p. 2.

6. In a recent study Theodore Zeldin points out that such consultations by mail were common, *France, 1848-1945: Ambition, Love and Politics*, vol. 1 (Oxford: Clarendon, 1973), p. 27.

7. Fouquier, p. 18.

8. Ibid., p. 32.

9. *La Presse*, July 9, 1844. (The place of publication for newspapers and journals cited throughout the text is given in the bibliography.)

10. *Correspondance de Madame Lafarge*, 2 vols. (Paris: Mercure de France, 1913).

11. Marie Lafarge, *Heures de prison* (New York: Lasalle, 1854).

12. Edward Shorter, *The Making of the Modern Family* (New York: Basic Books, 1975). For an outline of the thesis, see Introduction, pp. 3-21, and Chapter IV, "Romance," especially pp. 148-161, on the transformation of courtship.

13. Ibid., p. 148. Shorter's view that the "revolution" began from below is contested, but the book is full of fascinating material.

14. See John R. Gillis, *Youth and History: Tradition and Change in European Age Relations* (New York: Academic, 1974), esp. chap. 2.

15. In her study *L'Image de la France dans l'Angleterre victorienne* (Paris: Colin, 1967), Sylvaine Marandon uses memoirs and travel literature to demonstrate that the English were well aware of "the French system" of raising girl children in strict separation from men and with no access to romantic literature until marriage. Many observers correctly noted that the French girl was more strictly controlled

than her English counterpart and generally more socially backward. But even if their lives were restricted in most ways, it is probable that many young women of the class did read some of the forbidden literature. Marandon quotes one wry observer as saying that at age seventeen the French girl was plunged into hopeless ignorance "unless she had borrowed some novels from her mother's maid" (p. 284). And there were other means of access as well, such as the daily papers which contained serialized romances, the home library with books to be devoured while *Maman* was out visiting or the boarding school with its opportunities for arrangements with servants, à la Emma Bovary. For the French girl, indeed, literature appears to have been a more exclusive means for gaining some knowledge of an outside world than for the English girl, whose experience was more varied.

16. See Adeline Daumard, *La Bourgeoisie Parisienne de 1815 à 1848* (Paris: S.E.V.P.E.N., 1963), pp. 272-280. Daumard indicates that rural recruitment into the ranks of Parisian *négociants*, tradesmen, and industrialists was considerable and that the Parisian *bourgeoises* often married the young provincials moving to the capital to seek their fortunes.

17. Marandon remarks, in this regard: "[Young French women] were practically forbidden any reading (save for English novels, whose very origin—to the constant amusement of the English [commentators]—sufficed to guarantee their innocuousness" (p. 284).

18. Marie wrote the memoirs in prison to gain sympathy for her cause, and her dramatic introduction sets the stage for the lugubrious account that follows: "I remembered, I wept, I wrote." *(Mémoires,* 1:2).

19. Ibid., p. 61.

20. Ibid., p. 75.

21. Ibid., pp. 85 f.

22. Ibid., p. 85.

23. Ibid., p. 97.

24. *Edinburgh Review,* 75 (April-July 1842): 368.

25. *Memoirs of Madame Lafarge* (London: Colburn, 1841).

26. *Mémoires,* 1:92.

27. Ibid., p. 129.

28. *La Gazette des Tribunaux,* July 13, 1844.

29. *La Presse,* July 14, 1844.

30. *Mémoires,* 1:105.

31. *Procès,* 1:140.

32. *Mémoires,* 1:124.

33. Ibid., p. 125.

34. *Procès,* 1:84-98, 105 f. The *Progrès,* August 6, 1840, noted that Clavé was from the "Catholic school" of Hugo and Lamartine, that his verses "breathed a perfume of ingenuous virginity." For example:

Je t'aime comme le zéphire
Aime la rose du matin,
Comme le fleuve qui soupire
Les rives de son frais bassin,
Ton souvenir remplit ma veille
Et je te vois quand je sommeille
Comme le bel ange qui veille
Du haut des cieux à mon destin. *(Procès,* 1:105)

35. *Mémoires,* 1:133.

36. *Procès,* 1:90.

37. *Mémoires,* 1:165.

38. Ibid., p. 166.

39. Ibid., p. 167.

40. Ibid., p. 174.

41. *Procès,* 2:366-368. The episode was widely reported, including in the English papers such as the *Spectator* (September 12, 1840), though Marie chose not to include the sad end of her druggist in her memoirs. Young Guyot, son of a pharmacist from Montmédy, was demonstrated to have had the sort of relationship with Mlle. Cappelle which she described. His father wrote to the court and sent three notes which he said were not included in the packet of letters the Garats had reclaimed. He said his son had confessed the relationship to him and told him that Mlle. Cappelle was a dissembler. One of Marie's notes appears to refer to her aunt's discovery of their intrigue: "The story of Caroline has been discovered! They are going to write to you. Remember I am an orphan: God took away my father, and then my mother, everything in a word. Then my uncle became my guide and my aunt wanted to replace her sister [Marie's mother]. This morning she swore to me that if I were found to be mixed up in this affair she would never look at me again in her life.... I am mad.... I have lost my head.... You are a man of honor, I believe in you, save me by your absolute silence. May God and you have pity on me! Through an incredible piece of foolishness my honor lies in your hands" *(Procès,* 2:367 f.).

42. *Mémoires,* 1:198-200.

43. The overcrowding of the professions is discussed by Lenore O'Boyle in "The Problem of an Excess of Educated Men in Western Europe, 1800–1850," *Journal of Modern History,* 42, no. 4 (December 1970): 471-495.

44. *La Presse* and *Le National* showed sympathy for Euphémie Lacoste as an educated and intelligent young woman, wronged by her parents, her husband, and the small-

minded populace of Auch where the trial was held. They recounted Euphémie's many little services to her husband—shaving him and washing his feet—with some astonishment, but there was no outpouring of indignation over her parents' role in the accused woman's unhappiness, as there was over Marie's guardians. And even in Marie's case, the critics did not contest the right of the guardians to make the choice in the way they did, but rather the particular choice of Lafarge.

In England, where young women's role in choosing a husband was, within limits, more active, there was shock expressed over the procedure adopted by Marie's aunt and uncle. The *Edinburgh Review* (note 24) remarked that the uncle arranged the marriage of his niece "with a man of whom he knew nothing, whose face he had never seen three days before he determined to entrust to him for life the orphan child then under his charge. It is remarkable that this circumstance is passed by with indifference by all persons at the trial, and does not, as far as we learn, appear to have excited remark or astonishment in the minds of the Journalists of France. Are we, then, to assume that this *agent matrimoniale* is commonly employed in France by persons of respectability and honour?"

45. Shorter, p. 337. Indeed, the percentage does not begin to decline until the first quarter of the twentieth century. In the middle classes the age gap was even greater. Men in Bonnie Smith's sample from the Lille upper bourgeoisie averaged six years older from the 1840s to 1880s. ["The Bourgeois Women of Lille, 1860-1910" (University of Rochester, 1975), p. 72.]

46. Shorter, p. 221.

47. *La Gazette des Tribunaux*, July 14, 1844.

48. Advertisements such as the following from *Le National*, July 16, 1844, appeared frequently: "MARRIAGE—Persons who wish to marry can, with assurance of the strictest confidence, address themselves to Mme. de Saint-Marc. Her relations in *haute société* place her in a position to be informed about widows and young women with dowries and fortunes up to two million." The advertisements were not discreetly tucked away in want-ad sections; de Foy's normally took a third or a half of a page. The bureaus would then ask clients to submit dossiers, such as the one Charles Lafarge had, with letters of recommendation, indications of financial status, and so forth. In Marie's case the beautiful watercolors of Le Glandier included in Charles's dossier helped reconcile her to marrying him, at least until she saw the place.

49. *Le National*, September 21, 1840.

50. *Procès*, 2:201.

51. Ibid., p. 202. The father-in-law also reported that his daughter told him that Lafarge had had "attacks" and that once he was "rigid" for several hours and had saliva in the corners of his mouth. The father seemed to take this evidence of disease, perhaps epilepsy, as one more count against Lafarge, though it is clear that his daughter's happiness was not his primary concern. He acknowledged he had not had "time" to question her on the subject.

52. Quoted in Saunders, p. 22.

53. *Mémoires*, 1:103.

54. Fouquier, p. 32.

55. Ibid.

56. Ibid. Vergès admits that he alone had conducted his daughter before the makeshift altar in the priest's lodgings, since he was the only one in the family who could tolerate Lacoste's atheism. Euphémie, then, had been forced to marry in the absence of her mother, who disapproved the last-minute arrangements when Lacoste refused a church ceremony.

57. *Procès*, 2:403.

58. Ibid., p. 405.

59. Ibid., p. 404.

60. *La Gazette des Tribunaux*, July 14, 1844.

61. In her recent study, "The Bourgeois Women of Lille, 1860-1910," Bonnie Smith discusses the concept of the mistress of the home and the developing responsibilities of women in providing a smoothly functioning domestic routine through "thrift, order and charm" (chap. III, "Domestic Life of the Women of Lille"). Erna Hellerstein also stresses the emergence of a new bourgeois model in "French Women and the Orderly Household, 1830-1870," *Proceedings of the Western Society for French History* (forthcoming). She states, "Women's role in this system was two-fold: to establish and observe time and space marks within the space of the household, and to display clearly the boundaries of the group at home and in such public places as the street and theater. Within the household, routine, regularity, and separation of rooms according to function and of the hours of the day according to task absorbed much of the household administrator's energies" (p. 8). In her descriptions of how she set out to civilize and bring order to her little corner of the Limousin, Marie Lafarge provides a case study of the new attitude *(Mémoires, 2:1–180)*.

In many ways the French model of the mistress of the home presented in the new prescriptive literature was similar to the English model. Yet it is interesting to see that the "carping" tone of the British manuals, noted by Patricia Branca is absent in the early French household manuals [*Silent Sisterhood: Middle-Class Women in the Victorian Home* (Pittsburgh: Carnegie-Mellon University Press, 1975), p. 22]. Mme. E. F. Celnart, for example, in her *Manuel des Dames* (Paris: Roret, 1833), which is significantly subtitled "the art of elegance," spends a great deal of time on grooming, appearance, and practical tips for "charm" for those on limited budgets, and it adopts a cheerful tone in purveying to young provincials information on urban, especially Parisian, lifestyles. The book is full of reassuring remarks; in her description of visiting cards she says: "Of course you know all this, I am only saying it to remind you" (p. 235). Similarly, Madame Pariset, in her *Nouveau Manuel complet de la maitresse de maison* (Paris: Roret, 1852), tells women that happiness will come to them if they manage to be orderly and efficient, keep careful account books, and set aside time both for their personal grooming and for the development of their minds: "It is idiocy to believe that an educated woman gifted with pleasing talents cannot at the same time be a good manager and an essential woman" (p. 56). Pariset indeed urges "positive thinking" on her readers: "Regard yourself as a true minister of the interior, and never neglect the conduct of your administration" (p. 4).

By contrast, the most popular early English manuals, such as Mrs. Sandford's *Female Improvement* (London: Longman, 1836) and the volumes by Mrs. Ellis on the wives, mothers, and daughters of England, adopt a sour tone and frequently seem to give their readers the impression that their tasks are beyond their capabilities. There is little talk of elegance and charm, much criticism of luxury-loving women, and many efforts to humble the new bride in preparation for her role. Mrs. Ellis says, "In the first place, what is it you are expecting?—To be always flattered? Depend upon it, if your faults were never brought to light before, they will be so now. . . . Depend upon it, if you were never humble and insignificant before, you will have to be so now. Yes, you had better make up your mind at once to be uninteresting as long as you live, to all except the companion of your home. . . . It is quite possible you may have more talent, with higher attainments, and you may also have been generally more admired; but this has nothing whatever to do with your position as a woman, which is, and must be, inferior to his as a man" [*The Wives of England* (London: Fisher, 1843), pp. 116 f.].

These differences deserve further analysis, but it is possible that the more rapid appearance of a middle class in England, which early rejected aristocratic ideals of elegance for a stern puritan code, did not permit the combination of upper-class notions of female charm with the newer ideals of orderliness, planning, and efficiency which is evident in the French model. At the same time the traditionally greater sheltering of French girls made marriage a literal emancipation—a time when a variety of freedoms were finally theirs. By contrast, English daughters, in a wealthier society, were freer before marriage than their French counterparts and they perceived the state of marriage as a restriction of some of the freedoms of girlhood.

Contemporaries often noted the difference. Max O'Rell, in *Les Filles de John Bull* (Paris: Lévy, 1884) remarked, "The young girl is the heroine of English society. Free and accessible, she is more attractive as a woman, but perhaps less appealing as a future wife, than the timid and sweet French girl. . . . In marrying, the French woman gains her freedom, the English woman loses hers" (pp. 118 f.). In *Paris and the Parisiens in 1835*, 2 vols. in one (Paris: Galignani, 1836), Frances Trollope said much the same of the French woman: "All that exceeding charm and fascination which is forever and always attributed to an elegant French woman belongs wholly, solely and altogether to her after she becomes a wife" (1:232). Of course, this ideal could be realized fully only in the upper reaches of the class. It was accessible to the more fortunate of Marie Lafarge's circle, not to the likes of an Euphémie Lacoste.

62. *Mémoires*, 1:120-125.

63. For example, Karl Hillebrand, in his *France and the French in the Second Half of the Nineteenth Century* (London: Trübner, 1882), p. 33, claimed that the French woman still ruled supreme in the salon, in the family, and even in the house of business. It is true that her influence in salon and business by the time Hillebrand wrote had declined greatly, though there remained many wives who kept small shops. In Marie's time women still played very active roles in larger industrial operations (see Zeldin, p. 66).

It is intriguing to consider how Marie envisioned her own future familial role as a combination of bourgeois domesticity and aristocratic elegance. She explains that while her husband worked on his loan for the forge, "I built castles in Spain . . . or I should say dreams of trips to Paris. It would take ten years to put our plans in execution, or rather in full operation. During each of these years we would not go to spend more than a month in Paris, but in compensation my husband would give me enough money to create a delightful residence within our old walls. I would be able to receive my friends, and my family; I would have a little girl, perhaps even a little boy whom I would raise in English style, who would learn German, English and Italian from the cradle, etc. After these ten years of sensible saving, we would hire a good business manager, a steward, and would then spend six months a year in Paris and six at Glandier. We would travel; I would marry my daughter; my son would be a diplomat; and M. Lafarge, named a deputy, would finally succeed in bringing some sparks of enlightenment and civilization to [the department of] Corrèze" *(Mémoires,* 2:145).

64. Catherine Bodard Silver, "Salon, Foyer and Bureau: French Women in the Professions," in *Clio's Consciousness Raised: New Perspectives on the History of Women,* ed. Mary S. Hartman and Lois W. Banner (New York: Harper & Row, 1974), p. 78.

65. *Mémoires,* 2:94. Also *Procès,* 2:402-411: "I am at Glandier," she told her aunt, "which is to say I am in the most wild place, the place most a part of nature, the place most forgotten by civilization" (p. 405).

66. Celnart, p. 228.

67. *Mémoires,* 2:103.

68. *Procès,* 2:138.

69. *Mémoires,* 2:92.

70. Ibid, p. 189.

71. Ibid., p. 99.

72. Ibid.

73. Ibid.

74. Ibid., p. 102.

75. Ibid., p. 179.

76. *Procès,* 2:414.

77. Ibid., p. 76.

78. Zeldin comments: "The idealization of women placed even greater distances between them and men. The cult of their purity made them inaccessible" (p. 291).

79. See Daniel Scott Smith, "Family Limitation, Sexual Control, and Domestic Feminism in Victorian America," in *Clio's Consciousness Raised: New Perspectives on the History of Women,* pp. 119-136.

80. *Procès,* 2:437. As she wrote to her sister, "I so wish I, too, could be 'a little round.'"

81. Ibid.

82. Ibid.

83. *La Gazette des Tribunaux,* July 13, 1844.

84. Ibid.

85. Fouquier, p. 17.

86. *La Gazette des Tribunaux,* July 13, 1844.

87. Ibid., July 15, 1844.

88. Ibid., July 13, 1844.

89. Adeline Daumard (pp. 361 f.) notes that women of the "petite" and "moyenne" bourgeoisie were frequently better educated than their husbands.

90. *La Gazette des Tribunaux,* July 14, 1844.

91. Ibid.

92. French Penal Code, Article 324.

93. *La Gazette des Tribunaux,* July 13, 1844.

94. Ibid.

95. Zeldin, p. 304.

96. *La Gazette des Tribunaux,* July 14, 1844.

97. Shorter, pp. 77 f.

98. Cited in Zeldin, p. 304.

99. Ibid., p. 305.

100. *La Gazette des Tribunaux,* July 13, 1844.

101. Ibid., July 14, 1844.

102. Ibid., July 15, 1844.

103. John H. Winslow, *Darwin's Victorian Malady* (Philadelphia: American Philosophical Society, 1971), chap. 4.

104. *La Gazette des Tribunaux,* July 15, 1844.

105. Winslow, p. 35.

106. Ibid., esp. chap. 9, "'Fowler's Disease'—A Probable Victorian Malady."

107. In a letter of June 7, 1974, M. Henri Polge, Director of the Departmental Archives of Gers, informed me that while putting together materials for an ORTF broadcast on the Lacoste affair, "we found proof that Mme. Lacoste was completely innocent and a victim of scandalmongers. Lacoste bought in Toulouse (and not in Vic-Fezensac, where the inept police looked at the time) the medications with arsenic base...."

108. *Procès,* 2:417 f.

109. Ibid., p. 416.

110. Ibid., p. 418.

111. *Correspondance,* 2:61.

112. *Mémoires,* 2:165 f.

113. *L'Echo français,* Sept. 7, 1840.

114. *Procès,* 2:131 f.

115. Ibid., pp. 212 f.

116. Ibid., pp. 53 f.

117. In her trial for the theft *(Procès,* 1:1-172) Marie's elaborate tale was dismantled bit by bit. Clavé was shown to have been out of the country in Algeria and later Mexico.

118. *Procès,* 1:18. Marie tells her friend, "Why go on, why not answer your heart and conscience? Do you want to have my death to reproach yourself?" Marie warned that before priest, friends, and Christ himself she would declare that she was dying the victim of the friend who betrayed her (pp. 18 f.).

119. *L'Echo Français,* August 5, 1840.

120. Raspail published his doubts about his

rival Orfila's findings and called Marie *la malheureuse calomniée* (cited in Saunders, p. 235).

121. Her last years are described briefly in Saunders, pp. 246-253.

122. Saunders, p. 200. She continued to write to Lachaud. In 1841 she told him, "I felt the need to share my life and I entrusted it without discernment.... With him I suffered constantly, I was unhappy over everthing, we did not understand one another, or we understood one another too well" *(Correspondance,* 1:245).

123. *Correspondance,* 1:1-157.

124. Ibid., p. 118.

125. André Gayot, "La Littérature de Mme. Lafarge," *La Nouvelle Revue,* 5 (January-February 1913): 18-30.

126. Ibid., p. 26.

127. *La Phalange,* October 9, 1840, pp. 306-307. The article is signed by Louis Blanc.

128. In addition there was a flood of pamphlets with titles such as *L'Innocence de Mme. Lafarge démontrée.* The English press followed the case closely and was generally sympathetic. The *Edinburgh Review,* 75 (April-July 1842): 359-396, devoted a long article to an attack on the evils of the French judicial system using the case as a vehicle and referring to Marie as the "unfortunate prisoner." It pointed out, justly, that the court failed sufficiently to separate the question of whether or not the deceased died by arsenic from the question of whether arsenic in whatever amount was administered by Mme. Lafarge. The *Standard* (September 26, 1840) called the trial a "shameless mockery of justice" and declared Lafarge to have been "a most disreputable ruffian, who had married his unfortunate wife merely for the purpose of getting possession of her property, and who had made a most fraudulent representation of his position in life." The *Atlas* (October 3, 1840) noted and shared the near universal sympathy for Marie in France and England, but it did acknowledge that it was the prisoner's "birth, beauty and accomplishments" which drew sympathy, not her proved innocence.

129. *Procès,* 2:73 f.

130. *La Gazette des Tribunaux,* July 17, 1844.

131. Fouquier, p. 6.

132. *Correspondence,* 2:292.

CHAPTER 2

1. Lenore Davidoff considers the system

from a sociological perspective in *The Best Circles: Society Etiquette and the Season* (London: Croom Helm, 1973). Chapter III, "The Anatomy of Society and Etiquette," is especially relevant; although she deals primarily with the upper levels of the middle classes, much of the discussion is generally applicable. For France, Adeline Daumard's *La Bourgeoisie Parisienne de 1815 à 1848* (Paris: S.E.V.P.E.N., 1963), chaps. 4-5, contains much useful information on marriage patterns. See also Theodore Zeldin's *France, 1848-1945: Ambition, Love and Politics,* Vol. 1 (Oxford: Clarendon, 1973), Part 2, and Barbara Corrado Pope's "Angels in the Devil's Workshop: Leisured and Charitable Women in Nineteenth-Century France and England," in *Becoming Visible,* ed. Renate Bridenthal and Claudia Koonz (New York: Houghton Mifflin, 1977).

2. Sarah Ellis, *Daughters of England* (London: Fisher, 1843), p. 459.

3. The summary presented here is based on the published records of the trial in *The Trial of Madeleine Smith,* ed. F. Tennyson Jesse, Notable British Trials (New York: Day, 1927). Additional material, including several previously unpublished letters by Madeleine Smith, is contained in Peter Hunt, *The Madeleine Smith Affair* (London: Carroll and Nicholson, 1950) and in Nigel Morland, *That Nice Miss Smith* (London: Muller, 1957). Hunt's is the best full account of the case.

4. The account presented here is based on the verbatim record of the case in *La Gazette des Tribunaux;* the summary in Armand Fouquier, *Les Causes célèbres de tous les peuples,* 9 vols. (Paris: Lebrun, 1858-1874), vol. 7, cahier 35; and the dossier "Affaire Lemoine" in the Archives Départementales de l'Indre-et-Loire, which contains all the preliminary interrogations undertaken by the *juge d'instruction* (hereafter referred to as Dossier Lemoine, with the number of the cited document).

5. Originally over two hundred letters were found. Those introduced in evidence were printed in expurgated form in the Smith edition of the trial *(The Trial of Madeleine Smith,* A. Duncan Smith, ed. [Edinburgh: Hodge, 1905]) and subsequently in full in the Jesse edition. Some additional letters are quoted in Hunt and Morland.

6. Madeleine destroyed all of Emile's letters. Those quoted are copies of drafts found in his lodgings after his death which were not admitted in evidence at the trial, but from her replies, it is fair to assume that the versions Madeleine received were similar if not identical.

7. For reasons which will become clear, many of the local papers, such as the *Gazette,* the *Chronicle,* and the *Sentinel,* all published in Glasgow, failed to sympathize with Miss Smith, unlike the press elsewhere.

8. Fouquier, p. 17.

9. *Trial of Madeleine Smith,* p. 306.

10. Madeleine's reputation as an extraordinary creature who transcended her time has been kept alive more than Angélina's, and it is remarkable to what extent Miss Smith has been seen as anything but a product of her age. The dean of British true-crime writers, William Roughead, said in a foreword to Peter Hunt's study of Miss Smith: "Madeleine is not a maiden of her time. She was a pagan of an earlier age, untrammeled by, and disdainful of the hidebound traditions of her day" (p. vii). In her introduction to *The Trial of Madeleine Smith,* Jesse pictures Madeleine instead as a young girl who should have been born in the twentieth century—a plucky, vital girl who had unladylike and unvictorian qualities of determination, passion, and ruthlessness (pp. 1-38). In his recent study of the case, Richard Altick guards the image of the transcendent woman: "Part of her guilt, in contemporary eyes, was that she was disloyal to her sex; part of her fascination to us is that she was uninhibited by the age in which she lived" [*Victorian Studies in Scarlet* (New York: Norton, 1970), p. 176]. My study obviously takes issue with these assessments.

11. Morland, p. 16.

12. *Fraser's Magazine,* 31 (1845): 703-712.

13. Ibid., p. 703.

14. Ibid., p. 704.

15. "The Glasgow Poisoning," *United Presbyterian Magazine,* 1 (1858): 383 f.

16. Fouquier, p. 24; Dossier Lemoine, pièce 72.

17. Dossier Lemoine, pièce 158.

18. *Trial of Madeleine Smith,* p. 321.

19. "A girl's whole life from babyhood was oriented to the part she had to play in this status theatre. Although marriage was her greatest chance for expanding her role, it was not the end of the play by any means. It was the progression through sharply demarcated stages in the move from one status to the next which made her life so different from her brothers'. It also made what education she received meaningless to her future life. From the time the little girl entered the schoolroom at about the age of five until she 'came out' at seventeen or eighteen, there was nothing to mark her progress in the way of promotions, certificates or even variation in dress. Later in the period, some girls were sent away to school especially during their middle teens, some even to the Continent. Some were given a few added responsibilities at home in connection with running the house or less often with the younger children" (Davidoff, p. 51). Davidoff notes later that an educational sociologist "has argued that the classroom situation creates certain 'psychological capacities' that give children 'the abilities to engage in non-familial types of universalism.' Leaving home and embarking on graded tasks in the company of thirty or more peers of equal status and equal responsibility 'provides the first prolonged experience of impersonality,' teaching children how to deal with segmented attention, how to sever relationships without feeling personally bereft" (p. 93). Davidoff feels that the "typical small private boarding and finishing schools were hardly substitutes" (p. 93) for the above experience, though they clearly did provide elements of it which gave some women at least—Madeleine Smith included—experience in dealing with non-familial authority relationships.

20. "A Woman's Thoughts About Women," *Chambers' Journal of Popular Literature,* 6 (1857): 273 f.

21. Ibid., p. 274.

22. "Paying Daughters," *National Magazine,* 2 (1857): 31.

23. Ibid.

24. Quoted in Hunt, p. 61.

25. Quoted in Morland, p. 47.

26. A discussion of some of this literature is contained in C. Willett Cunnington, *Feminine Attitudes in the Nineteenth Century* (London: Heinemann, 1935), esp. chaps. 5 and 6.

27. Quoted in Hunt, p. 38.

28. Dossier Lemoine, pièce 158.

29. See Zeldin, pp. 315-342 on children, and Sylvaine Marandon, *L'Image de la France dans l'Angleterre victorienne* (Paris: Colin, 1967), pp. 259-307, on the family.

30. Dossier Lemoine, pièce 104.

31. Ibid.

32. Ibid.

33. Fouquier, p. 11.

34. Dossier Lemoine, pièce 137. The judge mentioned her remark to her in the trial: " 'My pregnancy,' you said, 'was not certain, and it was the only way to complete my novel.' Now there you used expressions that no magistrate would invent" (Fouquier, p. 12).

35. Quoted in Hunt, p. 36.

36. Ibid., p. 37.

37. Ibid., p. 39.

38. A typical article, "Women as They Are and Might Be," appeared in the *Lady's Com-*

panion, November 1857, pp. 240-246. "It is not the man but the state which women are taught to care for. . . . All people care about is what the man *has*" (pp. 242 f.).

39. *Trial of Madeleine Smith*, p. 323.

40. Ibid., p. 315.

41. Ibid., p. 305.

42. Ibid., p. 306.

43. Quoted in Morland, pp. 46 f.

44. Ibid., p. 47.

45. Quoted in Hunt, pp. 52 f.

46. Ibid., pp. 53 f.

47. *Trial of Madeleine Smith*, pp. 308 f.

48. Ibid., p. 309.

49. Quoted in Hunt, pp. 83 f.

50. *Trial of Madeleine Smith*, pp. 319-321. This long letter reiterated earlier themes of the necessity of Madeleine's paving the way for marriage, now more than ever, but Émile seems genuinely sorry that they were carried away: "I will never again repeat what I did until we are regularly married. . . . We did wrong. God forgive us for it. Mimi, we have loved blindly. It is your parents' fault if shame is the result; they are to blame for it all. . . . Oh! Mimi, be bold for once. do not fear them—tell them you are my wife before God." Emile still does not trust Madeleine, and with reason: "I cannot help doubting your word about flirting. . . . Mimi, the least thing I hear of you doing, that day shall be the last of our *tie*, that I swear. You are my wife, and I have the right to expect from you the behaviour of a married woman—or else you have no honour in you."

51. See *Trial of Madeleine Smith*, pp. 8-12.

52. Dossier Lemoine, pièce 132.

53. Ibid., pièce 104; Fouquier, p. 12.

54. Dossier Lemoine, pièce 73.

55. *La Presse*, December 10, 1859.

56. *Le Figaro*, December 14, 1859.

57. Dossier Lemoine, pièce 127.

58. Ibid., pièce 110.

59. Ibid.

60. Ibid., pièce 127.

61. Ibid.

62. *La Gazette des Tribunaux*, December 10, 1859.

63. Dossier Lemoine, pièce 110.

64. *Trial of Madeleine Smith*, p. 316. As was usual with Madeleine, she larded even this important letter with trivia and teasing: "I did not know (or I should not have done it) that I caused you to pay extra Postage for my stupid, cold letters—it shall not occur again. . . . I know you can have little confidence in me. But dear I shall not flirt. I do not think it is right of me. I should only be plesant [*sic*] to Gentlemen. Free with none, my pet, in conversation but yourself" (p. 317). She makes the regular promise to tell all to her parents and facilitate their marriage, but warns, "I shall consider about telling Mama. But I dont see any hope from her—I know her mind. You, of course, cannot judge of my parents. You know them not" (p. 317). Her sense of triumph in the matter of their lovemaking is clear, as is the insincerity in her reiterated and formulaic references to their future life together: "Tell me, pet, were you angry at me for allowing you to do what you did—was it very bad of me. We should, I suppose, have waited till we were married. I shall always remember last night. Will we not often talk about our evening meetings after we are married. . . . Adieu again, my husband. God bless you and make you well. And may you yet be very, very happy with your Mimi as your little wife" (pp. 317 f.).

65. *Trial of Madeleine Smith*, p. 237. The theme of Madeleine's brilliant defender, the Dean of Faculty John Inglis, was indeed that one who had been a "gentle and confiding and affectionate girl, the ornament and pride of her happy home" (p. 233) had been set upon by an "unknown adventurer" who was "vain, conceited, pretentious, with a great opinion of his own personal attractions, and a very silly expectation of admiration from the other sex" (p. 234). Accounting for the tone of Madeleine's letters, then, was easier. As Inglis proceeds: "And how corrupting that influence must have been!—how vile the arts to which he resorted for accomplishing his nefarious purpose, can never be proved so well as by the altered tone and language of the unhappy prisoner's letters. She had lost not her virtue merely, but, as the Lord Advocate said, her sense of decency. Gentlemen, whose fault was that—whose doing was that? Think you that, without temptation, without evil teaching, a poor girl falls into such depths of degradation? No. Influence from without—most corrupting influence—can alone account for a fall. And yet, through the midst of this frightful correspondence . . . there breathes a spirit of devoted affection towards the man who had destroyed her that strikes me as most touching" (p. 237). Madeleine, then, had it both ways: she was innocent of initiation in the sexual encounter and even got some little credit for being a dutiful fantasy wife. And, of course, Inglis would argue that she was innocent of murder as well and that the mercurial L'Angelier, suspected to have "dosed" himself with strange substances, had taken his own life.

66. Ibid., p. 295.

67. Ibid., p. 317. Emile's response demonstrated some concern over Madeleine's report and over the possible consequences of their act: "I do not understand, my pet, your not bleeding, for every woman having her virginity must bleed. You must have done so some other time. Try to remember if you never hurt yourself in washing, etc. I am sorry you felt pain. I hope, pet, you are better. I trust, dearest, you will not be ————. Be sure and tell me immediately you are ill next time, and if at your regular period" (p. 320).

68. Ibid., p. 336.

69. Ibid., p. 346.

70. William Acton, *The Functions and Disorders of the Reproductive Organs in Childhood, Youth, Adult Age and Advanced Life, Considered in their Physiological, Social, and Moral Relations* (Philadelphia: Blakiston, 1857), cited in the voyeuristic but useful study of Ronald Pearsall, *The Worm in the Bud: The World of Victorian Sexuality* (New York: Macmillan, 1969), p. 41.

71. Steven Marcus documents the immense popularity of Acton's study in his *The Other Victorians* (New York: Basic Books, 1966), pp. 1-33, but he points out that despite its title the book devotes little attention to women. Acton, in any case, appears to have been describing less a state of affairs than a state of mind, and one which was not shared by the entire medical community by any means, let alone by the middle classes in general. Patricia Branca has recently noted that the sexual strictures of much of the literature of the period were directed toward unmarried youth and that regular sexual relations in marriage were considered healthy for both sexes by many authorities. She argues too that the abundant documentation for women's increasing concern about their physical appearance and all their talk about flirting—Madeleine was not exceptional—is evidence of acceptance of sexuality. Finally, Patricia Branca maintains that widespread adoption of contraceptive devices in the middle classes argues against the notion that either abstinence or *coitus interruptus* must be accepted as the way middle-class people limited their families [*Silent Sisterhood: Middle-Class Women in the Victorian Home* (Pittsburgh: Carnegie-Mellon University Press, 1975), chap. 7]. In other words, without insisting that Victorian women were actually sexual enthusiasts, recent studies undermine the image of the sexless Victorian woman and also suggest that women were seeking to improve the quality of sex for themselves within marriage. See also Carl N. Degler, "What Ought to Be and What Was:

Women's Sexuality in the Nineteenth Century," *American Historical Review*, 79 (December 1974), pp. 1467-1490.

72. *Spectator* 30 (1857): 729.

73. Quoted in Hunt, p. 62. Madeleine goes on: "My heart burns this night with love for you—I grow excited while I write you—I long to be your wife then there will be no danger we may *love* each other."

74. *Trial of Madeleine Smith*, p. 321.

75. Dossier Lemoine, pièce 110.

76. Quoted in Hunt, p. 61.

77. Ibid., p. 91.

78. *Trial of Madeleine Smith*, p. 353.

79. Quoted in Hunt, p. 61.

80. Ibid., p. 62. She confided further: "It saddens me to tell you this but I know you will love me for the way I am situated with regard to papa. He cares not for what I say. Though I tell him my mind is made up he wont care. His character is decision—He is the same as the other Glasgow people. He wants heart. I do not think he understands the warm love of young people. He has forgotten all his youthful passions—that night I brought them to his recollections—But he did not mind [pay attention]." Madeleine of course claimed to understand her father, while denying that Emile did; and if the argument made here is true—that her confrontations with her father were not real, as she tried to persuade her lover—then the fantasized intensity of her parent's refusal to permit the marriage may have meant that, unconsciously, she wanted her father for herself.

81. *Trial of Madeleine Smith*, p. 387.

82. Fouquier, p. 22.

83. Ibid.

84. Ibid.

85. The letter was read into evidence at the trial. "You cannot doubt that since the day of my departure, I have known the deepest sorrow that ever a man can have, especially when I think about how I had to be separated from you without having the joy of pressing you again to my heart and giving you a kiss of the purest love and affection. . . . I worry greatly over not knowing how your mother is treating you, how she is ordering you about. I am sure that she is covering you with reproaches, but try not to notice, don't worry, that is all I ask. If I could be like the birds, I would quickly fly to your side to share the sorrows you are suffering. . . write me a few lines, my angel, to reassure me about what is happening between your mother and you. That would make me very happy, and it would not be difficult, since you can write the letters in your dressing room and give them to

your music teacher, who will surely deliver them, for it will be he who will bring you this letter" (Fouquier, p. 8). The music teacher may have backed off, for it was the widowed tailor who lived on the Lemoine property who accepted the commission. After proceedings began, this poor man, humiliated over his role in the affair, attempted unsuccessfully to commit suicide. He testified with his injured jaw in bandages. Jean, meanwhile, unable to get good references, had left town to find work. A desperate note he sent to his brother suggests that even his own family was refusing to deal with him. This is the only letter of Jean's included in the dossier which was his own effort. He complains that he cannot take field work since the dust and heat bother his eyes, and he begs for news of Angélina. She is, he says, in her last days: "she might die and you have not informed me about her confinement" ("elle pourai [sic] mourir et tu ne mas pas fait savoir lacoucheman [sic]") (Dossier Lemoine, pièce 165).

86. Fouquier, p. 11.
87. Ibid., p. 13.
88. Ibid., p. 3.
89. Dossier Lemoine, pièce 159.
90. Ibid., pièce 162.
91. Ibid., pièce 156.
92. Ibid., pièce 157.
93. Ibid., pièce 163.
94. Ibid., pièce 158.
95. Ibid., pièce 139.
96. Ibid., pièce 140.
97. *La Presse*, October 20, 1857.
98. Ibid.
99. Fouquier, p. 24.
100. Ibid., p. 30. Like Madeleine's defense counsel, Charles Lachaud adopted the explanation of seduction, but the task was more challenging in view of both Fétis's and Angélina's testimony. "Is it a rape? No, not in the law of men, but in the law of God, it is clearly such. There is an age, a difficult age, in which young girls experience mysterious sensations. The wretch profited from these dispositions of this innocent and frivolous girl, who was bound to succumb if his honesty did not protect her." In defending both women, whose stories were very different, Lachaud accepted most of Mme. Lemoine's account and argued that the mother, in hushing up the affair and in destroying the corpse of a child born dead, was performing a sacred duty: "This mother was stronger than a woman, more courageous than a man, she acted with a virility which inspires fear; yes, I acknowledge it, she acted with an energy inspired by the classical age; she had a daughter to save!"

(Fouquier, p. 31). Lachaud dismissed all of Mlle. Lemoine's behavior as irresponsible and the incriminating testimony against her mother as the foolish stories of a child. He shrewdly pointed out that the magistrates in the preliminary investigation had not followed the customary practice of confronting the mother and daughter with their contradictory stories for fear that Angélina would break down and return to her mother's version of events. Lachaud's speech was greeted with outbursts of cheers and applause, but it was noted that the audience consisted mostly of outsiders, many of them Parisian women who had traveled to Tours for the event. Such persons used different standards than the citizens of Chinon to judge Mme. Lemoine's behavior. The presiding judge, who was infuriated by their disturbance, accused them of being paid, but their behavior instead expressed a newer bourgeois code which endorsed all means to defend against scandal (Fouquier, p. 32).

101. The writer for *Le Figaro* (December 14, 1859) remarked, "I know nothing more lamentable than the position of this unhappy mother, put upon by the opinion of a jealous and scandal-mongering village populace." *La Presse* (December 11, 1859) expressed pity for the mother and ventured the opinion that her celebrity, unfortunately, was bound to pursue her. The local paper from Tours, the *Journal de l'Indre-et-Loire* (December 10, 1859), announced it was refraining from printing the act of accusation because of "unseemly details" and remarked that Angélina had been raised in a way which demonstrated her mother's "deplorable abandon."

Several London papers, including the *Times* (November 12, December 14, 1859), gave full accounts of the case, and the *Saturday Review* (December 17, 1859) commented that it would refrain from censure: "Still less do we think it a suitable text for a heavy homily on the comparative excellence of English education and home morals. Merely as regards the crime, we are not in a position to cast stones." The journal had developed some detachment from its admittedly reserved endorsement of acquittal in the Madeleine Smith case, however. "We must remember that precisely the same class of motives which influenced a Scotch jury to find Madeleine Smith's guilt not proven has weighed with the Tours jury to acquit Angélina Lemoine. In either case the miserable character of the paramour saved the accused. That is to say, both in Scotland and France a sentimental sort of gallantry was considered a sufficient ground for neglecting evidence." So it was; and in England, at least, there were signs of a new distrust of allegedly innocent young girls.

102. "I felt truly astonished to have my last letter returned to me. . . . This may astonish you, but you have more than once returned me my letters, and my mind was made up that I should not stand the same thing again. And you also annoyed me much on Saturday by your conduct in coming so near me. Altogether I think owing to coolness and indifference (nothing else) that we had better for the future consider ourselves as strangers. I trust to your honour as a Gentleman that you will not reveal any thing that may have passed between us. I shall feel obliged by your bring [sic] me my letters and Likeness on Thursday eveng. at 7. . . . You may be astonished at this sudden change—but for some time back you must have noticed a coolness in my notes. My love for you has ceased, and that is why I was cool. . . . What has passed you will not mention. I know when I ask you that you will comply. Adieu" *(Trial of Madeleine Smith*, pp. 373 f.).

103. *Trial of Madeleine Smith*, p. 375.

104. Peter Hunt offers this hypothesis (pp. 117 f.).

105. After the trial, L'Angelier's minister at St. Jude's Episcopal Church in Glasgow came forward to say that L'Angelier had told him that he believed he was legally married according to Scottish law (Hunt, p. 79).

106. *Trial of Madeleine Smith*, pp. 376 f.

107. The *Times* (July 10, 1857) labeled L'Angelier's conduct "base and unmanly in the last degree" and agreed with the verdict. Like many, the *Times* suspected that Madeleine had done the deed, but excused her (though without enthusiasm) as the victim of seduction: "A Mr. Minnoch had proposed in all innocence to her, and in spite of stolen interviews and boarding-school heroes, she thought it better to have a solid Glasgow man of business than a French clerk on 30 pounds a year who boasted to everybody of his successes with women in general and herself in particular." The *Examiner*, the *North British Daily Mail*, the *Guardian*, the *Illustrated London Times*, and indeed most English papers, as well as the Edinburgh dailies, accepted the verdict and either argued Madeleine's innocence or contended that if she were guilty, her victim deserved what he got. The medical journal the *Lancet*, adopting the line that Madeleine was seduced and corrupted, reserved its harshest words for L'Angelier, the "miserable little fop." Remarking that "he seems to have been a vain and impulsive little coxcomb," the *Lancet*

suggested that his death was the result of arsenic taken for cosmetic purposes, "in his anxiety to regain her affection by the good looks which had once won her" (July 18, 1857, p. 64).

Nearly all the accounts nonetheless expressed considerable alarm over the revelations about Madeleine's behavior and what these suggested both about the hidden evils within proper society and the inadequacies of female education. The Manchester *Guardian* (July 15, 1857) complained, "It is the fashion of our time to set the young free from all restraints. They may read French novels, choose their own acquaintances, and decide a thousand questions for themselves which their grandmothers would not have dreamed of proposing to their daughters at all." The *Illustrated London Times* (July 11, 1857) also voiced the troubled concern with change: "We cannot but think that among our 'respectable' classes there prevails a want of confidence between parents and children in affairs of the heart, which it is painful to contemplate. A 'good match' is of course duly introduced into the drawing room, and recommended to the daughters, and with regard to all other attachments, they are ignored, though it must be perfectly well known that they exist. Worldliness is the rule, and hence worldliness is every now and then shocked by tragedy. . . . The whole question of the relation between the sexes, and the vital points which it involves, is neglected by those who would think themselves very wrong if their daughters did not learn music and embroidery. Such awful exposures as this Glasgow one should teach people—above all, heads of families—to take more care of what may be called the sentimental education of their offspring. . . . Above all, let the lessons of our moralists be attended to in the matter of marriages, and let society cease to treat the marriage of daughters as only an event answering to the putting [of] sons in a profession."

The *Scotch Thistle* (July 18, 1857) was one of the only Edinburgh papers to condemn popular sympathy for Madeleine, though like many of the Scottish papers, it joined the chorus of attack on the fashion of sending daughters away to school, either to London or to the continent. The *Ayrshire Express* (July 11, 1857) found the explanation for Madeleine's fall in such boarding schools "at which foreign governesses or foreign actresses (it is not very clear which) preside, and during which elegant selections from travels, etc., are read, whereby the use of arsenic (among other things) . . . by Styrian peasants, blowsy and breathless, is indelibly imprinted on the youthful female imagination [it was demonstrated that Madeleine had seen articles on arsenic-eating in *Chambers' Journal* and *Blackwood's Magazine*]; and to which, doubtless, a due supplementary addition of popular novels and talk 'about marriage' with hints from accomplished actresses on the use of cosmetics for the one grand absorbing object of existence would be vouchsafed."

108. *Spectator*, 30 (1857): 27.

109. Ibid.

110. Max O'Rell, *Les Filles de John Bull* (Paris: Lévy, 1884), p. 33.

111. Quoted in Hunt, p. 188.

112. Madeleine's remarkable ability to recoup her losses should not obscure the fact that her plans for her life were quite different. She intended to marry William Minnoch, the approved suitor, and she almost did so. A Monsieur de Mean, Chancellor to the French Consul and the only witness who knew both L'Angelier and Mr. Smith, testified in the trial that shortly after the death of Emile he had visited Mr. Smith to inform him that certain letters from Madeleine had been discovered in the dead man's lodgings. De Mean offered his services to Smith in recovering those letters before they fell into the hands of authorities, but Smith, unaware of the gravity of the situation, merely gave his assent without personally pursuing the matter. De Mean's testimony clearly indicates that he considered the situation so delicate that he did not give Mr. Smith sufficient warning about the letters. Since L'Angelier had led de Mean to believe that Mr. Smith was fully aware of the relationship between himself and Madeleine, de Mean assumed that Mr. Smith would have acted promptly to recover the letters himself. If he had done so, Madeleine might never have been brought to trial. She would have married Minnoch and retained a blameless reputation. But she was not that lucky [quoted from Mary S. Hartman, "Murder for Respectability: the Case of Madeleine Smith," *Victorian Studies*, 16, no. 4 (June 1973): 400].

113. Fouquier, p. 32.

114. *Sentinel*, July 11, 1857.

115. *Daily Express*, July 11, 1857.

CHAPTER 3

1. J. Hajnal, "The European Marriage Pattern in Perspective," in *Population and History*, ed. D. V. Glass and D. E. C. Eversley (London: Arnold, 1965), p. 102.

2. Patricia Branca makes this point in discussing the position of the single woman in *Silent Sisterhood: Middle-Class Women in the Victorian Home* (Pittsburgh: Carnegie-Mellon University Press, 1975).

3. Frances Trollope, *Paris and the Parisians in 1835* 2 vols. in one (Paris: Galignani, 1836), vol. 1, p. 287.

4. See the well-known essay by W. R. Greg, "Why Are Women Redundant?" in his *Literary and Social Judgments* (Boston: Osgood, 1873), pp. 274-308.

5. See the article by Tamara Hareven, "The History of the Family as an Interdisciplinary Field," in *The Family in History*, ed. Theodore Rabb and Robert Rothberg (New York: Harper & Row, 1973), pp. 211-226.

6. The main sources for the Doudet affair are Armand Fouquier, *Les Causes célèbres de tous les peuples*, 9 vols. (Paris: Lebrun, 1858-1874), vol. 3, cahiers 12, 13; *La Gazette des Tribunaux*; and *La Tribune judiciare* (Paris: Borrani et Droz, 1855), pp. 1-193. The main sources for the case of Constance Kent are Yseult Bridges, *The Tragedy at Road-Hill House* (New York: Holt, Rinehart & Winston, 1955) and John Rhode (pseud. of C. J. C. Street), *The Case of Constance Kent* (New York: Scribner, 1928). Bridges's book is the best account of the case, although it mistakenly places the runaway episode in 1857 rather than 1856.

7. Her full statement is reprinted in Bridges, p. 206: "I, Constance Emilie Kent, alone and unaided, on the night of 29th June 1860 murdered at Road Hill House, Wiltshire, one Francis Savile Kent. Before the deed was done no one knew of my intention, nor afterwards of my guilt. No one assisted me in the crime, nor in the evasion of discovery."

8. *Worcestershire Chronicle*, May 7, 1855.

9. Fouquier, p. 23.

10. Ibid., p. 3.

11. Ibid., p. 4.

12. Ibid., p. 7.

13. Ibid., p. 6.

14. Ibid., pp. 7, 37.

15. Ibid., p. 8.

16. Alex Comfort, *The Anxiety-Makers* (London: Panther, 1968), pp. 84 f.

17. For a full discussion and extensive bibliography, see René Spitz, "Authority and Masturbation, Some Remarks on a Bibliographical Investigation," *The Psychoanalytic Quarterly*, 21 (1952): 490-527; also E. H. Hare, "Masturbatory Insanity: The History of an Idea," *Journal of Mental Science* 108 (1962): 1-25.

18. Comfort, p. 106, chap. 3 passim. Masturbation was among the evils regularly cited as prevalent at boarding schools for both sexes. Concern over the issue seems to have been greater in England than in France, although S. A. Tissot's mid-eighteenth century work, *Onanism: A Treatise on the Disorders Produced by Masturbation,* was regularly republished throughout the nineteenth century. A review of a new edition of Tissot in *Archives générales de médecine,* December 1855, p. 763, notes that since the first edition in 1758, the book had sold over 100,000 copies. There is a discussion of the belts similar to those ordered for the Marsden girls in an article by Gerhart S. Schwartz entitled "Devices to Prevent Masturbation" in *Medical Aspects of Human Sexuality,* 7 (May 1973): 141-153.

19. Quoted in Bridges, p. 24, from Dr. John Bucknill, who examined Constance Kent for mental disorders in 1865.

20. Joseph W. Stapleton, *The Great Crime of 1860* (London: Marlborough, 1861), p. 21.

21. Bridges, p. 27.

22. Ibid.

23. Stapleton, p. 29. Richard Altick *(Victorian Studies in Scarlet* [New York: Norton, 1970], p. 283) quotes the memoirs of the Victorian writer E. E. Kellett, who was persuaded that such diagnoses often covered foul play among the respectable classes. "A doctor once told me that he did not believe that there was a single medical practitioner in London of twenty years standing, who had not serious reason to believe that wives in his practice had poisoned their husbands, and husbands their wives, but in the vast majority of cases the doctors could not utter their suspicions."

24. Ibid., p. 28.

25. Ibid.

26. Ibid., p. 32.

27. Ibid., p. 28.

28. Ibid.

29. In addition to the inquest, which was held on July 2, 1860, the Trowbridge magistrates held inquiries *in camera* beginning on July 9 directed toward the nurse Elizabeth Gough. After the failure of this effort, Scotland Yard was called in in the person of Chief Inspector Jonathan Whicher, and local magistrates resumed their sessions on July 16. Consequent to Whicher's suspicion of Constance, the girl was arrested on July 20 and brought before the magistrates on July 27. After her release the magistrates of Bath petitioned the Home Secretary, George Lewis, for a special commission to investigate the crime; this was denied, although Lewis

authorized a local solicitor to conduct a private inquiry of the case in his own office. The solicitor was not permitted to reveal the source of his authority or to take evidence upon oath, which meant that witnesses could not be compelled to answer summons or to respond to questions. The inquiry was conducted in September and resulted in the arrest of Elizabeth Gough, who was questioned by Trowbridge magistrates in October and released. Local magistrates then held further inquiries *in camera* into the revelation that local police had been locked in the kitchen by Mr. Kent while investigating the crime. In November a local magistrate received permission from the Home Secretary to conduct an open inquisition; this resulted in the discovery that a piece of important evidence, a bloody night shirt, had been discovered and had then disappeared under mysterious circumstances. A new inquiry was held in late November with no results, but finally the Attorney-General, on November 24, applied to the Queen's Bench for the issuing of a writ *ad melius inquirendum.* If successful, the application would have quashed the verdict of the coroner's jury on technical procedural grounds and permitted a new inquiry, but it was denied by the Court of the Queen's Bench in January 1861. There the formal efforts to find a killer stopped.

30. Cited in Bridges, p. 119, from the *Trowbridge and North Wilts Advertiser.*

31. Stapleton, p. 129.

32. Ibid.

33. Ibid.

34. Ibid., p. 131.

35. Ibid., p. 132.

36. Ibid.

37. Ibid.

38. In a letter which she sent to Rowland Rodway, her father's solicitor, Constance said, "It has been stated that my feelings of revenge were excited in consequence of cruel treatment. This is entirely false. I have received the greatest kindness from both the persons accused of subjecting me to it. I have never had any ill-will towards either of them on account of their behavior to me, which has been very kind. I shall be obliged if you will make use of this statement in order that the public may be undeceived on this point" (quoted in Bridges, p. 233). The statement, if true, left Constance without a motive for the crime.

39. Quoted from a local newspaper (unattributed) in Bridges, p. 239.

40. The letter, dated August 30, was widely published and is quoted here from the *British Medical Journal,* September 2, 1865, p. 239.

41. *La Tribune judiciare,* p. 148.
42. Fouquier, p. 9.
43. *La Tribune judiciare,* p. 53.
44. Fouquier, p. 24.
45. *La Presse,* February 25, 1855.
46. *La Tribune judiciare,* p. 148.
47. Fouquier, p. 13.
48. Ibid.
49. Ibid.
50. James Loftus Marsden, *Notes on Homeopathy* (London: Headland, 1849), p. 24.
51. James Loftus Marsden, *The Action of the Mind on the Body* (Great Malvern: Lamb, 1859), pp. 36, 46 f.
52. *La Tribune judiciare,* p. 63. It is possible that Marsden was made to feel a kind of hereditary role in his children's corruption. Because of his interest in writings by the water-cure reformers of the period, he may have seen a contemporary study on marriage by the American Mary Gove Nichols and her husband Thomas Low Nichols, who both later practiced at Malvern. Mrs. Nichols was concerned about what she called the evils to children resulting from marriages involving "amative excesses." She wrote that "masturbation in children, and every evil of sensuality, spring from the polluted hot-bed of a sensual and unloving marriage, where woman is subject to a destroying sensualism during pregnancy and lactation" *(Marriage: Its History, Character and Results: Its Sanctities and Its Profanities; Its Science and Its Facts. Demonstrating Its Influence, as a Civilized Institution, on the Happiness of the Individual and the Progress of the Race* [Cincinnati: Nicholson, 1854], p. 223). Ideas like Mrs. Nichols's were, in any case, part of Marsden's milieu. (She figures in another case and will be discussed at greater length in Chapter 5.) Marsden's first wife had borne children annually for the seven years of their marriage; she had died giving birth to the last child, who was stillborn.
53. *Berrow's Worcestershire Journal,* March 31, 1855. Mary Marsden did not attend the trials, and her deposition is not given in the French accounts.
54. Ibid.
55. Ibid.
56. It was Emily, his second daughter, whom Marsden found the brightest, but he was also most troubled about Emily's "bad habits." In a letter of October 15, 1852, he told Doudet, "Her composition is very nice, but I beg you to look upon her as a child, treat her like a child, don't ask for her opinion and don't speak to her as though she were a woman; if you do not follow my advice, she may seem pleasing enough, but she will be

come a most intolerable creature through impertinence and extravagance. There is no danger of overworking her. She is headstrong and it is necessary to prevent her from misbehaving" *(La Tribune judiciare,* p. 60). In the same letter Marsden mentions receiving "poor Lucy's" efforts and remarks that at least they show she is trying to learn. Returning to Emily, he stresses the female qualities which he wishes developed: "I want Emily to see that conduct, goodness, and unselfishness are on a higher plane than gifts of the mind, and I would rejoice to learn that she was cultivating these qualities. Are they learning to dance?"
57. *Berrow's Worcestershire Journal,* March 31, 1855.
58. Ibid.
59. *Comfort,* pp. 96 f., 105, cites examples from memoirs and prescriptive literature on the practice. One woman recalls that her nurse was extremely severe on the subject: "Believing, as she told me years later, that self-abuse was 'the evil rotting the world,' she insisted on supervision in the lavatory, and put us to bed with our hands tied, sometimes too tightly: I remember my piano teacher commenting on my scarred wrists" (p. 97).
60. Fouquier, p. 14.
61. The *British Mothers' Magazine,* published between 1845 and 1863, has equal love for all children in a family as one of its constant themes. To cite only two examples, the editor Mrs. J. Bakewell serialized her novel *The Second Marriage: or Prejudice Removed* in volumes 8 and 9 (1852, 1853). One of its most important aspects is the striving of the new wife to establish a loving relationship with the children of the first marriage and to give the same treatment to them as to her own children. The poem "To a Step-Child" (vol. 8, p. 201) also illustrates the advice and sentiments typical in these publications: "Child of the lost, the buried, and the sainted, I call thee mine,/ Till fairer still, with tears and sin untainted, her home be thine."
62. I am grateful to Elizabeth Jenkins, who kindly showed me a copy of her unpublished paper "The Young Step-Mother, A Sensational Source," which discusses the startling similarities between the Constance Kent case and the novel by Charlotte Yonge entitled *The Young Step-Mother.* Miss Jenkins suggests that the Kent case might have prompted Charlotte Yonge to re-write the story with a benevolent stepmother whose actions averted the sort of disaster which happened at Road-Hill House. Miss Jenkins notes that although a portion of the novel had already appeared in serialized form before the crime, the possibility of some

influence cannot be ruled out. The parallels which she draws between characters and incidents are most intriguing.

63. Stapleton, p. 40.

64. *Frome Times,* November 7, 1860. This paper also noted that although Kent was not hated by his neighbors, as he insisted at the time of the crime, he was considered "reserved" and was less well liked than the rest of his family. There were some reasons for the neighbors' feelings. In his capacity as sub-inspector of factories, Kent had reportedly dismissed twenty to thirty local children from factory work, as they were barred by child labor legislation. In addition, he had taken steps to prevent neighbors from fishing in the river near his home and had enclosed his premises to prevent poaching. Cottagers who had considered the land public property were aggrieved, and it did not help matters that Kent prosecuted some local boys for stealing from him *(Frome Times,* October 17, 1860).

65. The document was sent to John Rhode after *The Case of Constance Kent* appeared in 1928, but he used it in a shorter essay on the case which was included in a later collection, *The Anatomy of Murder* (New York: Macmillan, 1937), pp. 43-86. The original document was destroyed in World War II, and portions here are taken from the passages in the Rhode essay reprinted in Bridges.

66. Bridges, p. 254.

67. Stapleton, p. 33.

68. Bridges, pp. 254 f.

69. Ibid., p. 257.

70. The *Frome Times* cited the incident as reported at the time in a Bath paper: "The elder boy [William, though younger, was the taller and taken for the elder] said little, but the younger boy [Constance] told him to mind his own business, more than hinting that his conduct was impertinent." One of the policemen claimed to have guessed that "the younger boy" was a girl by observing the way she sat and crossed her legs. When the truth was out, the policemen's response was sympathy and respect for the little girl who had played her part so well. The reporter for the *Frome Times,* who questioned the officers after the crime, noted, "The little girl, we are told, acted like a little hero, acting the part of a boy to the admiration of all who saw her" (July 25, 1860).

71. Bridges, p. 39. There are few precise textual references given in Bridges and almost no notes to her sources. Although I have found confirmation of nearly all her statements in the *Trowbridge and North Wilts Advertiser,* the *Somerset and Wilts Journal,* the *Frome Times,*

the *Bath Chronicle,* and other papers, as well as a reference to Kent's summoning before the Board of Factory Commissioners in the study by his friend Stapleton (p. 30), I have not located the source for these allegations beyond Bridges. However, I am confident they are accurate.

72. Berryer, Célestine Doudet's defender, noted the greater use of manual punishment in England than in France, but cited recent articles in educational journals, the *Bulletin de l'Instruction primaire* (May 1854), and the *Quarterly Review of Education* (May–June 1854, nos. 18, 19), which discussed a trend in England toward reduced use of physical correction.

73. In her *Mothers of England* (London: Fisher, 1843), p. 34, Mrs. Ellis, one of the most popular authorities, argues that children who are regularly beaten merely become hardened. She believes in the undisputed authority of parents, but maintains that parents should try to understand that children think differently from adults and require reasoning along with discipline.

74. See the discussion in Branca, pp. 108-110.

75. *Queen,* December 1865, January 1866; *Englishwomen's Domestic Magazine,* March 1870. From April through November the supplements of the "Conversazioni" column were published separately. The supplements have been bound together and are located where the pornography is kept in the private cases of the British Museum, probably because they were given the collective title "On the Whipping of Girls."

76. *Englishwomen's Domestic Magazine,* May 1870.

77. Ibid., April 1870 (supplement).

78. Ibid., March 1870 (supplement).

79. Ibid., July 1870 (supplement).

80. For information about the present state of medical opinion on the question, I owe special thanks to Marc H. Hollender, M.D., Chairman of the Department of Psychiatry at Vanderbilt University and author of several historical studies on female sexuality. Dr. Hollender told me that his experience and study have revealed no way of detecting the regular masturbator through genital examination. He also communicated to me the following remarks, which appeared in *Medical Aspects of Human Sexuality,* 7 (July 1973): 107-109. J. P. Semmens, M.D., Associate Professor of Obstetrics and Gynecology at the Medical University of South Carolina, responded as follows to the question, "Does the size of the clitoris increase with frequent

sexual stimulation?" "To my knowledge, there is no documented evidence that increased activity causes the clitoris to become hypertrophic or any larger on a permanent basis. Inferences have been made in the less responsible sexual literature suggesting that labial hypertrophy and clitoral hypertrophy are related to excessive female masturbatory activity. This probably stems from the concept that oftentimes this hypertrophy may be purely of the left or right side paralleling the right-handedness or left-handedness of the individual. I would admonish any professional drawing such a conclusion about a client purely on the basis of physical observation."

81. James Manby Gully, one of Dr. Marsden's partners at Malvern, who figures in another of the cases discussed here, stressed the necessity of well-cooked foods for general health and warned that undercooking produced excessive stimulation of the ganglionic centers liable to exacerbate nervous conditions [*An Exposition of the Symptoms, Essential Nature and Treatment of Neuropathy or Nervousness* (London: Churchill, 1837), p. 128].

82. Fouquier, p. 29.

83. Ibid., p. 24.

84. Ibid., p. 26.

85. Ibid., p. 33.

86. Ibid.

87. Ibid., p. 32.

88. Ibid., p. 34.

89. *La Presse*, February 26, 1855.

90. Ibid.

91. Fouquier, p. 28.

92. Ibid.

93. *La Presse*, February 23, 1855.

94. *La Tribune judiciare*, p. 43.

95. Berryer added, " 'Bad habits,' which caused their physical decline and which, once they were overcome, allowed the restoration to glowing health—there you have the whole case in a nutshell" (Fouquier, p. 53).

96. Fouquier, p. 26.

97. *Le Figaro*, March 4, 1855.

98. Ibid. *Le Figaro* states that in this session, as usual, women were a majority of the audience. Several mothers reportedly brought their children, and the president ordered one boy of about ten to be taken out. Other women were said to have left voluntarily after some of the revelations.

99. Ibid.

100. Ibid.

101. *La Presse*, February 22, 1855.

102. Fouquier, p. 44.

103. Bridges reprints the account in an appendix (pp. 259 f.).

104. Ibid.

105. Stapleton, pp. 40 f.

106. *Frome Times*, October 10, 1860.

107. In October 1860, on the only known occasion Kent gave testimony before the local magistrates, he claimed to have known of the blanket's disappearance before he left, but all the earlier testimony contradicted his statement *(Frome Times*, October 3, 1860).

108. Stapleton, p. 72.

109. Ibid.

110. The local press, by and large, remained suspicious. The *Frome Times* for August 8, 1860, spoke of the "false delicacy of the coroner and foreman of the jury" and called their action a public insult.

111. *Frome Times*, October 10, 1860.

112. Bridges, p. 110.

113. *Frome Times*, November 7, 1860.

114. Stapleton, p. 114.

115. Joseph Stapleton had been the family's doctor, but maintained in his book that he had had limited social acquaintance with Mr. Kent (pp. 70 f.). His study is invaluable for the information it provides from one who was present within hours of the crime, and it clearly helped to shape the perceptions and prejudices of those who quoted from it several years later, after Constance confessed.

116. Stapleton, p. 26.

117. Ibid., p. 26.

118. Ibid., p. 48.

119. Ibid., p. 73.

120. Ibid., p. 79.

121. Ibid., p. 65.

122. Ibid., p. 109.

123. Bridges, p. 203.

124. Ibid., p. 204.

125. Yseult Bridges ·shows that A. W. Wagner. influenced by Newman's Oxford Movement, was viewed by his fellow high churchmen as a kind of hero who had seized upon the opportunity of Constance Kent's presence in the nursing establishment to gain attention for the confessional. Bridges quotes from the foreword of a pamphlet on Wagner by a sympathizer, Canon Hutchinson: "I am especially grateful to the author for the information he gives of the case of Constance Kent, and the almost nation-wide stir it made, and the prominence given by it to the integral place of the confessional in the economy of the English Church. All the great guns were brought up and trained on Wagner of Brighton in that connection.

"He stood his ground, and a great—a really great—victory was won. One might almost say that from that time the confessional in the Church of England remained unchallenged" (p. 249). In the end, however, it was not endorsement of the sanctity of the confessional, but their own reluctance to reopen an affair they wanted closed which kept the authorities from refusing Constance's plea of guilty.

126. *Brighton Gazette,* May 11, 1865.

127. A sampling of this press reaction of 1865 follows. "Is the Confessional of the Anglican Church sealed against the law of the land?" *(Brighton Gazette,* May 11). "Now instances of false confession certainly have occurred, and it might be said with some plausibility that such an occurrence was particularly likely to take place in the case of an enthusiastic young woman of a strong devotional temperament, who might work herself up into the notion that it was a good work to denote herself for the sake of her family and who by the mere fascination of the event, passing as it were under her very eyes, might have had her imagination so deeply affected that she might bring herself to think she had really done it" *(Pall Mall Gazette,* April 26). "We simply attach no judicial importance to her confession, drawn up at 'St. Mary's Home . . .,' and we think it would have been far wiser and better, and more legal, had no private gentleman escorted this young girl from Brighton to Bowstreet, in order that she might confess herself a murderess" *(Standard,* April 26). "What life was possible for Miss Kent after Mr. Wagner had begun to tell the inmates of the house that one of their number was a murderer?" *(Express,* May 13). "It seems tolerably clear that the cause of Miss Kent's voluntary deposition against herself was the influences exercised upon her mind by Mr. Wagner and Miss Green [sic], the 'Lady Superior' of the 'hospital' into which she had been removed" *(News of the World,* May 14).

128. *Bath Chronicle,* May 4, 1865; Bridges, p. 218.

129. Bridges, p. 218.

130. *Bath Chronicle,* May 4, 1865.

131. Ibid., May 11. Miss Greame did in fact request a "mother-daughter" immunity but was refused.

132. *Somerset and Wilts Journal,* May 5, 1865.

133. *Lancet,* May 20, 1865, contains a copy of the letter.

134. Quoted in Bridges, p. 237.

135. Ibid.

136. One local paper, the *Somerset and Wilts Journal,* had consistently maintained belief in Constance's guilt and reminded its readers of the fact at her confession (April 24, 1865). The *Trowbridge and Wilts Advertiser,* however, had supported Constance right along

and greeted the confession with suspicion (April 29, 1865). Many papers, including the *Daily Telegraph* (July 22, 1865), the *Morning Post* (July 22, 1865), the *Daily News* (July 22, 1865), the *Express* (July 22, 1865), and the *Times* (July 22 and 28, 1865) accepted the confession but complained of unsatisfactory evidence.

137. *Law Times,* September 2, 1865.

138. *Saturday Review,* April 29, 1865. After commutation of the sentence, the *Saturday Review* expressed approval and, unsurprisingly, more sympathy for Wagner and Greame than most others. "Their influence told, and told for good, on the stony heart of the God-forgetting murderess; and we trust that the work of penitence begun under religious auspices may advance under the severe and life-long seclusion which is now, except for its possible religious uses, a life worse than death" (September 2, 1865).

139. *Times,* April 27, 1865.

140. *Medical Times and Gazette,* July 22, 1865. The article concludes, "The moral lesson to be learned is the existence of evil passions in the breasts of even young children, which require to be kept in subjection by proper moral and religious training, and the existence of which alone, in however frightful a degree, does not constitute insanity." The *Lancet* echoed the view, in combination with the more popular opinion of hereditary madness: "How far such an hereditary predisposition may have been influenced by subsequent sympathetic changes in the female constitution—how for a critical moment in a girl's life she may have developed that ephemeral though special form of mental disturbance which the late profound psychologist, Dr. Wigan, characterised as the 'motiveless crimes of the young,' is a question most deserving investigation" (May 20, 1865).

141. *Bath Express,* April 29, 1865.

142. Bridges, p. 204.

143. Bridges speculates on this possibility (pp. 28 f.).

144. In England the Doudet affair elicited criticism characteristic of a general reaction against girls' finishing schools, which were increasingly attacked as centers of fine ladyism. Many critics, such as this one, directed their hostility toward the boarding schools across the channel: "For ourselves, we are content to believe in the innocence of four little English girls rather than in that of a Frenchwoman whose mind seems to have been so tainted with vicious thoughts as to have no room for womanly grace or virtue." The article proceeds to demand more practical

education for women and laments current practice: "our children are sent abroad by the hundreds, far from the wholesome moral influence of home and the holy ties of family love.... Our girls are worse off than their brothers.... Why be obliged to send our children to the continent to teach them how to live in England, and run the chance of Mlles. Doudet . . .?" *(Daily News,* April 3, 1855).

145. *La Tribune judiciaire,* pp. 187 f.

146. Fouquier, p. 47.

147. Ibid., p. 56.

148. Arthur Griffiths, *Secrets of the Prison-House or Gaol Studies and Sketches* (London: Chapman and Hall, 1894), pp. 10 f.

149. Bridges, p. 240.

150. B. A. Marsden and J. A. Marsden, *Geneological Memoirs of the Family of Marsden* (Birkenhead: Griffith, 1914), p. 113. Marsden's one son died at sea in 1869.

151. Marsden's will bestowed some property he still held in Malvern on his wife and created a trust fund for her daughter to be administered by her throughout the girl's minority [Registry of Wills, Somerset House].

CHAPTER 4

1. Lee Holcomb, *Victorian Ladies at Work: Middle-Class Working Women in England and Wales, 1850-1914* (Hamden, Conn.: Archon, 1973).

2. This was more true of England than of France, though the study of middle-class women and religion for both countries remains to be done. Bonnie Smith's recent dissertation, "The Bourgeois Women of Lille, 1860–1910" (University of Rochester, 1975), makes a strong case for the existence of a deeply felt religious faith and an all-embracing ritual which enveloped the lives of women of the upper bourgeoisie from birth to death. "There was hardly an important moment in a woman's life which the Church did not sanctify; there was hardly a task in her daily life, hardly a relationship for which the Church did not have its teachings or its own manual" (p. 238). As Smith shows, however, the church was not merely a traditional force in women's lives; women adapted its ideology and its functions to their own growing urge for expanded social functions and used religious and especially charity organizations as a vehicle to effect their own transition to more modern roles. "Neither could accept any change in the other without feelings of dissonance. In a symbiotic way religion and women, as forces of tradition, faced change in nineteenth-century life" (p.

250). It is true, of course, that some of the intense religiosity did represent a reaction against change among more privileged segments of the bourgeoisie.

In her study of Victorian women, *Silent Sisterhood: Middle-Class Women in the Victorian Home* (Pittsburgh: Carnegie-Mellon University Press, 1975), Patricia Branca suggests that by the second half of the century middle-class women as well as men appear to have experienced declining religious faith. Such a development is hard to measure, but Branca suggests one index in the "increasing secularism of the material read by women" (p. 147). She points out that the *Englishwoman's Domestic Magazine* made it a policy to exclude religious material. "Looking through the hundreds of magazines printed in the nineteenth century for women, one is left with the impression that women were more concerned with the condition of their wash or the nature of their complexions than the state of their souls" (p. 147).

3. Peter Cominos presents a good though somewhat abstract discussion of this transition in "Innocent Femina Sensualis in Unconscious Conflict," in *Suffer and Be Still,* ed. Martha Vicinus (Bloomington: Indiana University Press, 1972), pp. 155-172.

4. See discussion in Branca, chap. 2. "Above all, the tone of most manuals was naggingly critical of middle-class women" (p. 22).

5. E. L. Linton, "The Girl of the Period," *Saturday Review,* 25 (March 14, 1868): 339 f.

6. Ibid., p. 340.

7. Jules Barbey d'Aurevilly, *Les Bas-bleus* (Paris: Dentu, 1874).

8. Louis Delzons, *La Famille française* (Paris: Colin, 1913), p. 61.

9. Linton, "The Girl of the Period," p. 340, on the new woman as closet prostitute.

10. Delzons, p. 64.

11. The major source for the Bravo affair is the account of the inquest entitled *The Balham Mystery. A Complete Record of the "Bravo" Poisoning Case* published as a serialized feature with illustrations by the *Daily Telegraph* (hereafter referred to as Balham). Two excellent studies of the case were also most useful: Elizabeth Jenkins, *Dr. Gully's Story* (New York: Coward, McCann & Geoghegan, 1972), a fictionalized version solidly based in the evidence, and John Williams, *Suddenly at the Priory* (London: Heinemann, 1957).

The account of the Francey affair is based on testimony from the preliminary interrogations undertaken by the *juge d'instruction* and on the trial testimony in *La Gazette des Tribunaux.* Documents from the preliminary interrogations are hereafter referred to as Dossier Francey. I should note that in gaining permission to use this dossier, I agreed to change the name of the victim, whom I have called Hippolyte Bazard.

12. Balham, p. 45.
13. Ibid., p. 40.
14. Ibid., p. 42.
15. Ibid., p. 26.
16. Ibid.
17. Ibid., p. 7.
18. Ibid., p. 27.
19. Ibid., p. 47.
20. Ibid., p. 26.
21. Ibid., p. 2.
22. Ibid., p. 11.
23. Ibid., p. 18.
24. Ibid., p. 52.
25. Quoted in Williams, p. 254.
26. Elizabeth Jenkins provides the most convincing account of what probably happened that night at the Priory; John Williams provides some excellent speculation about motive. Jenkins's study concentrates on the character and role of Dr. Gully. I have attempted to look a bit closer at Florence.
27. Dossier Francey, pièce 52.
28. Ibid.
29. *La Gazette des Tribunaux*, March 27, 1885.
30. Dossier Francey, pièce 82.
31. Ibid., pièce 114.
32. Ibid., pièce 117.
33. *Le Figaro*, March 25, 1885.
34. Dossier Francey, pièce 40.
35. Ibid., pièce 25.
36. Ibid., pièce 54.
37. See Chapter 6.
38. Dossier Francey, pièce 28.
39. *Le Petit Moniteur* (March 28, 1885) referred sarcastically to the "heroine of the trial, since that is what we now call women who kill men." *Le Soleil* (March 30, 1885) remarked that women owed a good deal to the man who invented nervous crises. *Le Figaro* (March 27, 1885) noted that Henriette had become "the heroine of a novel for all the little *petites bourgeoises* of Yonne." As it turned out, there was good reason for this scepticism from an otherwise normally receptive audience.
40. Balham, p. 45.
41. Ibid., p. 35.
42. Ibid., p. 48.
43. *Times*, June 12, 1876.
44. Ibid.
45. Ibid.
46. *Medical Times and Gazette*, August 19, 1876.
47. *Le Petit Journal*, March 29, 1885.

48. Dossier Francey, pièce 59.
49. Ibid., pièce 62.
50. Ibid., pièce 58.
51. *Le Figaro*, March 27, 1885.
52. *La Gazette des Tribunaux*, March 27, 1885.
53. Ibid.
54. Dossier Francey, pièce 70.
55. The dossier includes several of Bazard's letters to the *juge d'instruction*, urging him to investigate this or that person and providing details about their alleged knowledge. Unless indicated, as in this instance, all the evidence cited is taken from the formal interrogations.
56. Dossier Francey, pièce 62.
57. Ibid., pièce 64.
58. Ibid., pièce 30.
59. Ibid., pièce 68.
60. *La Gazette des Tribunaux*, March 28, 1885.
61. Dossier Francey, pièce 28.
62. Ibid., pièce 53.
63. *Le Figaro*, March 27, 1885.
64. The dossier contains both the letter she sent to Bazard and the copy. The press reprinted the letter in its entirety. The excerpts here were taken from *La Gazette des Tribunaux* (March 27, 1885) and compared with the originals, since Mme. Francey's handwriting was tiny and hard to decipher.
65. Ibid.
66. Ibid.
67. Ibid. *La Gazette des Tribunaux* used the word *poésie* rather than *poste* in printing the letter, but *poste* (mails) makes more sense in context.
68. *Le Figaro*, March 27, 1885.
69. Dossier Francey, pièce 35.
70. *La Gazette des Tribunaux*, March 27, 1885.
71. Ibid.
72. Ibid.
73. Much was made of the incident by the presiding judge, who clearly disbelieved Henriette's story. It is more than likely that the maid was telling the truth, for a floor plan of the home included in the dossier indicates that the salon was at the back of the house. A light there would not have been seen from the street to illuminate the mistress's return, and she would not have passed through the salon on her way up to bed.
74. *La Gazette des Tribunaux*, March 28, 1885.
75. Ibid., March 27, 1885.
76. Dossier Francey, pièce 111. This and the following statement were made to the police, who were checking reports of Bazard's attempted rapes.

77. Ibid. In one pathetic deposition the wife of a bricklayer reported that Bazard had offered her money and tried to seduce her, but that since she was unmarried at the time, she had not attempted to file a complaint.

78. Ibid., pièce 113.

79. Ibid., pièce 115.

80. Ibid., pièce 116.

81. Ibid., pièce 127.

82. Ibid., pièce 122.

83. La Croix, March 30, 1885.

84. Dictionnaire de Biographie française, ed. Roman d'Amat and R. Limouzin-Lamothe (Paris: Letouzey, 1965), vol. 10, p. 958.

85. La Gazette des Tribunaux, March 28, 1885.

86. For a description, see Brian S. Smith, A History of Malvern (Leicester: Leicester University Press, 1964).

87. The writings of James M. Gully include The Water Cure in Chronic Disease (London: Churchill, 1846); A Guide to Domestic Hydrotherapia (London: Simpkin, 1863); Lectures on the Moral and Physical Attributes of Men of Genius and Talent (London: Savill, 1836); and A Monograph on Fever and Its Treatment By Hydrotherapeutic Means (London: Simpkin, 1885).

88. James Manby Gully, An Exposition of the Symptoms, Essential Nature and Treatment of Neuropathy or Nervousness (London: Churchill, 1837), p. 77.

89. Ibid., p. 2. This is one of the few instances Gully uses the term "hysterical," and it appears to be employed in a more popular rather than a clinical sense. With their general sympathy for women and women's ailments, the water-cure specialists may have been sensitive to the increasingly pejorative usage and diagnosis of more orthodox practitioners. See Carroll Smith-Rosenberg, "The Hysterical Woman: Sex Roles and Role Conflict in Nineteenth-Century America," Social Research, 29 (Winter 1972): 652-678.

90. Gully, Neuropathy, pp. 76 f.

91. See Kathryn Kish Sklar, Catherine Beecher: A Study in American Domesticity (New Haven: Yale University Press, 1973), pp. 205-209. "[At the water-cure establishment] female communality replaced the characteristic isolation of American domestic life, bodily sensuality could be freely indulged, and an unwanted pregnancy might even be terminated" (p. 206).

92. Ibid., p. 207.

93. Jenkins, p. 193.

94. In a memorial written on the doctor's retirement from Malvern, J. Morris remarks that although Gully himself was not in the Temperance movement, he believed that medical men generally had been responsible for augmenting the drinking habits of the middle and upper classes. Morris quotes a letter from Gully of January 16, 1872: "The 'distinguished' man in London and his humble imitators have to answer for a vast amount of tippling in well dressed and well housed families" [Dr. Gully and Malvern (Malvern, 1872), p. 28].

95. Suspicion of the doctor's practice is apparent in the questioning at the inquest (Balham, pp. 50 f.).

96. Jenkins, p. 24. Full citation for Drysdale in bibliography.

97. Ibid.

98. Balham, pp. 50 f.

99. Such conclusions must be based in part upon inference from their sympathetic treatment of women's reproductive ailments in general. Gully made no published pronouncements on the subject and was careful to observe the social code in his public relations with Florence. But his private actions, fortuitously revealed, provide a strong argument for the case.

100. Vanity Fair, August 5, 1876. The same publication was less gentle in its weekly cartoon by "Spy" which portrayed a repulsive, oily-faced creature with a tap for its nose, presumably for the water-cure.

101. Balham, p. 38.

102. Ibid.

103. Ibid.

104. Ibid., p. 42.

105. Ibid.

106. Ibid., p. 30.

107. Ibid., p. 23.

108. Ibid., p. 15.

109. Ibid., p. 26.

110. Ibid., p. 47.

111. Ibid.

112. Ibid., p. 48.

113. Ibid., p. 50.

114. Ibid., p. 7.

115. Ibid., p. 32.

116. Ibid., p. 30.

117. Ibid.

118. Ibid.

119. Ibid., p. 16.

120. Ibid.

121. The deposition appears in Balham, pp. 44-46.

122. Ibid., p. 45.

123. Ibid.

124. Ibid.

125. Ibid.

126. Ibid.

127. Williams, pp. 275 f., was, as far as I know, the first to suggest this motive, which occurred to no one who got into print at the time.

128. Her grief and terror when she was confronted with Charles's agonies suggest this possibility, as well as the albeit tardy summoning of several experts. But this may simply have been a frightened response to the reality of her having committed the act with intent to kill.

129. The phrase is the title of a contemporary pamphlet on the case from collections in the British Museum. It voiced the popular theme that the affair with Gully was still on.

130. *Times*, June 12, 1876.

131. Quoted from the *World* in Balham, p. 55.

132. In England, as will be seen in Chapter 6, there was no parallel wave of women's crimes.

133. The summary here is from the account in *Le Figaro*, January 8-9, 1885.

134. *L'Illustration*, December 6, 1884. Clovis Hugues was a poet elected as a radical in 1881 who had joined the socialists and then shunned them when they disapproved his attending Louis Blanc's funeral [Theodore Zeldin, *France, 1848–1945: Ambition, Love, and Politics*, vol. 1 (Oxford: Clarendon, 1973), p. 770]. Ironically, he himself had fought a duel with a Bonapartist who had insulted his wife, but he strongly disapproved his wife's methods of revenge against her former friend in 1883.

135. Dossier Francey, pièce 41.

136. Ibid., pièce 30.

137. Ibid., pièce 18.

138. Ibid., pièce 11.

139. Ibid., pièce 28.

140. Ibid., pièces 21-23.

141. Ibid., pièce 23.

142. Ibid., pièces 45, 46.

143. Louis Proal, "La Criminalité féminine," *Le Correspondant*, May 1890, pp. 479-500.

144. Ibid.

145. Louis Proal, *Le Crime et le suicide passionels* (Paris: Alcan, 1900), p. 177.

146. French Penal Code, Article 337.

147. Some of the same terrors which drove Madeleine Smith in 1857 affected Henriette Francey.

148. See the excellent article by Theodore Zeldin on sexual jealousy as fuel for anti-clericalism in nineteenth-century France: "The Conflict of Moralities: Confession, Sin and Pleasure in the Nineteenth Century," in *Conflicts in French Society*, ed. Theodore Zeldin (London: Allen & Unwin, 1970), pp. 13-50.

149. Jules Michelet, *Le Prêtre, la femme et la famille* (Paris: Lévy, 1899).

150. Dossier Francey, pièce 132.

151. Balham, p. 15.

152. Ibid., pp. 24, 30.

153. Ibid., p. 10.

154. Ibid., p. 48.

155. Ibid., p. 30.

156. Ibid., p. 38.

157. *Portsmouth Times and Naval Gazette*, September 21, 1878. In drink, if not in murder, Florence appears to have had considerable female company by the 1870s. C. Willett Cunnington, in *Feminine Attitudes in the Nineteenth Century* (London: Heinemann, 1935), pp. 206-209, remarks that in England by the 1870s correspondence columns of the women's magazines began to feature the "horrors of married life," including the increased consumption of alcohol. Doctors, including James Gully, noted the problem as well, and the *British Medical Journal* for August 1875 published an article on "Intemperance in Women" (cited in Branca, p. 148). The "horrors of married life" do not appear to have been any worse, but women were noticing them more, and some at least were unable to cope with their new perceptions that they were unhappy.

As the *Portsmouth Times and Naval Gazette* remarked, "no one knows to this hour whether she [Florence] died with a secret or not, whether it was the secret which rendered alcohol a necessity, or whether she was a harmless, albeit, of course, culpable, vinomaniac." This paper expressed a view which was general in the press at the time of the inquest two years before, namely, that Florence was a bad woman, but probably not a guilty one, that the real culprit was Gully. "She was an adulteress and an inebriate, selfish and self-willed, a bad daughter, and a worse wife. . . ." (September 21, 1878). "Meantime, by means of cold water and cool temperament, a fellow delinquent still enjoys a frosty and kindly old age. Dr. Gully, at whose door in reality lies this wretched death, trots up and down in health and vigor, the sun shining benevolently on his white head and ruddy face. At the famous Bravo enquiry he came into the room 'smiling.' Does he smile still? Serene and beautiful old man! How we envy him his retrospections, and, since he is an ardent spiritualist, the shining apparitions which he is able to conjure up" (September

24, 1878). The doctor, who hardly deserved such invective, died in 1883; the wife whose death would have permitted him to marry Florence had survived her youthful rival by a year and a month (Jenkins, p. 316).

CHAPTER 5

1. Unless otherwise indicated, general material on the Fenayrou case is based on the full record of testimony which appeared in the two major legal journals *Le Droit* and *La Gazette des Tribunaux* for the two trials in August and October 1882, and also on the summary by A. Bataille, court reporter for *Le Figaro*, in *Les Causes criminelles et mondaines*, 18 vols. (Paris: Dentu, 1883), vol. 3, pp. 205-312. Unfortunately, the records of the preliminary interrogations undertaken at Versailles no longer exist.

The account of the Bartlett case is based on the complete testimony and records in *The Trial of Adelaide Bartlett*, ed. John Hall, Notable British Trials (London: Hodge, 1927). The interpretation of Adelaide's behavior presented here owes much to the fine study of the case by Yseult Bridges, *Poison and Adelaide Bartlett* (London: Hutchinson, 1962).

2. For a discussion of some of the lesser known French literature see Theodore Zeldin, *France, 1848-1945: Ambition, Love, and Politics*, vol. 1 (Oxford: Clarendon, 1973), chap. 11. See also Patricia Branca, *Silent Sisterhood: Middle-Class Women in the Victorian Home* (Pittsburgh: Carnegie-Mellon University Press, 1975), esp. chaps. 7, 8.

3. Bridges, p. 29.

4. Edward Clarke, *The Story of My Life* (London: Murray, 1918), p. 246.

5. Edward Clarke, "Leaves from a Lawyer's Casebook: The Pimlico Mystery," *Cornhill Magazine*, 49 (December 1920): 667.

6. *Times*, April 19, 1886.

7. Alfred Leach, "The Case of Edwin Bartlett," *Lancet*, May 22, 1886, pp. 968-970.

8. *Times*, February 9, 1886.

9. Ibid., February 12, 1886.

10. Richard Altick, *Victorian Studies in Scarlet* (New York: Norton, 1970), p. 246.

11. Clarke, "Leaves from a Lawyer's Casebook," p. 667.

12. Gustave Macé, *Les Femmes criminelles* (Paris: Charpentier, 1904), p. 237.

13. The Archives of the Prefecture of Police in Paris contain several letters from Gabrielle Fenayrou to Gustave Macé (Dossier Fenayrou). Gabrielle was grateful to Macé for

having spared her children the information that she was being arrested on a murder charge at the time the officers came to their home. Her notes to Macé are fond, inquire after his health, and ask for permission to see her children.

14. *Le Figaro*, August 5, 1882.

15. René Fabre, *Histoire de la Pharmacie* (Paris: P.U.F., 1963), p. 66.

16. *Le Droit*, August 10, 1882.

17. Ibid.

18. *Le Figaro*, August 6, 1882.

19. Macé, p. 243.

20. *Times*, February 9, 1886. This statement was quoted at the inquest by her husband's attending physician, Dr. Alfred Leach, to whom Adelaide confided many details of her life with Edwin.

21. *Le Figaro*, August 7, 1882.

22. Ibid., August 10, 1882.

23. *Le Voltaire*, August 14, 1882.

24. *Times*, February 9, 1886.

25. *Trial of Adelaide Bartlett*, p. 229.

26. Thomas Low Nichols, *Esoteric Anthropology (The Mysteries of Man): A Comprehensive and Confidential Treatise on the Structure, Functions, Passional Attractions and Perversions, True and False Physical and Social Conditions, and the Most Intimate Relations of Men and Women* (New York: Arno, 1972).

27. *Trial of Adelaide Bartlett*, p. 372.

28. Nichols, *Esoteric Anthropology*, p. 113.

29. *Trial of Adelaide Bartlett*, p. 183. Judge Wills retracted his earlier comments when Clarke informed him that Nichols's book, far from recommending sexual license, was in fact quite limited in its endorsement of sex, with more restrictions on indulgence than Clarke thought most persons could follow.

30. Nichols, *Esoteric Anthropology*, p. 114. Clarke quoted this passage in court *(Trial of Adelaide Bartlett*, p. 184).

31. *Times*, February 9, 1886.

32. Clarke, "Leaves from a Lawyer's Casebook," p. 653.

33. Ibid., p. 648.

34. *Times*, April 14, 1886.

35. Ibid., February 16, 1886.

36. Ibid., April 14, 1886.

37. Ibid.

38. Leach, "The Case of Edwin Bartlett," *Lancet*, May 29, 1886.

39. *Trial of Adelaide Bartlett*, p. 218. It was Dr. Leach who reported the incident, and Adelaide had allegedly replied: "That is a nice story. Imagine him standing for two hours and doing anything."

40. Leach, "The Case of Edwin Bartlett."

41. *Le Siècle*, August 14, 1882.

42. Macé, pp. 255 f.

43. *Le Figaro*, August 10, 1882.

44. Marin alleged in the trial that he had been "deaf and blind" to Gabrielle's behavior with Aubert *(Le Figaro*, August 10, 1882). The presiding judge, in his memoirs, suggested a character trait in Marin which several of the couple's acquaintances intimated: "As a husband, he wanted his wife to be pious so that she would be faithful to him; but as a pharmacist, he wanted her to be coquettish in order to attract customers" [Anatole Bérard des Glajeux, *Souvenirs d'un Président d'Assises, 1880-1890* (Paris: Plon, 1892), vol. 1, p. 58].

45. *Le Figaro*, June 15, 1882.

46. Ibid.

47. Ibid.

48. Ibid.

49. Ibid.

50. *L'Intransigeant*, October 18, 1882.

51. *Le Droit*, August 10, 1882.

52. The literature is discussed in Zeldin, chap. 11.

53. In her recent paper, "Secular Rules and Secular Sanctions: The Regulation of Female Sexuality in Nineteenth-Century France," Erna Hellerstein of Stanford University examines this study (A. Debay, *Hygiène et physiologie du mariage)* among others and shows that manuals such as Debay's, which sold for just three francs in 1880, contained a surprisingly frank and detailed description of the sex act. Debay recognized women's capacity for sexual enjoyment as about the same as men's and urged that sex, in moderation, was good for health and contributed to family and social stability. Nonetheless, while their sexual needs were recognized, women were urged to please their husbands in bed as a means of hanging on to them. While husbands were also encouraged to try to please their wives, wives were effectively ordered to feign orgasm if they did not experience it. This amounted to a declaration of the male right to the female orgasm in the name of marital stability.

54. Macé, p. 230.

55. Ibid., p. 231.

56. Ibid. Macé said of her, "This singular creature, who almost totally lacked amorous feeling, in spite of her ideas and her lewd desires, wronged her husband and two lovers at the same time. A living doll, a statue made out of flesh, she did not find a Pygmalion to animate her. A rebel against marital duties, she submitted out of duty to her husband and out of fantasy to her lovers" (p. 234). Macé marveled over her managing to "wrong" all three men at the same time, and he also occasionally referred to her as the "adulter-ess," but he came closer to understanding her than many, despite his lapses into stereotype.

57. *Le Droit*, August 11, 1882.

58. *Le Figaro*, August 11, 1882.

59. Ibid., August 5, 1882.

60. *Le Droit*, August 11, 1882. Grousteau commented without further explanation that he had remarked that the "moral level of Gabrielle's mind" had progressively declined when he knew her, and that he had been surprised to hear recent reports that she was getting on well with Marin and attending church again after a lapse of six or seven years.

61. Ibid., August 10, 1882.

62. Ibid., August 11, 1882.

63. *Trial of Adelaide Bartlett*, pp. 103 f.

64. Ibid., pp. 177 f.

65. Leach, "The Case of Edwin Bartlett."

66. *Times*, February 12, 1886.

67. *Trial of Adelaide Bartlett*, p. 145.

68. *Times*, February 12, 1886.

69. *Trial of Adelaide Bartlett*, p. 178.

70. *Times*, April 19, 1886.

71. *Trial of Adelaide Bartlett*, p. 366.

72. Ibid.

73. Ibid., pp. 398 f.

74. Ibid., p. 372.

75. The explanation offered here follows the one suggested by Yseult Bridges, with variations which will be noted. So far as I know, Bridges is the only one to have "solved" the case as it probably happened. I have discovered no contemporaries. as there were in the Kent case, who guessed the probable truth and published it.

76. Altick, p. 246.

77. Leach, "The Case of Edwin Bartlett."

78. *Times*, February 9, 1886.

79. Ibid., April 17, 1886.

80. Ibid.

81. I am grateful to Rudolph Binion of Brandeis University for some remarks he made in a letter to me (November 9, 1974) about patterns in women's lying and in Adelaide's lies in particular. It may well be, as he suggests, that women's falsifications are more intricate, "with huge elaborations through which the distorted facts are visible." For them, as a subordinated group, lying has been a survival tactic, as for any other such group. Moreover, I suspect that the internalization of expected codes of behavior for their sex makes their need to explain deviations from such behavior to themselves, as well as to others, more critical. As a result, the lies necessarily become more elaborate, contrived as they are not only to convince others, but to convince, and relieve, the self.

82. *Times*, February 16, 1886.

83. Ibid.

84. See John B. Blake, "Mary Gove Nichols, Prophetess of Health," *Proceedings of the American Philosophical Association*, 106 (June 1962): 219-234.

85. For a discussion, see Blake, p. 223, who also includes references to other materials on Nichols.

86. Thomas Low Nichols and Mary S. Gove Nichols, *Marriage: Its History, Character and Results: Its Sanctities, and Its Profanities; Its Science and Its Facts. Demonstrating Its Influence, as a Civilized Institution, on the Happiness of the Individual and the Progress of the Race* (Cincinnati: Nicholson, 1854), p. 252.

87. Blake, p. 231.

88. Mary Nichols alleges that the ovarian tumors on display in a medical college in Albany, some of them as large as twenty pounds, were the result of "amative excess" (p. 207).

89. Her statement, as delivered to her counsel, was presented in the trial by Clarke. "For six years that contract [marriage without physical union] was kept between us, and then there came to me my heart the wish that I too, might be a mother, and have a child at my knee to love me, and on my entreaty my husband broke through the contract that had been made. Once and once only I was admitted to my husband's love, and when the months had gone by, instead of the child there came the weeks of agony, and of life nearly lost in the labor-struggle, and from that time my hope and wish for a child went, and we resumed our old relations" (*Trial of Adelaide Bartlett*, p. 326). Without realizing its possible significance for his client's decision to have a child, Clarke paraphrased a key passage in Thomas Nichols' work *Esoteric Anthropology* to prove to Judge Wills that the book had no "vicious object": "It lays down the rule that it is only for the continuation of the species that the indulgence of sexual passion is permissible, that the moment that indulgence is supposed to have resulted in a natural and legitimate consequence, from that moment the wife is sacred from the husband until the time of the nursing of the child has expired" (*Trial of Adelaide Bartlett*, p. 319).

90. See the previously mentioned discussion in Branca, chap. 7.

91. There is a good discussion in Linda Gordon, "Voluntary Motherhood: The Beginnings of Feminist Birth Control Ideas in the United States," in *Clio's Consciousness Raised: New Perspectives on the History of Women*, ed. Mary S. Hartman and Lois W. Banner (New York: Harper & Row, 1974), pp. 54-71.

92. Blake, p. 229.

93. *Trial of Adelaide Bartlett*, pp. 371 f. Wills continues, "and it is such reading as this that helps to unsex them, and to bring them to a place like this day after day to listen willingly to details which even to men of mature life . . . are distasteful and disgusting." Again and again, the women are singled out for their "improper" interest in the proceedings. But as his remarks suggested, Wills was talking about women of another age, one which perhaps had existed only in imagination. The *Evening Standard* remarked that at the trial the gallery was occupied almost exclusively by well-dressed women and girls, armed with "luncheon packets, sherry, sandwiches and eyeglasses." The women, it appears, were quite unmoved by the judge's concern: "in spite of the plainest hints from the learned judge, Mr. Justice Wills, women and young girls, fashionably dressed, maintained their places, and in the intervals of adjournment, tittered and laughed over the judge's prudery" (April 19, 1886). The indignant *Reynolds' Newspaper* contended that the judge should simply have cleared the women out: "Who were these petticoated ghouls who sat and gloated over a fellow-woman's misery?" (April 18, 1886). It was more comfortable, surely, to assume that they were gloating over a fellow-woman than that they were identifying with her.

94. *Times*, March 20, 1886. A former servant revealed this information.

95. *Trial of Adelaide Bartlett*, p. 186.

96. Altick, p. 243.

97. Certainly there were enough clues. Leach himself reported at the trial that Edwin had asked him about this possibility. When Leach inquired why his patient thought it might be so, Edwin replied, "Well, I am doing such absurd things, things against my common sense; in fact both my wife and I are doing so" (*Trial of Adelaide Bartlett*, p. 245).

98. Ibid.

99. Ibid., p. 116. Bartlett's business partner reported that Adelaide ordered the brandy, along with fruit cake, walnuts, and mango chutney. He said that Adelaide remarked at the time, "I know these things are not fit for Edwin to eat but he fancies them."

100. *Evening Standard*, February 26, 1886.

101. Blake, p. 226. At the trial itself, Mrs. Nichols was described as "a spiritualist advising ladies in all their problems, social and domestic, either by letter, in the strictest confidence, or by appointment at her private

consulting rooms" *(Trial of Adelaide Bartlett,* p. 45).

102. Bridges presents the theory in chap. 4, pp. 240-247.

103. *Trial of Adelaide Bartlett,* p. 113. Edwin Bartlett, Sr., who had lived with his son and daughter-in-law for five years, reported that he had "scores of letters" from Frederick. The Bartletts' landlord, a Mr. Doggett, also related a curious incident. Adelaide, he said, received a New Year's greeting card from Frederick shortly after Edwin's death. Her response on opening it, he said, was "Oh, how cruel!" *(Trial of Adelaide Bartlett,* p. 134). On one level the remark expressed the irony of such a greeting at a time of bereavement, but might Adelaide have been thinking that Frederick was carrying their grim game a bit too far with this jest?

104. *L'Intransigeant,* October 8, 1882.

105. *Le Droit,* August 10, 1882.

106. Macé reports Marin's remark: "Je suis en possession d'une femme au tempérament froid, incapable de me tromper" (p. 247).

107. *Le Petit Journal,* August 15, 1882.

108. So far, work has concentrated more on the prescriptive literature on the subject (see note 53 of this chapter) than on the more difficult issue of practice. In a context in which the middle classes had long practiced birth control, it will be a challenge to uncover women's initiative in the matter.

109. *Le Droit,* August 10, 1882. Gabrielle told Macé the story. Marin and the maid confirmed it.

110. Macé, p. 249.

111. *Le Droit,* August 10, 1882.

112. *Le Figaro,* October 12, 1882.

113. *Le Droit,* August 11, 1882.

114. *Le Petit Journal,* August 15, 1882. The papers included *Le Voltaire, Le Petit Parisien, La Petite République, Le XIXième Siecle,* and *Le Figaro.*

115. *L'Intransigeant,* October 12, 1882. In an article in *Le Figaro,* which was written less than half in jest, the writer Octave Mirbeau said Lucien alone was guilty: "Marin is ugly and a pharmacist, but he is married and . . . wronged, and on these two accounts, he is sacred. . . . She [Gabrielle] obeyed her feminine instinct, which is always to betray and kill, if not by physical blows, at least by blows to the heart. Gabrielle Fenayrou is also sacred, for all women are condemned if she is. Her husband alone has the right of life or death over her, because she belongs to him alone, like a cat or a dog, like all the beasts of the domestic menagerie" *(Le Figaro,* October 12,

1882). A lone writer for the *Gaulois* complained that his editor was attacking him for going against public opinion in defending Gabrielle. The law already regarded her as a subordinate with inferior status, he argued, so it should not condemn her when she merely stated that she had been dominated by her husband (October 13, 1882).

116. Bérard des Glajeux, p. 63.

117. Ibid.

118. Macé, p. 257. In a letter pleading for her daughter's release, she wrote that Gabrielle "tried prayer and tears in order to prevent this vengeance, but unconscious of this crime that she had never asked for, that she had never wanted, that she would have been so happy to prevent, she gave way in the face of her husband's implacable will, believing, in her unconsciousness, as he perhaps did and as her endlessly repeated to her, that she would thereby reinstate herself with him, that she would raise herself up from her errors according to how much help she offered to his legitimate vengeance."

119. *Le Droit,* August 10, 1882.

120. Dossier Fenayrou.

121. The *Evening Standard* (August 14, 1882) declared that business failure was the "real motive." The *Times,* in an editorial of October 16, 1882, declared that the vengeance theory was not tenable and adopted the view that Aubert must have been blackmailing Marin Fenayrou.

122. Clarke, "Leaves from a Lawyer's Casebook," p. 656.

CHAPTER 6

1. The chief source for this account is the testimony and documents in *The Trial of Mrs. Maybrick,* Notable British Trials, ed. H. B. Irving (London: Hodge, 1912). My presentation is also heavily indebted to the study by Trevor L. Christie, *Etched in Arsenic* (London: Harrap, 1969), which is the best treatment of the case, and to the materials in the Christie Collection at the University of Wyoming, which include correspondence with contemporaries who knew the family, notes, newsclippings, and photographs related to the affair. My account also relies on newspaper reports, especially from the Liverpool press, and on documents and information in a book edited by J. H. Levy, entitled *The Necessity for Criminal Appeal as Illustrated by the Maybrick Case* (London: King, 1899). Levy, a leader in the campaign to free Mrs. Maybrick, called

the case "one of the most extraordinary miscarriages of justice of modern times" and was one of many who likened it to the Dreyfus Affair (p. vii).

The chief sources for the case of Claire Reymond are A. Bataille, *Les Causes criminelles et mondaines,* 18 vols. (Paris: Dentu, 1881–1898), 13: 247-267, *Le Figaro* and *La Gazette des Tribunaux.* Important interviews appeared in *Le Petit Journal* and *Le Petit Parisien.* The preliminary interrogations, unfortunately, have either been lost or destroyed.

2. Some of these gains are considered in the previously cited work by Patricia Branca, *Silent Sisterhood: Middle-Class Women in the Victorian Home* (Pittsburgh: Carnegie-Mellon University Press, 1975), and Bonnie Smith's Ph.D. dissertation, "The Bourgeois Women of Lille, 1860-1910" (University of Rochester, 1975). Both these studies emphasize the material gains of women as well as their increased domestic authority, but they also speculate on the resulting rise in expectations which occurred.

3. Christie Collection, Aunspaugh letters. These letters were written between Mr. Christie and Florence Aunspaugh in the early 1940s, and though some of Miss Aunspaugh's recollections were used by Mr. Christie in his study, they were not directly attributed at the author's request. After the deaths of Miss Aunspaugh and Mr. Christie, Mrs. Christie donated the letters as part of the Christie Collection to the library of the University of Wyoming. Miss Aunspaugh's extended memoir of her visit relied on her own experiences and on accounts given to her by her family and especially her father, who was a New Orleans cotton broker who had business dealings with Edwin Maybrick. Miss Aunspaugh provided a very full study, including descriptions of all the principals, assessments of their character and roles, and much detail about the Maybricks' physical surroundings, daily routine, and social position.

4. *Trial of Mrs. Maybrick,* pp. 230 f.

5. Ibid., pp. 343 f.

6. *New York Herald* (London Edition), August 14, 1889.

7. *Saturday Review,* August 17, 1889.

8. *Times,* August 8, 1889.

9. *Liverpool Daily Post,* August 9, 1889. The statement is from one of the letters to the editor.

10. *La Gazette des Tribunaux,* July 13, 1892.

11. Ibid.

12. Ibid.

13. Quoted in Christie, p. 32.

14. Ibid.

15. Ibid., p. 40.

16. Ibid., p. 43.

17. Christie Collection, Aunspaugh letters.

18. Quoted in Christie, p. 46.

19. Ibid., p. 47.

20. Levy, p. 435. This information was included in the signed deposition of Florence's solicitors, Arnold and Richard Cleaver.

21. *Trial of Mrs. Maybrick,* p. 109.

22. Levy, p. 451. The citation is reportedly from an article by Dr. Stevenson of Guy's Hospital, an expert in toxicology who testified at the trial. Levy questions its accuracy, but Florence Aunspaugh, in a description of the Maybrick home a year before James's death, mentions that the couple then slept in separate bedrooms (Christie Collection).

23. There were rumors reported about Florence's other affairs at the time of the trial, and Miss Aunspaugh says that her father told her they were true. She reports the following event relating to Florence and her brother-in-law Edwin Maybrick: "The first incident my father ever had of anything being amiss was the night of the formal dining the year I was with him in England. There were twenty couples, which, of course, made a long table. My father had the seat of honor—to the right of Mr. Maybrick.... Mr. Edwin Maybrick was near Mrs. Maybrick, and they were laughing and talking. My father happened, involuntarily, to glance at Mr. James Maybrick. Just as he did, he heard Mrs. Maybrick say to Edwin with a laugh, 'if I had met you first things might have been different.' As that remark was made, Mr. James Maybrick dropped his knife, clinched [*sic*] his fist, his eyes glared and his face flushed the color of fire. In a second he recovered himself, picked up his knife and everything passed on smoothly for the remaining part of the evening." Miss Aunspaugh reports that a year later, just after James's death, another brother, Michael Maybrick, searched Florence's bedroom when she was out and "found in Mrs. Maybrick's writing desk thirteen love letters from Edwin Maybrick, seven from Alfred Brierley [the only man mentioned in the trial as Florence's lover], and five from lawyer Williams of London." Miss Aunspaugh's father knew Brierley well and remained his friend after the trial, so her information may be correct. Miss Aunspaugh adds that Michael Maybrick was responsible for keeping the information about Edwin and the lawyer out of the investigations. "Michael Maybrick suppressed Edwin Maybrick's let-

ters to Mrs. James Maybrick and also made an agreement with lawyer Williams of London, that he would return his [Williams's] letters to him if he would not assist in any way with the defense."

24. Quoted in Christie, p. 49.

25. Ibid., p. 51. Miss Aunspaugh's account indicates that Florence and Alfred Brierley had been "sweet" on one another for some time before her visit with her father and that therefore their relations had been going on for more than a year by the time James died. However, Aunspaugh corroborates the notion that Brierley was getting cold feet after the Flatman Hotel incident and states that several cotton men took him aside and warned him that the episode might get to Maybrick's ears (Christie Collection).

26. Levy, p. 415. This woman, a Mrs. Samuelson, gave her statement prior to the trial, but she managed to avoid appearing at the trial by taking a trip to the Continent. In the preliminary hearing she had stated that while she and her husband were on holiday with the Maybricks the previous March, she had got into a tantrum over a card game and told her husband she hated him. Florence, she said, had tried to calm her down by saying, "You must not take serious notice of that. I often say I hate Jim without meaning a word of it."

27. *Trial of Mrs. Maybrick*, p. 89. The statement was reported in testimony by the nursemaid.

28. Ibid., p. 59.

29. Levy, p. 438. Brierley remarked at the preliminary hearing that he had burned the letters in question.

30. Ibid. Brierley had said, "When we so parted on the 24th of March it was distinctly understood that we would not meet again except in public, and I for my part had finally resolved that I would not again be tempted into a similar position."

31. Christie, p. 55.

32. *Le Petit Parisien*, May 25, 1892.

33. Bataille, p. 249.

34. *Le Petit Parisien*, May 24, 1892.

35. La Baronne Staffe, *Les Usages du monde* (Paris: Havard, 1890), pp. 256 f. This message, as will be seen, was actually appearing with more frequency toward the end of the century in prescriptive literature for women.

36. *Le Figaro*, July 13, 1892.

37. *La Gazette des Tribunaux*, July 13, 1892.

38. *La Lanterne*, May 26, 1892.

39. *Le Petit Parisien*, May 25, 1892.

40. Ibid.

41. *Le Petit Journal*, May 25, 1892.

42. *La Lanterne*, May 26, 1892.

43. *Le Petit Journal*, May 25, 1892.

44. *La Lanterne*, May 26, 1892.

45. *Le Figaro*, July 13, 1892.

46. *La Lanterne*, May 26, 1892.

47. *Le Petit Parisien*, May 25, 1892.

48. *La Gazette des Tribunaux*, July 13, 1892.

49. *Le Figaro*, July 13, 1892.

50. Ibid.

51. Summarized in Theodore Zeldin, *France, 1848–1945: Ambition, Love, and Politics*, vol. 1 (Oxford: Clarendon, 1973), p. 343.

52. *Le Figaro*, July 13, 1892.

53. Ibid.

54. Ibid.

55. See Sylvaine Marandon, *L'Image de la France dans l'Angleterre victorienne* (Paris: Colin, 1967), chap. 4; Smith, chap. 3.

56. *La Lanterne*, May 25, 1892.

57. Many contemporaries remarked on this feature. In her chapter on the family, which cites numerous nineteenth-century commentators, Marandon summarizes: "In France parents—insofar as they are capable—continue to watch over the young who have left the nest, by contrast with the practice of the English (who are closer to nature in their habits), where it appears that past the period of dependency, during which the young require care, the generations live in a certain material and affective autonomy" (p. 277). Max O'Rell, who married a Frenchwoman, described Englishwomen for the French in his *Les Filles de John Bull* (Paris: Lévy, 1884) and stressed that after marriage the Englishwoman was far more independent. He notes wryly, "The English girl leaves her mother [at marriage] with the same emotion and ceremony with which we [French people] leave a landlord" (p. 110). More recent surveys continue to point out the relatively greater closeness of French families and of mother-daughter relationships and point out that it was not until after World War II that the pattern began to change markedly. In a recent study of contemporary France, John Ardagh stresses the persistence of family ties and mother-daughter relationships and notes that women's clubs and female solidarity in general have not been marked features of French life. "Until recently the strength of family links made up for this lack of clubbiness and in fact was a cause of it. But with the dispersal of families and the move to new suburban homes, the French housewife is beginning to feel her isolation. 'Put the young bourgeoise down in a new flat,' said one critic of this mentality, 'and what'll she do?'

Still spend half the morning telephoning to Maman to discuss what to cook her husband for dinner.' " *(The New France: A Society in Transition, 1945-1973* [Harmondsworth: Penguin, 1973], p. 356). See also Priscilla Robertson, "The Home as a Nest: Middle-Class Childhood in Nineteenth-Century Europe," in *The History of Childhood* ed. Lloyd de Mause (New York: Harper & Row, 1975).

58. Patricia Branca discusses the problems of English middle-class women in this regard: "It is interesting to note that in all the various sources used for this study, there is no mention of any type of family relationship beyond the nuclear family. Never was there a reference to the role of grandparents, aunts, uncles or cousins. This lack of relationships beyond the immediate family was particularly striking in the discussions on pregnancy. It would seem likely that at this very important event in a woman's life she would have her mother or sister or some other close relative to assist her. However, the middle-class woman was advised to seek the aid of a friendly neighbor" (p. 146). Florence Maybrick had lived in three homes since her marriage, Adelaide Bartlett had lived in four, and Florence Maybrick, though a widow part of the time, had lived in six different residences since her first marriage.

59. Christie, p. 47.

60. Ibid.

61. In a chapter on religion in her study on the bourgeois women of Lille, Bonnie Smith remarks that "on a national scale, the movement of women into convents blossomed during the nineteenth century.... Though the history of women entering convents in the nineteenth century and the feminine tinge afforded Catholicism by virtue of their superior numbers has not yet been written, many founders have their biographies...." (p. 234). Smith notes the special appeal of teaching orders: "From a psychological point of view, nuns in boarding schools, instead of mothers, became models to emulate, and perhaps after living in an atmosphere which all alumnae professed to enjoy, young women found in the convent an appealing alternative to home.... In considering bourgeois women of Lille the temptation to explain away the celibate life as deviant is not helpful. Certain female orders played a visible and vigorous role in urban society as they controlled the distribution of charity through the Bureau de Bienfaisance, as they taught rich and poor girls alike, and as they managed most hospitals and institutions for the orphaned, aged, and ill.... Another trend in the selection of religious orders does

raise questions, for a quarter of the sample of Lille's wealthy nuns [Smith's sample was ninety nuns from 1800 to 1914 from Lille's upper bourgeoisie] committed themselves to the cloistered or contemplative life" (pp. 235 f.).

62. Christie Collection, Aunspaugh letters.

63. *New York Herald* (London Edition), August 18, 1889.

64. *Trial of Mrs. Maybrick*, p. 46.

65. *Porcupine* (Liverpool), August 10, 1889.

66. See Leonore Davidoff, "Mastered for Life: Servant, Wife, and Mother in Victorian and Edwardian Britain," *Journal of Social History*, 7, no. 4 (1974): 406-428. In her excellent recent study *The Domestic Revolution: The Modernisation of Household Service in England and France* (London: Croom Helm, 1976), Theresa McBride discusses the perception of nineteenth-century commentators that their problems with servants were novel and that servant-employer relationships had deteriorated since the *ancien régime*: "Correctly or not, they often insisted that the servants of the eighteenth century had been more attached to their employers, more loyal, and more willing to accept their proper 'place' in society. This theme of the eighteenth-century servant as a model of loyalty reflected their deep sense of dissatisfaction with the nineteenth-century servant situation, but its implication of a total shift in the problems was unjustified" (p. 16). McBride later shows how in more rapidly modernized England, the paternalistic servant-employer relationship actually gave way to a contractual relationship quite early in the nineteenth century, but that in both countries, and especially in France, the "middle classes were more likely to complain of contemporary servants and cling to their image of the faithful retainer who could be considered a member of the family" (p. 119).

67. *Le Figaro*, June 8, 1892, comments on Reymond's stupidity in trusting a coachman allegedly being paid by Claire to reveal her husband's whereabouts. Sympathy for Mrs. Maybrick caused many papers to comment on the domestic "cabal" against the accused. The weekly journal *Truth* (London), willing enough to accept Florence's guilt, remarked that the case "shows up 'lady friends' and woman servants in a rather baleful light" (August 15, p. 310). Christie quotes the editor of that journal: "I sincerely trust that Nurse Yapp will never again obtain a situation in a private house.... The woman was guilty of a gross abuse of trust, and it is to be regretted that the law cannot punish her. Had the mob

caught her and ducked her [during the trial] I cannot say that my regret would have been poignant" (p. 159).

68. "Mrs. Briggs from the outset was a potent factor in the household. She kept a general eye upon affairs" [*New York Herald* (London Edition), August 14, 1889]. Miss Aunspaugh is more explicit on the subject, as one who witnessed daily life there, and her account goes far to demonstrate how little Florence Maybrick was mistress of her own home. "There was a Mrs. Briggs, who was invited to the formal dining, and remained in the house about ten days afterwards. This woman's position in the house was a most puzzling one. There [*sic*] little tête-à-têtes in groups of two and sometimes three of the servants went on more frequently while she was there, and she was included in them. . . . Both Mrs. Briggs and Nurse Yapp despised and hated Mrs. Maybrick, and the most pathetic part about it was Mrs. Maybrick did not have the brain to realize their attitude towards her. . . . Mrs. Briggs took all kinds of authority around the place and with the servants. She would address Mr. Maybrick as James. At the table I have heard her say things like this—'James grazing the horses on the grounds would save so much expense in cutting grass—James dont you think a roof on the porch by the side of your den would be much better—James I would suggest you wear your heavy coat; it is so much cooler this morning—James a pork roast would be nice for dinner today.' Not one time did she ever address Mrs. Maybrick. While it is in my thoughts, I want to say that during my entire visit in Mr. Maybrick's home, I can not recall one instance where Mrs. Maybrick gave an order or instructions to a servant. . . . When Mr. and Mrs. Maybrick were gone, she [Briggs] would go in every room in the house. Mr. Maybrick's bed room and Mrs. Maybrick's bed room. Only one room escaped her—that was Mr. Maybrick's 'den.' Mr. Maybrick had a Yale lock on the door. . . . Mrs. Briggs was supposed to be Mr. and Mrs. Maybrick's guest. Yet she was on far more intimate terms with Yapp than she was with Mrs. Maybrick. Mr. Maybrick addressed her as Mrs. Briggs, and was always very reserved and dignified towards to [*sic*] her (Christie Collection, Aunspaugh letters).

69. *New York Herald* (London Edition), August 18, 1889. This source also revealed the unsurprising fact that Yapp wore her mistress's cast-off clothes, but added that she also tried on Florence's dresses when she was out and that

she had carried Florence's umbrella for her appearance in court.

70. Ibid.

71. Christie (American edition, Philadelphia: Lippincott, 1968), p. 38.

72. *Trial of Mrs. Maybrick*, p. 105.

73. Ibid. Christie quotes an important letter from Florence to Dr. Hopper, the man to whom Florence had previously confided her revulsion for James in the belief that the doctor was her friend, but who had sided with James in an effort to effect a reconciliation. On the day James died, Florence, who still believed that the doctor was sympathetic to her, dashed off a desperate pencil note to him begging for help. At the trial the note was merely mentioned but not produced, and Christie states that it did not come to light for nearly forty years. Christie makes the observation that if Hopper, who acknowledged receiving it, had submitted the letter, it might have altered the verdict. "Dear Dr. Hopper. I am sure you must have heard of Jim's dangerous illness, and no doubt feel that I ought to have called you in to see him. My misery is great and my position such a painful one that when I tell you that both my brothers-in-law are here and have taken the nursing of Jim and management of my house completely out of my hands, you will understand how powerless I am to assert myself. I am in great need of a friend!

"Michael, whom Jim informed of the unhappiness existing between us last month, now accuses me as being the primary cause of Jim's present critical state, to which want of proper care from me as regards his nourishment and medical attention may be added. Michael hardly speaks to me. I am neither cheered nor told the worst. I am a mere cypher in my own house, ignored and overlooked. I am too utterly broken-hearted to struggle against myself or anyone else; all I want is to die. . . .

"It is terrible. How shall I bear it? I have no one to turn to, and my husband's brothers are cold-hearted and brutal men. Because I have sinned once, must I be misjudged always? Yours Distractedly. F. E. Maybrick" (Christie, pp. 62 f.).

74. In a recent paper entitled "Social Relationship and Sexual Liberation Among the Utopian Socialists," presented at the Third Berkshire Conference on the History of Women (June 9-11, 1976) at Bryn Mawr College, S. Joan Moon uses evidence from the writings of women in these movements to show that they mistrusted some of the men's notions about socialization of sex, at least until the economic basis of society had been trans-

formed to permit women to enjoy economic independence. "[The socialist women] seized upon the provisional nature of the new morality, cautioned against the egotistical implications of its practice, and subordinated it to general social change" (pp. 9 f.).

75. This view, already noted in Branca, was voiced in her previous discussion, with Peter N. Stearns, in *Modernization of Women in the Nineteenth Century* (St. Charles, Mo.: Forum, 1973). The notion was argued earlier in the American context in a paper by Daniel Scott Smith, "Family Limitation, Sexual Control, and Domestic Feminism in Victorian America," in *Clio's Consciousness Raised: New Perspectives on the History of Women*, ed. Mary S. Hartman and Lois W. Banner (New York: Harper & Row, 1974), pp. 119-136. Smith uses the phrase "domestic feminism" to describe evidence for women's gains in authority in the home and in decision making about family limitation. Countering earlier views of middle-class women's declining status in the nineteenth century, he argues that they effectively extended their autonomy in the domestic sphere in their roles as wives and mothers. "The perspective suggested above helps to explain why the history of the suffrage movement involved a shift from the woman-as-atomistic-person notion toward the ideology of woman as wife-and-mother. Drawing on the perceptions gained from their rise within the family, women finally entered politics in large numbers at the turn of the twentieth century. Given the importance of family limitation and sexual control in domestic feminism, it is not surprising that women were involved in and strongly supported the temperance and social purity movements—reform attempts implicitly attacking male culture" (p. 133). See also the article by Linda Gordon, "Voluntary Motherhood: The Beginnings of Feminist Birth Control Ideas in the United States," in the same volume.

76. Under the Napoleonic Code, execution of the so-called crime of passion was restricted to men, who alone could not be tried for premeditated murder (though they could be indicted and tried on a lesser charge) if they killed either wife or lover in circumstances of *flagrant délit* (Article 324). Popularly, the crime of passion had a broader definition and included all manner of crimes motivated by sexual jealousy and hatred.

77. Louis Proal, *Le Crime et le suicide passionels* (Paris: Alcan, 1900), p. 291.

78. Paul Aubry, *La Contagion du meurtre* (Paris: Alcan, 1894), pp. 107-130. Aubry, in noting the Francey affair as one such case, states, "Does anyone believe that if the former [Mme. Clovis Hugues] had not been made into a heroine . . . , if all the newspapers had not trumpeted this unfortunate affair . . . , that the latter [Mme. Francey] would have permitted her imagination to become so aroused, that she would not instead have feared to use a revolver against a man who was so easy to get rid of by legal means?" (p. 128).

79. Bataille, 1:174-193.

80. Ibid., p. 186. This was her official explanation. She was more candid in earlier testimony when she acknowledged having known of the affair some time, but having decided to act only when she realized that the whole town knew!

81. Proal, pp. 114 f., says that the revolver had replaced the acid used by the seduced and abandoned in the past. Aubry, who titles his chapter on the subject "Murders Committed by Aid of Acid and the Revolver," states that he sees the revolver killings as a variety of the "crimes of disfiguration" through acid (p. 109). The first widely discussed revolver case involving a bourgeois woman occurred in 1880. A young woman named Marie Bière, from a modest middle-class family, had studied music at the Paris Conservatory and in 1887 became the mistress of a young man of good family. Discovering she was pregnant by him, she agreed to get an abortion; but she wanted the baby and postponed the operation until it was too late, hoping that having the child would induce her lover to marry her. He did not, and six months after its birth, the infant girl, who had been put out to nurse, died. Marie continued to sleep with her lover and to try to persuade him to marry her, but he steadfastly refused and she finally shot him, wounding him seriously. She pleaded that she had continued to have relations with her victim because she wanted another child and stated dramatically: "All mothers will understand me!" The jury's acquittal was enthusiastically applauded [Bataille, 1:13-51].

82. Bataille, 11:147-149. The woman was acquitted.

83. *Le Petit Parisien*, May 25, 1892. Significantly, she did not make this statement again at the trial, but relied instead on her lawyer's decision to gain acquittal through her rival's letters rather than through any plea for her own rights as a wife.

84. Proal, p. 606.

85. Ibid.

86. *La Liberté*, July 13, 1892, argued that the legal possibility of divorce made the "crime

passionel" obsolete, but even if Claire Reymond had wanted divorce, she could not have got it on the grounds of adultery, since Reymond's liaison was not conducted at home. She might have attempted the grounds of cruelty and injury, which were being loosely interpreted by the courts (Zeldin, p. 358), but for Claire, as for most unhappily married women, the step was unthinkable.

87. *Le Figaro,* May 27, 1892.

88. Ibid., June 8, 1892.

89. Howard Zehr, Jr., points out that in general, attempts to describe crime take one of two approaches: either they begin with a set of empirical data from which they derive a variety of explanations or they "attempt to develop general theories of delinquency that presumably can be tested empirically later on." The general theories, as he indicates, have tended to find the causes of delinquency either in peculiarities of the individual or in general social conditions ["Patterns of Crime in Nineteenth-Century Germany and France: A Comparative Study," Ph.D. dissertation (Rutgers University, 1974), 1:4 f.].

90. See citation in note 77.

91. Proal, p. 603. Proal names Alexandre Dumas *fils* as the major offender among the literati for having written plays endorsing male crimes of passion. The plays, Proal says, summoned husbands to destroy the "monsters" who dared to be unfaithful with the injunction *Tue-la!* ("Kill her!"), which became a popular by-word (pp. 583-585). Dumas was indeed a mouthpiece for male antagonism against alleged new female sexual infidelity, and he did not use his plays to convey the same message to women. Indeed, though Proal does not mention the fact, Dumas was alarmed by the women's crimes of passion and wrote a pamphlet entitled "Les Femmes qui tuent et les femmes qui votent" ("Women Who Kill and Women Who Vote"), which argued that frustration over their lack of a political voice was the chief motive prompting women to the new violence. Dumas contended implausibly that if the vote were conceded, women would cease their attacks. Neither Dumas nor Proal opined that the real cause of their violence might lie in a new consciousness, as yet largely prepolitical, on the part of some women whose grievances had nothing to do with their impotence in the public realm.

92. Obviously, it is impossible to discover actual behavior or to demonstrate trends with any precision. Many commentators, such as the author of *My Secret Life,* noted the decline

after midcentury in the *public* display of sexual immorality. Peter Cominos, in "Late-Victorian Sexual Respectability and the Social System," *International Review of Social History,* 8 (1963): 46, notes the reduction of brothels after the 1850s and 1860s and suggests that there was an actual reduction of male marital infidelity in the last decades of the Victorian era. Then, too, as Cominos remarks, late Victorian men were the products of those mid-Victorian public schools, with their new emphasis on sexual virtue and self-restraint (p. 40).

93. The public adherence of English men to the campaigns of the 1870s and 1880s against the Contagious Diseases Acts, which were argued to enshrine the double sexual standard, set an example at any rate, as did their participation in the social purity campaigns. Some of the major figures, such as Gladstone, have recently been shown to have led rather different sorts of private lives than their public behavior would suggest, but it would be hazardous to dismiss so many public statements by men as evidence of mere hypocrisy.

94. Quoted in W. J. Reader, *Life in Victorian England* (London: Batsford, 1964), p. 141.

95. See discussions in Smith; Edward Shorter, *The Making of the Modern Family* (New York: Basic Books, 1975); and Catherine Bodard Silver, "Salon, Foyer, and Bureau," in *Clio's Consciousness Raised: New Perspectives on the History of Women,* ed. Mary S. Hartman and Lois W. Banner (New York: Harper & Row, 1974). In a recent paper entitled "Patriarchal Feminism in Mid-Nineteenth Century France," presented at the Third Berkshire Conference on the History of Women (June 9-11, 1976) at Bryn Mawr College, Karen Offen discusses the "male-feminist" phenomenon in France. She argues that men such as Ernest Legouvé, who argued for the separation of sex roles but the improvement of women's status within their sphere (see his *Histoire morale des femmes* [Paris: Sandré, 1849]), reflected views widely held by French women, which blended well with the continued appeal of the aristocratic tradition in assigning women powerful but separate roles and which emphasized motherhood in a context in which early family limitation had deprived women of the children they may have wanted to have. "In short, domesticity within a framework of separate spheres must have looked extremely good to women who had not yet had the chance to fully test its limitations. . . . For a long time, therefore,

most Frenchwomen could hardly envision breaking out of their separate sphere to pursue either public professions or the vote; they were primarily interested in further exploration of education opportunities that would serve them in private life" (pp. 14 f.).

96. Howard Zehr, Jr. (1:18-28), provides an excellent introductory discussion to the relative deprivation theory developed by Ted Robert Gurr in *Why Men Rebel*, (Princeton: Princeton University Press, 1971). Zehr notes some problems with the theory, but it appears to offer new ways to look at many sorts of behavior, including that of these women.

97. Staffe, p. 258. The baroness advises that if a wife senses she is loved by another man, she should tell her husband and ask him to protect her. If the husband is the violent sort, she warns, the wife must defend herself alone, "and the best means is to remove any hope from the very first moment. . . . Do not hope to be a friend . . . ; that is playing with fire."

98. Ibid., p. 206. Similar themes were voiced in the popular marriage manual by Dr. Charles Montalban, *La Petite Bible des jeunes époux* (Paris: Flammarion, 1885). This work, which is more a sex manual, stresses the healthiness of limited marital sex for both men and women, but warns against the evils of female boredom and especially the "fatal literature" which some women read, which can destroy marriages. Montalban urges husbands to keep all such literature, especially George Sand's *Lélia*, away from wives (p. 97). The positive tone of the manuals earlier in the century, when newly married women were urged to regard themselves as true "ministers of the interior," appears to be giving way to a frightened response to social change and its dangers to the purity of the woman in the home.

99. Zehr, 2; 3: chap. 4. (This chapter begins in vol. 2 and carries into the next volume of the work.)

100. In the annual French report, the *Compte général de l'administration de la justice criminelle*, prepared by the Ministry of Justice, the only index for estimating class is a rough division of offenders by crime category into educational levels which are not consistent. By the 1880s even these were dropped for individual crime categories relevant here. However, my survey of the annual volumes in the Bataille series (covering the causes célèbres from 1880 through 1898) revealed just two cases of crimes of passion by men who were clearly middle-class, both of which have the distinct air of exceptions which prove the rule.

The first, an affair from 1889, involved a businessman from Montpellier who shot a legal consultant who was having an affair with his wife (11:101-116). Immediately afterwards the businessman summoned a doctor, a priest, and the police; he later pleaded that his victim, who survived, had refused to sign a document recognizing that he had forfeited his honor and would leave town. This case, with its aura of efficient planning and the prior arrangement of a "business agreement" to avoid revenge by violence, displays a masculine transition phase in which older styles of passion killing were giving way to the more discreet modes of retribution adopted by the middle classes.

The second case, from 1884 (5:278-280), involved an executive in a manufacturing concern in Thiers who had attempted to shoot his wife's lover, a white-collar worker employed by the railroad. To avoid further scandal the lover's employer insisted on transferring him out of town, but once when the lover returned on a visit, the husband sought revenge again, and succeeded this time in wounding his victim. The assailant was acquitted, as in the other case, but the intervention of the lover's employer to prevent a revenge killing signals again the changing climate of opinion.

The more traditional crime of revenge for sexual infidelity did survive among lower-class men (Bataille notes several cases) and also among "transitional" groups. In this latter category I would place the single remaining case featured in Bataille (9:289-293) which could be labeled "middle class." The case involved a Parisian pharmacist who in 1888 murdered an apprentice discovered in the act of making love to his wife. The case is reminiscent of the Fenayrou affair, and the description suggests that this man, like Marin, was responding to more traditional impulses which reflected a pre-bourgeois mentality.

The Bataille volumes for the same years display the dramatic feminization of the crime of passion. They describe no less than seven cases of middle-class women who shot their victims with revolvers in what were labeled crimes of passion (only two victims survived) and one middle-class woman who disfigured her rival with sulfuric acid. In addition, there is an even larger representation of lower class women who turned to acid and the revolver.

An article on female criminals in *La Grande Revue*, 1889, pp. 393-427, devotes most of the discussion to an attack on the avenging women in the acid and revolver cases (after alleging that twice as many French women as men commit adultery). The article is the only one of which I am aware which, albeit inadvertently, touched upon part of the explanation for the women's actions offered here. It suggests that troublesome matters such as the large numbers of such revenge crimes do not bother the women at all, since they view themselves not as criminals but as enforcers of justice, and that furthermore "nothing touches a woman less than such considerations. She does not understand their importance, she is not imbued with ideas of social peace as we men are, we who make the laws and consider their application" (pp. 416 f.). In suggesting that the women did not have the same stake in preventing scandal, the author was quite correct.

101. *Le Petit Journal,* May 28, 1892.
102. *Trial of Mrs. Maybrick,* p. 199.
103. Ibid., pp. 200 f.
104. Ibid.
105. Ibid., pp. 196-198, 203. Miss Aunspaugh confirmed that Maybrick was a hypochondriac who bought every patent medicine that came out. "My father once said—'Maybrick has got a dozen drug stores in his stomach'" (Christie Collection, Aunspaugh letters).
106. *Trial of Mrs. Maybrick,* p. 152.
107. Levy, p. 467. The gentleman, Valentine Blake, son of an Irish MP, said he had given Maybrick the substance in February 1889.
108. The medical expert for the prosecution was Dr. Thomas Stevenson, lecturer on forensic medicine and chemistry at Guy's Hospital, London. The expert for the defense was Dr. Charles Tidy, examiner of forensic medicine at London Hospital.
109. Several such letters appeared in the Liverpool papers, which carried the largest number of responses. The *British Medical Journal* (August 17, 1889, p. 393) disagreed with the verdict, pointed out that the tiny quantity of arsenic found was consistent with the theory of an arsenic habit, and later printed a letter (October 12, p. 830) from an authority who argued that arsenic withdrawal would not produce death as arsenic was not addictive. The *Lancet* (August 17, 1889) accepted the verdict.
110. *Trial of Mrs. Maybrick,* p. 45.
111. The *Times* acknowledged the justice of American protests about this usage in an editorial of August 8, 1889.
112. *Trial of Mrs. Maybrick,* p. 236.
113. Levy, p. 15.
114. *Trial of Mrs. Maybrick,* pp. 344 f.
115. Ibid., p. 347.
116. Christie, p. 149.
117. Ibid. One of the rallies held in London was led by Alexander MacDougall, a Scottish

barrister, who wrote to the *Times* (letter of August 9) reminding the public of his role in fighting against an unjust decision in the Penge case twelve years before and urging the "solemn duty of the public to zealously watch over our criminal trials." An estimated fifteen hundred attended MacDougall's rally, and later MacDougall published a book, *The Maybrick Case* (London: Baillière, Tindall & Cox, 1896) which suggested that all the poison had been planted by the "Suspecting Five," that is, Michael and Edwin Maybrick, Mrs. Briggs and her sister, and Miss Yapp. The more likely theory is that James had the poison there which he got from Blake (see note 107). However, Edwin Maybrick did later admit that he had removed a box of pills from among James's collection which listed arsenic as an ingredient. Edwin had no explanation for his action and it is probable that since he suspected Florence, he wished to remove any evidence which suggested that his brother was an arsenic-eater (Levy, pp. 13 f.).

118. Christie, pp. 150 f. Interestingly, one of the most influential religious leaders, the preacher Charles Spurgeon of the Metropolitan Tabernacle, was reported to have "invited the ladies of the congregation to sign a petititon praying the Queen to alter the sentence on Mrs. Maybrick, on the ground that the case was surrounded with ever-increasing doubt" [*New York Herald,* (London Edition), August 20, 1889].
119. Christie, pp. 152 f.
120. Ibid., p. 153.
121. Ibid.
122. The Brooklyn *Daily Eagle* (August 11, 1889) published an interview with a man called Matthew Howard who knew Mrs. Maybrick and her mother. Of the baroness, he said, "She seemed to be tinctured with the demoralizing social heresies of the Woodhull school of philosophy. ... Her example and teachings must have imbued the daughter with loose ideas of the marriage relation. If I am not mistaken as to the Socialistic theories of the baroness at the time I speak of, under such tuition the daughter would hold lightly her obligations to a husband who had deceived and abused her and for whom she had an aversion." Of Florence, Howard said, "She seemed to be unusually amiable, winning and gentle in her manners, and of a timid and affectionate nature which would induce her to step aside rather than risk hurting a worm." Howard thought Florence was innocent.
123. *Daily Post,* June 19, 1889.
124. Florence says that the publisher and her friends "persuaded me that the public

would give me their tenderest regard, and that possibly the humanities might be furthered a bit if the story of a woman—whatever might be her failings in other directions—wholly guiltless of the terrible charge of wilful murder, and for which in her innocence she was made to suffer so cruelly, be given in fullest heart detail to a sympathetic world" (Florence E. Maybrick, *Mrs. Maybrick's Own Story: My Fifteen Lost Years* [New York: Funk and Wagnalls, 1905], pp. 14f.) Unfortunately, the volume gives next to nothing of what it promises. It is intriguing to compare it with the intensely personal memoirs of Marie Lafarge. Mme. Lafarge knew she had to sell herself as a romantic creature; Florence Maybrick, in an age disabused about women's alleged guilelessness, opted for an appeal to public causes of the injustice of the court and prison systems.

125. Maybrick, p. 368.

126. "Mrs. Chandler" was found by a neighbor who visited her three-room cottage and discovered the old woman's shriveled body lying on the bed. "And in the bedroom some one found a scrapbook, thick with saffron clipping, telling who the recluse really was" (Christie Collection, *New York Post*, October 24, 1941).

127. *Times*, August 15, 1889.

128. The largest number of letters appeared in the Liverpool papers, especially the *Daily Post*, the *Echo*, the *Morning Courier*, and the *Evening Express*. Many appeared in the London and New York papers and especially the London edition of the *New York Herald*. And sales made records: the *Daily Post* (August 9, 1889) reported that the *Echo* sold over a million copies the week of the trial.

129. *Daily Post*, August 8, 1889.

130. *Porcupine*, August 3, 1889.

131. *Truth*, August 15, 1889. *Moonshine* (London) of August 17, 1889, asked, "Had these ladies of Liverpool forgotten that Mrs. Maybrick (apart from the poisoning charges) had confessed to gross immorality; or . . . had she told so many fibs that when she admitted having been naughty they did not believe her?" The *Spectator* (August 24, 1889) stated, "In the Maybrick case there has been an element of partisanship which we can hardly be mistaken in referring to something like a claim for women of the right to observe or disregard the obligations of marriage at their own pleasure. . . . There seems to be at the present time a sort of partisanship for unfaithful wives, which has long disappeared, if it ever existed in precisely the same form, for unfaithful husbands. Doubtless there was a time when libertinism was regarded almost as a sort of distinction in a man. But we cannot remember that there ever was a tide of the sentimental sympathy and admiration for it which seems to have been felt towards Mrs. Maybrick."

132. *Truth*, August 15, 1889.

133. Ibid.

134. *Daily Post*, August 9, 1889. In her letter "Faemina" adds that she doubts that any jury of her own sex would have convicted Mrs. Maybrick. Another woman, answering her own question about why there were no women on the jury, said "Husbands must be protected from adulterous and murderous wives, and they gave their judgment accordingly" (August 12, 1889).

135. L. Forbes Winslow, *Recollections of Forty Years* (London: Ouseley, 1910), p. 149. A Ladies Central Committee was promptly formed, which announced it had received "an immense number of postcards and letters of sympathy from women of all classes, including many families of distinction, expressing their strong and unanimous desire that the verdict against Mrs. Maybrick should be quashed. The committee say that they are determined that their efforts shall not be relaxed until Mrs. Maybrick is released" [*New York Herald* (London Edition), August 20, 1889].

136. Quoted, unattributed, in Christie, p. 148.

137. *Daily Post*, August 12, 1889.

138. Ibid., August 15, 1889.

139. Quoted, unattributed, in Christie, p. 148.

140. Ibid.

141. *New York Herald*, (London Edition), August 14, 1889.

142. "Ought Mrs. Maybrick to be Tortured to Death?" *Review of Reviews*, 6 (October 1892): 390-396. W. T. Stead apologized for paying little attention to the case but made up for lost time with his usual hyperbole. James Maybrick, he claimed, had been "a seducer, an adulterer and a debauchee" (p. 392). Stead hinted that the arsenic habit was the result of Maybrick's efforts to cure himself of syphilis, and then produced an incredible letter which he claimed proved that Maybrick had been murdered by a man who had confessed just before dying after escape to South Africa. The letter was doubtless a fraud, and Stead's hints about Maybrick's disease appear to have been made for sensational effect.

143. *Liverpool Review*, August 17, 1889. Butler notwithstanding, some men of high rank, at least, were feeling the new sting of criticism; most visible were the politicians.

Dilke had learned—as Parnell was soon to do—that the private morals of statesmen had become a public concern. Cominos notes the fact, but fails to give enough importance to the influence of new attitudes among increasingly vocal women (p. 48). The hostility toward Dilke and Parnell and the sympathy toward Mrs. Maybrick, all accused of the crime of adultery, can be reconciled if the women's new attack on the male preserve of the double sexual standard is taken into account.

144. Christie describes the campaign in chapters 12-13 of his study. There is material on Mary Dodge's efforts in *Gail Hamilton's Life in Letters,* ed. B. H. A. Dodge (Boston: Lee & Shepard, 1901). (Gail Hamilton was Mary Dodge's pen-name.) Helen Densmore, another of Mrs. Maybrick's supporters, wrote an article on the affair entitled "The English Dreyfus Case" published in *The Arena,* 22 (1899): 598-613. Densmore, an American doctor living in London, denied in her article the "rumor" that Florence had wounded herself to get sympathy. Christie, however, learned that the rumors were true and that Florence, perhaps at the instigation of her mother who was orchestrating attempts to get her daughter released, had shown some blood to the prison doctor which she claimed came from her lungs. The suspicious doctor had the prisoner watched through the peephole in her door at night and, according to Christie, "the warders observed some scenes which were macabre even for Woking." As Christie states, "the prisoner had inserted a tin knife into her vagina during the menstrual period and had drawn forth the blood which she mixed with sputum and exhibited to the doctor. In so doing, she accidentally severed the vaginal artery, produced a hemorrhage, and nearly bled to death before she was found stretched out in her cell" (p. 178). Christie reports that the Home Secretary, Asquith, agreed to have the report shown to Mary Dodge, head of the Women's International Maybrick Society, since, as the secretary said, "it is worthwhile stopping her mouth." To her credit, Miss Dodge was not deterred by this crass maneuver (p. 199).

145. Christie, p. 207.
146. *Echo,* June 12, 1889.
147. Christie, p. 225.

CONCLUSION

1. Patricia Branca discusses the problems of these nonadapters with reference to evidence for the increased use of drugs and alcohol among middle-class women toward the end of the century. See *Silent Sisterhood: Middle-Class Women in the Victorian Home* (Pittsburgh: Carnegie-Mellon University Press, 1975), pp. 174-250. Others, such as Ann Douglas and Carroll Smith-Rosenberg, have described the passive resistance of women through illness. See Carroll Smith-Rosenberg, "The Hysterical Woman: Sex Roles and Role Conflict in Nineteenth-Century America," *Social Research,* 29 (Winter 1972): 652-678; Ann Douglas, " 'The Fashionable Diseases': Women's Complaints and Their Treatment in Nineteenth-Century America," *Journal of Interdisciplinary History,* 4, no. 1 (Summer 1973): 25-52, reprinted in Mary Hartman and Lois W. Banner, *Clio's Consciousness Raised: New Perspectives on the History of Women* (New York: Harper & Row, 1974), pp. 1-22.

2. Such work might supplement the findings in Theresa McBride's comparative study of servants, *The Domestic Revolution: The Modernisation of Household Service in England and France* (London: Croom Helm, 1976). The nearly five hundred volumes of the London Central Criminal Court, for example, contain a great many cases with testimony from servants and their employers.

3. *Daily News,* August 12, 1876.

4. This summary is taken from the account of the case in *La Gazette des Tribunaux.* A recent summary of the case points out that the young officer, Emile de la Roncière, was completely exonerated in 1848, long after he had finished his sentence, when the case was reopened by one of the original prosecuting attorneys. This account points out that Mlle. de Morell did have some special provocation for her accusation. Young de la Roncière, in his rage over Marie's false accusations in the matter of the forged letters, had bet some fellow officers that he could produce proof of having slept with the girl by presenting a lock of her pubic hair! The matter was arranged through his mistress, Mlle. de Morell's governess, who slept next door and who admitted de la Roncière to her charge's room. Mlle. de Morell claimed that the young man had effected his entry by means of a ladder which he had placed beneath her window. It was pointed out at the trial, however, that the evidence showed that the window had been broken from the inside, that is, by Marie herself, and that it would have been impossible in any case to reach the window latch through the small aperture which had been made in the glass. This evidence was not considered sufficient at the time, and it is understandable that

the young officer refrained from pointing out what had actually happened. It was not an attempted rape, but it was a very compromising adventure for one who hoped for an honorable military career. [René Floriot, *Les erreurs judiciares* (Paris: Flammarion, 1968), pp. 23-28].

5. *La Gazette des Tribunaux,* June 30, 1834.

6. *National Review,* (October 1858): 350.

7. A. Bataille, *Les causes criminelles et mordaines* 18 vols. (Paris: Dentu, 1881-1898), 12: 236-255.

8. See William L. O'Neill, *Divorce in the Progressive Era* (New York: F. Watts, 1973), esp. chap. 1.

9. Richard Altick, *Victorian Studies in Scarlet* (New York: Norton, 1970), p. 42.

10. Ibid.

11. Elaine Showalter, *A Literature of Their Own: British Novelists from Brontë to Lessing* (Princeton: Princeton University Press, 1977).

12. Ibid., MS chap. 6, p. 182.

13. Ibid., p. 182.

14. Ibid., p. 183.

SELECTIVE
BIBLIOGRAPHY

BACKGROUND STUDIES

Albert, P., and Terrou, F. *Histoire de la presse*. Paris: Presses Universitaires de France, 1970.
Altick, Richard. *Victorian Studies in Scarlet*. New York: Norton, 1970.
Ardagh, John. *The New France: A Society in Transition, 1945-1973*. Harmondsworth: Penguin, 1973.
Banks, J. A. *Prosperity and Parenthood*. London: Routledge & Kegan Paul, 1954.
Barker-Benfield, G. J. *The Horrors of the Half-Known Life: Male Attitudes Toward Women and Sexuality in Nineteenth-Century*. New York: Harper & Row, 1976.
Bellanger, Claude et al. *Histoire générale de la presse française*. 2 vols. Paris: P.U.F., 1969.
Best, Geoffrey. *Mid-Victorian Britain, 1851-1875*. New York: Schocken, 1972.
Blake, John B. "Mary Gove Nichols, Prophetess of Health." *Proceedings of the American Philosophical Association* 107 (June 1962): 219-234.
Branca, Patricia. *Silent Sisterhood: Middle-Class Women in the Victorian Home*. Pittsburgh: Carnegie-Mellon University Press, 1975.
———, and Stearns, Peter N. *Modernization of Women in the Nineteenth Century*. St. Charles, Mo.: Forum, 1973.
Chevalier, Louis. *La Formation de la population parisienne au XIXᵉ siècle*. Paris: P.U.F., 1950.
Cominos, Peter. "Late-Victorian Sexual Respectability and the Social System." *International Review of Social History* 8 (1963): 18-48, 216-250.
Cunnington, C. Willett. *Feminine Attitudes in the Nineteenth Century*. London: Heinemann, 1935.
Daumard, Adeline. *La Bourgeoisie parisienne de 1815 à 1848*. Paris: S.E.V.P.E.N., 1963.
Davidoff, Leonore. *The Best Circles: Society, Etiquette and the Season*. London: Croom Helm, 1973.

307

————. "Mastered for Life: Servant, Wife, and Mother in Victorian and Edwardian Britain." *Journal of Social History* 7 (1974): 406-428.

Ellenberger, Henri. *Criminologie du passé et du present.* Montreal: Les Presses de L'Université de Montréal, 1965.

Esmein, A. *A History of Continental Criminal Procedure.* Boston: Little, Brown, 1913.

Filene, Peter Gabriel. *Him/Her/Self: Sex Roles in Modern America.* New York: Harcourt Brace Jovanovich, 1974.

Gattrell, V. A. C., and Hadden, T. S. "Criminal Statistics and Their Interpretation," *Nineteenth-Century Society.* Edited by E. A. Wrigley. Cambridge: Cambridge University Press, 1972.

Griffiths, Arthur. *Secrets of the Prison-House or Gaol Studies and Sketches.* London: Chapman and Hall, 1894.

Guy, William A. "On the Executions for Murder That Have Taken Place in England and Wales During the Last Seventy Years." *Journal of the Statistical Society* 38 (1875): 463-486.

Hare, E. H. "Masturbatory Insanity: The History of an Idea." *Journal of Mental Science* 108 (1962): 1-25.

Hartman, Mary S., and Banner, Lois W., eds. *Clio's Consciousness Raised: New Perspectives on the History of Women.* New York: Harper & Row, 1974.

Hellerstein, Erna. "Secular Rules and Secular Sanctions: The Regulation of Female Sexuality in Nineteenth-Century France." Unpublished paper presented at the Third Berkshire Conference on the History of Women, June 9-11, 1976, at Bryn Mawr College.

Kamm, Josephine. *Hope Deferred. Girls' Education in English History.* London: Methuen, 1965.

McBride, Theresa M. *The Domestic Revolution: The Modernisation of Household Service in England and France.* London: Croom Helm, 1976.

McGregor, O. R. *Divorce in England.* Toronto: Heinemann, 1957.

McLaren, Angus. "Doctor in the House: Medicine and Private Morality in France, 1800-1850." *Feminist Studies* 2 (1975): 39-54.

Marandon, Sylvaine. *L'Image de la France dans l'Angleterre victorienne.* Paris: Colin, 1967.

Marcus, Steven. *The Other Victorians.* New York: Basic Books, 1966.

Moon, S. Joan. "Social Relationship and Sexual Liberation Among the Utopian Socialists." Unpublished paper presented at the Third Berkshire Conference on the History of Women, June 9-11, 1976, at Bryn Mawr College.

Offen, Karen M. "Patriarchal Feminism in Mid-Nineteenth Century France: The Case of Ernest Legouvé (1807-1903)." Unpublished paper presented at the Third Berkshire Conference on the History of Women, June 9-11, 1976, at Bryn Mawr College.

O'Neill, William L. *Divorce in the Progressive Era.* New York: New Viewpoints, 1973.

Pearsall, Ronald. *The Worm in the Bud: The World of Victorian Sexuality.* New York: Macmillan, 1969.

Perkin, Harold J. *The Origins of Modern English Society, 1780-1880.* London: Routledge & Kegan Paul, 1969.

Pollak, Otto. *The Criminality of Women.* Philadelphia: University of Pennsylvania Press, 1950.

Proal, Louis. *Le Crime et le suicide passionels.* Paris: Alcan, 1900.

Rabb, Theodore, and Rothberg, Robert, eds. *The Family in History.* New York: Harper & Row, 1973.

Ranulf, Svend. *Moral Indignation and Middle Class Psychology.* Copenhagen: Levin & Munksgaard, 1938.

Reiss, Erna. *Rights and Duties of Englishwomen.* Manchester: Sherrat & Hughes, 1934.

Schwartz, Gerhart S. "Devices to Prevent Masturbation." *Medical Aspects of Human Sexuality* 7 (May 1973): 141-153.

Sklar, Kathryn Kish. *Catharine Beecher: A Study in American Domesticity.* New Haven: Yale University Press, 1973.

Smith, Bonnie. "The Bourgeois Women of Lille, 1860-1910." Unpublished Ph.D. dissertation, University of Rochester, 1975.

Spitz, René. "Authority and Masturbation, Some Remarks on a Bibliographical Investigation." *The Psychoanalytic Quarterly* 21 (1952): 490-527.

Tobias, J. J. *Urban Crime in Victorian England.* New York: Schocken, 1972.

Vanier, Henriette. *La Mode et ses métiers: Frivolités et luttes des classes, 1830-1870.* Paris: Colin, 1960.

Vicinus, Martha, ed. *Suffer and Be Still: Women in the Victorian Age.* Bloomington: Indiana University Press, 1972.

Villeneuve, Roland. *Le Poison et les empoisonneurs célèbres.* Paris: La Palatine, 1960.

Wilson, Patrick. *Murderess.* London: Michael Joseph, 1971.

Winslow, John H. *Darwin's Victorian Malady.* Philadelphia: American Philosophical Society, 1971.

Zehr, Howard, Jr. "Patterns of Crime in Nineteenth-Century Germany and France: A Comparative Study." Unpublished Ph.D. dissertation, Rutgers University, 1974.

Zeldin, Theodore. *France 1848-1945: Ambition, Love, and Politics.* Vol. 1. Oxford: Clarendon Press, 1973.

————. ed. *Conflicts in French Society: Anti-Clericalism, Education and Morals in the Nineteenth Century.* London: Allen and Unwin, 1970.

NINETEENTH-CENTURY SOURCES

Acton, William. *The Functions and Disorders of the Reproductive Organs in Childhood, Youth, Adult Age and Advanced Life, Considered in their Physiological, Social and Moral Relations.* Philadelphia: Blakiston, 1857.

Aimé-Martin, Louis. *De l'Education des mères de familles.* Paris: Gosselin, 1834.

Beeton, Isabella. *The Book of Household Management.* London: Beeton, 1861.

Celnart, Elisabeth F. *Manuel des dames.* 4th ed. Paris: Roret, 1830.

Droz, Gustave. *Monsieur, Madame et Bébé.* Paris: Hetzel, 1866.

[Drysdale, George.] *The Elements of Social Science; or Physical Sexual and Natural Religion. An Exposition of the True Cause and Only Cure of the Three Primary Social Evils: Poverty, Prostitution, and Celibacy.* London: Truelove, 1886.

Ellis, Sarah. *The Daughters of England.* London: Fisher, 1843.

————. *The Mothers of England.* London: Fisher, 1843.

————. *The Wives of England.* London: Fisher, 1843.

Granier, Camille. *La Femme criminelle.* Paris: Doin, 1906.

Hillebrand, Karl. *France and the French in the Second Half of the Nineteenth Century.* London: Trubner, 1881.

Icard, S. *La Femme et la période menstruelle.* Paris: Alcan, 1890.

Joly, H. *Le Crime.* Paris: Cerf, 1889.

Lacassagne, A. "Notes statistiques sur l'empoisonnement criminel en France." *Archives d'Anthropologie criminelle* 25 (1886): 260-264.

Linton, E. Lynn. *The Girl of the Period, and Other Social Essays.* London: Bentley, 1883.

Macé, Gustave. *Les Femmes criminelles.* Paris: Charpentier, 1904.

Montalban, Charles. *La petite Bible des jeunes époux.* Paris: Flammarion, 1885.

Nichols, Thomas Low. *Esoteric Anthropology (The Mysteries of Man): A Comprehensive and Confidential Treatise on the Structure, Functions, Passional Attractions and Perversions, True and False Physical and Social Conditions, and the Most Intimate Relations of Men and Women.* New York: Arno, 1972.

Nichols, Thomas Low, and Nichols, Mary Gove. *Marriage: Its History, Character and Results: Its Sanctities, and its Profanities; Its Science and Its Facts. Demonstrating Its Influence, as a Civilized Institution, on the Happiness of the Individual and the Progress of the Race.* Cincinnati: Nicholson, 1854.

O'Rell, Max. *Les Filles de John Bull.* Paris: Lévy, 1884.

Pariset, Madame (pseud.). *Nouveau Manuel complet de la maitresse de maison.* Paris: Roret, 1852.

Puibaraud, L. "La femme criminelle." *La Grande Revue* 12 (1899): 393-427.

Sandford, Mrs. John. *Female Improvement.* London: Longman, 1836.

Staffe, Baronne. *Les Usages du Monde.* Paris: Havard, 1890.

Trollope, Frances. *Paris and the Parisians in 1835.* 2 vols. in one. Paris: Galignani, 1836.

STUDIES RELATED TO THE CRIMES

The Balham Mystery. A Complete Record of the "Bravo" Poisoning Case. London: *The Daily Telegraph,* 1876.

Bataille, A. *Les Causes criminelles et mondaines.* 18 vols. Paris: Dentu, 1881-1898.

Bridges, Yseult. *How Charles Bravo Died.* London: Jarrolds, 1956.

———. *Poison and Adelaide Bartlett.* London: Hutchinson, 1962.

———. *The Tragedy at Road-Hill House.* New York: Rinehart, 1955.

Christie, Trevor L. *Etched in Arsenic.* London: Harrap, 1969.

Clarke, Edward. "Leaves from a Lawyer's Casebook: The Pimlico Mystery." *Cornhill Magazine* 49 (December 1920): 641-667.

Correspondance de Madame Lafarge. Paris: Mercure de France, 1913.

Fouquier, Armand. *Les Causes célèbres de tous les peuples.* 9 vols. Paris: Lebrun, 1858-1874.

Gril, Etienne. *Madame Lafarge devant ses juges.* Paris: Gallimard, 1958.

Gully, James M. *An Exposition of the Symptoms, Essential Nature and Treatment of Neuropathy or Nervousness.* London: Churchill, 1837.

Hall, John, ed. *The Trial of Adelaide Bartlett.* London: Hodge, 1927.

Hunt, Peter. *The Madeleine Smith Affair.* London: Carroll and Nicholson, 1950.

Irving, H. B., ed. *The Trial of Mrs. Maybrick.* London: Hodge, 1912.

Jacomet. *Les Drames judiciaires du XIX' siècle.* Paris: Payot, 1929.

Jenkins, Elizabeth. *Dr. Gully's Story.* New York: Coward, McCann & Geoghegan, 1972.

Jesse, F. Tennyson, ed. *The Trial of Madeleine Smith.* New York: Day, 1927.

Lafarge, Marie. *Heures de prison.* New York: Lasalle, 1854.

[Lafarge, Marie.] *Mémoires de Marie Cappelle, veuve Lafarge, écrits par elle-même.* Brussels: Jamar, 1841.

Levy, J. H. *The Necessity for Criminal Appeal as Illustrated by the Maybrick Case.* London: King, 1899.

Marsden, B. A., and Marsden, J. A. *Geneological Memoirs of the Family of Marsden.* Birkenhead: Griffith, 1914.

Marsden, James Loftus. *The Action of the Mind on the Body.* Great Malvern: Lamb, 1859.

———. *Notes on Homeopathy.* London: Headland, 1849.

Maybrick, Florence Elizabeth. *Mrs. Maybrick's Own Story: My Fifteen Lost Years.* New York: Funk & Wagnalls, 1905.

Morland, Nigel. *That Nice Miss Smith.* London: Muller, 1957.

Rhode, John. *The Case of Constance Kent.* New York: Scribner, 1928.

Saunders, Edith. *The Mystery of Marie Lafarge.* Paris: Pagnerre, 1840.

Stapleton, Joseph W. *The Great Crime of 1860.* London: Marlborough, 1861.

Williams, John. *Suddenly at the Priory.* London: Heinemann, 1957.

MANUSCRIPT SOURCES

Dossiers of preliminary interrogations for the Lemoine and Francey cases, from departmental archives in Tours and Auxerre.

Dossier on the Fenayrou case, from the Archives de la Préfecture de Police, Paris.

Christie Collection (Maybrick case), from special collections, University of Wyoming.

NEWSPAPERS AND JOURNALS

Paris

Le Cabinet de Lecture; Le Charivari; Le Commerce; Le Constitutionnel; Le Courrier Français; Le XIXeme Siecle; Le Droit; L'Echo Français; L'Estafette; Le Figaro; La France; Le Gaulois; La Gazette de France; La Gazette des Tribunaux; L'Intransigeant; Le Journal des Débats; La Lanterne; La Liberté; Le National; La Patrie; Le Petit Journal; Le Petit Parisien; La Petite Republique; La Phalange; La Presse; Le Siècle; Le Temps; La Tribune Judiciaire; L'Univers; Le Voltaire.

French (except Paris)

L'Album (Tulle); *L'Echo de la Baise* (Condom); *Le Facteur* (Ussel); *L'Indicateur Corrèzien* (Tulle); *Le Journal de Chinon; Le Journal de l'Indre-et-Loire* (Tours); *L'Opinion* (Auch); *Le Progrès de la Corrèze* (Tulle); *L'Utilitaire* (Brives).*

London

The British Medical Journal; The British Mothers' Magazine; Chambers' Journal; The Cornhill Magazine; The Daily News; The Daily Telegraph; The Evening Standard; The Examiner; The Express; The Illustrated London Times; The Lady's Companion; The Lancet; The Law Journal; The Law Magazine; The Medical Times and Gazette; The Mother's Friend: A Monthly Magazine; The News of the World; The Observer; The Pall Mall Budget; The Pall Mall Gazette; Public Opinion; The Queen; Review of Reviews; Reynolds' Newspaper; The Saturday Review; Solicitor's Journal; The Spectator; The Times; Truth; Vanity Fair.

British and American (except London)

The Arena (New York); *The Ayrshire Express; The Bath Chronicle; The Bath Express; Berrow's Worcestershire Journal; Blackwood's Magazine* (Edinburgh); *The Brighton Gazette; Chambers' Journal* (Edinburgh); *The Chronicle* (Glasgow); *The Citizen* (Glasgow); *The Citizen* (Liverpool); *The Courier* (Glasgow); *The Daily Express* (Edinburgh); *The Daily Post* (Liverpool); *The Daily Scotsman* (Edinburgh); *The Dublin Review; The Eagle* (Brooklyn); *The Echo* (Liverpool); *The Edinburgh Courant; The Edinburgh Review; The Evening Post* (Edinburgh); *The Examiner; The Frome Times; The Gazette* (Glasgow); *The Guardian* (Manchester); *Journal of Jurisprudence* (Edinburgh); *Liverpool Daily Post; The Malvern Advertiser; The New York Herald* (London Edition); *The New York Tribune; The Porcupine* (Liverpool); *The Review* (Liverpool); *The Scotch Thistle* (Edinburgh); *The Sentinel* (Glasgow); *The Somerset and Wilts Journal; The Trowbridge and North Wilts Advertiser; The Worcestershire Chronicle; The World* (New York).

INDEX

Abortion: in Bravo case, 159–60; in Fenayrou case, 207; in Reymond case, 229; and water-cure doctors, 157–58

Acton, William, on female sexuality, 72

Adultery, 4; concern over rising incidence in France, 169; as a factor in all later cases, 133–34, chaps. 4–6 *passim;* in French law, 37, 231; French views on, 241–42; and "modernity," 263–65; possible declining incidence among late-Victorian men, 301 n. 92–93; probable rising incidence among English and French women, 133–34

Advice manuals for women, 32–33; and changing French views on the double standard, 245, 302 n. 97–98; *Daughters of England* (Sarah Ellis), 52; English and French compared, 273 n. 61; on sexuality, 192, 293 n. 53. *See also* Marriage; Sexuality

Albert, Prince, 101, 175

Alcoholism: and Florence Bravo, 139, 156, 173; doctors' role in, 290 n. 94; and Alexander Ricardo, 136, 158; among "respectable" women, 157, 291–92 n. 157

L'Angelier, Emile, chap. 2 *passim*

Animal magnetism. *See* Mesmerism

Antimony (tartar emetic): and death of Charles Bravo, 139–40; used to doctor horses and "cure" alcoholism, 165. *See also* Poison

Arsenic: in Lacoste, Lafarge, Maybrick, and Smith cases, chaps. 1, 2, and 6 *passim;* as aphrodisiac, 41, 247; "arsenic eating," 246–47; as cosmetic, 54, 281 n. 107; as cure for syphilis, 41; and flypapers, 216, 226; in Fowler's Solution as cure-all, 40–42; and Marsh test, 46

Aubert, Louis (pharmacist lover of Gabrielle Fenayrou), chap. 5 *passim*

Barbey d'Aurevilly, Jules, 132

Bartlett, Adelaide, 3, chap. 5 *passim,* 218, 257, 259, 263, 267

Bartlett, Charles (elder brother-in-law of Adelaide), 175

Bartlett, Edwin (husband of Adelaide), chap. 5 *passim,* 259, 263

Bartlett, Frederick (younger brother-in-law and probable lover of Adelaide), 176; possible role in murder, 205

Bazard, Charles (brother of Hippolyte), 148

Bazard, Hippolyte (author's pseudonym for victim in Francey case), chap. 4 *passim*

Berens, Hippolyte (admirer of Euphémie Lacoste), 21–22

Berryer, Antoine (defense counsel for Célestine Doudet), 115, 117

Birth control: and Adelaide Bartlett, 197–98, 201–2; in England, 201–2; and Gabrielle Fenayrou, 192–93, 207–8; in France, 295 n. 108; and free-love literature, 186, 294 n. 89; and Mary Gove Nichols, 200–202

Bourgeoisie: ideals of romantic love versus "interest" in courtship, 17; image of the "mistress of the home," 10–11, 32, chap. 1 *passim,* 273 n. 61

Bravo, Charles (second husband of Florence Campbell Ricardo), chap. 4 *passim,* 263

313